W9-BRV-235

## DATE DUE

| | | | |
|---|---|---|---|
| | | | |
| | | | |
| | | | |
| | | | |
| | | | |
| | | | |
| | | | |
| | | | |
| | | | |
| | | | |
| | | | |
| | | | |
| | | | |
| | | | |
| | | | |
| | | | |
| | | | |
| | | | |
| | | | |

William Dwight Whitney and the
Science of Language

The Johns Hopkins University Studies in
Historical and Political Science
*123rd Series (2005)*

W. D. Whitney

# William Dwight Whitney and the Science of Language

Stephen G. Alter

The Johns Hopkins University Press
*Baltimore and London*

#55487335         4-26-05

© 2005 The Johns Hopkins University Press
All rights reserved. Published 2005
Printed in the United States of America on acid-free paper

9  8  7  6  5  4  3  2  1

The Johns Hopkins University Press
2715 North Charles Street
Baltimore, Maryland 21218-4363
www.press.jhu.edu

*Library of Congress Cataloging-in-Publication Data*

Alter, Stephen G.
  William Dwight Whitney and the science of language / Stephen G. Alter.
    p. cm.
"W.D. Whitney's main works in general linguistics": p.
Includes bibliographical references and index.
ISBN 0-8018-8020-3 (hardcover : alk. paper)
1. Whitney, William Dwight, 1827–1894.  I. Title.
P85.W478A78 2005
410′.9 — dc22          2004012070
A catalog record for this book is available from the British Library.

*Frontispiece:* W. D. Whitney portrait photo. Charles R. Lanman, ed., *The Whitney Memorial Meeting* (Boston: Ginn and Co., 1897).

*To Ann L. Alter*
*And to the memory of Fred C. Alter*

# Contents

# Preface

Some years ago, I considered it a mark of intellectual maturity *not* to aspire to write a biography. I'm embarrassed to admit this now, so I blame it on having attended graduate school. Cutting-edge historians, we were led to believe, did not go in for historical biography. This was fine with me because my own ambition (I thought) pointed in a different direction. I wanted to write a book about the rise of the "cultural" sciences in America. It seemed simple enough: I just needed to make my topic a bit more specific.

I was rescued from my subsequent wanderings when I learned of an important omission in the literature on my subject — an omission, it turned out, that involved biography. No full-length study had been done of William Dwight Whitney (1827–94), a renowned Orientalist as well as nineteenth-century America's leading writer on general linguistic theory — what was known at the time as "the science of language." That field, I soon discovered, was connected with nearly everything in the surrounding intellectual landscape. In this context, therefore, the story of a particular career could nicely serve my original purpose; it could open a wide window on the human sciences of that era.

Viewed from this perspective, W. D. Whitney's life and legacy were not the main point. I wanted to use Whitney only as a lens through which to view the environment in which he worked. In addition, I grew skeptical of the notion that Whitney had exerted significant influence on recent linguistics. Historians had made a number of claims to that effect, but most of these struck me as either vague or lacking in proportion. Accordingly, in an encyclopedia article about Whitney that I wrote several years ago, I soft-pedaled the idea of his ongoing relevance.

Then I changed my mind. Increasingly, the evidence formed a pattern I had not fully grasped at first, and I became convinced that Whitney, in addition to achieving a towering reputation in his own day, had made permanent contributions to Western language study. Still, setting forth that case has proved a complicated proposition.

The first two chapters in this work recount Whitney's early life and the beginnings of his career as an Orientalist — focusing on things that foreshadowed his approach to general linguistics. Chapter 3 surveys Victorian-era debates about language in relation to science and religion, which formed an important ideological context for Whitney's theorizing. Chapter 4 presents the basic features of Whitney's linguistic system and describes the dismayed response his views provoked among America's religious intellectuals. Chapter 5 looks at Whitney's efforts to organize his field professionally.

Chapters 6 and 7 take up the central problem of language study as one of the human or social sciences, while exploring Whitney's views on ethnology, anthropology, and Darwinian evolution. Then comes an account of Whitney's sensational public quarrel with the Oxford-based linguist F. Max Müller, the single most dramatic episode in Whitney's career. More significant in the long run, however, was his complex relationship with the German "Neogrammarian" movement, which is the subject of Chapter 9. Chapter 10 brings Whitney's story to a close and considers the other main components of his legacy: his ironic influence on Ferdinand de Saussure's linguistic theory, and the way in which Whitney's ideas have been vindicated by modern sociolinguistics.

I add here a note on terminology. Throughout the nineteenth century, English-language writers used the older term *philology* and the newer term *linguistics* virtually interchangeably: either could denote language study as a whole. I continue this practice for the sake of stylistic variety, except where I indicate that one or the other term is being preferred for a specific purpose.

Many have given of their time and expertise throughout this book's preparation. I am grateful first to those who read all or part of the manuscript in its various stages: Richard W. Bailey, Graeme Bird, Kenneth Cmiel, Paul Conkin, Madhav Deshpande, Damon DiMauro, Thomas L. Haskell, David A. Hollinger, Stanley Insler, Stephanie Jamieson, Konrad Koerner, Ronald Numbers, Ross Paulson, Elaine Phillips, Rosane Rocher, Michael Silverstein, Talbot Taylor, Thomas R. Trautmann, and James Turner. Michael Silverstein and James Turner, who read the entire work more than once, gave invaluable guidance. I also owe an extraordinary debt to Craig Christy and John E. Joseph, major interpreters of the Whitneyan legacy. Each read multiple revisions of key chapters, led me to make innumerable improvements, and encouraged me to sharpen the message. Patricia Casey Sutcliffe helped as well by correcting some of my facts based on her own Whitney research. The deficiencies that inevitably remain are my own responsibility.

An Andrew W. Mellon Foundation dissertation fellowship at the University of Michigan helped me launch this project; a year at Harvard's Charles Warren Center for the Study of American History allowed me to develop it. I am grateful to the Warren Center's directors, staff, and fellows for providing such an ideal setting in which to work. Donald Fleming deserves particular credit.

The staffs of libraries in the United States, Britain, and Germany have made this research possible. My thanks go especially to William Massa, Judith Schiff, and others working with the Manuscripts and Archives Department at Yale University's Sterling Memorial Library. Ron Ritgers, William Vance, and Richard Whitekettle furthered the cause by retrieving additional materials from Sterling Library. Barbara Burg of Harvard's Widener Library graciously and professionally traced stray bits of bibliographic information, thus saving me a number of headaches.

For help in finding information on the *Century Dictionary,* I thank Cathy Clark and the other staff of the Charles Sanders Peirce Edition Project, Indianapolis, Indiana, as well as Margaret R. Leavy of New Haven, Connecticut. Kenneth Minkema of Yale, and Elise Feeley and Kathryn Gabriel, both of Northampton, Massachusetts, helped me sort out Whitney family genealogy and church affiliation. Professor Frederick Rudolph of Williams College supplied me with a copy of the Williams Catalogue of 1845. For their assistance with language translations, I thank my colleagues Damon DiMauro and Lenore Weiss. And for supplying me with good company and a spare bed after days spent in the archives, I am grateful to Martin Appold, Larry and Elise Rifkin, and Genzo Yamamoto.

Finally, the dedication of this book is one I am proud to make, although in my perfect world I would never need to do so.

William Dwight Whitney

# Introduction

## A Pathclearer in Linguistic Science

From start to finish, this book pursues a single thread of argument, intended to explain how William Dwight Whitney helped inspire some of the fundamental themes in modern linguistics. Whitney's eminence in that field was already manifest in his own day. He was a mainstay of the American Oriental Society and a founder and the first president of the American Philological Association, these being the nation's first organizations wholly dedicated to linguistically based research. Whitney's own specialty was Vedic Sanskrit, the oldest language of the Indian subcontinent. Yet he did pioneering work in other fields as well, including articulatory phonetics, modern language pedagogy, and lexicography. He made his chief impact in this last area by editing the *Century Dictionary* (1889–91), a landmark of nineteenth-century scholarship. Whitney also wrote as a linguistic generalist on subjects ranging from dialect geography to spelling reform. Finally, he accomplished all of this while teaching Sanskrit and modern European languages for nearly forty years at Yale College in Connecticut.[1]

In addition to being America's first fully professional linguist, W. D. Whitney was one of the few Americans of that era, in any field, to gain a high reputation among scholars in Europe. Recalling this preeminent status years later, the Johns Hopkins University classicist B. L. Gildersleeve struck an elegiac note: "Whitney has left no successor, and indeed, so far had he risen even in his lifetime, that we, his close contemporaries, hardly considered him as one of us, and I cannot trust myself to remember that he was a fellow-student of mine in Berlin half a century ago."[2]

Our focus will be on Whitney's work in general linguistics, the field that explores the essential nature of language and the fundamental principles of language study. His views on these subjects appeared in public lectures (first sponsored by the Smithsonian Institution), in two major books, and in a large number of shorter writings. The best medium-length summation of his ideas was his article "Philology: The Science of Language in General," prepared for the 1885 edition of *Encyclopedia Britannica*.

Through this body of work, Whitney left a special mark on three major schools of modern linguistics. First, he inspired the late-nineteenth-century German *Junggrammatiker* (the Neogrammarians), whose essential perspective has dominated historical linguistics down to the present. Members of that group said that Whitney anticipated key aspects of their teachings.[3] He also helped to inspire Ferdinand de Saussure, the most celebrated among the founders of linguistic structuralism. In his *Cours de linguistique générale* (1916), Saussure famously taught that words are "arbitrary and conventional signs," having no intrinsic connection with the things they signify. That thesis would become a staple of postmodern cultural theory, yet Saussure credited it to a New England Yankee: "Whitney quite rightly insisted upon the arbitrary character of linguistic signs. In so doing, he pointed linguistics in the right direction."[4] This and other comments from Saussure constitute Whitney's most striking claim to fame.

Less eye-catching but actually more important were the theoretical foundations Whitney supplied for sociolinguistics, the movement that would form the capstone of his legacy. Soon after launching that school in the late 1960s, its main architect, William Labov, pointed to Whitney as his earliest intellectual predecessor.[5] Other prominent linguists have offered similar tributes over the years. In the early decades of the twentieth century, Leonard Bloomfield described Whitney as "the greatest of English-speaking linguistic scholars," whose writings contained "little to which we cannot today subscribe." And in 1979, Charles F. Hockett declared that most of Whitney's achievement still "stands unscathed."[6]

Explaining precisely what Whitney achieved, however, presents an interpretive challenge. There is an apparent contradiction between the glowing accolades he received and the elusiveness of his concrete influence. The ideas and research techniques usually associated with either the Neogrammarians or the structuralists were a far cry from Whitney's teachings. Accordingly, as the linguist Benvenuto Terracini pointed out in the late 1940s, "No 'school of Whitney' exists."[7] That is, that is, no group had thus far built upon clearly Whitneyan foundations. The same would appear to be true when comparing Whitney's teachings with the highly technical sociolinguistic research that came later; at most, the two approaches seem only faintly related.

And what of all the effusive praise Whitney received? As it turns out, these remarks were largely ambivalent. First of all, many writers credited Whitney with maintaining principles so basic that they themselves considered them truistic. And even then, they took back some of what they gave. Saussure, who said that Whitney had pointed linguistics in the right direction, went on to declare that a whole new orientation was needed. And Bloomfield hinted that Whitney's achievement actually had been something quite modest—a mere preserving of sanity in the face of the nineteenth-century penchant for "mystic vagueness and haphazard theory."[8]

This book will argue, however, that preserving sanity was itself a major feat. Nearly everyone later agreed that an exceptional amount of wrong-headed linguistic theory had circulated during Whitney's lifetime, and that against this, Whitney stood for solid good sense.[9] Specifically, he elaborated the Anglo-Scottish Enlightenment conception of language as a *social* product—as opposed to the German-romanticist notion that language resembles a living organism. At the same time, Whitney addressed the single biggest challenge faced by nineteenth-century linguists: the need to prove that their field was a genuine "science." (This goal was being pursued long before its more familiar twentieth-century phases.)[10] Against the romantic-era belief that linguistics study constituted a kind of *natural* science, Whitney argued that the field belonged with the social or cultural sciences, alongside history, ethnology, and anthropology.

Whitney approached these questions with a mixture of calm didacticism and hardball polemics. He had a gift for clarity in exposition, yet he also enjoyed dishing out unsparing criticism—especially of prominent European linguists. His main target was Friedrich Max Müller of Oxford University. Although German by birth and upbringing, Max Müller became, hands down, the Victorian world's most widely read Orientalist and language theorist. The rivalry between Müller and Whitney was long-running, culminating in an international dispute in the mid-1870s. Recalling that episode years later, the American social critic Henry Adams remarked: "In the combative days of Whitney and Max Müller, I had more than enough to do in merely trying to keep out of the range of weapons." Indeed, Müller himself once spoke of the "tomahawks and Bowie knives" that seemed to appear whenever Whitney leapt into battle.[11] The remark was characteristically malicious, yet there was something to it.

Ultimately more fitting, however, was the Neogrammarians' description of Whitney as a *Wegweiser,* or pathclearer, someone who had helped blaze a "methodological pathway" in linguistics. He did this in part by cutting down wrong ideas that stood (as he saw it) in the way of progress. Like an American backwoodsman, he put his hand to the axe and did this rude but necessary work.[12] Yet he also, as Saussure said, pointed the path in the right direction. In addition to promoting a socially oriented view of language, Whitney adopted the "uniformitarian" principle made famous in nineteenth-century geology. This was the assumption that the same kinds of forces one sees in effect today must have operated as well in all other historical epochs. As the linguist Craig Christy has shown, Whitney was the leading advocate of this kind of thinking in his field: other language scholars had touted the idea, but Whitney applied it consistently.[13] The practical effect was to break the nearly exclusive fascination with ancient tongues that had held earlier generations of linguists in its thrall. Henceforth, greater emphasis would be placed on current processes of language change as well as on synchronic language states. It was this outlook that did the most to link Whitney, at a deep and sometimes hidden level, to the Neogrammarians, to Saussurean structuralism, and to sociolinguistics.

This story is made richer and more complex by several factors, mostly having to do with the way nineteenth-century language study intersected with issues of science. First of all, the definition of *science* itself was in flux—a semantic trend of tremendous yet little-appreciated significance for the development of modern linguistics. Second, that field faced the same challenge as the human sciences as a whole in Whitney's day: the juggernaut biological, chemical, and other physically oriented disciplines threatened to absorb the study of society and behavior, including speech behavior. How could linguists meet this threat?

A further complicating factor was the Darwinian revolution, along with the

Victorian debate over "man's place in nature." Some of the most colorful episodes in that period's "warfare" between science and religion revolved around issues of language, especially the question of how language first originated. In this context, W. D. Whitney and Charles Darwin themselves entered into a trans-Atlantic partnership. Whitney defended Darwin against attacks from Max Müller, and Darwin cited works by Whitney in the revised (1874) edition of his *Descent of Man.* Darwin also offered to pay to have one of Whitney's articles reprinted in England. Even so, the link between Darwin and Whitney was not at all simple, and their intellectual relationship made for one of the most convoluted aspects of Whitney's career.

Finally, spectacular developments in the historical study of languages give further depth to our story. The nineteenth century was a heroic age of discovery—of old texts and especially of previously unsuspected kinship ties among the world's widely scattered tongues. Language study thus became an eclectic meeting ground of the humanities and the social sciences, presenting an attractive challenge to someone like W. D. Whitney who aspired to sum up the whole. He resolved to do this, however, like everything else he did, strictly on his own terms.

# CHAPTER ONE

# An American Orientalist

Two months after his wedding, in the fall of 1856, twenty-nine-year-old William Dwight Whitney sat down to pen a brief autobiography. He likely did this as a last-minute chore, since he and his wife were preparing at that time for an extended trip to Europe. It would not be Whitney's first trans-Atlantic journey; he had already spent three years as an advanced student in philology at the universities of Berlin and Tübingen. That had been an exhilarating yet austere experience, requiring a decidedly Spartan mode of living. And even now, travel on this scale was no easy thing financially: the money had to be borrowed. Still, he hoped to make the coming trip much more of a vacation than the previous one had been. In addition to affording the newly married couple a leisurely honeymoon, it would give Whitney a chance to recuperate from a uniquely stressful academic year. It would also give him the opportunity, while visiting Paris and Rome, to meet the famous Orientalist scholars in those cities. These were pleasant prospects, yet overseas travel was always an uncertain venture. Whitney must have thought it prudent to leave a written account of his life, a precaution lest his story go untold.

As it turned out, this "autobiography" was not a particularly revealing document. Probably written in haste, it filled a mere two and a half pages, and it read like a *curriculum vitae*. Here were listed the various local, often home-based, schools that Whitney had attended as a boy. Then came college, then postgraduate study, and finally his present position: for two years he had taught Sanskrit and modern European languages at Yale College in New Haven.[1] This fact-based and scholastically centered narrative was, in its own way, a telling reflection of Whitney's personality. Yet it said remarkably little about the family and social environment in which that personality had been nurtured. Can we supplement his own account and thus supply what the biographer demands — elements of Whitney's early life that foreshadow his later calling?

## Community and Character

His mother died when he was seven years old, and his father's remarriage led to a total of seven children. Such a large household put a strain on the father's finances. Josiah Dwight Whitney, Sr. (1786–1869) once remarked on his "long life of plodding in a very moderate way." Nearly half of that life was spent as a retail merchant. He then served for seventeen years as cashier, and for one year as president, of the main bank of Northampton, Massachusetts. One of his son's colleagues later described the elder Whitney as "a liberal and enlightened man, though not a man of education"; that is, he had not attended college. He was, however, the son of a Harvard graduate, and he was fitted for more than business pursuits alone. Esteemed by his neighbors, Josiah Whitney served as Justice of the Peace of Hampshire County for over twenty years.[2]

Josiah's letters to his children reveal a man who was long-suffering, self-denying, and conscientious, intent on equipping both sons and daughters for useful callings. For his sons, this meant doing all that he could to help them acquire the formal education he himself had missed. The daughters received substantial schooling as well; they were trained at home in Latin, French, and basic natural science. (An "astral lamp" kept in the family parlor introduced all of the children to astronomy.) If the senior Whitney sometimes doubted the value of postcollegiate study, especially when gained at the expense of a long stay in Europe, he deferred to his sons' larger knowledge of such matters. Yet of one thing he was certain: training of the intellect was no excuse for neglecting the affairs of the soul. The family attended Northampton's main Congregational church, which Josiah Whitney had joined in 1826, the year before the birth of his son William. By then he had already removed his eldest boy from the town's famed Round Hill School because of the unorthodox character of the religious instruction given by its Transcendentalist proprietors.[3]

Through Josiah's mother's family, the Dwights, the Whitneys were linked to a network of kinsmen, descended from the early Puritan settlers and spread throughout New England. The most prominent among these forebears was the Reverend Jonathan Edwards, the theologian of Northhampton's famed 1730s revival. (As it happened, the Whitney home stood next to what had once been Edwards' parsonage.) The Dwight family had long sent its sons to Edwards' alma mater in New Haven to complete their formal education: Josiah Whitney's grandfather, Josiah Dwight (1715–68), had graduated in the class of 1736. Despite these ties, however, the Whitneys were not lineally related to Jonathan Edwards or to his descendants who became presidents of Yale College: Edwards' grandson Timothy Dwight (1752–1817) and, later, Theodore Dwight Woolsey (1801–89). (Nor were the Whitneys related to New Haven's famous son Eli Whitney, the inventor of the cotton gin.) Rather, the Whitneys' branch of the Dwight family had split off from what would become the more famous line nearly four generations earlier, around 1700. However close in proximity, the two lines did not intermarry in the intervening years.[4]

The Whitneys of Northampton were not, therefore, among the region's leading families. Yet they did enjoy local distinction, and along with this came high expectations. Did Josiah Whitney's second son measure up to community standards? In most respects he exceeded the mark, for young "Will" Whitney demonstrated character and ability well beyond his years. His boyhood pastimes of botany and ornithology afforded practice in the empirical arts of observing, collecting, and classifying diverse phenomena. And his countryside rambles, gun in hand, soon led him to shooting, stuffing, and mounting his best bird specimens for display. Already as a youth, William became an expert taxidermist.

Aptitudes of a different sort can be seen in the architectural drawings he prepared under the instruction of a local draftsman. Still held in the Whitney archive at Yale, these pages bear clean lines, neatly labeled, detailing the interior beams of houses and bridges—all of this suggesting a bent toward precise and painstaking labor. A precocious intolerance of shoddy workmanship also showed in the seriousness with which he took his schoolwork. As a fourteen-year-old, William complained of the errors he found in his student edition of Cicero and of the "imperfect" Latin dictionary his family owned.[5]

For their part, that family had long noted the boy's diligence. Yet what kind of career did this suggest? William exuded the Protestant work ethic, and this, coupled with his academic leanings, suggested some kind of a learned calling.[6] He would not, however, model himself after the ubiquitous New England clergyman, for it became clear that the boy lacked all taste for theology. Nor would his model be the patrician man of letters, for the Whitney children could not aspire to join the ranks of patricians. He patterned himself, rather, on a newer and scrappier intellectual type, and in this his older brother set the example.

More than seven years separated William from Josiah Dwight Whitney, Jr. (1819–96), and the two differed markedly in temperament. William was generally steady and circumspect; Josiah, impetuous and often tactless. Still, the brothers grew to be intimate. William admired Josiah's intellectual ability, and he emulated his brother's enthusiasm for science. As a student at Yale, Josiah fell captive to astronomy and chemistry, the latter taught by Benjamin Silliman, America's first professor in that subject. He took added inspiration from the Scottish geologist Charles Lyell, whom he heard lecture at Boston's Lowell Institute several years later. This event led Josiah to decide on a career in chemical geology. For training in the latest research techniques, one needed to do advanced study at a German university, and Josiah soon set out for Europe. This kept him far from home during a critical period in his younger brother's life; he left the country just as fifteen-year-old William was entering college. Still, even from a distance, his example and encouragement had a marked effect.

Josiah would later direct a number of government-sponsored geological surveys in the American west, the most important of these in the newly acquired state of California. (There his co-workers christened the state's highest point of elevation Mount Whitney.) Eventually Josiah came back east to teach geology and economic mineralogy at Harvard College, the position he would occupy for the remainder of his career.[7]

Three of W. D. Whitney's younger siblings also found their way into scholarly work. A sister, Maria (1830–1910), taught modern languages briefly at Smith College; a half-brother, James Lyman Whitney (1835–1910), served as director of the Boston Public Library; and another half-brother, Henry Mitchell Whitney (1843–1911), became a professor of English at Beloit College. The seven Whitney children were an attenuated group, scattered in age and eventually in location. Yet they were mutually supportive. "Brother Will" was a favorite with the younger ones, since he was always ready to sympathize with their concerns and offer dependable counsel. To confide his own thoughts, however, William looked to Josiah and to a sister between them in age, Elizabeth Whitney Putnam (1822–63).

William D. Whitney was almost wholly unremarkable in appearance. Photographs taken when he was in his twenties show a man of medium build with wavy brown hair, a prominent forehead, and a deadpan expression. The only notable features then and later were his weary and unsentimental eyes. This did not mean that he lacked a sense of humor. Among siblings and friends, William indulged an irreverent wit as well as a considerable taste for the absurd. The latter quality was on display in a letter he wrote to his married sister Elizabeth, then residing in Wisconsin, during his first year on the Yale faculty. He had just returned from a visit home, and in reporting the local news, he described the sensation created by a traveling stage production of *Uncle Tom's Cabin* (1851):

> Think of a low strolling theater for a whole week in the Northampton Town Hall, and with crowded houses every night; almost all the strict respectable people as Uncle Payson even, going themselves or sending their children! And all because the subject is "Uncle Tom"! It is one of the most striking of the wonderful phenomena which have gone about the world with that book. I am getting rather disgusted about it. It is a very moving drama: *three* deaths on the stage: Eva, her papa, and the good old nigger: and so affecting that people (as Mrs. Gorham) don't shed tears simply, but cry and sob, like to break their hearts, and little boys, like Eddy Conwell, go out and leave at ten o'clock because they cry so hard it hurts 'em and they can't stand it. Can you beat that out your way?[8]

The wry cynicism was typical. Whitney's gaze on the world at times resembled that of a Mark Twain—indeed, he would later enjoy Twain's *Roughing It* (1872).[9] Certainly he did not embrace the sentimental humanitarianism commonly associated with antebellum reform movements. Whitney did hate slavery, however, and he became a typical New England advocate of "free soil" in the West. In the same year (1854) that he ridiculed the mania for *Uncle Tom*, he vehemently condemned efforts to open the Kansas and Nebraska territories to slaveholders. (He concluded a letter to a friend at that time: "Can't close without the customary formula: Down the Nebraska bill [*sic*] and its authors and supporters!!!!!") And finally, when the southern states withdrew from the Union, he wished for a policy of no compromise with rebels.[10]

Whitney always set a high estimate on his own abilities. He also made a point of avoiding all displays of deference toward those of high academic or social reputation. As one of his Yale colleagues later observed, "No one was ever less influenced than he by the authority of great names."[11] This spirit of self-reliance reflected a lifelong intellectual habit: Whitney was anxious to show that he had embraced the things he held true only after independent investigation. Here again he manifested a classic Protestant disposition, the desire to read the evidence for himself, chapter and verse. It was actually wrong, Whitney felt, to get one's convictions at second hand. Conversely, once he had made up his mind on a subject, his opinion was ironclad.

These matters of intellectual temperament, set early in Whitney's life, would eventually pervade his scholarship—including his "linguistic science." Meanwhile, his college years introduced the philosophical underpinnings of his thinking on that subject.

## Collegiate Science and Philosophy

Josiah Whitney, Jr. had followed Dwight family tradition by attending Yale, but William, as a younger son, did not enjoy that privilege. His father sent him instead to Williams College, situated among the Berkshire hills of western Massachusetts. He was allowed to bypass the first year of classwork—a practice not uncommon in that era—yet he still found college "rather an easy life. I never study more than an hour and a half a day, and plenty of time is left for reading, writing, hunting, and skinning and stuffing" (that is, he continued doing taxidermy). He also kept a journal in which he recorded his bird sightings and listed the specimens he had shot and mounted. Here he occasionally waxed eloquent. Of a springtime Sabbath morning he described sparrows lifting up "their sweet, melodious voices in songs of praise, more genuine, without doubt, than those ascending from the gallery of the church, and interrupted by no sermon."[12]

W. D. Whitney's leisure pursuits actually complemented one of the college's official aims: like other schools at that time, Williams was increasing its offerings in natural science. Classical languages and mathematics still dominated the first two years of study, but botany, mineralogy, and astronomy had been added for juniors. Williams even boasted the first astronomical observatory at an American college, installed shortly before Whitney's arrival. There was also a student-run Natural History Lyceum, which conducted field expeditions, maintained a small museum, and held regular meetings at which members presented papers.[13] Whitney made good use of these opportunities. He became a leader in the Lyceum, plus he developed an intense new interest in astronomy.

Despite this increased attention to natural science, the antebellum colleges did not attempt to train their students for scientific careers. Rather, they aimed to inculcate an informed theistic worldview. Central to this thinking was the idea that nature showed the marks of intelligent design, hence of a Grand Designer. Accordingly, seniors at Williams College rounded out their scientific studies with Bishop Joseph Butler's *Analogy of Religion, Natural and Revealed* (1736) and William Paley's classic *Natural Theology* (1802).[14] The subtitle of Paley's book was apt: "Evidences of the Existence and the Attributes of the Deity Collected from the Appearances of Nature."

Seniors also attended a course of lectures, standard for that period, on "Mental and Moral Philosophy." The content was broader than the name implied, for the course was intended almost as a grand tour of knowledge. Presidents of colleges usually gave these lectures, and in this role the patriarch of Williams College made himself exemplary. Annually during his thirty-six-year tenure at that institution, Mark Hopkins (1802–87) surveyed the combined natural, social, and psychological order from the dust of the ground up to its human pinnacle. Scores of Williams graduates testified to his effectiveness at this task. As one alumnus noted, if students did not always remember the details of Hopkins' lectures, they still picked up an orderly habit of mind that would aid them in almost any future endeavor. W. D. Whitney expressed his own sincere appreciation of Mark Hopkins during his final year in college. To a cousin, he declared: "The Prex is the greatest teacher entirely that was ever suffered to appear on this earth." And, as he told his father, "I should be much inclined to take for gospel what the Prex says."[15]

What Mark Hopkins did say differed little from what was presented at most American colleges. Hopkins taught that the universe played no tricks and that the five senses could be trusted; nature could therefore be known with accuracy through empirical investigation. This was the essence of Scottish "Common Sense" realism, the official philosophy of the colleges in that day. Rather than challenge young minds, the goal of this doctrine was to confirm the untroubled epistemology that boys brought with them when they first stepped onto campus.

Mark Hopkins expounded this viewpoint with great conviction and little subtlety. He was dismissive of all philosophical wrangling, whether David Hume's hyper-empiricist skepticism, which questioned the certainty of all knowledge other than the smallest sensory impressions, or the cloudy idealism commonly associated with the Germans. Hopkins did seek to acquaint his students with the teachings of Immanuel Kant, although mainly to exhibit "specimens of nonsense." He acknowledged the existence of Kant's categories of the mind — the fundamental notions of being, identity, time, space, number, and resemblance — yet he interpreted these in a strictly Common Sense fashion, rejecting the idea that consciousness structures one's perception of reality. Of the mind's categories, Hopkins declared: "Everybody knows them, and not only so but always has known them, and could not help knowing them." They were things "such as nobody thinks of denying except a philosopher, or possibly a fool."[16]

W. D. Whitney found this anti-speculative outlook congenial, one result being that the three years he would later spend at German universities produced little inclination toward German philosophy. He later spoke of "the valuelessness of metaphysics for anything but amusement."[17] This outlook would eventually pervade Whitney's language theory. Likewise, many of the more specific themes in his theoretical system also had their source in his collegiate training. Especially influential, as we will see in later chapters, were his assigned readings on ethics and political economy, which taught that humans were freely choosing and morally accountable beings. Readings in logic and rhetoric supplied crucial themes as well.

Whitney firmly resisted certain other aspects of the collegiate ethos, however. Likely under Josiah's influence, he had already become one of the era's quiet dissenters from New England religiosity. This alone probably did much to produce an anomalous situation at Williams College at that time. Student-led revivals swept most American campuses annually during the middle decades of the nineteenth century. Yet it is a telling fact that fervor burned low at Williams precisely during Whitney's student years — neither he nor a majority of his classmates experienced spiritual conversion.[18] A conscientious student, Whitney no doubt read Paley's *Natural Theology* and *Evidences of Christianity* (1794), both assigned texts. In this respect, his education seems to have paralleled that of the young Charles Darwin, who benefited from the close reasoning he found in Paley's works yet was not finally convinced by their arguments.[19] A further indication of Whitney's leanings appeared soon after his graduation when he read the Scotsman Robert Chambers' *Vestiges of the Natural History of Creation* (1844). This huge best-seller set forth a naturalistic hypothesis of biological evolution years in advance of Darwin's *Origin of Species* (1859).[20]

During his final year of college, W. D. Whitney added a new field to his informal curriculum: he began teaching himself to read German. Josiah had urged his brother to learn European languages, and he helped materially by shipping home the books he had been purchasing while abroad. William soon developed such a love for his new-found subject "that there is no fear of my ever becoming tired and giving it up." Indeed, he said, he had "not paid a great deal of attention to Natural History lately, further than to read my paper before the Lyceum when it came my turn: it has been crowded out by the German."[21] A crossroads had been reached. Although he would never abandon his interest in the study of nature, events soon pointed Whitney toward a very different kind of scientific calling.

## Yankee Ambition and the Lure of Language

W. D. Whitney was only eighteen years old when he graduated, valedictorian, in the thirty-six-member Williams class of 1845. Josiah was back in New England at this time. He needed money, so he had interrupted his studies in order to work for a number of months with the state geological survey of Vermont. However brief, Josiah's visits to Northampton during this period had a marked influence on his brother's future. Josiah brought glowing reports of German academic life, based on his own broad experience. On first arriving at Berlin, he had followed the standard practice of that day by hearing lectures in a variety of subjects before settling down to his specialized training. Among this sampling was comparative Indo-European philology, a bright new star in the scholarly constellation.

Philology of the more traditional kind had a long and distinguished history: its modern roots lay in Renaissance humanism, and by the eighteenth century it stood at the center of Western learning. Its special province was unlocking the meaning of old texts—whether Roman legal documents, Old Norse sagas, or the books of the Bible. *Comparative* philology, however, focused not on textual content but on the history of languages themselves, especially on the genealogical interrelationships among groups of languages. Most early researchers in this field concentrated on some branch of the Indo-European family.

Before the latter part of the eighteenth century, few had guessed that this family of languages even existed. The first widespread realization of that fact came with the arrival in India of an extraordinary group of British colonial officials. Preeminent among these was Sir William Jones (1746–94), a jurist by vocation, yet also a linguistic polymath. In 1786, in his annual address as president of the Asiatic Society of Bengal, Jones made a striking observation. He pointed to the structural similarity between Sanskrit, the ancient language of the Indians, and classical Greek and Latin. So close was this similarity, he said, that it could not have been produced by accident; it could only be explained by supposing that all three languages had "sprung from some common source."[22] German and Scandinavian scholars followed up this insight, demonstrating that most of the modern European, Indian, and Iranian languages, along with their predecessor tongues, constituted a vast yet interconnected family. These scholars also invented the comparative mode of research, which aimed to reconstruct the history of the Indo-European family tree.

As a student at the University of Berlin, Josiah Whitney attended lectures in this new *Sprachwissenschaft,* or "linguistic science." He heard two of the pioneers of that field, Franz Bopp (1791–1867) and Jacob Grimm (1785–1863). Listening to "dear old Bopp and Grimm," he later said, produced in him "a longing desire to turn up double, some day, and set one half to work on philology." Such enthusiasm clearly made an impression on his younger brother, for William soon decided that he too wanted to hear the famous German scholars.[23] His father, however, had a different plan in mind. The senior Whitney considered medicine a fit calling for a young man of such obvious scientific bent, so he arranged for his son to train with a Northampton physician beginning in the autumn following William's graduation from college. The physician's office, however, proved to be an unhealthy place; on the second day of his apprenticeship, William contracted measles. At that point, his medical career came to an end.

During the convalescence that followed, William came to a bold decision. Once recovered, he took a job as a clerk in his father's bank—although he hoped not to stay there long. His real objective he described in a letter to Josiah, who had recently returned to Berlin:

> The change of plan was rather of the suddenest, but I am very well pleased with it. My love for the medical profession never was anything well worth mentioning, and I have found out that father had no particular idea of making a year's study of it or more subservient to a plan of general education, but fully intended that the practice should follow. The height of my ambition is to go to Berlin and

study Philology until I have fitted myself to take a not very low stand among educated men, and anything of that kind I fear I never shall do unless I raise the shino [as in "shiners"—gold coins] to aid myself in good part. I endeavor to spend my evenings now as profitably as possible, chiefly in studying Italian and in reading some German and French.[24]

Not yet nineteen years old when he wrote these lines, William had marked out his path far into the future. He had decided to study philology, and he intended to make that field his professional calling. His father's plans for his medical training would have dispensed with a "general education" of the kind Josiah was getting. Yet William yearned for such an education, vocationally serviceable but also intellectually thorough. He also longed to join America's academic aristocracy, a practicable way for a talented youth of modest background to bolster his social status.[25] The first step, however, was to earn the money to finance his studies, which would have to come out of the $600 annually that he would be making at the bank. Josiah advised his brother that an advanced course in philology would require at least three years.[26] As it turned out, it would take him nearly as long to save the money he would need.

After days bent over bank records, Whitney gave his evenings to study. He followed a definite plan, beginning with the modern languages and working his way back. Having surveyed Swedish and Danish, for instance, he then took up "Icelandish." He had a clear view of the task before him, so it was frustrating to find his progress slowed by a lack of appropriate books. And his banking chores weighed on him increasingly as the months wore on; he was impatient, he said, to go "over the puddle" to Europe as soon as possible.[27] Still, the activities of Whitney's banking years made for a fitting preparation, as the historian Carl Diehl shows in a fine pen portrait:

The long, meticulously neat columns of figures and notations progressing to precise and unarguable conclusions were in many ways emblematic of W. D. Whitney's personality. These careful accounts were replicated in the long lists of geological and botanical observations that he had begun compiling for himself in college and the exact observations of the daily weather that he was to note every day in his diaries for fifty years. On the weekdays he labored over the bank's account books and on the weekends he added to the long lists of birds sighted, birds shot, and birds stuffed and mounted. For he was as cool and precise a marksman as he was an accountant. And his skill at stuffing and mounting his specimens rivaled the best professionals of the day. Naturally, every speci-

men was neatly catalogued and mounted in his own well-built bird cases, catalogued in the same neat and unadorned handwriting in which even then he had
started the innumerable declensions and grammatical forms of Old Norse, modern Swedish and German, and — ancient Sanskrit.[28]

Making a start on that language was Whitney's logical next step, for Sanskrit
was considered the royal tongue of nineteenth-century comparative philology.
Josiah helped out by sending home a copy of Franz Bopp's beginning Sanskrit
textbook.[29] Taking that step was still a frightful thing, however, as Whitney
told his hometown friend Freeman ("Free") Bumstead: "I have really com-
menced the Sanscrit. Free, I almost shudder at my own audacity in so doing,
for, if I can form any opinion, it is likely to prove worse than French, Spanish,
Italian, and German, all stewed down in Latin and Greek. I shall not calculate
on doing much this summer besides learning to read its uncouth characters
readily, when combined into words: (there are fifty of them, like to nothing on
[sic] heaven above or in earth beneath that ever a man saw before) but next
winter I shall grapple it vigorously."[30]

At least he was not alone: Whitney found a study partner in the reverend
George Edward Day (1815–72), his father's pastor and a future professor of Hebrew at Yale's Divinity School. For a time, the two worked at Sanskrit together.
Seeing the young man's diligence, George Day soon gave Whitney a letter of
introduction to Edward Elbridge Salisbury (1814–1901), a Yale College language professor and a leading member of the American Oriental Society. This
allowed Whitney to travel to New Haven to attend a meeting of that organization as Salisbury's guest.[31]

W. D. Whitney's labors at the Northampton bank finally came to an end
with the arrival of summer 1849. At that point a new opportunity beckoned.
Like Mark Twain in *Roughing It,* he jumped at the chance to travel west, working as an assistant to an older brother in a government-appointed position.
Josiah had become director of the Lake Superior Geological Survey, which explored the copper region of Michigan's Upper Peninsula; William thus got a
job on the survey crew. His responsibilities included botanical and baromet-
ric observations as well as the financial accounts. This did not mean, however,
that he took a break from philology; along with gear and provisions, into the
wilderness went Bopp's Sanskrit textbook.[32] Already by this time, Whitney had
translated and abridged a German treatise on the structure of the Sanskrit language. This work, his first publication in the field of Indology, would appear

in the Congregationalist quarterly *Bibliotheca Sacra,* owing to the assistance of George Day, who was one of the journal's editors.[33]

His summer in Michigan come and gone, W. D. Whitney returned East. He still planned to go abroad, but first, to better prepare himself, he had decided to spend a year at Yale College. His mentor there, at least officially, was E. E. Salisbury, America's first European-trained Orientalist. (Salisbury had studied Arabic at the University of Paris and Sanskrit with Franz Bopp at Berlin.) Perhaps more importantly, Salisbury had helped organize Yale's postgraduate Department of Philosophy and the Arts. It was in this fledgling department that Whitney enrolled in the fall of 1849.

Among his handful of fellow students was the classicist James Hadley, a talented young member of Yale's faculty. Together, Whitney and Hadley constituted the first—and last—Sanskrit class ever taught by Salisbury. Even at that, they took much of their instruction on their own, reciting by themselves from eight until nine each morning. Whitney also attended a class in advanced Greek taught by Yale's President Theodore Dwight Woolsey, and he did weekly exercises in Anglo-Saxon under Josiah W. Gibbs (1790–1861), the college's Professor of Sacred Literature.[34] Judging from letters Whitney wrote at this time, one would hardly guess how important a role Josiah Gibbs played in American philology, for Whitney barely mentioned him. Yet as we will see, Gibbs's influence as a language theorist had spread far beyond Yale during the previous decades.

Whitney liked and admired James Hadley, who proved to be an extremely able scholar as well as an ideal companion. Portrait photographs reveal Hadley as alert and sympathetic, yet also full of self-deprecating humor; he always seemed to have a half-ashamed smirk on his face. Whitney described Hadley's intellectual character thus: "He has studied language, while Prof. Salisbury has rather studied languages, and he is of more profit to me in the class than the Prof. himself." This phrase, "language rather than languages," was a commonplace among nineteenth-century philologists, suggestive of their quest for the essential principles on which all of the world's tongues were constructed. Whitney wanted to make this quest his own. As he told his friend Freeman Bumstead: "What I wish to study is Comparative Philology generally, which, you know, is not the science of languages only, but of language. At present I hardly know more than that it is a most vast, important and interesting field."[35]

As Whitney admitted, he had at this time only a vague notion of what comparative philology entailed. Yet his ignorance made the subject all the more attractive: in its apparent breadth, comparative philology seemed to hold the promise of an all-embracing "science" of language. Again writing to Bumstead, who was studying medicine, Whitney defended his own vocational choice: "Stupid stuff too you might perhaps call it. . . . But I think you would be surprised to learn what wonders have been accomplished in the investigation of language within the past half century, and how near Comparative Philology has come to a complete analysis thereof, and to turning back the vast and complicated body of languages as they at present exist to a few simple principles working among and upon a few simple utterances."[36] Whitney would make it his goal to search out those "few simple principles."

His efforts were frustrated, however, by the vagaries of the book trade. While at Yale, Whitney tried to obtain a copy of Bopp's groundbreaking *Vergleichende Grammatik* (volume 1, 1833), a "comparative" grammar embracing Sanskrit, Greek, Latin, Persian, Gothic, Zend-Avestan, Armenian, Lithuanian, and Old Latvian. By listing in parallel columns the paradigms of word inflection from each of these languages, Bopp gave impressive evidence of their common structure and ancestry. Yet as Whitney discovered, Bopp's volume was out of print and nearly impossible to find, and detailed information about comparative philology was otherwise hard to come by.[37] As a result, although he had made a good start on the various Indo-European languages, Whitney could not begin his comparativist work until he traveled to Berlin and met Professor Bopp face to face.

He grew in his sense of calling nonetheless, even to the point of passing up a vacation to New York City with Josiah: "I could not tear myself away from my beloved Sanskrit." Whitney clearly was committed to philology, but would this lead to a paying job? He responded to his father's query with a formal description of the prospects:

> Within not many years past, owing chiefly to the introduction of Sanskrit to the knowledge of European scholars, an entirely new province of study, and one of the highest importance, that of comparative philology, has been opened to the world. In consequence of it, as great a revolution has been effected in the study of language and of languages as has been effected in the other departments of science. The old system and methods are being superseded and discarded, and everything is assuming new forms. As yet it has received but little attention in this country, as the old men are too old for it; but it must inevitably be introduced and occupy as high a position as any other branch of study in the requirements

of American scholarship and the task of accomplishing this is committed to the rising generation.[38]

These remarks, apparently so full of confidence, betrayed an underlying trepidation: Whitney knew he was taking a gamble, for Indological studies had hardly been heard of in America's academic institutions. Still, he also knew that this very situation spelled potential. Like Benjamin Stillman launching the study of chemistry at Yale a generation earlier, Whitney saw the opportunity to pioneer a "new science" in his own country.[39] Gaining expertise in a specialized field, and one thus far known mainly in Europe, surely would win him distinction among his peers.

The Reverend Day of Northampton was pleased to hear of Whitney's plans to go overseas for advanced study and so commit himself to a philological career. "But," he asked, "is there not *one friend* you will need—even him 'who sticketh closer than a brother'?" Others had posed the same question—a college classmate who had gone on to theological seminary; a cousin, Dwight Whitney Marsh; and his father's sister—all urged William to embrace the Christian faith. Soon his father warned him to avoid any "taint of German rationalism or German infidelity" while abroad, for "scientific men and literary men are peculiarly apt to overlook the one thing needful." The elder Whitney appealed to his son to keep the Sabbath during his stay in Berlin, and to hear an Evangelical clergyman there whom George Day recommended.[40]

It is easy to imagine the recipient of all this advice growing restive. And yet it was much too sensitive an issue to confront directly. How must Whitney have felt, for instance, when he read this heartrending plea from his father, written several years later?

> The Bible *may be* true and there *may be* a neverending hereafter! Many, a very large portion of the best and soundest intellects do believe it. You yourself know that you have a soul and you don't know where it came from or how it got here and cannot tell any better what will be its future state unless you believe the Bible to be true. Will you then run the awful hazard of going into eternity blindfolded?[41]

It was, arguably, a question worth considering. Yet in response to these pleadings, Whitney kept silent. He always replied in friendly fashion, even as he avoided all mention of things spiritual. Casual remarks to his more intimate friends, however, suggested his general attitude. He had little respect for Yale's religious life: he found the Divinity School students lacking a spirit of Christian service, and he once told of how, after hearing a particularly bad sermon at the College Chapel, he had needed "a strong dose of the Skandinavian mythology at noon to revive me."[42]

On the other hand, Whitney sincerely admired the Reverend Horace Bushnell (1802–76), whom he aptly described as a "great disturber of the modern church." A Congregationalist pastor and theologian from Hartford, Bushnell often lectured in New Haven, and Whitney was glad, "after all the insipidities to which I had before been a victim, to hear a man who had something of his own to say." These remarks raise the question of Whitney's familiarity with Bushnell as a *linguistic* thinker — especially since Whitney said these things late in 1849, the year that Bushnell's "Preliminary Dissertation on Language" was published as an introduction to perhaps his most provocative theological treatise.[43] Whitney could hardly have been unaware of Bushnell's linguistic ideas, yet he appears never to have commented on them directly. Later we will see the reason for this silence.

## On Indian Ground

Whitney finally attained his dream in September of 1850, when he sailed for Germany to begin three years of advanced philological study. With him he carried a letter of introduction from E. E. Salisbury, addressed to the renowned Professor Bopp. He soon discovered, however, that the man was less impressive than the reputation. Josiah must have neglected to tell his brother that Bopp was notorious for conducting class simply by reading aloud from his published works. "I don't find lectures at the University of Berlin so great shakes as I had supposed," Whitney complained. Not the least cause of his vexation was the sense of being cheated financially. He wrote in his diary concerning fees owed to the professor: "Twenty-nine thalers for what has been worth no more than as many groschen to me! To think of the books that might have been purchased with so much money; and how ill my second quarter's account will look with such a spot on it! I have had the last experience with the old gentleman, and never really want to see his face again. . . . Bopp's lecture this afternoon, stupid enough as usual."[44]

A redeeming alternative appeared in Albrecht Weber, the university's young professor of Sanskrit. Unlike Bopp, who focused on comparative philology, Weber was an expert in ancient Indian literature. His specialty was the Vedas, the four collections of hymns and religious incantations that comprise the earliest Indian lore. These were in fact the oldest literary works known at that time. For this reason, European scholars saw them not only as the key to the early history of the Indian people but also as the chief source of insight into primeval human experience. Seen in this light, the Vedas were profoundly important. Whitney quickly became fascinated with the idea of doing groundbreaking research on these texts, a shift in interest that effectively redefined his field of specialization.

Hitherto Whitney had regarded the study of Sanskrit only as a means, however indispensable, to the pursuit of comparative philology; now Sanskrit was becoming an end in itself. He explained this change in perspective to Yale's E. E. Salisbury, anxious to justify his new course:

> You may recollect that you protested, or perhaps that is too strong a word to be properly used, against my pursuing the Sanskrit for simply its linguistic value, and will therefore, I hope, experience satisfaction in hearing that I have found myself quite unable to resist the attractions of the study of Indian antiquity, which are especially strong in the present rather anomalous transition-period, when, in the Vedas, a firm foundation is just beginning to be laid and a true scientific treatment of the subject is becoming possible. It is my ambition now to become an Orientalist, standing on Indian ground and proceeding from there out as far as possible to all that has a relation with it, not by any means losing sight at the same time of Comparative Philology, as indeed it is hardly possible to do if one wanders with his eyes open over such ground, but rather subordinating it to the other than the other to it. . . . Of course, since my plans took this direction, I have been led more away from Bopp, who rather represents the linguistic, to Weber, who more directly represents the archaeological department of the study. He has given a very interesting course of lectures this winter on the history of Sanskrit literature.[45]

In describing his new field of interest as "archaeological," Whitney used that word in its older inclusive sense, suggesting the study, not just of material artifacts, but of a group's entire culture.[46]

Here once again, Whitney accurately forecast his future. He would not, after all, become a comparative philologist. Instead, he now set his sights on becoming "an Orientalist." If anything, this was an even more specialized, and therefore hazardous, field. As he said in his letter to Salisbury, "I am almost frightened myself at the resolution to which I have come considering on the one hand how little call there is in practical America for such studies, while I have got my bread to earn in some way and on the other how few of the helps in the pursuit of such studies are to be found in American libraries and how far they are beyond the reach of any means which I can command, but I am determined to make the trial and not thwart my inclination until it shall plainly appear to be leading me into difficulties."[47] Again, his words were prophetic: "practical America" would hardly support a full-time expert on Oriental languages.

Even so, Whitney pursued studies that fit with his new goal. In addition to the all-important Sanskrit, he acquired the basics of Arabic, Persian, Egyptian, and Coptic—the latter two languages studied under the famed Karl Richard Lepsius (1810–84). His training thus reflected Europe's recent burst of interest in the languages and literatures of the ancient East. After the original British Indologists had laid a foundation in Sanskrit, progress on other fronts came through a series of breakthroughs. European researchers decoded the Babylonian cuneiform script in 1803, deciphered the Egyptian hieroglyphs in 1822, and placed Zend-Avestan, the language of Persia's Zoroastrian scriptures, in its historical relationship to Sanskrit in 1832.

W. D. Whitney reveled in his induction into these mysteries. A typical diary entry from this period describes lectures in the morning, study throughout the afternoon, a performance of Beethoven's *Fidelio* after supper, and reading from the Vedas and the Koran late in the evening: "Most superb day."[48] Yet while he delighted in Orientalist study, Whitney would increasingly subordinate the intrinsic charm of its literature to the severe demands of historico-philological investigation. This scholarly asceticism could be seen already in his personal habits—testified to many years later, when one of his former students recounted an interview with the daughter of Whitney's Berlin landlady:

> Fräulein Schaal spoke of the delight her mother and herself had felt at the messages sent them by the professor who had become so celebrated, but who had not forgotten them, and showed the visitor Professor Whitney's room, all unchanged, a typical *Studentenzimmer;* in the middle, a long plain table, and by it an uncushioned arm-chair. That, said she, was Professor Whitney's chair, and in it he used to sit for hours at that table, almost without moving. When he moved the chair more than a little, I knew that it was time for me to take him his mug of beer, and perchance a bit of bread. And, as a very small girl then, I wondered at the table, which was covered with little bits of paper, which he had arranged

in a certain order, and was very particular that no one should disturb. The only adornment which he had in the room was an American flag draped over the mirror; and on the Fourth of July he said he would work an hour less than usual, as it was the anniversary of American independence.[49]

Such seriousness set Whitney apart from the typical American student-tourist. This *Wandervogel,* a bird of passage, visited a number of German universities, each only long enough to hear the famous lecturers. Whitney did enjoy meeting fellow countrymen such as Francis Child and Basil Gildersleeve, dedicated students who would later become major philologists in the United States. Yet he decided to steer away from Berlin's "American colony." He found that attending its social functions robbed him of opportunities to practice his spoken German. And as he confided in his journal: "I am beginning to conclude that the great majority of Americans in the city are thorough asses and that the fewer acquaintances we have among them the better."[50]

Finding Whitney an able student, Albrecht Weber recommended him to Europe's premier Vedic specialist, Rudolph von Roth. Whitney thus spent two summers studying under Roth at the University of Tübingen. The result was a major scholarly collaboration: Roth recruited Whitney's assistance in editing the second oldest of the four Vedas, the *Atharva,* as yet unpublished and thus hardly known in the West.[51] (The oldest and most important of these texts was the *Ṛg Veda.*) Whitney continued this project after he wound up his studies in Berlin in the spring of 1853. (He did not earn an advanced degree, as that was hardly needed for an academic career in the United States at the time.) Taking leave of Germany, he spent six weeks in Paris, three in Oxford, and seven in London, collating and copying all of the *Atharva Veda* manuscripts then held in European libraries. These labors laid the foundation of the Roth-Whitney edition of the *Atharva Veda;* the Sanskrit text was published in two parts in 1855–56. Whitney thus got an early start doing original research, a step toward joining the elite circle of European Indologists.

These activities mightily impressed his colleagues at home. Before going abroad, Whitney had attended several meetings of the American Oriental Society—naturally enough, since E. E. Salisbury managed that organization almost single-handedly at that time—and soon he received word of his election as a member. The AOS had been established only ten years earlier by the Salem, Massachusetts, lawyer John Pickering (1777–1846) and a handful of other part-time philologists. Its constitution defined "Oriental" broadly, as embracing Asian, Near Eastern, African, and Polynesian languages and cultures, although Pickering himself urged the group to concentrate on India and Egypt.[52]

In actual practice, however, miscellaneous factors steered the Society's subject matter in the early years. Papers presented at the group's meetings usually included several dealing with Arabic and Sanskrit, but more dealing with biblical Hebrew, since the membership included a large number of clergymen. An assortment of other topics was addressed in the form of communications sent by the Society's "corresponding members." Mostly American foreign missionaries, with an occasional diplomat in Asia or the Near East, these individuals supplied hard-to-get information about the languages and cultures in the vicinity of their postings. (Whitney often expressed admiration for the character and scholarly contributions of the missionaries he met through the organization.)[53]

The AOS held its annual meeting in Boston and its semi-annual meeting in New Haven, these being the two centers of its New England–based membership. The semi-annual meeting, held in October, was naturally the smaller affair, enough so usually to be accommodated at the home of one of the Yale faculty. The Society officially sponsored a scholarly journal, yet there were not enough high-quality contributions for it to appear on a regular basis. The first volume came out in 1843, but the second not until four years later. So despite the group's lofty aims, the American Orientalists had little to show for their early efforts.

It was against this backdrop that the Society received a heartening letter from Albrecht Weber of Berlin. He wrote to congratulate the AOS members for their advancement of Indological studies, particularly through the labors of their young colleague William Whitney. Following a well-established tradition among German Orientalists, Weber used this occasion to point out British lethargy in the field, only now contrasting this with American drive and ambition. It was true that William Jones and his peers had done important work in the early days, yet British Indology had slowed dramatically after that first generation retired. Weber pointed especially to the failings of Horace Hayman Wilson (1786–1860), who occupied England's first professorship in Sanskrit, established at Oxford in 1827. Although a good scholar himself, Wilson had succeeded in training not a single professional Sanskritist during his long teaching career. As a result, Weber boasted, most of the Sanskrit positions in

British universities had been filled by Germans. In the same way, although the East India Company had done much to promote the publication of the Vedic texts, it found no native Englishmen equipped to do the work itself. The company had been obliged, therefore, to sponsor the efforts of a young German, Friedrich Max Müller, who was then in the process of editing the *Ṛg Veda*.[54]

This letter from Professor Weber of Berlin must have delighted its audience (E. E. Salisbury read it aloud at the annual AOS meeting). Although full of national self-congratulation, it suggested nonetheless that American youth and vigor — under wise German tutelage — had handily beaten the complacent British. W. D. Whitney could have received no higher commendation in the eyes of his colleagues in New England.

Soon after receiving the letter from Weber, Salisbury came to a momentous decision. He wanted to see Oriental languages represented at Yale, yet he had become convinced, apparently with good reason, that teaching was not his strong suit. Financially independent, he planned to retire. Salisbury would continue to offer his services as an instructor in Arabic whenever needed. (They never were.) Yet the task of teaching Sanskrit, he proposed, should be transferred to Whitney. Under this plan, Whitney would become "Professor of the Sanskrit and its relations to the kindred languages, and of Sanskrit literature."

Salisbury envisaged this mainly as a post for graduate instruction in Yale's Department of Philosophy and the Arts. Yet his proposal also called for Whitney to teach modern languages in the undergraduate college. (Those subjects had traditionally been handled by visiting Europeans, contracted on a yearly basis.) Fees from this extra teaching would add about $300 a year to Whitney's earnings. Salisbury himself would pay his base salary — $700 — to the College treasury. This arrangement would be set under a five-year contract, with Whitney's option to renew and the College's pledge to do the same unless Salisbury suffered financial incapacity. Salisbury also expected Whitney to assist him in editing the AOS journal. Finally, Salisbury hoped that Whitney would be able to begin these duties in September, immediately upon his return from Europe.[55]

Taken by surprise, Whitney responded to this offer with real gratitude but also considerable caution. He told Salisbury that he would need to stay abroad until late in the summer in order to complete his *Atharva* research. Once he was home, moreover, he would want to visit family and friends and to give his eyes a rest before he began any new exertions. All of this told against his being ready to teach in the fall term. Salisbury promised to take no action on the matter until Whitney returned, effectively extending the offer to the following year.[56]

At bottom, Whitney was reluctant. He was daunted by the proposed responsibility, and he especially disliked the idea of teaching modern languages. In part he felt unprepared (he pled his slight command of French), but mainly he wanted to avoid such mundane teaching chores. James Hadley assured him that the faculty was unanimous in wanting him to join them, and he predicted — wildly optimistically — that the teaching load would be light. Whitney's brother Josiah, on the other hand, raised a further objection. Yale, he noted, lacked the "liberality of religious opinion" that William would enjoy were he perhaps to land a position at Harvard. "If being at New Haven would lay any restraint on you, so that you would be unable to publish and write your opinions in the course of your researches, then I would not go there." Fortunately, however, no immediate decision needed to be made. Whitney's presence was not required for the coming academic year, so there would be ample time to discuss these questions once he got home.[57]

Whitney arrived in Northampton in August of 1853, the beginning of a year spent renewing old ties, working odd jobs, and eventually continuing his studies. He took things easy at first. There were, of course, many Whitneys to be visited. He also indulged in leisure reading, including the famous account by the naturalist Darwin of the world-circling voyage of the *Beagle*. January found Whitney rooming with Josiah in Cambridge, Massachusetts, the home of Harvard College. He spent part of his time there preparing statistical tables for a book his brother was writing, a survey of the metallic resources of the United States. He also commuted to Boston to work at organizing the American Oriental Society's library, whose books and manuscripts lay piled in a corner of the Athenaeum Building located on Beacon Hill. And soon he was preparing reviews of recent scholarly works for the Society's *Proceedings* of 1854. Through these latter endeavors, Whitney placed himself, as he put it, "in the service of Oriental philology."[58]

Meanwhile, in the absence of other prospects, and with scant rejoicing, he accepted the teaching position at Yale. Salisbury was pleased, although he warned that a career as an Orientalist would not prove materially rewarding.[59] As the one holding the purse strings, he was in a good position to know.

## Early Years at Yale

An illuminating portrait of Whitney's new surroundings can be found in Louise Stevenson's *Scholarly Means to Evangelical Ends* (1986), an examination of the social and intellectual milieu at nineteenth-century Yale. Here are described the daily community of Christian learning, the local literary societies and discussion groups, the intermarriages among faculty families, and related institutions such as the Congregationalists' *New Englander* magazine—all of which revolved around the life of the College.

The New Haven scholars sought to integrate sound religious doctrine with the best that the arts and sciences had to offer. This actually was a goal of most American colleges of that day, yet Yale stood out in two respects. First, its faculty was committed, however tentatively, to producing original research. Several members in addition to Whitney spearheaded this effort, for they too had trained at German universities. Second, the New Haven scholars took at least partial inspiration from philosophical idealism. This latter point belies a common stereotype: not only did German philosophy nurture the New England Transcendentalists and the beginnings of American theological liberalism, but it also brought a stimulating influence to conservative and evangelical Yale.[60]

In this setting, W. D. Whitney was in many ways an odd man out. Unlike most of his new colleagues, he was not a Yale graduate. Neither was he an ordained clergyman as were many of the faculty. Especially important, Whitney's religious and philosophical beliefs differed from those of nearly all of his colleagues—including his patron E. E. Salisbury, his good friend James Hadley, the College's preeminent philologist J. W. Gibbs, its leading natural scientist James Dwight Dana, its president T. D. Woolsey, and an up-and-coming spokesman for the New Haven scholars, Noah Porter, who taught the bellwether subjects of moral philosophy and psychology. Nearly all of these figures sought to combat what they called the "new infidelity," an increasing indifference to religion found especially in the academic disciplines. Yet Whitney did not share this concern; neither was he imbued with the idealist philosophy that informed the work of colleagues such as Gibbs and Porter. He therefore cannot be classed either religiously or philosophically among most of those with whom he would associate daily for nearly forty years. Despite his long tenure at Yale, Whitney would never be completely of Yale. Not, that is, until the final decade of his career when Yale itself began to change.

Whitney's early years in New Haven would be marked by an undercurrent of dissatisfaction, stemming largely from the issue of religion. Other sources were financial constraints and the burden of modern language teaching. None of these problems seemed insuperable at first, however, and despite his reservations, Whitney was glad enough to have a position to step into. And in many respects he found Yale a congenial environment. He settled into rooms on campus—located, ironically, in the Divinity School. Soon his walls displayed a map of ancient India, an etching of Cologne Cathedral, and cityscapes of Berlin and Tübingen. Dominating his study were a black walnut bookcase and a large table, the latter strewn with an assortment of dictionaries.

For the first two years Whitney boarded with the Hadleys, who introduced him—with some prodding—to New Haven's social life. (He told his sister, "I go out into society just as much as I can't help . . . and make no more calls than are required of me.") Whitney did enjoy the community's oratorio society, for he loved the choral music of Bach, Handel, and Mendelssohn. He also enjoyed the local intellectual circles. He was invited almost immediately to join "The Club," a group made up mostly of Yale men that met for discussion at President Woolsey's home. And he was elected a member of the Connecticut Academy, a scientific association dominated, again, by Yale. Not least, he took an active part in New Haven's newly founded philological society, which had been established while he was abroad.[61]

Whitney would acquire his first student in Sanskrit only in his second year of teaching, yet his hands were already full. He continued to organize the AOS library, now housed at Yale, and he began work on several new Indological projects. There were also general-interest papers to prepare for the Oriental Society's meetings, with a view toward making those occasions a bit more stimulating. Taxing his time most of all was his modern language teaching. In addition to conducting his regular recitations in the College, he led an extracurricular German class for five young women.[62] With these various endeavors in mind, Whitney described his divided feelings in the spring of his first year: "I don't believe a teacher ever taught anything under pleasanter circumstances than I have been doing hitherto, or that many people are in a pleasanter situation generally, only that I feel all the time as if I were on the edge of a gulf, and liable at any moment to plunge over in."[63]

These were all good activities, but would they keep body and soul together? His father wanted to know the bottom line. Whitney alleged that he would make do "by the aid of lecturing, bird-stuffing, gardening, marrying heiresses, etc." He did in fact do taxidermy (eagles mostly) for pay in those years. But he still needed occasional cash advances from home. Under these circumstances, his extracurricular language teaching proved a boon. It also paid a nonfinancial dividend. Writing to a hometown friend, Whitney laconically mentioned a Miss Baldwin in his ladies' German class, "which has naturally bro't us into connection somewhat." He went so far as to express admiration for the young woman's character. Four months later, in April of 1856, Whitney became engaged to Elizabeth Wooster Baldwin (1824–1912); they would marry that August. It was an upward move for Whitney socially: Elizabeth (a second "Lizzie" in his life) was the daughter of Roger Sherman Baldwin of New Haven, an ex-governor of Connecticut (Whig Party) and a one-term U.S. Senator.[64]

Whitney's engagement was a happy event, yet it came after one of the most anguished—and revealing—periods in his personal life. Whitney experienced multiple crises during those months, all of them in some way connected to the issue of religion. His views on that subject continued to trickle out. Home for Thanksgiving during his first year on the Yale faculty, he described for his older sister the day's church service:

> We filed into our pew with a good deal of effect, and set the rest of the congregation a good example by looking hard at Mr. Hall and keeping awake. We had just such a sermon as Mr. Hall always preaches: his text was "Rejoice with Trembling," and he thought the trembling was so much the most important part of it that he didn't mind the rejoicing at all. He thought that if we only shook in our shoes enough we couldn't fail of doing our duty in the premises: I regarded it as a humbug, and have expressed my indignation accordingly. But Mr. Hall is a consistent man: he, his looks and his sermons are all alike grim and fierce: he never took a happy view of anything.[65]

Again Whitney's words contained a touch of Mark Twain: beneath the amused veneer lay considerable resentment.

Tension in connection with Yale began to surface the following year as Whitney discovered that his lack of religious commitment obliged him to lead a life of "concealment." He felt placed in a false position, and he agonized over whether he should continue to work "among the people of New Haven, who think and believe so differently from me." He reproached himself for having accepted the job in the first place, thus allowing the predicament to arise. On the other hand, he feared the possibility of being asked to resign and the humiliation that would entail. Most of all, he dreaded telling his father where he stood, knowing the pain it would cause him.[66]

Josiah at least provided a sympathetic ear. Writing to his brother, William wondered aloud whether, as a matter of personal honor, he ought to seek another position: "I should without the least hesitation accept an invitation to a Professorship of Oriental Languages in any Western institution where they would take me with a full knowledge of my irreligiousness." He asked, for instance, if Josiah knew anything about the University of Michigan's policy concerning its faculty's beliefs. In a more pessimistic mood, he concluded that Yale was his only option: "Another Professorship I certainly cannot hope to obtain elsewhere, as of course I would not accept another place without making my sentiments distinctly and explicitly known; and there is not probably an institution in the land where they would not be shy of an avowed materialist."[67] What exactly he meant by the term "materialist" we will see better as we go along. In any case, Whitney was right: it was rare in that day for someone of openly irreligious opinions to hold an academic post in America.

Meanwhile, his father was pleased to hear of the strong faith of the Baldwin family of New Haven, especially among its females, with whom his son was becoming so friendly. But for good measure, the senior Whitney invoked the authority of a past president of Yale College, a figure who had contended with "deistical" beliefs earlier in the century: he urged his son to read Timothy Dwight's *Theology Explained and Defended* (1818). He also recommended that William seek out the current Yale president for spiritual counsel. As usual, William made no reply. And instead of reading Timothy Dwight's defense of the faith, he soon read David Friedrich Strauss's notorious *Leben Jesu* (1835), a naturalistic account of Jesus' life and legacy that epitomized the "German rationalism" his father had earlier warned about.[68] As with his reading of *Vestiges of the Natural History of Creation* years earlier, Whitney apparently left no record of what he thought of *Leben Jesu*. Still, his intellectual drift was clear enough.

He could read what he wanted in private, but his independent thinking still placed Whitney in an awkward position among his friends and colleagues. And it threatened infinitely more his growing intimacy with Elizabeth Baldwin. Here once again, Whitney's situation paralleled that of the young Charles Darwin, whose own religious doubts had been the source of considerable anxiety during the courtship of *his* future wife. Whitney's skepticism, however, was significantly more advanced than Darwin's at this point in his life.

Whitney had begun confiding his views to Elizabeth early in their relationship. Yet he increasingly feared that he had not made himself clear enough and that he had thus allowed Elizabeth to hope that those views might change. Had he unwittingly betrayed her by erring on the side of discretion? As springtime arrived, he became so conscience-stricken that he had difficulty concentrating on his work: "I can do nothing here of any profitable employment till my mind is bro't to calmness."[69]

Things came to a head in early April. Elizabeth went to visit relatives in Worcester, Massachusetts, and Whitney was obliged to communicate with her by letter. He wrote almost daily, and in doing so, he left probably the most unguarded record of his religious opinions that exists. It should be said, first, that he gave in these letters all of the indications of a young man sincerely in love. Indeed, he showed a greater sensitivity and tenderness than one might have expected, judging from his irreverence on other occasions. At the same time, however, he was decidedly plain-spoken. He reproached himself for not having been more forthright with Elizabeth earlier, and he now sought to make amends: "You cannot perhaps understand, certainly I cannot tell you in words, how deep and satisfying my convictions are, how entirely I believe that I am right and you are wrong, with what grimaces even I reject the creeds of orthodoxy, even when I most heartily recognize all the good and beautiful that is attached to them, and most strongly admire and love those who hold them. You do not do justice to the strength of my persuasions because they are as yet so quiet and unaggressive, but that is owing partly to their strength and partly to my weakness."[70]

What was the actual substance of Whitney's outlook? About sacred scripture, he said: "I approach that which claims to be God's word with the deepest distrust. . . . I find there written so much that seems to me a false science, false history, false or at any rate crude and imperfect morality and religion even, that I cannot help saying this is from man's hand and not from God's." Whitney declared these things even at the risk of losing the relationship that had come to matter to him the most. As he said, "I have written with calmness but oh, Lizzie, I feel in my heart of hearts what momentous interests hang upon this point: I have been far enough from calm when I have thought upon it." Even so, he was committed to making sure that Elizabeth knew exactly what she was getting were she to have him. And as he told her, she certainly could not want him if he betrayed his conscience and lost his own self-respect by denying his true beliefs.[71]

These intimate matters of love and religion also had links to Whitney's job situation. He could hardly consider marriage while his position at Yale, for all he knew, was hanging by a thread. And so, sometime during the week after he wrote his anguished letters, Whitney went to talk things over with the stern and respectable T. D. Woolsey. His purpose was not to get spiritual counsel, as his father had hoped, but to come clean. The result of this meeting was as much a surprise as a relief, and Whitney's relief was profound. As he told his sister Elizabeth, he had discovered that "there is liberality indeed throughout New Haven to a degree which even I, well as I know them, did not comprehend. . . . Even President Woolsey, whom I went to consult with as the highest authority, told me that he saw no necessity for my leaving them, at least at present."[72] This took care of one of Whitney's worries: he could remain at Yale — "at least at present" — without doing so under false pretenses.

Having this problem settled helped to clear the way for a second break-through. Just after getting the benign word from Woolsey, William and Elizabeth came to a meeting of the minds: although grieved by his lack of faith, she loved him nonetheless. William attributed this result to an underlying kindredness of spirit. As he told his sister, "Much as our beliefs are unlike, they are but the outward shell of our [similar] inward character." He could also report the joyful outcome: "I have decided now, Lizzie, that I may stay in New Haven as I have done, and allow myself to be happy: and I am engaged to Miss Lizzie Baldwin: we have promised to love and help one another till death part us."[73]

Two months after their wedding the new couple traveled to Europe for a seven-month sabbatical; they took with them Whitney's sister Maria. A journey of this length was an extravagance for someone of Whitney's means. His father arranged the financing through his contacts with Boston bankers. A chief goal of the trip was to restore Whitney to good health. He had been nearly prostrate during the previous months, a result, no doubt, of the emotional strain he had been under. The travelers initially went southward, enjoying Florence and Rome for many weeks before settling in Paris for the main part of their stay. These locales also allowed for the further study of European languages.

The latter had not been on Whitney's original list of goals for the trip; he had wanted to spend his time in Paris, for instance, mainly conferring with the leading French Orientalists.[74] Yet it was uncertain when Yale would hire a regular faculty member in modern languages, so Whitney felt obliged to expand his teaching repertoire. Still, Europe had its pleasures. The journey also brought the beginnings of two significant relationships. While in Rome, the Whitneys became friends with Charles Eliot Norton (1827–1908), a young Boston man of letters and the future editor of the *North American Review.* (Norton was there studying Italian art and collecting books on Dante.) Earlier, while passing through England, Whitney had paid a brief visit to Oxford Sanskritist F. Max Müller, the celebrated student of the *Ṛg Veda*.[75]

The return to New Haven brought the beginning of a new academic year and a tremendous letdown. No one had been hired in his absence to handle the modern languages, so Whitney was expected to continue teaching German and to add French as well. He told Josiah how he felt about these duties: "I abominate and grudge the time for it more and more, and I feel as if I must manage to get emancipated." Yet where else could he go? When they arrived home from Europe, Whitney and his wife went to live with her parents in order to reduce expenses, and two months later their first child arrived. The next year Whitney was in debt to his father.[76] He signed on again, therefore, this time without hesitation, when his five-year contract with Yale came up for renewal. Salisbury made the appointment for life or until Whitney chose to leave.[77] His salary did not increase, but at least his position seemed secure.

That fall (1859), Whitney had nearly one hundred students, very few of them studying Sanskrit. And the next year he began offering a German class in Yale's Sheffield Scientific School — this in addition to what he taught in the College. Other activities held more interest: Whitney did piece work for the 1864 revision of Webster's *American Dictionary of the English Language,* edited by Yale's Noah Porter; he also wrote several articles on Orientalist subjects for the *New American Cyclopedia.* Yet these jobs did not produce much income, and they brought no lessening of his classroom chores. Thus, after a decade as a college professor, Whitney declared in exasperation: "I feel as if I were fast turning into a mere teacher of German and French: my weekly exercises are to be nine this year."[78] Relief would come eventually, yet only at the point of a new crisis in Whitney's official relations with Yale.

## Additional Sites of Endeavor

Ambivalent about his work at the College, Whitney showed more enthusiasm for other scholarly venues. One of these was the New Haven Philological Society. Although officially autonomous, this group was made up mostly of Yale faculty. Among its original members were T. D. Woolsey and E. E. Salisbury, both European-trained, as well as James Hadley and Josiah Gibbs. Given this pool of talent, the society had high potential. Yet the meetings, at which members took turns reading papers, were not always productive in the early days. Soon after Whitney went to Berlin as a student, Hadley sent him the following report—one of his affectionately sardonic depictions of New Haven life. He referred here to William L. Kingsley, a graduate of the College and the Divinity School, a local lawyer, and the future proprietor of the *New Englander:*

> Mr. Kingsley follows me alphabetically in the Philological Society. In March he had not made any preparation, and thought we had better go and hear Dr. Bushnell of Hartford, who was to lecture on the regular evening of our meeting. . . . Well March passed and April came and the Society convened at Pres. Woolsey's. . . . We began as usual with miscellaneous talk, until at last Mr. Kingsley suggested that we might as well organize. The members tacitly acquiesced, and maintained for some time an unbroken silence of expectation. At last I ventured to observe that we had hoped to receive some communication from Professor Kingsley. Yes, he said, but men do not always obtain what they hope for. He had intended to prepare something, but various causes had prevented—he would not give his excuses like a Sophomore. The long and short was that he had no communication for the Society. So there we were. . . . Well, [after a discussion of Latin poetic metre] we Philologs went off upon other matters, told stories, talked politics and so on til about 10 o'clock when we adjourned. Such was our last meeting.[79]

Twelve years later, under new leadership, things had changed considerably. Whitney described the Philological Society at this time as "quite a pleasant little institution. . . . Mr. Hadley and I are the two old folks in it, the rest are chiefly tutors and University [graduate] students, with one or two teachers and other outsiders. . . . I regard it as an especially valuable institution for the advanced students in philology."[80]

For his own scholarly activity, Whitney found his main stage in the American Oriental Society—this in spite of his initial discouragement with that organization. By the mid-1850s the AOS had grown stagnant and appeared unlikely to achieve national, much less international status, unless big changes were made. The group was dominated by a handful of members from Boston and New Haven, and the semi-annual meetings at the latter site suffered from chronic low attendance.[81] Still, Whitney discovered an advantage in the group's small size and weak leadership, for under such conditions his own influence could be considerable. He served first as the Society's Librarian and soon added the job of Corresponding Secretary—a position, despite its modest title, that included management of the journal and the published *Proceedings*.

Especially important was his labor on an ad hoc committee charged with promoting "increased efficiency" in the Society's administration, which Whitney used to overhaul the entire setup. He prepared the committee's report, in which he made a number of interlocking proposals. The ultimate goal, he said, should be the rejuvenation of the AOS journal. A volume of four to five hundred pages, published annually, would earn the society international respect and encourage substantive exchanges with European scholars.[82] The financing of this effort would require an increase in the number of dues-paying members, and that meant recruitment. Whitney organized a letter-writing campaign for this purpose. He also moved to tighten the rules for current members. As for those delinquent in their dues—"dead heads" he called them—"I should be in favor of striking them all off." Similarly, retired missionaries should be dropped from the list of corresponding (courtesy) members and required to pay their own way.[83] These initiatives would eventually bring substantial results, especially once Whitney began to supply the final ingredient: high-quality material for publication in the journal.

Whitney discovered a further means by which to stimulate Orientalist studies in America. Soon after he took the job at Yale, he began hearing reports about money having been willed for a Sanskrit professorship at Harvard College. He hoped that this post would be created and that they would offer it to him. At least in that way, he calculated, "Mr. Salisbury, or someone else, might be started into providing a little better for me here."[84] Yet there was no word of the Harvard chair actually being established.

Several years later, Whitney took matters into his own hands and tried to goad Harvard into making the rumored chair a reality. He also tried to secure that position for someone other than himself. The person he had in mind was an expatriate American named Fitzedward Hall (1825–1901), whose unusual career began just after his graduation from Harvard in 1846. Hall went adventuring at sea and was shipwrecked in India, where he stayed and studied the native languages, became a teacher, and worked his way up in the Anglo-Indian educational establishment. Eventually, he made plans to retire in England. Before he did so, however, he visited the United States, and it was at this time (the fall of 1860) that Whitney made his acquaintance. Whitney regretted Hall's decision to settle abroad, not least because Hall's valuable collection of

Sanskrit manuscripts would likely end up in Oxford's Bodleian Library. Besides, a friendship of sorts had developed. As Whitney told Josiah, he had "established a personal relation with him [Hall] that will be of the greatest advantage to me in all time to come."[85]

Whitney was not angling for his own advantage, however, when he tried to bring Fitzedward Hall permanently back to America. This took place two years later, after Hall was offered a professorship in Sanskrit at King's College, London. Whitney tried to use this event to provoke a counteroffer. Attempting to enlist Yankee pride, he contacted G. W. Wales, a brother of the deceased Bostonian who was said to have willed his fortune to establish the Harvard Sanskrit chair. Whitney argued that the position should now be created and that Hall should be invited to fill it: "His loss to us if he were finally to cut loose from America would be a great one, as his acquisition would be of the highest value to the science of our country and would do much to establish Oriental Studies here with that firmness and give them that consideration in the eyes of the world which we ought to strive earnestly to win for them."[86]

Whitney must have winced at the reply he received. Writing from Beacon Street, G. W. Wales said that he too hoped that Mr. Hall would decide to return to his native land, "though from what you say I should think him very much wanting in patriotism, to carry to England the fruits of his labours." Wales also alluded to various obligations that had taken up a large share of his brother's estate. Still, he tossed down a scrap: if local gentlemen wanted to raise the money to bring Hall to Harvard, Wales certainly would do his part. Taking his cue, Whitney tried to organize a funding committee in Boston and Cambridge, carefully explaining that, thus far, no open position for someone of Hall's abilities existed in the United States.[87] Yet his efforts failed, and the Harvard Sanskrit chair again proved to have been a mirage.

Whitney later confessed to Charles Eliot Norton, a college classmate of Hall's, his mixed feelings about the abortive attempt to bring Hall back to America: "It was a great shame to let such a man become expatriated. Two years ago, it would have been very easy to fasten him here, and I tried as hard as I could to make your people at Cambridge see that they could and ought to retain him; but it was in vain. Now, I fear that he is too strongly rooted for transplantation. Anyhow, one takes a kind of wicked satisfaction in seeing that England has to come even to America for her scholars in that department of Oriental study which it is most her duty and interest to cultivate. There is no native Englishman who is nearly Hall's equal in Sanskrit."[88] Whitney's "wicked satisfaction" was accompanied by a more practical compensation. In addition to his London professorship, Fitzedward Hall was appointed to the influential post of Librarian of the East India Company, through which he gained an insider's knowledge of the British Indological scene. Over the years, Hall would keep Whitney abreast of developments in that arena.[89]

The most striking feature of this episode is Whitney's willingness to sacrifice his personal interest in an effort to promote the scholarly eminence of his country. For at this early point in his career, he gave up any claim to the one position in America that could have relieved his frustrations at Yale, seeking it for another man for the sake of the larger good. Even if he did covet access to Hall's manuscript collection, Whitney still showed a considerable degree of unselfish patriotism. This affair also illustrates how prominently the relationship between Harvard and Yale figured in Whitney's vision for improving American scholarship. It was crucial, he believed, to promote healthy competition between these leading colleges, so that each could spur the other to greater efforts. He would always keep an eye, therefore, on the relative strength of these institutions.

There is yet another lesson to be learned from the affair of the Harvard Sanskrit professorship. It comes from what might seem a mere detail, being only a point of terminology. In his letter to G. W. Wales, Whitney described America's efforts in the Orientalist field as an aspect of "the science of our country." Used in this sense, "science" was the rough equivalent of scholarship as a whole. This comprehensive definition of the term was embraced nearly universally at the time Whitney began his career, as much so in its English version as in its German equivalent *Wissenschaft*. Yet it was also a definition that—at least in English—would soon begin to pass from the scene.

# CHAPTER TWO

# Indological Foreshadowings

As a young graduate student at the University of Berlin, William Dwight Whitney had taken his stand, as he put it, "on Indian ground." He decided to concentrate his life's work on the oldest writings in the Sanskrit language and on the unique historical insights they afforded. There was no obvious connection between this highly specialized field of research and the general linguistic theory he would eventually espouse. Even so, as in a glass darkly, Whitney's approach to Orientalist investigation foreshadowed key aspects of his linguistic science. It will be useful, therefore, to delve further into Whitney's work as an Indologist, for here one finds the earliest traces of his views about science itself as applied to language study. Here also, in the remote realm of Orientalist scholarship, events took place that would lead Whitney toward an intense new interest in theoretical linguistics.

## Baconian Indology

W. D. Whitney produced an astonishing amount of original research during his career. Each project took years to complete, and several filled entire issues of the *Journal of the American Oriental Society.* His work began with the 458-page Roth-Whitney edition of the *Atharva Veda* text, published in 1855–56. (An additional volume, consisting of philological commentary, was projected for later.) Next Whitney prepared a preliminary 50-page index of the *Atharva*'s lexical and grammatical forms, and then he began the much larger task of compiling an exhaustive *Index Verborum,* which he would finally complete in 1881.[1]

Whitney was obliged to take on much of this work because Rudolph von Roth became distracted by a new venture: he was named co-editor of a comprehensive Sanskrit lexicon being sponsored by the Russian Academy of Sciences. Yet Whitney played an important role here as well. As one of four principal contributors to that work (apart from the editors themselves), he selected passages from Vedic literature to illustrate early Sanskrit word usage. This he did during most of the twenty-three years it took to prepare the lexicon's seven volumes.[2] Another of Whitney's endeavors was a translation, with explanatory notes, of the *Suryasiddhanta,* an early Indian astronomical treatise. That work earned him his first honorary doctorate, awarded by the University of Breslau in 1861.[3]

Labors of this kind exemplified the sober, *wissenschaftlich* side of nineteenth-century Orientalism. There was, however, another side to this movement, one that built on solid scholarship yet added an intense interest in Eastern religion and literature for their own sakes. For instance, by producing the first Western translation of the *Bhagavadgita* in 1785, the Englishman Charles Wilkins inspired German romantic philosophical writers from Goethe to Schopenhauer. This enthusiasm for the East was short-lived in Britain itself, especially after the appearance of James Mill's *History of British India* (1817) with its jaundiced depiction of Indian culture. On the Continent, however, the venerating spirit increased. Some believed that the ancient East had nourished the entire Hellenic, hence European, intellectual tradition. Others saw Western religion as a debasing of the more pristine revelation given to the earliest Hindus. An American observer (not W. D. Whitney) described the latter outlook in the 1860s: "According to the philologers of Berlin, . . . it is from India that the last word of wisdom is to come to us, not, like Christianity, corrupted on its way, but fresh with the vigorous thought and the profounder intuitions of the earliest ages and the wisest men."[4]

For his part, Whitney deplored this celebratory kind of Orientalism. He called, instead, for a more dispassionate approach to Indological investigation, based on the ideal of inductive science typically associated with the English philosopher Francis Bacon (1561–1626). Central to this "Baconian" method was the meticulous gathering and classification of facts. Whitney pursued these objects especially through quantification, often through measuring the frequency of occurrence of each grammatical form appearing in a given text.

Also characteristic of the Baconian spirit was an aloofness toward past intellectual authority. As Whitney once said, the "scientific" treatment of a subject "excludes the admission as coordinate evidence of all opinion, by whomsoever and at whatsoever time expressed."[5] This distrust of unsubstantiated testimony was foundational to modern historical scholarship, as developed most famously in the German universities. It was also a key to philologically based biblical criticism, one of the most advanced centers of which was Tübingen, where Whitney had trained under Roth. Whitney's admiration for the new methods showed, for instance, in his review of a Frenchman's study of ancient Chinese civilization. He noted the author's "astonishment that the world is not satisfied with the works of the old Jesuit missionaries on the science, chronology, and history of China . . . as if those unimpeachable authorities had not already settled it. It is plain that a man who could betray such a state of mind has no idea of what historical criticism is, as practiced in our times. Why unsettle anything which great and good men in former times have agreed in believing? Why, indeed, but that we are taught to 'prove all things,' that we may 'hold fast that which is good.'?"[6] Whitney quoted here from the New Testament, invoking the common culture of that age. He did this, moreover, with a fair degree of sincerity, for despite his doubts about the substance of Christianity, he still enjoined a classically Protestant approach to old writings. The ideal was to set aside interpretive tradition and make an unmediated examination of the texts alone.

Whitney found this outlook reinforced by the Indological training he received in Germany. The first professorships in Sanskrit in that country were created in 1818, one for August Wilhelm Schlegel at the University of Bonn, and the other for Franz Bopp at Berlin. Schlegel and his students sought guidance from works written by the Indian experts on Sanskrit language and literature. (Few of the Continental Sanskritists spent time in India itself.) Bopp, however, doubted the worth of these sources, and so did his students Rudolph von Roth and Albrecht Weber. W. D. Whitney followed suit. By adopting this perspective, he distanced himself not only from the Sanskritists of the Bonn school but also from the pioneers of British Orientalism, who had worked in close collaboration with the Indian pandits. He was relieved, therefore, to find that the American Fitzedward Hall took a different approach, even though Hall had trained under the Anglo-Indian system: "I had rather feared that he would be too assertive of the Hindu [that is, Indian] methods and authorities; but he fully appreciates the advantages also of European study, and thinks as freely as one could ask."[7]

The Berlin school faulted the Indian linguists for their apparent inattention to the historical evolution of Sanskrit. In Whitney's day and since, scholars have estimated that the language's earliest period, the Vedic, began between 2000 and 1500 B.C.E., and continued for about a thousand years. Roth and Whitney considered the Vedic texts, although recorded by a priestly class, as reflecting a popular oral tradition expressed in a living vernacular. They found it hardly surprising, therefore, that the Vedic canon itself reflected gradual changes occurring in that language.

The Vedic period was followed by the era of "classical" Sanskrit, which differed from the Vedic dialect as much as nineteenth-century English differed from that of Milton or Shakespeare. Classical Sanskrit was a fixed and stylized language used mainly by the scholarly elite; Whitney compared it to Ecclesiastical Latin. The Indians developed a complex system of grammatical analysis during this period, all keyed to the classical tongue. And yet, Whitney complained, those techniques were used to analyze Sanskrit in all of its phases, including the Vedic. He concluded that the Indian scholars, by idealizing Sanskrit as something perfect and unchanging, had effectively denied its historical development. (Indeed, as Whitney noted, the name Sanskrit itself meant "perfect, polished, highly elaborated.")[8]

What Roth and Whitney wanted was a straight description of Sanskrit grammatical usage as found in the literary texts, wholly apart from the native analysis of those works. This method appeared at its best in the St. Petersburg lexicon, which cited passages from the entire history of Sanskrit writing in order to show the changes the language had undergone. Yet this approach also meant that a grammatical form had to be attested in a literary work in order to be considered valid. Whitney discounted the Indian scholars' interest in what would later be called "generative" grammar, which derived rules for the ongoing production of meaningful utterances, including utterances perhaps never before spoken. Instead, Whitney and his teachers treated Sanskrit as a "dead" language, regarding it as defined exclusively by a body of old texts.[9]

Whitney made a second complaint against Indian grammatical scholarship. That tradition was built on the work of Pānini, the presumptive author
of some four thousand grammatical rules, written in the form of terse poetic
aphorisms. Whitney acknowledged that these rules were based on minute observation, yet he found them to be unsystematic, characterized by "obscu-
rity and false proportion." Here again he framed his critique with reference to
nineteenth-century science, only in this case he reflected a growing *criticism*
of the Baconian spirit. By the 1830s and 40s, British and American intellectuals were reassessing the ideal of science as mainly a fact-gathering enterprise. Physicists and astronomers charged that the life sciences, especially, were
piling up too much undigested data at the expense of meaningful generaliza-
tion; the main offender was the overburdened Linnaean system of plant and
animal taxonomy.[10] Similarly, Whitney faulted Pānini and his followers for
failing to construct their rules in a way that would subordinate the complex
and particular to the simple and general. As a result, he said, they were obliged
to present a "chaos of exceptions."[11]

Whitney looked forward to the time when European scholars would gain
a better purchase on the Vedic tongue, so that Pānini could be allowed "to retire more and more into the background, until we are able at last to declare
ourselves quite independent of him." After all, this was the path that European science had taken for centuries: it had "broken the yoke of too many an
asserted authority to submit itself blindly to the lead of Hindu guides."[12]

Whitney had more respect for the native school of phonetic analysis, a contrast that can be seen in his own scholarship. Although he never made an in-
tensive study of an Indian grammatical treatise, he devoted two of his major
editing projects to phonetically oriented works known as *Prātiśākhyas*. Each of
these served as a guide to the correct pronunciation and metric accent of one of
the four Vedas. Whitney praised the phonetic science embodied in these writings, citing the "nicety of its observations and the subtlety of its distinctions."
An example was the differentiation between sonants, voiced articulations such
as the b-sound, and surds, unvoiced articulations such as the p-sound. (Another such pairing was g and k.) As the Indian scholars pointed out, the sounds
in each of these pairs were identical except for the initial activation of the vocal
cords in the sonant version.[13]

Even as he acknowledged such insights, however, Whitney still found fault
with Indian phonetics as a whole. The problem, once again, was an excess of

empirical data collection, an "over-refinement of analysis" and an "exaggeration of the subordinate, accidental or doubtful elements of articulation." Thus, although European phoneticists could learn from the Indians, their truer sense of proportion would lead them to construct a better system.[14]

Yet what did Whitney say about the actual content of the old Eastern literature? He had been intrigued as a student by his first taste of Indian mythology, but this did not last. He later specified, for instance, the kinds of things one should *not* expect to find in the *Avesta*, the sacred Zoroastrian scriptures of ancient Persia: "We do not go to them to learn religion, or philosophy, or science, not to have our hearts touched and swayed by the surpassing power of poetic thoughts and fancies."[15] Likewise, Whitney found neither wisdom nor beauty in Hindu writings. His description of the Brahmana texts was typical: "While they contain valuable fragments of thought and tradition, they are in general tediously discursive, verbose, and artificial, and in no small part absolutely puerile and inane."[16] And, late in his career, he said of the *Ṛg Veda*'s "Cosmogonic Hymn": "The unlimited praises which have been bestowed upon it, as philosophy and as poetry, are well-nigh nauseating."[17]

Yet to the serious scholar, Whitney suggested, the intrinsic worth of the old Oriental texts was not the point anyway. Rather, the value of these works was almost exclusively historical, in a dispassionately "scientific" sense. After making the above remark about the Cosmogonic Hymn, for instance, Whitney affirmed that this text was "of the highest historical interest as the earliest known beginning of such speculation in India, or probably anywhere among Indo-European races."[18] The Vedas also supplied the only available window onto the primordial Indo-Europeans' practical mode of life. Such information had to be gleaned indirectly from passing references to tools and shelter or to local flora and fauna. This approach was necessary, Whitney said, owing to "the lamentable lack of a historic sense which has ever been one of the most remarkable characteristics of the Indian mind, rendering all direct native testimony to a historic fact nearly worthless."[19]

The essence of what we have seen here—the pervasive anti-romanticism, the suspicion of acclaimed authority, and the empiricism balanced by a search for simple unifying principles—all would eventually reappear in W. D. Whitney's general linguistic writings. The Orientalist world, however, also provided a more event-specific backdrop to Whitney's career as a language theorist.

## The Boden Election

From the beginning of his professional career, Whitney kept a close eye on developments in European philology. One item that interested him especially was the question of who would fill a vacant professorship in Sanskrit at Oxford University. This was the prestigious Boden chair, the prize in a hotly contested election held in December of 1860. The chair's original incumbent, Horace Hayman Wilson, had died earlier that year.

The chief contenders for this position were the Englishman Monier Monier-Williams (1819–99) and Friedrich Max Müller, individuals who hailed from strikingly different backgrounds. An Oxford alumnus, Monier-Williams had studied Sanskrit in India and then had taught at the East India Company College in Haileybury, England. Max Müller, a native of Saxony, had earned a doctorate in Sanskrit at the University of Leipzig and had trained further in Berlin and Paris. He then set out to produce the first authoritative edition of the *Ṛg Veda* text. It was this project that brought him to Oxford in 1846 to consult manuscripts held at the Bodleian Library.

Once in England, Müller found a patron in Baron Christian K. J. von Bunsen, the Prussian minister to the Court of St. James and himself an amateur Orientalist. Bunsen used his influence to secure support from the East India Company for his young friend's research. This backing in place, Müller settled in Oxford, and the university press brought out the first volume of his *Ṛg Veda* edition in 1849. Müller also began giving lectures in the modern European languages, and soon he was appointed to an Oxford professorship in that subject. The chance to teach in his own specialty, however, arose with H. H. Wilson's death.[20]

The Boden election campaign lasted for nearly six months and had all the trappings of a contest for a seat in Parliament: there were handbills, letters to newspapers, and petitions of testimony. The intense partisanship was due largely to the character of the position itself. When Lieutenant-Colonel Joseph Boden of the East India Company bequeathed the University £25,000 to endow a chair in Sanskrit, he stipulated that the post should help promote the Christianization of India. Monier-Williams admitted that he was not the best man for the job if Oxford wanted to produce first-rate scholarship. Yet he was the better qualified, he argued, for what Boden had envisaged. He was familiar mainly with the writings of India's classical era, which, he said, would prove useful in translating the Bible into Hindi. By contrast, Müller's research on the Vedas, the literature of a much earlier period, would do little to illuminate the contemporary Hindu mind. Müller had other strikes against him as well: he was a foreigner; he was not an Oxford graduate; and he was suspected, rightly enough, of holding ultra-liberal theological views.[21]

W. D. Whitney probably first heard of Max Müller while studying in Germany in the early 1850s—the launching of Müller's *Ṛg Veda* project at that time caused considerable excitement in Orientalist circles. He soon arranged to have Müller elected as a corresponding member of the American Oriental Society, a move he urged, in part, because Müller's access to manuscripts in England could prove useful to scholars such as himself. Yet he also held Müller to be genuinely deserving. The two men subsequently met when Whitney paid a call on Müller at Oxford during his post-wedding trip. Four years later, in the midst of the Boden campaign, Müller contacted Whitney in order to secure the endorsement of E. E. Salisbury, the senior statesman among American Orientalists. Passing along this request, Whitney vouched for Müller's superior qualifications for the Oxford position.[22]

Most European scholars agreed: Whitney's friends told him that opinion on the Continent was decidedly pro-Müller.[23] Yet the Oxford voters followed their own inclinations, and Monier-Williams won the election hands down. Whitney was "desolated" by this outcome, which he described as "a downright shame." Yet at the same time he expressed ambivalence. Müller partly deserved his defeat, Whitney believed, "as he has been mildly toadying Wilson and the English for it [the professorship] these many years, and softening or hiding his opinions on many points to humor them."[24] Whitney still admired Müller as a scholar, yet it rankled him to hear of someone using flattery—and keeping secret his religious convictions—in an effort to improve his job prospects.

As his acquaintance with Müller was only slight, Whitney viewed the election mainly in terms of its effect on British Orientalist scholarship. For Müller, on the other hand, the result was a bitter disappointment; it meant failure to secure England's most prestigious post in his own field of expertise. Yet Müller did not wallow in self-pity. Instead, he rechanneled his considerable energy into a very different branch of philology. It was an amazingly quick transformation, for within a mere six months of his Boden defeat, he presented to a distinguished London audience a series of highly acclaimed lectures on "The Science of Language." The battle for the Oxford Sanskrit professorship was thus immensely important for the future of linguistics. Not only did Max Müller's lectures revive his own career, but they also set the stage for W. D. Whitney to take up the same subject. For those lectures would become the single most important factor prompting Whitney to give sustained attention to "linguistic science."

## Indian Astronomy

In the years just before he composed his own lectures on language, Whitney took part in an international debate about an apparently unrelated subject — the origins of Indian astronomy. The main question was this: Did the Indians invent their own astronomical system, or had their achievements in this field been shaped by outside influence, perhaps from Mesopotamia or from ancient Greece? This issue, which had far-reaching implications for the history of science, had attracted European scholars since the 1600s. It was popular especially among the French savants of the *ancien regime;* most influentially, the astronomer Jean-Sylvain Bailly (1736–93) championed the high antiquity of Indian science. The early British Orientalists entered the discussion as well. William Jones believed that the Indians had invented the first lunar zodiac, while H. T. Colebrooke concluded that the Indian system was at least partly indebted to the Greeks.

A new round of debate began in the years 1859–62 when the astronomer Jean-Baptiste Biot (1774–1862) proposed that the lunar zodiac had been invented jointly by two separate nations. Biot suggested that the Chinese had first conceived of lunar mansions, the series of star clusters used to track the moon's path across the nighttime sky each month. Yet it was the Indians, he argued, who had then constructed an actual zodiac for the measurement of time, using the Chinese mansions as their basis.[25] This hypothesis found a critic in the Sanskritist Albrecht Weber, who believed that the Indians had invented the entire system.

Weber held a built-in advantage over Biot on this subject, since the question was largely one of textual exegesis: how should one interpret the apparent references to stellar phenomena found in the Vedas? Those texts mentioned *Nakṣatras,* a term presumably denoting the asterisms (star clusters) that formed the lunar mansions. Yet these references came clothed in myth and were highly allusive, as in the passage from the *Ṛg Veda* which declared that "the king Soma lives with all the nakṣatras." That is, the moon-god visited, on successive nights, each of the twenty-eight sisters who comprised his harem. (The number twenty-eight presumably referred to the days in the lunar month, one mansion for each day.) Based on these references to *Nakṣatras* dating from the early Vedic period, Weber concluded that the Indians had invented the lunar zodiac. The Chinese and Arabic systems were therefore derivative.[26]

W. D. Whitney joined the discussion at this point, opposing not only Biot's theory but also the position held by Weber, his friend and former teacher. Whitney acknowledged that the Vedas alluded to celestial phenomena, yet the specific things referred to, he said, were not at all clear. His conclusion: literary evidence alone could prove the priority of neither the Indian nor the Chinese nor any other ancient system. The historical relationship between these developments was therefore "yet to be discovered."[27]

Scholars had been attracted to the celestial references in the Vedas for a further reason. Could these not be used to fix dates for the Vedic texts themselves, thus helping to establish a chronology of early Indian history? Modern researchers had tried to glean such dates with the help of native cosmological treatises dating from the previous millenium. Yet here again Whitney was skeptical. While it was true that the writers of those treatises had developed an elegant mathematical astronomy, they did not, he said, employ Baconian methods: "Their science is not a science of observation; it is a system whose data are absolute and perfect, handed down from inspired sages, or revealed by divine beings. . . . So far as is known, the astronomical literature contains no record of any native Indian observations." And, Whitney reasoned, if these more recent Indian astronomers had failed to follow empirical procedure, the allusions to stellar phenomena included in the nation's oldest literature could be trusted even less.[28]

Whitney elaborated his views on these subjects, along with considerable technical discussion, in a ninety-four-page article published in the 1863 *Journal of the American Oriental Society*.[29] (He had presented several shorter papers on these topics already.) He disclaimed any bias in the matter, for he was content, he said, to leave unsettled the question of national priority in scientific invention. Yet he believed that even this negative conclusion was useful, since it would clear the ground for future researchers. Whitney did suggest that the Indian cosmology likely had derived from the Greeks and that this probably did not take place until the early Christian era. He also judged the work of the Indians to be "the most complete and correct of all the ancient systems excepting the Greek."[30]

Whitney thus admitted at least the possibility of original Indian contributions to astronomical science. Yet he did not encourage this view, and he based this opinion on his overall appraisal of the Indian intellectual style: "They were not a people of such habits of mind that we should expect to see arise among them an institution like the lunar zodiac, of so practical a bearing, founded upon faithful and persevering observations of the heavenly bodies, and intended for chronometrical uses. In the Hindus as students of the heavens, as observers of celestial conditions and phenomena for other than superstitious ends, my faith, I must acknowledge, is of the smallest."[31] Whitney concluded that the Indians had, at best, produced brilliant ratiocination based on inadequate empirical data. And to his mind, such procedure was but a few steps short of mysticism.

Although Whitney singled out the Indians for special condemnation, his pronouncements in this respect were little different from what he said about anyone, regardless of nationality, whom he considered deficient in the empiricist spirit. Just as he faulted European Sanskritists who implicitly trusted the native linguistic sages, he had little patience with Europeans who venerated ancient Indian science. As he declared in the midst of the astronomy controversy, "the clear light of modern investigation has forever dispelled the wild dreams of men like [Jean-Sylvain] Bailly, who could believe India to have been the primitive home of human knowledge and culture."[32]

## An Emerging Rift

The Indian astronomy debate demonstrated Whitney's growing self-confidence as a scholar—clearly, he regarded himself as an equal of the major European savants. The debate also showed that Whitney would not keep silent in the face of views he thought untenable, no matter who expressed them. He criticized not only Biot, who had recently died, but also his friend Weber. In doing the latter, Whitney was plainspoken but not offensive. Weber responded by saying that he would not let their "literary duel" affect their friendship. And as Whitney himself remarked several years later, of all his acquaintances in Europe, Weber was the one to whom he was "most warmly attached, and to whom I owe most."[33]

A very different spirit, however, began to manifest itself in his relations with F. Max Müller. Whatever his ambivalence about Müller personally, Whitney had thus far respected Müller's scholarship. He approved, for instance, of much that he thought useful in the latter's *History of Early Sanskrit Litera-*

*ture* (1859).[34] But then Müller weighed into the astronomy debate with a distinctive new argument, one that managed to combine elements of Biot's and Weber's contrasting views on the beginnings of the lunar zodiac. In a paper entitled "Are the Indian Nakṣatras of native or of foreign origin?" Müller set forth a qualified version of the native-invention thesis. Paradoxically, however, he built this case on Biot's hypothesis that the Chinese had first discovered the series of star clusters and that the Indians and others had then borrowed this. Müller explained that Indian astronomers had incorporated this outside influence into their own preexisting schema of portioning out the lunar transit.

In other words, Müller claimed that the Indians had originated the idea of dividing the heavens into a segmented pathway, and he therefore defined *Nakṣatras* (as referred to in the Veda) as the divisions themselves. Müller thereby championed Indian originality in conceptualizing the *function* of the *Nakṣatras:* the only borrowed element consisted of the asterisms that marked and named those divisions. He based this interpretation on what he understood to be the temporal sequence in which three variant definitions of a term like *Nakṣatra* naturally would have arisen. First of all, Müller said, it would simply have meant a star, then it would have referred to the twenty-eight equal divisions of the heavens, and finally it would have specified the asterisms that marked those divisions. The Indian writers would have adopted this third definition, Müller argued, only in the process of borrowing the asterism concept with which they completed their zodiac.

W. D. Whitney responded to this unique theory in an addendum to his lengthy essay of 1863, where he especially considered Müller's etymological reasoning. Müller had suggested that a term's abstract definition (the divisions of the sky) would develop earlier than its concrete definition (the star clusters). Yet Whitney thought Müller had got things backwards. Surely, he argued, the name *Nakṣatra* would have been applied to the idea of star clusters prior to its being assigned to the idea of divided space.[35] Whitney thus drew on a staple teaching of British-empiricist linguistic philosophy: a concrete definition always forms the basis of any term denoting a general or abstract concept. By contrast, Müller adopted the viewpoint of post-Kantian idealism: a general concept is always inherent in any concrete definition. The question of the meaning of *Nakṣatra,* therefore, had ramifications far beyond the debate over ancient astronomy. As we will see in a later chapter, this philosophical disagreement lay at the root of Whitney's and Müller's opposing explanations of the origin of language itself.

In private, Whitney admitted that personal considerations had influenced his response to Müller's zodiac theory: "It seems to me only a very easy task to demolish the views of my three antagonists [Biot, Weber, and Müller] . . . but Müller is the only one of them for whom and whose opinion I feel anything like contempt. I have borne down upon him much more strongly than I would otherwise have cared to do, on account of his abominably mean treatment of Weber, in all his works."[36] Apparently Müller had attacked Weber personally while critiquing his Indological work, and it was loyalty to his former mentor that put the flint into Whitney's response.

There was, however, more to the story. Several months before Whitney's astronomy essay was published, Max Müller had written Whitney a friendly letter, requesting his endorsement of a petition to secure continued funding for his *Ṛg Veda* work. Unaware of what was coming, he also expressed his hope that Whitney would approve of his views on Indian astronomy: "It seems to me that we are pretty well agreed on the main points." Müller went on to complain that Weber had written a "silly reply" to his work on that subject: "However I do not mean to quarrel with him, but I wish his friends would tell him that he does himself no good by always snapping at me."[37]

Müller wrote to Whitney again nine months later, lamenting that a host of obligations had thus far kept him from reading Whitney's review of his article on the *Nakṣatras*. (By then, Whitney had distributed copies of his essay, in cluding his response to Müller, "pretty liberally" among the Indologists of Germany, France, and Britain.)[38] Yet if Müller had not read the essay itself, he certainly was aware of Whitney's disagreement with Weber, which he tried his best to exploit. As he told Whitney, "By his [Weber's] indiscriminate assertions, by his unscholarlike manner of [illeg.], by his confused conjectures . . . , he has done more harm than good to our studies."

Finally, Müller asked Whitney for advice. Because U.S. law did not recognize foreign copyrights at that time, he sought the name of an honest American publisher for his new book on "the science of language," which he wanted to keep from being pirated.[39] Whitney responded by helping to bring about a long-term arrangement between Müller and the Charles Scribner Company of New York. Scribner would later become the American publisher of a number of Whitney's books as well.

Whitney and Müller would continue, over the years, to do routine scholarly favors for one another.[40] Even so, considerable animosity had already developed on Whitney's side, stemming from the cutting remarks Müller had made about Albrecht Weber. Soon to become mutual, this antagonism would eventually add bile to some of the most important nineteenth-century debates about the nature of language and linguistic study.

Thus far we have followed a labyrinthine path through Whitney's early career as an Orientalist. This aspect of his life will reappear on occasion throughout our story, for Indology would always constitute Whitney's primary field. Still, it was but one of several lines of scientific and philological discussion that would inform his language theory. We turn next to other sources, both learned and popular, that shaped his thinking on that subject.

# CHAPTER THREE

# Victorian Language Debates

Although Orientalist matters dominated the early part of his career, William Dwight Whitney did not ignore the wider discussion about language taking place at this time. Victorian thinkers on both sides of the Atlantic were giving considerable attention to linguistic study, a subject that touched on some of the central intellectual issues of the age. It bore particularly on the mystery of human origins and on the related question of humanity's status within the natural order. As that question famously presented itself in the wake of Darwin's *Origin of Species* (1859), was mankind closer to the angels or the apes? Indeed, even before Darwin's book appeared, religious writers were looking to "scientific" philology for aid in their fight against the increasingly naturalistic worldview of the sciences themselves.

Our eventual goal is to see how W. D. Whitney responded to this popular linguistic debate and how others, in turn, responded to his views. Yet in order to pursue that story, we must first place Whitney temporarily into the background, making him but a single figure on a larger canvas. We pause, then, to take an interpretive sounding of Victorian-era linguistic debate, beginning with its remoter sources.

## Locke's Essay on the Meaning of Words

The seventeenth-century founders of British empiricism took a decidedly practical interest in language. Experience — especially the rancorous theological battles of post-Reformation Europe — had shown that words themselves often gave rise to intellectual disagreements. The solution, these thinkers insisted, was clarity of expression. Plain and precise word definitions were essential to learned discourse — especially, as the charter members of England's Royal Society pointed out, to the collaborative labors of science. John Locke supplied the philosophical underpinning of this outlook in Book III, "Of Words," in his *Essay Concerning Human Understanding* (1690).

A word, said Locke, stood for nothing other than an idea in the mind of its speaker. Hence, the same word used by different speakers did not necessarily mean the same thing. Although the surrounding community agreed more or less on the relationship between a given word symbol and its referent, each individual had his or her unique understanding of that relationship. Word definitions were characterized, therefore, by a significant degree of subjectivity. Here already, Locke said, language betrayed inherent "imperfections" as a medium of communication.[1]

A related theme was that the linkage a speaker did create between a word and its definition was purely arbitrary: it was not something given by Nature. This point was not original with Locke. Plato had famously considered it in his dialogue *Cratylus.* More recently, Francis Bacon had characterized words as merely "the tokens and signs of notions," and Thomas Hobbes had said much the same. Following in this tradition, Locke declared that certain words stood for certain ideas, "not by any natural connexion . . . for then there would be but one Language amongst all Men; but by a voluntary Imposition, whereby such a Word is made arbitrarily the Mark of such an Idea." Because the connection between an idea and its verbal representation was not inherent, Locke concluded that that connection had to be voluntarily re-created with a speaker's every utterance.[2]

These notions about the subjectivity, arbitrariness, and voluntariness of word definitions were unsettling, for they suggested that shared knowledge was highly problematic. Indeed, Locke's philosophy of language called into question the very notion of mutual intelligibility. Still, Locke offered this analysis, not as a body of truth to be contemplated, but as a survey of obstacles to be overcome. To help his readers surmount those obstacles, he recommended the use of words that were literal rather than figurative in meaning. This practice, he suggested, would lead to more consistent definitions and would thereby create a more communal mode of "human understanding."

In this context, Locke made what he hoped would be a helpful observation. Wanting to encourage a greater attentiveness to word definitions, he declared: "It may also lead us a little towards the Original of all our Notions and Knowledge, if we remark, how great a dependence our Words have on common sensible Ideas." The emphasis here was on "*sensible* ideas," that is, those got through the five senses. Locke noted that even "abstruse" terms, such as "to Imagine, Apprehend, Comprehend, Adhere, Conceive, Instill, Disgust, Disturbance, Tranquillity, &c.," were based on physical, sense-based metaphors. (W. D. Whitney later built on this assumption when he insisted that the concrete definition of a word, as with the Sanskrit *Nakṣatra,* always appeared prior to its abstract definition.) Locke went on to suggest that this metaphorical basis of abstract terms pointed toward a program of etymological research: "I doubt not, but if we could trace them to their Sources, we should find, in all Languages, the Names, which stand for Things that fall not under our Senses, to have had their first rise from sensible Ideas."[3]

Although scarcely more than a passing observation, this insight into the "sensible" metaphors underlying abstract terms would profoundly affect Western linguistic theory during the 150-year period after Locke's essay appeared. It did this, moreover, in a number of different ways. Later writers interpreted Locke's analysis each according to his own philosophical point of view. As a result, a principle that was intended to promote community of understanding would actually lead to new rounds of controversy.

## The Materialist Strain in Enlightenment Linguistics

Locke's *Essay* contributed significantly to each of nineteenth-century Europe's three main branches of linguistic theory. These we may label Common Sense, idealist, and materialist. In our next chapter we will see how W. D. Whitney embraced the first of these, the Common Sense tradition, even as he fought against the second; that struggle will be a focus of our story. The immediate concern, however, is with the third and most radical of these viewpoints, which would cast a shadow over the whole of Victorian language debate.

The materialist tendency in modern linguistics began with the writings of the English barrister, philosopher, and political gadfly John Horne Tooke (1736–1812). Horne Tooke had been deeply impressed by Locke's insight into the metaphorical basis of abstract terms, including the notion that all such words derived from the name of some physical condition. Yet he pushed this teaching to an unwarranted conclusion: he argued that by tracing word histories in this way the etymologist arrived at the only real meaning a word had ever had. For example, "A RIGHT line is that which is ordered or directed, the shortest between two points. . . . A RIGHT conduct is [likewise] that which is ordered. . . . To do RIGHT is to do that which is ordered to be done." Similarly, "TRUTH" was merely what one "troweth," or promised, to do. Horne Tooke devoted the bulk of his two-volume *Diversions of Purley* (1786, 1805) to etymologies such as these. His point was to show that inherited ideals of truth and good conduct were really only names and that those names registered strictly sensory impressions upon passive minds. His conclusion: the so-called operations of the mind, humanity's noblest sentiments among them, were "merely operations of language."[4]

Horne Tooke's views became surprisingly popular in the early part of the nineteenth century, despite their obvious radicalism as well as the often fanciful character of his etymologies. This popularity stemmed from the way his theory apparently furnished a "scientific" mode of analysis applicable to language. As one admirer said, Horne Tooke "treated words as the chemists do substances; he separated those things which are compounded from those which are not decompoundable." Even some religious thinkers were impressed by this procedure.[5]

Nevertheless, a substantial body of criticism was aimed at Horne Tooke's philosophical impiety. According to one writer, *The Diversions of Purley* espoused nominalism — the doctrine that general conceptions are names only — "in its lowest and worst form, as an instrument in the hands of materialism."[6] The two most eminent critics of that outlook represented two distinct philosophical viewpoints. The Scotsman Dugald Stewart hailed from the Common-Sense tradition, while the English poet and religious thinker Samuel Taylor Coleridge taught a version of Continental idealism. Each of these alternatives to Horne Tooke's materialism would soon gain a significant following, yet one of them was clearly ascendant. Although German in its origin, the idealist strain of linguistic thought would become by far the most popular in Victorian-era Britain and North America. And especially important for our purposes, the idealist writers opposed not only their real enemy — linguistic materialism — but also the far more moderate Common Sense perspective. For in their calculation, the three branches of nineteenth-century language theory increasingly boiled down to only two.

## Linguistic Natural Theology

Surely the best-remembered exponents of linguistic idealism in America have been the New England Transcendentalists. Ralph Waldo Emerson set the pattern in his book *Nature* (1836) by offering a new response to John Locke's analysis of conceptual terms. While it was true that words expressing abstract concepts were based on physical metaphors, those metaphors were more than mere conventionalized mental associations. For the world itself, said Emerson, was "emblematic." Every natural fact symbolized a spiritual fact, with the result that appropriate sense-based metaphors sprang up readily in the minds of language users. Emerson's friend Henry David Thoreau suggested a similar thesis in *Walden* (1854).[7] Here already one sees how Locke's insight was shared alike by materialists and idealists.

The "Emersonian" style of language theory was actually commonplace in mid-nineteenth-century America, yet the Transcendentalists played only a small part in making this so. Much more influential were orthodox religious writers, chiefly from the evangelical mainstream. For that group, the embrace of linguistic idealism was a part of their involvement in a much larger intellectual trend — the creation of a new kind of natural theology. Traditionally, works in this genre were of the sort W. D. Whitney was assigned as a college undergraduate: they focused on physical nature, examining the cosmos, the earth, and the biological sphere for marks of intelligent design. When spokesmen such as William Paley dealt with humanity, they again pointed to physical features, especially to finely adapted organs such as the human eye. These, said Paley, were difficult to account for without invoking an all-wise Creator.

In the early part of the nineteenth century, a number of writers began to supplement this approach by focusing on humanity's unique moral and intellectual faculties — including the faculty of speech. These too revealed supernatural origins, they argued, only in a deeper way, suggesting a more profound spiritual significance than could be inferred from mere anatomy and physiology. The language-oriented version of this new outlook we will call *linguistic natural theology*.

Almost all writers who embraced this perspective ultimately drew from the works of Johann Gottfried Herder and Wilhelm von Humboldt, dating, respectively, from the 1770s and the 1830s. Herder championed the idea of language as a spontaneous growth from within the soul; it was not just something the speaker acquired from the surrounding community. Herder also taught that language and reason were inextricably connected, each being dependent on the other. Words, therefore, did not merely serve as labels for preexisting ideas; rather, they molded ideas from their very inception. Humboldt added the corollary that language functioned primarily as the handmaid of *Bildung,* or self-formation; its communicative role was only of secondary importance.[8]

Yet what of the more "scientific" aspect of linguistic natural theology—was there anything here corresponding to the traditional natural theologian's study of nature? The key lay in the intertwining of the life sciences and philosophical idealism in Europe in that era. The late-eighteenth and early-nineteenth centuries saw the vogue of *Naturphilosophie,* the transcendentalist biological thought associated with Goethe and Geoffroy, and later, in Britain and America, with Richard Owen and Louis Agassiz. These figures were interested, not in mere physical anatomizing, but in discovering the ideal principles on which living things were constructed. They wanted to imbue the life sciences with more penetrating insights than those of the Enlightenment, which had been infatuated with Newtonian mechanism.[9] This fusion of idealism and empirical science had its parallel, in a general sense, in German philology, for language scholars in that country were renowned for their "scientific" methods. This linkage in turn buttressed the scientific aura of linguistic natural theology.

The idealist perspective on language was not necessarily religious in character, yet it could easily be adapted to religious purpose. A number of American thinkers took this step, having been inspired by S. T. Coleridge's *Aids to Reflection* (1825). That work served as an all-important conduit, bringing a somewhat mystical version of German philosophy to the English-speaking world. In America, Coleridge's *Aids* influenced not only the avant-garde writers of Concord and Brook Farm but also the conservative religious academics who held forth in New Haven. The key figure there was Josiah W. Gibbs, Yale's longtime professor of sacred literature and the college's chief language theorist until his death in 1861.

Up to a certain point, Josiah Gibbs was thoroughly Lockean in outlook. Borrowing directly from the *Essay Concerning Human Understanding,* he declared that language "has no immediate expression for intellectual ideas." He also affirmed that this need was supplied by metaphors based on sensory experience.[10] Gibbs went on, however, to apply this teaching to the study of religious concepts, noting that the word *spirit* originally had meant "breath" or "wind"; *heaven*, likewise, was something "heaved" or "arched." He offered these illustrations, not in the debunking mode of Horne Tooke, but rather to emphasize the necessity of sense-based language for describing the unseen realm. Figurative terms like these were indispensable, Gibbs argued, because religious concepts such as "spirit" simply could not be named in any other way. To this Gibbs added a further observation: once part of routine speech, words like *spirit* constituted "faded metaphors." The original derivation having been forgotten, their literal sense was no longer apparent to the average speaker.[11]

Gibbs's argument shows once again how Locke's insight into word origins supplied the basis not only of Horne Tooke's linguistic materialism but also of the nineteenth century's idealist language theory. What made these outlooks distinct from one another was the divergent ways in which they built on their common Lockean foundation. Gibbs added an idealist superstructure—like Emerson's, only more elaborate. How, he asked, did sense-based figures of speech, such as spirit, convey the intended concept to the mind of the hearer? His answer: "In the organic process of language, the person addressed is not a passive recipient of thoughts and ideas from the speaker, but by an independent activity of his own he reproduces the thoughts and ideas out of what is presented to him." Gibbs characterized this activity as the "reproduction of ideas by spontaneous action"—a classically Herderian notion.[12]

Continuing in this vein, Josiah Gibbs flatly rejected Locke's other main teaching about language, that the connection between a word's form and its meaning was a purely arbitrary matter. Instead, he declared that words enjoyed "natural significancy." First writing on this subject in 1839, Gibbs said that this thesis, although neglected of late, was assuming its place once again as "one of the deepest and most important doctrines in philology. . . . In order to explain the existence of language, it is not enough that man has the organ of speech, that he has sensations and ideas, and that he has a desire to communicate them to others; but it is also necessary that sounds should have a natural adaptedness to express the particular sensations and ideas." Language was therefore "not entirely arbitrary or conventional."[13] This theme neatly reinforced the perspective of linguistic natural theology. For as Gibbs suggested, there was in language a deep psychological dimension, an element that brute sense perception and improvised mental associations by themselves could not readily explain.

Josiah Gibbs's most famous student extended these lines of thought. A member of the Yale class of 1827, Horace Bushnell was the Hartford theologian who attracted so much attention among the New Haven academic community by virtue of his provocative writings and lectures. In his "Preliminary Dissertation on Language" (1849), Bushnell set forth a theory of religious rhetoric emphasizing imagination and intuition. Revisiting Gibbs's question, he again asked how it was that different minds could agree so readily in their metaphoric leaps, rendering mutually understandable even those words denoting abstract concepts. He answered by positing a "hidden analogy" or "Logos" in the world of physical nature resonating with the inner logos of abstract thought. Nature itself constituted a "vast dictionary and grammar" that supplied all the material the mind needed for purposes of representation.[14] If this was almost exactly what Emerson had said, it was because Emerson, Gibbs, and Bushnell all had drawn from the same source: German-idealist language philosophy as interpreted by Coleridge.

Yet Bushnell parted company with Emerson (and to a degree with Gibbs) in that he made his case in order to affirm the mystery of the Trinity, the cornerstone of orthodox Christian faith. (His "Preliminary Dissertation" served as an introduction to his treatise *God in Christ.*) Bushnell held that Trinitarian doctrine, being so far removed from any physical reality, simply did not lend itself to precise description. He argued, therefore, that the believer's apprehension of the divine was more a matter of poetic insight than of theological exactitude.[15] Although directed toward orthodox ends, this conclusion proved unsettling to mainstream evangelical thinkers, and it embroiled its author in controversy for many years.

A lesser-known yet complementary theme in Bushnell's "Dissertation" was its endorsement of linguistic natural theology. Borrowing Josiah Gibbs's phrase, Bushnell declared that the "natural significancy" of words offered unmistakable proof of a universe suffused with divine intelligence. And it did a better job of this, he said, than did a stack of books on traditional natural theology "piled even to the moon."[16]

How did William Dwight Whitney respond to this idealist and religiously tinged strain of language theory? The full answer will have to await our next chapter, for his initial reaction was silence. He appears to have had no personal contact with the Transcendentalists, even though R. W. Emerson was a nominal member of the American Oriental Society. He also rarely mentioned Josiah Gibbs, although he could hardly have been unaware of his language theory. After all, Gibbs was still teaching and publishing during Whitney's first five years on the Yale faculty. Finally, Whitney apparently never commented on Horace Bushnell's linguistic teaching, although he surely must have been familiar with it as well. His reticence is not surprising. In Bushnell's case especially, to have spoken out would have involved Whitney in a religious debate he naturally thought it best to avoid. Also, as we have seen, Whitney sincerely admired Bushnell for his role as a courageous "disturber of the modern church." Still, he could not have missed — and he could not have liked — the romanticist philosophy of language that was growing so popular in this period. Whitney's response to that tendency would eventually form the core of his own system of language theory.

## The Challenge of Evolutionism

By the time Horace Bushnell published his "Preliminary Dissertation on Language," many lesser-known writers had already embraced the philosophy underlying that work. They did this in order to address the Victorian-era challenge to theism that was implicit in the growth of scientific naturalism. The threat arose especially from naturalistic explanations of humanity's mental and moral capacities.

A milestone in that trend came with the publication of *Vestiges of the Natural History of Creation* (1844) — the anonymous work on biological evolution that W. D. Whitney read in the summer after graduating from college. *Vestiges* devoted a chapter to the subject of human origins, including the question of the origin of language. Here the writer suggested (in an argument likely borrowed from Jean-Jacques Rousseau) that the earliest humans uttered spontaneous and inarticulate cries, their vocal cords functioning like an "Eolian harp placed in a draught." To these random sounds the community gradually would have attached conventional meanings. Language was thus "no new gift of the Creator to man"; it was essentially the same as animal vocalisms, only enhanced by long practice so as to produce symbolic communication.[17]

This passage prompted a redoubling of the emphasis on linguistic natural theology. Already by this time American journals were combining reports on the latest developments in technical philology with touches of idealist language theory. The number of these articles shot up dramatically, however, in the wake of *Vestiges*. The Congregationalist *Bibliotheca Sacra* and the nonsectarian *North American Review* both decried the notion of a mere "outward and mechanical connection" between language and thought; they also rejected the idea of speech as an "arbitrary, artificial, and gradual invention." Language, they said, was a spontaneous product of the soul, called forth by something more than the purely practical need to communicate. Even the Presbyterian-run and Scottish-leaning *Princeton Review* embraced the German outlook, praising J. G. Herder's teaching on "the unity of cognition and language; to speak is to know."[18]

The response to *Vestiges* also included discussion about how language actually originated. All who spoke from the standpoint of linguistic natural theology rejected the idea that language could have been invented through human ingenuity alone. Although many of these writers did accord some role to human artifice, they insisted that this could have produced nothing without a divinely bestowed language instinct implanted in the first human minds.[19]

A further voice in this chorus came from a distant relative of W. D. Whitney's. Benjamin Woodbridge Dwight (1816–89) of Clinton, New York, was a clergyman and schoolmaster as well as a grandson of Yale's president Timothy Dwight. He was also one of the first Americans to discuss knowledgeably the work of Franz Bopp and Jacob Grimm. His writings on that subject originally appeared in *Bibliotheca Sacra* and the *New Englander* and were collected in his book *Modern Philology* (1859). There Dwight declared, with little supporting evidence, that the most recent linguistic research confirmed the account of human origins set forth in the Bible. This again was a discussion that could hardly have escaped Whitney's notice, for his friend James Hadley wrote a favorable review of Dwight's book.[20]

Of course the greatest challenge to this religio-linguistic consensus came from Darwin's *Origin of Species* (1859). That work did not discuss human evolution, much less the emergence of language, yet its implications were clear enough. In response, long before Darwin addressed those subjects in *The Descent of Man* (1871), an army of writers endeavored to show that human mental capabilities were vastly superior to those of animals. And as part of this effort, they presented a familiar message about language. Articles in Boston's *Universalist Quarterly,* for instance, affirmed that speech "did not progress from the bleatings of herds to vocal articulations by slow lessons" and that language existed, not just to facilitate communication, "but to originate thought."[21] And so, in the post-*Origin* decade of the 1860s, the idealist banner continued to fly high over popular philological discourse in America. This, however, was nothing compared to what was happening in England.

## A Victorian Apotheosis

Friedrich Max Müller faded fast from the scholarly pantheon after his death in 1901, and he has since been remembered chiefly as a popularizer. Müller does deserve credit for editing the *Ṛg Veda* as well as for virtually founding the discipline of comparative mythology — achievements that made him the Atlantic world's most celebrated Orientalist in his day. Yet Müller's larger popular success actually resulted from the denial of one of his chief ambitions in the Orientalist field: this took place in December of 1860, when he lost his bid for Oxford's Boden chair in Sanskrit. The university would later create a chair in Comparative Philology expressly for Müller, thus making his position there secure. Yet by then he had long since found his niche in an auxiliary calling. As noted already, his defeat in the Boden election, rather than thwarting his drive, served instead as a creative stimulus. For within a stunningly brief amount of time — just six months after that event — Müller delivered the first of his two lecture series on "the Science of Language."

The setting of those lectures was the prestigious Royal Institution of Great Britain, a forum established in London in 1799 for the genteel popularization of natural science. Physicists and chemists had been featured there especially, Humphrey Davy and Michael Faraday among them. Securing this venue was a master stroke. Arranged by Müller's friend Baron Bunsen, sponsorship by the Royal Institution brought court patronage and thus a guaranteed audience made up of England's social and intellectual elite. Among those who reportedly attended were Prince Albert, F. D. Maurice, John Stuart Mill, and Michael Faraday himself.[22] There were yet further advantages to addressing this forum: it allowed Müller to circumvent the Oxbridge university establishment as well as the socially prominent amateurs of the London Philological Society. In this way he created an entirely new public interested in linguistics, and one that looked to him alone as its guide.

Max Müller set out to mold that public's understanding of what language study meant for modern civilization — something he accomplished more successfully than any other individual in the nineteenth-century English-speaking world, W. D. Whitney included. It was a vocation for which he was eminently well suited. Handsome, suave, and ingratiating, Müller spoke fluent English and had a flair for brilliant exposition. He used his talents, on one level, to provide a lively survey of the current state of comparative philology, a field still relatively unknown outside the European continent at that time. His more ambitious goal, however, was to conduct a tour de force of linguistic natural theology.

Like the other writers we have seen, only with infinitely greater scholarly authority, Müller used linguistic data to argue for the uniqueness and supernatural origin of the human mind. The timing of this message was no accident: he turned to these issues just over a year after the publication of *The Origin of Species,* and he took every opportunity in his lectures to combat the materialist views that were already being insinuated in Darwin's name. Confronting the language issue head-on, Müller denied that speech could have originated through a Darwinian process: "It admits of no caviling, and no process of natural selection will ever distill significant words out of the notes of birds and the cries of beasts." And, he said, the fact that animals did not speak spoke volumes about the chasm between them and humans, for language was "the one great barrier between the brute and man." It was the most telling piece of evidence against the idea that humans had evolved from ape-like ancestors.[23]

What exactly did language reveal about this subject? Drawing on his early training in Kantian philosophy, Müller regarded the ability to use language as but the outward manifestation of the uniquely human capacity for abstract reflection. And that capacity, he argued, could never have developed from something less than itself. Pushing the point further, Müller reemphasized J. G. Herder's notion that words were necessary for the conduct of reasoning. Or, as he put it in his second lecture series, "*Without speech no reason, without reason no speech.*"[24]

Like Josiah Gibbs and Horace Bushnell, Müller rejected the Lockean notion that the connection between a sign and its meaning was purely arbitrary. He acknowledged that the original metaphoric essence of most words had long been obscured by the subsequent growth of conventional definitions. Yet he suggested that the trained philologist could reveal those essences anew. Tracing word derivations would thus form a kind of metaphysical recovery project—only in a sense that was the very opposite of Horne Tooke's. If etymologies were pursued back far enough, to the earliest glimmerings of human speech, they would reveal a golden age of pristine consciousness, of pure identity between word and thought. Müller thereby presented the philologist as the "scientific" counterpart of the romantic poet. Indeed, he hinted that the philologist, not the poet or philosopher, was the figure best equipped to recapture humanity's original paradisiacal state of being.[25] At the same time, he suggested that language study provided the new master key to the human sciences.

Müller thus positioned himself as an ambassador between conflicting Victorian worlds. He aimed his diplomacy at reconciling the contradictory impulses of that age, at reintegrating a culture torn between the claims of religious faith and scientific advancement, between nostalgia and progress.[26] Ironically, much of Müller's ability to cast himself in this role stemmed from the fact that he was a foreigner, someone for whom German romanticism, including idealist natural science, came as a birthright. It was in serving up this *Weltanschauung* so learnedly yet attractively to his London audience that Müller excelled all of the other spokesmen for linguistic natural theology. And by so doing, he made himself a mid-Victorian cultural hero.

W. D. Whitney could not have been pleased with most of the popular language writing produced in these years. Still, he did his best to ignore this work, which in any case was largely the product of amateurs rather than the Continental scholars he saw as his legitimate peers. Then, however, Max Müller gave his virtuoso performance, and ideas that had appeared mainly in theological works or denominational journals now came from a highly authoritative source, posing a much greater threat, as Whitney saw it, to the foundations of a genuinely scientific linguistics. In response, his own priorities as a language scholar soon began to shift.

# CHAPTER FOUR

# Building a System of General Linguistics

In March of 1864, William Dwight Whitney traveled to Washington, D.C., to deliver a set of lectures under the auspices of the Smithsonian Institution. His topic was "The Principles of Linguistic Science." At least outwardly, this series suffered by comparison with Max Müller's series given at London's Royal Institution. That had been an illustrious affair in every way—in its setting, its attendees, and its style of presentation. Washington, by contrast, was hardly an auspicious venue. Moreover, it was a city distracted: the Republic's ordeal of civil war was then about to enter its fourth exhausting year. The audience Whitney attracted was accordingly small and not particularly distinguished. Nor were they treated to any notable rhetorical display.

Yet if the outward occasion was humble, the goal Whitney pursued was quite the opposite. He aimed to do nothing less than beat Max Müller's achievement by presenting a substantively superior version of language theory. Whitney's material was indeed rich in insight, and his lectures were appreciated on this score. Nevertheless, certain things Whitney said invited controversy. Many of America's religious intellectuals, including a number of his colleagues at New Haven, were dismayed at his failure to embrace a more reverential philosophy of language. This criticism from close to home represented only the beginning of the challenges Whitney would face.

## A Supplemental Vocation

When he turned his attention to linguistic theory, W. D. Whitney actually recovered his original ambition. After graduating from college, he had set his sights on studying comparative philology; this he hoped would reveal the "few simple principles" underlying all linguistic phenomena.[1] But then he changed his area of specialization during his first semester at the University of Berlin. Now focusing on Vedic Sanskrit, he set aside the idea of investigating language in general.

Eventually Whitney joined the Yale College faculty, and in the years that followed he threw himself into the affairs of the American Oriental Society, taught various language classes, and worked on his Indological projects. He also got married and started a family. At times he expressed an interest in speaking outside the classroom. As he told his sister during his second year of teaching, "I absolutely must crawl out of my hole, and say something to a larger public than I have been in the habit of addressing." What he had in mind at this point, however, was giving a public lecture on the current state of Orientalist studies.[2] It would be several more years before he began to consider issues of a more theoretical nature.

He started that new venture in a small way by presenting two separate papers to the American Oriental Society on the question of the origin of language. Each of these was chiefly a criticism of what others had said on that subject, and they were intended mainly to add variety to the society's meetings. Still, these papers previewed themes that he would eventually develop more fully.[3] Also at this time, Whitney gave a talk on a broader theoretical topic: "The Scope and Method of Linguistic Science." Presented at the 1859 meeting of the American Association for the Advancement of Science, this paper contained the earliest systematic statement of his thinking on general linguistics. Yet it was only a first draft, and in large part it repeated what others had already been saying. Here Whitney described comparative philology's investigative procedures, noting their resemblance to the methods used in the better-established sciences such as geology. He also gave various examples of the field's empirical discoveries. The real point of interest in this paper, however, is what it did *not* say: it omitted a number of themes that would become central to Whitney's mature linguistic thought. Most importantly, it said nothing about the Common Sense principles that would pervade his system.[4]

Whitney started working toward that fuller elaboration of his ideas in the fall of 1861 when he began giving his handful of Sanskrit students an additional weekly lecture on general linguistics.[5] A local event no doubt cleared the way for this new departure: Yale's senior language scholar, Josiah W. Gibbs, had died the previous spring. This allowed Whitney to steer a course away from linguistic idealism without directly challenging an older colleague.

The changed situation at Yale, however, was not the only factor drawing Whitney toward linguistics at this time. He began teaching on that subject only a few months after Max Müller presented his first lecture series in London. As Whitney later recalled, that event did more than anything else to goad him into formulating his own theoretical views.[6] Müller, after all, was a major European scholar as well as the preeminent spokesman for what Whitney considered a most uncongenial kind of language philosophy. His lectures soon appeared as articles, then as a published volume, attracting an enthusiastic readership both in Britain and in the United States. In a typical response, Boston's *North American Review* praised the liveliness and clarity with which Müller treated even "the most abstruse questions connected with the science."[7]

The sensation created by Müller's *Lectures on the Science of Language* (1862) must have caught the attention of the physicist Joseph Henry, the longtime secretary of the Smithsonian Institution. Henry soon contacted Whitney and invited him to present his own lecture series as part of the Smithsonian Institution's annual public offerings. What he wanted, he said, was "a course on philology exhibiting the history, the methods, and the results of the science, in connection with history and ethnology." Henry's choice of Whitney is not surprising. Whitney already had links to the Smithsonian as a consultant to its ethnological fieldworkers. Perhaps Henry also had been aware of Whitney's "Scope and Methods" paper delivered at a scientific meeting two years earlier. In any case, Whitney gladly accepted the offer. It was, in fact, the kind of opportunity he had been hoping for. When he began giving his weekly classroom lectures the previous year, he regarded them as "the germ, perhaps, of a more public course bye and bye."[8]

As he prepared his Smithsonian material, Whitney found his usual priorities turned upside down. He reported to his brother Josiah, a month prior to the event: "My main interest is still my lectures, which are advancing toward completion. Meanwhile, the *Prātiśākhya* makes rather slow progress, and other matters nearly none at all." This large investment of time brought little reward monetarily: the Smithsonian paid only $30 for each of his six lectures. Joseph Henry compensated by recommending Whitney to John Lowell of Boston, director of the famed Lowell Institute. This led to his presenting a revised series, twice as long as the original, in Boston that next winter. Yet Whitney still did not expect a large attendance. As he acknowledged, "The subject, however really and generally interesting it may be, is not a very taking one." His speaking style may have played a part in this as well. According to a Boston newspaper, he delivered his lectures "without flourish."[9]

If few came to hear him, Whitney could still pursue a larger audience. He did this by writing for journals, most often for the *North American Review*. That venerable publication had been in decline of late, yet it was being resuscitated under the editorship of Charles Eliot Norton. Whitney became friends with Norton in Italy during his post-wedding trip, and now, years later, Norton made Whitney one of the *North American*'s leading scholarly contributors. It was the beginning of a relationship that would last for over a decade.[10] Most of Whitney's articles were adapted from his lectures, although he also wrote book reviews. In either case, he usually aimed these writings at something in current philology that he considered in error. His first piece was a review of Max Müller's second (1864) volume of lectures. This task, Whitney discovered, afforded a special kind of pleasure: while reading Müller's new work, he could "hardly help stopping at every page to rail at it."[11]

Whitney's urge to do battle was strong, and it would grow stronger in the coming years. He was already in a mood to find fault with Müller; he began preparing his Smithsonian series just after their run-in on the subject of Indian astronomy. As we saw, he had "borne down" on Müller so strongly at that time because of the latter's "abominably mean treatment" of Albrecht Weber.[12] In public, Whitney always insisted that his attacks on fellow linguists were a matter of disinterested scholarship, unprejudiced by personal considerations. Clearly, this was not always true. Yet he convinced himself that whatever animus he might feel in these situations was irrelevant so long as the substance of his criticism was warranted. If he "bore down" harder in some cases, he still tried to make judgments based on intellectual merit. In addition, he regarded giving criticism as a kind of civic responsibility: each member of a scholarly community thereby helped improve the group's collective output.

Of course, engaging in polemics was also a way for Whitney to attract attention to his own views, something he was especially anxious to do in Europe.

Even though most of his articles appeared in American journals, he always requested extra offprint copies to circulate among his acquaintances abroad. This made his views well known among scholars, yet not among the reading public that had become so enamored with Max Müller. Whitney complained of the "stupid unanimity" in this regard among the British in particular.[13] The charge was exaggerated, yet there was in fact a gaping disparity between his and Müller's renown—a source of considerable vexation. In response, Whitney would eventually exceed the bounds of scholarly civility of his day, raising eyebrows even among his friends.

Meanwhile, he set out to produce his own full-length volume on language—a venture that proved both time-consuming and frustrating. A scheme for the immediate publication of his Smithsonian lectures fell through, and as a stop-gap, he settled for preparing a detailed abstract to be included in the *Smithsonian Annual Report*. It was not a good beginning; his work came sandwiched between long lists of donations to the Institution's coffers and collections. Moreover, the entire volume arrived behind schedule. "The Smithsonian Report with my 'abstract' in it is out at last," Whitney noted. "Whether it was good policy to furnish said abstract I somewhat doubt."[14]

In reality, these false starts were a blessing. It would have been premature to have produced a book before delivering the expanded Lowell series. And further revising after that was useful as well. Still, his heavy teaching load made this a slow process, and Whitney knew he would need to push hard if he was going to finish the project during the next summer's vacation. Otherwise, he said, "the world will have to wait an extra year for the true system of linguistic philosophy!" Even when he had completed the manuscript, there were additional delays at the printer. Meanwhile, Max Müller's popularity soared. Said one of Whitney's correspondents, a Latin scholar at a Midwestern college: "Müller is read a great deal and I hope you will be read more. . . . When do you appear?"[15]

To make matters worse, a current (1866) issue of Boston's *Universalist Quarterly* omitted Whitney's name from a roster of English-language philological writers—this nearly two years after he had lectured on the subject at the Lowell Institute. The list did include his relative B. W. Dwight and his Yale colleagues J. W. Gibbs (now deceased) and Noah Porter, the latter because of his work revising Webster's dictionary. It also, of course, included Max Müller. For Whitney to find his own name missing must have been galling. To top things off, the article in which the list appeared specifically championed language philosophy in the Humboldtian mode—thus confirming his suspicion that by contrast his own brand of linguistics was considered passé.[16]

Despite these delays and discouragements, Whitney's volume of lectures finally appeared in October of 1867 under the title *Language and the Study of Language*. Whitney had contracted with both Charles Scribner in New York and the house of Trübner in London so that the book would be published simultaneously in both cities. He also made the complicated arrangements required to secure a British copyright. Obliged to appear for notarization within Commonwealth territory on the same day that the book was published in London, Whitney made a quick trip to Montreal—a journey he otherwise considered a waste of precious time.[17]

## A Revival of Common-Sense Theory

Leafing through the pages of Whitney's first book, one finds few references to other writers. Whitney did rely on various specialists in technical philology—this he acknowledged in the book's Preface. Yet he conspicuously avoided references to well-known writers on theoretical subjects. Partly a matter of stylistic economy, this silence also reflected Whitney's ideal of knowledge itself. If a proposition accorded with the facts and made sense, what else was needed? He would not seek to support his views by appealing to famous names.

This did not mean, however, that Whitney dispensed with all guidance from the past. Despite his image of intellectual self-reliance, he actually inherited his leading ideas from Scottish Common Sense linguistic theory, a subset of Common Sense philosophy as such. (In private Whitney used the phrase "common sense," written with lower-case letters, to describe his linguistic views.) Common Sense philosophy was the school of epistemological realism that was standard in the early-nineteenth-century American academy. Whitney had learned a textbook version of that philosophy during his senior year in college. Common Sense realism represented the moderate wing of the British Enlightenment, and its linguistic version accordingly stood opposed to both Herderian idealism on the one hand, and Horne Tooke's materialism on the other. As we have seen, in contrast to Horne Tooke, the Common Sense thinkers regarded the mind as active in language formation, not merely as a passive receiver of physical sensations. Interestingly enough, W. D. Whitney purchased and presumably read a copy of Horne Tooke's *Diversions of Purley* while revising his lectures for publication.[18] Yet that work obviously exerted little influence on his thought.

The leading Common Sense philosophers, Thomas Reid and Dugald Stewart, had been interested in language mainly in relation to the operations of the mind. It was lesser-known figures such as Hugh Blair and George Campbell who worked out the implications of Common Sense for language itself.[19] These writers did not produce an elaborate theoretical system; rather, they offered a handful of principles based on what John Locke had said in his *Essay* of 1690. Following their lead, W. D. Whitney insisted, as of first importance, that there was no "internal and necessary tie" between a word and the idea it represented. For, he said, "every word handed down in every human language is an arbitrary and conventional sign."[20] Today readers tend to associate the notion of arbitrary and conventional signs with Ferdinand de Saussure's pioneering *Cours de linguistique générale* (1916) as well as with the avant-garde literary and anthropological theories Saussure's work inspired.[21] Yet this pairing of concepts actually began with the eighteenth-century Scots. Moreover, during at least the first half of the nineteenth century, this teaching was run-of-the-mill fare for most of the teenage boys who attended American colleges.

Whitney and his peers did not learn these principles through the actual study of languages—the daily recitations in Latin and Greek. Rather, they learned them from standard textbooks in logic and rhetoric. Whitney's class at Williams College read the following, for instance, in Hugh Blair's *Lectures on Rhetoric and Belles Lettres* (1783): "The connexion between words and ideas may, in general, be considered as arbitrary and conventional, owing to the agreement of men among themselves; the clear proof of which is, that different nations have different Languages." College seniors reading George Campbell's *Philosophy of Rhetoric* (1776) would have found much the same thing. Even as sophomores, Williams students learned from Levi Hedge's *Elements of Logick* (1816) that "Words possess no natural aptness to denote the particular things, to which they are applied, rather than others; but acquire this aptness wholly by convention." As for the term "arbitrary sign," its original use was in mathematics; Whitney would have seen it still employed in this context in Richard Whately's *Elements of Logic* (1826).[22] (As these references suggest, the themes of linguistic natural theology did not necessarily inform the language philosophy taught in the colleges.)

The Scottish language theory amounted to a significant improvement on John Locke's views. Locke had said that words were "arbitrary signs," but he did not say that they were "conventional." The point is significant because the latter term adds a substantially different perspective. "Arbitrary" suggests that one word-symbol is theoretically as good as any other for a particular purpose, while "conventional" suggests that the tie that *does* exist between a word symbol and its content is produced by social consent. The fact that English speakers say "tree" rather than *Baum* is an arbitrary matter; the fact that *all* English-speakers say "tree" is a matter of convention. W. D. Whitney summed up the distinction thus: "Every vocable was to us [as children] an arbitrary and conventional sign: arbitrary, because any one of a thousand other vocables could have been just as easily learned by us and associated with the same idea; conventional, because the one we acquired had its sole ground and sanction in the consenting usage of the community of which we formed a part."[23] (Whitney said this in his first book, but the same passage would appear again in subsequent articles. His shorter works tended to recycle sections of previously published material, and his ideas themselves showed a remarkable consistency over time.)

Locke wrote of arbitrariness alone in order to stress the completely voluntary as well as private nature of word formation. Because there was nothing inherent in a given sign that made it mean what it did, each speaker was free to establish a unique association between that sign and the correlate idea in his own mind. Locke was aware that this teaching raised the specter of linguistic anarchy, and for this he proposed a practical solution: he urged clearer word definitions. By contrast, the Common Sense writers added a theoretical corrective in the form of the notion of conventionality. That concept suggested an implicit social compact among speakers, which replaced anarchy with cooperation. A speaker could not, after all, make a sign mean whatever he wanted it to mean.

This viewpoint still preserved a place for voluntary choice, however, because the Scottish writers assumed that conventionality entailed, not forced imposition, but active conformity. Social conventions, they suggested, were really tacit agreements. Although such agreements were passed down through the generations and hence were binding to a fair degree on the future, they were also subject to revision and so were ultimately under the control of the human will. (Whitney construed "conventional" in precisely this sense when he referred to the "*consenting usage* of the community.") So while the Common Sense writers retained the idea of arbitrariness, they detached it from Locke's hyperindividualist understanding of voluntarism and paired it with a socially oriented conventionality; thus they produced the now-familiar coupling of terms.[24]

When W. D. Whitney first encountered this teaching as a college student, it likely struck him as merely truistic. Indeed, by 1853 the notion of words as conventional tokens was the standard view in Webster's *American Dictionary of the English Language:* "Language consists in the oral utterance of sounds, which usage has made the representatives of ideas. When two or more persons customarily annex the same sounds to the same ideas, the expression of these sounds by one person communicates his ideas to another."[25] It is hardly surprising, therefore, that Whitney's earliest papers on general linguistics made no mention of the arbitrariness and conventionality of the sign: those concepts would have been familiar already. Yet why then take the trouble, only a few years later, to revive those themes and make them central to his Smithsonian and Lowell lectures? The answer, of course, lay in the two series of lectures that Max Müller presented in the intervening period. In these, Müller emphasized what the New Haven scholars had called the "natural significancy" of words, thus throwing the Common Sense viewpoint onto the defensive.

Whitney was eager to meet this challenge. As he told C. E. Norton when he submitted one of his first articles to the *North American Review,* "It will by many be thought rather low-style philology to pronounce language simply a system of signs, and these signs nothing ineffably and mysteriously significative, but of arbitrary and conventional nature. But I hope to persuade a great many people of sense, and yourself among their number, that it *is so,* and that *low style* is better than 'highfalutin.'"[26] Whitney was right: Common Sense linguistics was held in low regard at that time, especially among Continental thinkers but also in Britain and America — so that Whitney felt surrounded on all sides. To be precise, Common Sense theory had come to be disparaged from two almost opposite perspectives: British and American religious intellectuals found it spiritually deadening, while many Continental thinkers found it philosophically unsophisticated. As Whitney complained to Josiah concerning the latter view, the "fundamental doctrines as to language which seem to you and me almost too obvious to admit of discussion are to the leading linguists of Europe superficial platitudes."[27]

Later, in a review of Whitney's book *The Life and Growth of Language* (1875), the Oxford philologist Archibald Henry Sayce neatly summed up this European climate of opinion: "Professor Whitney is the leading representative of what may be termed the common-sense school of philology, which has found its advocate among our Anglo-Saxon brethren in America. The same objections of superficiality and narrowness which the followers of Kant and Hegel have raised against Reid or Stewart, or the later representatives of Utilitarianism in this country, will doubtless be brought forward against Professor Whitney's philological system; but none at least will be able to deny its simplicity, its clearness, and its commendability to common sense."[28]

Self-consciously embracing these latter qualities, Whitney made it his mission to demystify language. He saw little need for linguistic thinkers to engage in profound psychological inquiry. As he once told a European correspondent, "I do not at all think that language emanates from the deeper and more mysterious parts of the mind, but from the more superficial and simpler." Whitney conceived of language as an instrumentality largely external to the psyche. It was, he said, a social institution, located primarily in the external world of communicative interaction.[29]

Even if he did not delve deeply in a psychological or philosophical sense, Whitney did more than probably any other theorist before or since to work out the main implications of Common Sense linguistics. Most significantly, he supplemented the notions of arbitrariness and conventionality with what we may call *semantic presentism*.[30] Here Whitney pointed to a striking paradox. He affirmed, on the one hand, that every word in every language had gained its meaning through an historical process and that word histories constituted the "foundation and substructure of all investigation in language." On the other hand, he argued that an awareness of a word's history had no practical bearing on one's understanding or use of that word. All that really mattered was the conventional definitions shared by contemporaneous speakers and hearers. From this perspective, he said, etymological investigation was "merely a matter of learned curiosity."[31]

Whitney thus denied the notion popular among Victorian-era language writers that the derivation of a word captured its "proper" sense, "its true original meaning and force."[32] He argued, on the contrary, that a knowledge of word origins was not in any sense practical: "To the greatest etymologist who lives, not less than to the most ignorant and unreflective speaker, the reason why he calls a certain idea by a certain name is simply that the community in which he lives so call it, and will understand him when he does the same."[33] Whitney thus showed that a *diachronic* (historical) emphasis alone did not accurately reflect the implications of the conventionality thesis. Equally important was what Ferdinand de Saussure would later call a *synchronic* perspective, a focus on the relationship between linguistic phenomena at a particular moment in time.[34]

## Practical Applications

Whitney applied these principles to a number of practical questions concerning proper English usage, modern language pedagogy, and spelling reform. The first of these categories, proper usage, presented a special challenge to the "scientific" philologist, and in Whitney's case produced a fair amount of ambivalence. On the one hand, his two major books included blunt condemnations of popular speech errors. He said in his 1875 volume that "the uncultivated have current in their dialect a host of inaccuracies, offenses against the correctness of speech — as ungrammatical forms, mispronunciations, blunders of application, slang words, [and] vulgarities." As he had noted earlier, these were the kind of practices "against which we, as Americans, have especially to guard and to struggle."[35] Whitney agreed to this extent with the genteel language critics of his day, writers (both American and British) who bewailed the erosion of proper English.[36]

For the most part, however, Whitney disdained the critics. As he remarked in 1868: "No literary business, certainly, ranks lower than this verbal criticism, which goes with a microscope over the surface of one and another writer's style, spying out cracks and roughness, making a big mark across them, and calling upon the world to stand aghast at their enormity."[37] Here Whitney stood alongside his professional colleagues Francis A. March, Fitzedward Hall, and Thomas R. Lounsbury — philologists who accorded an unprecedented degree of legitimacy to popular speech styles. Indeed, Whitney's own correspondence vividly attests to his enjoyment of American slang. It is true that he was biased in favor of elite standards, yet he still adopted a position that was considerably relativistic.[38] His outlook was in fact an *elitist relativism,* embodied in the ideal of "cultivated usage."

Whitney presented an optimistic view of history, in which upper-class influences increasingly shaped the languages of entire nations. As he said in his published lectures, "In any cultivated and lettered community, the cultivated speech, the language of letters, is the central point toward which all the rest gravitate." Whitney thus welcomed what he took to be the actual tendency in modern societies: the mass of speakers approximated the speech of the best educated.[39] In earlier times, the conservative influence on language had been active mainly within the bounds of a learned or priestly caste; examples included Brahmanic Sanskrit and ecclesiastical Latin. By contrast, "modern enlightened communities" tended to diffuse cultivated speech across class lines.[40]

Happily, Whitney found this trend especially well advanced in America, a country whose "desirable conditions" included relative social equality, easy communication between classes and regions, and above all, widespread availability of primary schooling. Here Whitney expressed a northern Whig-democratic cultural sensibility, having come of age in Massachusetts in the 1840s, in the heyday of Horace Mann's common school movement. Moreover, he first wrote on these topics in the years 1864–65 as the Union was achieving victory in the American Civil War. Along with most northerners, Whitney expected that what remained of America's distended social and political conditions would soon give way to national consolidation. Hence, he was confident that the nation's language would continue to consolidate as well.[41]

The ideal of cultivated usage was inherently relativistic because "usage" in this case consisted of whatever was spoken by the educated class at a given time. Whitney therefore adopted a laissez-faire attitude, bowing to a *kind* of prevailing practice as normative. Here again he followed George Campbell's *Philosophy of Rhetoric,* which offered the following criteria for standard speech: "reputable use," "national custom," and "present use." Elaborating this principle in his *Essentials of English Grammar* (1877), Whitney emphatically declared: "By good English we mean those words, and those meanings of them, and those ways of putting them together, which are used by the best speakers, the people of best education; everything which such people do not use, or use in another way, is bad English."[42] Whitney therefore scorned New York's Richard Grant White, a leader among the genteel critics, for preaching the "old dogma that usage does not govern language." In fact, he said, "usage does govern language, and absolutely," for there was "no such thing as taste and reason absolute in language."[43]

Although he both wanted and expected to see the increasing popular diffusion of upper-class speech standards, Whitney could not deny that lower-class and colloquial speech also shaped elite dialect. Yet he argued that the latter trend was not all bad. While popular influence was often corrosive of good speech habits, it also served a regenerative function: a language became petrified if cut off from it completely. And in any case, nothing could fully repress the appearance of new pronunciations, slang words, grammatical usages, and dialects. The best one could do was to set reasonable limits on speech innovations, thus slowing the rate of change.[44]

In a remarkable passage in his published lectures, Whitney summed up this balanced and optimistic vision:

> True linguistic conservatism consists in establishing an educated and virtuous democracy, in enlisting the whole community, by means of a thorough and pervading education, in the proper and healthy preservation of the accepted usages of correct speech — and then in letting whatever change must and will come take its course. There is a purism which, while it seeks to maintain the integrity of language, in effect stifles its growth: to be too fearful of new words and phrases, new meanings, familiar and colloquial expressions, is little less fatal to the well-being of a spoken tongue than to rush into the opposite extreme.[45]

In short, popular practice could be trusted once education had done its work.

What were the implications of these themes for modern language pedagogy, especially for teaching proper grammatical usage? By the time he wrote his *Essentials of English Grammar* (1877), Whitney had concluded that the usual justification for grammatical study, to promote "correctness" of speech, was "surely a most fundamental and unfortunate error." Rather, the scholar in this field should be "simply a recorder and arranger of the usages of language, and in no manner or degree a lawgiver; hardly even an arbiter or critic." Of course, schools still needed to teach proper grammar. Yet they should do this, Whitney said, in the same way that parents teach it to children: they should model it through good speech, encourage it through good literature, and impose it through sheer authority. Trying to explain why certain grammatical conventions were correct while others were not often amounted to "a false show of reason which is not really there." In reality, grammatical systems were abstracted from speaking norms: they merely codified "arbitrary usage."[46]

Similar principles guided Whitney's advocacy of spelling reform. Although usually remembered as an enthusiasm of nineteenth-century visionaries, the movement to promote simplified English spelling held serious intellectual credentials. It took inspiration, for instance, from efforts to construct a universal phonetic alphabet, a tool useful for transcribing unwritten languages. Like other pro-reform scholars, Whitney noted the frequent discrepancy between a word's spoken sound and its historic orthography — obvious examples appearing in the "silent" letters used in spelling words such as *knight*. The parallel with Whitney's general principles is clear: just as the link between a sign and its meaning was arbitrary and historically contingent, so also, to a large degree, was the link between the spoken word and its written form.[47]

Whitney therefore saw nothing sacred about traditional spelling: it was "only defensible on the ground that it exists, and cannot be got rid of without infinite trouble." This reality, he admitted, presented a formidable argument in favor of the status quo. Yet he found most other objections to spelling reform, especially those based on appeals to literary tradition and historical continuity, to be "nothing better than subterfuges under which the inertia of habit seeks to hide itself." At bottom, he said, the issue was one of altruism. Could contemporary English-speakers be persuaded to change their spelling habits so that future generations of school children, as well as foreigners, could learn the language more easily? Whitney had strong doubts on this score, so he never devoted himself to spelling reform with the zeal of an advocate such as F. A. March. He was content, rather, to await the majority decision.[48]

## Comparative Philology Under Harness

In preparing his two series of lectures, and later, in expanding these into his first book, Whitney did the job of a typical textbook writer: he summarized mounds of data supplied by others. He relied especially on experts in comparative Indo-European philology as well as on specialists in the world's other language families. Like his fellow writers of linguistic survey texts—Max Müller being the most obvious example—Whitney made his chief contribution through adopting a particular philosophical framework, in his case, based on Common-Sense principles. This choice of framework was all-important; it was the means by which to organize and interpret the many technical facts that philologists basically agreed upon. Like others, Whitney took these various elements, both technical and theoretical, and wove them into a system of general linguistics—not *the* system, but a particular attempt to bring coherence to the available material.

Pursuit of this goal placed Whitney in a curious relationship with comparative philology, a field with which he would never gain more than a secondhand acquaintance. As he confessed midway through his career, "I do not feel myself at all independently strong in that department."[49] Conscious of this limitation, Whitney showed sincere respect for the accomplishments of scholars such as August Schleicher and "Heinrich" (Heymann) Steinthal. In the Preface to his first book, he said that the works of these figures had constantly been at his elbow in the process of writing. At the same time, he declared that he had been "obliged to differ most strongly from some of their theoretical views."[50] Here Whitney hinted at a distinction he would make frequently. Comparative philology, he said, dealt with the facts of a given body of languages—"classifying them, tracing out their relations, and arriving at the conclusions they suggest." Linguistic science, on the other hand, dealt with the "laws and general principles" of language itself. Unfortunately, few scholars were adept in both areas: "One may be extremely well versed in the manipulation of its [philology's] special processes while wholly wrong as regards its grander generalizations."[51]

By drawing this distinction, Whitney sharpened a complaint that writers had been making for some years past. Linguistics, they said, needed to be founded on a more systematic set of principles so as to make the field more "scientific." A writer in New York's *Methodist Quarterly Review,* for instance, complained that etymological investigations had produced "accumulated masses of incoherent and unmeaning particulars," bereft of "logical laws." In truth, the writer said, there was a "deep distinction between the etymological and the scientific methods of philology." Others besides Whitney, then, had already been applying to language study the critique of excessive Baconianism, the same charge that Whitney would later make against traditional Indian linguistics—characterized (he said) by its over-emphasis on the particular. As the Methodist writer noted, the call for a purely inductive science, unprejudiced by generalizations, constituted the "philosophical cant of our day."[52]

This and other statements like it appeared in familiar periodicals, including the *New Englander* and the *North American Review*—two of them during W. D. Whitney's year of postgraduate study at Yale in 1849–50. These ideas likely came before his eyes at that time, for it was then that Whitney first expressed his own desire to find "a few simple principles" that would bring logical coherence to language study.

## The Mechanics of Word Formation

Whitney's two survey texts (1867 and 1875) conveyed standard information about comparative philology in the tradition of Franz Bopp—for despite his disappointment with Bopp as a lecturer, Whitney would in most respects adhere to his teachings. Like perhaps the majority of Western linguists at that time, Whitney held Indo-European to be the language family par excellence, one that afforded insights into the universal history of language.[53] The hallmark of that family was its highly developed inflective grammar. Many of the words in its constituent languages were composed of a stem plus an inflected suffix or prefix, producing their familiar paradigms of conjugation and declension. It should be noted that this emphasis on individual words was the norm in that day; grammatical analysis focused more on word structure (morphology) than on sentence structure (syntax).

Much of the detail in Whitney's books described the process by which inflective word constructions had arisen — based on Franz Bopp's conclusion that all inflective grammar consisted of syllables derived from preexisting words. The *-ly* in *godly* and *fully*, for example, was an abbreviated version of the word *like*, as in *God-like*. *Godly* and *fully* had thus been formed by combining two elements, each of which had a prior independent meaning. The formation of *godly* from *God-like* thus entailed both abbreviation and combination, two of the three processes Whitney found at work in the external construction of inflective words. The third process consisted of the substitution of word elements — seen, for example, in the transition from the Greek *episkopos* to its English equivalent *bishop*. In this case, not only were the first and last syllables dropped (abbreviation), but the *p* was replaced by a *b*, and the *sk* by an *sh*.[54]

As part of this analysis, Whitney made the common distinction between a word's "material" (independently significant) and "formative" (purely grammatical) elements. In the process of constructing *godly*, the word *like* had been reduced to the formative element *-ly*, whose independent origin and meaning had been disguised. Like Franz Bopp, Whitney taught that all formative (or "formal") elements at one time had been material — the same as saying that all morphological grammar had derived from formerly independent words.[55] Once established in a cluster of words, moreover, a formative element was free to be extended to still other, similar word stems. Thus was produced *fully*, *brotherly*, *lovely*, and so on.

Whitney devoted a substantial amount of attention to this last principle, known as grammatical "analogy." The tendency was to apply the prevailing morphological features of a language to more and more words so as to reduce the number of exceptions to that rule. For example, the *-s* suffix came to indicate the plural form of nouns in modern English much more so than it had in Anglo-Saxon.[56] The principle of analogy was actually a subject of some controversy among nineteenth-century philologists, so it will be useful to briefly examine Whitney's two-edged stance on this subject — an extension of his ambivalence about "standard usage" as a whole.

In both of his major books, Whitney condemned grammatical analogy as a source of improper usage among the uneducated, for the "tendency toward extension of prevailing analogies" often went "beyond their historically correct limits." In the worst instances, some speakers carried childhood usage, such as *gooder* and *goodest,* into adulthood. And many extensions of verb forms (*I done* instead of *I did*) "are still blunders and vulgarisms; and we may hope that they will always continue so."[57] Such were "deviations from the best usage, offences against the propriety of speech, kept down in the main by the controlling influence of good speakers, yet all the time threatening to rise to the surface."[58]

Counterpoised against these warnings, however, was Whitney's more acquiescent, laissez-faire stance. As he said in his published lectures, analogic usages "are, in their inception, inaccuracies of speech," yet often "become finally the norm of the language." Indeed, "prevailing usage has in our language already ratified a host of such blunders." And in his 1875 volume, while he continued to decry analogic "blunders," Whitney also declared that "the force of analogy is, in fact, one of the most potent in all language-history."[59] This *normalization* of the analogy principle was becoming a highly important theme in European linguistics at the time Whitney's later volume appeared, as we will see when we examine Whitney's relationship with the German Neogrammarian movement.

Whitney's analysis of word change included a second grand category: in addition to changes in the spoken symbol, there were also shifts in meaning. *Episkopos,* for instance, originally indicated merely an inspector or overseer, yet in time the word came to designate a high church official. There was, however, no inherent connection between a semantic change, on the one hand, and the purely phonetic history of a word, on the other. As Whitney pointed out, in the transition from *episkopos* to *bishop,* while the office so designated had grown in its responsibility, the phonetic symbol had shrunk in size. Other words changed in meaning while retaining their phonetic form. *Planet* originally meant "wanderer" and was used to designate any celestial body that moved independently of its neighbors. After Copernicus, this same phonetic symbol came to be applied only to those objects that orbited a central sun. The meaning had changed, but the form had not. One result, Whitney noted, was that hardly anyone other than etymologists recalled the metaphor on which *planet* was based.[60]

Here, of course, we have come full circle, back to the Common Sense principles of arbitrariness, conventionality, and semantic presentism — together suggesting that word symbols and word meanings were held together only by loose historical associations, which were continuously being reestablished. Indeed, said Whitney, these principles accounted for the entire process by which language has evolved.[61]

From this basis Whitney drew one last observation. Everyday language use, he said, requires a kind of collective amnesia: "Language would be half spoiled for our use by the necessity of bearing in mind why and how its constituents have the value we give them. . . . All significant transfer, growth of new meanings, [grammatical] form-making, is directly dependent upon our readiness to forget the derivation of our terms, to cut loose from historical connections, and to make the tie of conventional usage the sole one between the thing signified and its spoken sign."[62] After all, "individuals do not go on indefinitely to repeat the act of transfer which first allotted a word to its use; they establish a direct mental association between the idea and the sign, and depend upon that."[63] By their very nature as arbitrary and conventional signs, words were constantly being "cut loose" from their original meaning and redefined in the synchronic moment.

Here, we should add, Whitney did something unusual: his discussion of forgetting word origins was probably the single major instance in which he borrowed from the teachings of Yale's Josiah Gibbs. He was able to do this, however, only because Gibbs himself had built on John Locke's insight about the physical metaphors at the base of terms such as "Imagine, Apprehend, Comprehend," and so on. As Gibbs had pointed out, terms like these were really "faded metaphors": "the literal or physical sense is lost in the mind of him who uses the term." Here, no doubt, was the source of Whitney's notion of etymological forgetfulness. As Whitney noted, "the relics of forgotten derivations, *of faded metaphors,* are scattered thickly through every part of vocabulary."[64]

Finally, what motivated this impulse to make changes in word construction and word usage? Modifications of the spoken sign, Whitney said, usually entailed an easing of muscular effort in the lungs, throat, or mouth. No sooner was a "new" word coined than people found ways to conserve the "time and labour expended in its utterance." As to the redeployment of old semantic material, this too was done to conserve labor, to avoid having to invent an entirely new symbol for every new or modified conception. Historical association, a sense of continuity with the past—these constantly gave way before the over-riding tendency to avoid mental exertion.[65] As we will see in later chapters, Whitney placed great emphasis on this urge to economize effort, which he regarded as one of the few overarching "laws" of language development.

## On the Origin of Language

In the first two theoretically oriented papers he ever wrote, Whitney dealt with the problem of how language originated. Later, his first book included an entire chapter on that subject. It was, he said, "a perfectly legitimate scientific question, and one which even thrusts itself upon the attention of every profound linguistic student." Still, he judged that much of the past writing on this issue had not been very profitable.[66]

Whitney found more promising several newer works that had recently appeared in England, reviving the idea that language had developed through purely naturalistic means. There were two main theories of this kind. The first, developed in the eighteenth century by Condillac and Rousseau, suggested that humans had formed their earliest words from their own instinctive utterances, such as grunts, groans, and mating calls. We saw an updated version of this notion in *Vestiges of the Natural History of Creation* (1844).

The second naturalistic theory suggested that speech had begun with primeval man's *imitation* of sounds occurring in nature, his own grunts and groans included. Several writers elaborated this idea at the very time that W. D. Whitney was formulating his general linguistic views. Among these were the Anglican churchman F. W. Farrar and the anthropologist E. B. Tylor.[67] The writer who influenced Whitney the most, however, was the London philologist Hensleigh Wedgwood—who happened to be both a cousin and a brother-in-law of Charles Darwin. Wedgwood set forth his version of the imitation theory in the Introduction to his *Dictionary of English Etymology* (first volume, 1859) and, more elaborately, in his *Origin of Language* (1866).[68]

Whitney drew extensively from Wedgwood's writings as he prepared the final chapter of his 1867 book. Thus far he had avoided committing himself to any particular hypothesis; in his early papers and his Smithsonian lectures, he said only that language must have developed gradually, beginning from the simplest utterances. He was concerned mainly—and this was true throughout his career—with correctly framing the theoretical issue. He knew there could be no empirical answer. There was, he once said, "no prospect that we shall ever be able to say '*these* are the very first utterances of speaking men; now let us see how they originated.'" Not a matter to be solved with direct evidence, the origins question fell "within the province rather of linguistic philosophy."[69]

Philosophy was indeed the main area in which Whitney differed from his chief opponent, F. Max Müller. On the technical aspects, the two often agreed. First of all, they both expected to find clues to the origins puzzle in Franz Bopp's theory of monosyllabic *roots.* Roots were not actual words. They were, hypothetically, what would be left remaining if one could reverse the historical process by which grammatical inflections had been created. Stripped of all such "formal" elements, roots were thus the earliest building blocks of the Indo-European languages.[70] The first attempts to reconstruct root-utterances were made by the eminent comparative philologist August Schleicher, writing in the 1850s and 60s. Extrapolating from the oldest attested Indo-European languages, Schleicher generated a list of conjectured roots. These, he said, approximated the Indo-European proto-tongue, the long-lost "common source" of that entire linguistic family.

Although skeptical of Schleicher's specific reconstructions, Whitney too believed that the original Indo-European language had been composed of monosyllabic utterances. It mattered little, he said, that this could not be proved empirically, for "the firm foundation of the theory of roots lies in its logical necessity." Taking this argument a giant step further, Whitney and Max Müller each concluded that root-theory went a long way toward solving the problem of the origin of language. Both writers warned against confusing *Indo-European* roots with humanity's first words. Yet they both assumed (dogmatically, as it turned out) that monosyllabic roots of some kind had comprised the proto-tongue of *every* language family. As Whitney therefore suggested, the idea of roots brought one "very near to . . . the actual beginnings of speech."[71]

Whitney and Müller also agreed that the first things named by the earliest humans would have been individual objects, not groups of objects.[72] Here they both drew (at least tacitly) from the Scots philosopher Adam Smith's *Considerations Concerning the First Formation of Languages* (1759). Like most eighteenth-century philosophers who wrote about language, Smith focused less on language itself than on epistemology. He harked back to the old question of whether general terms or proper names held logical priority. For his part, Smith favored proper names. Originally, he surmised, the words *cave, tree,* and *fountain* would have named that particular cave, that particular tree, and that particular fountain with which the earliest speakers were most familiar. Only wider experience would have led them to make each of these terms the "common name of a multitude."[73] Whitney and Müller both held this supposition. From this point onward, however, their paths mostly diverged.

Max Müller used Kantian philosophy to dig beneath Adam Smith's *cave.* How, he asked, would such a word have come to be used as a proper name in the first place? In order to name a particular object, Müller argued, one first needed to discover some general quality that was characteristic of that object. The word *cave,* he said, derived from an Indo-European root meaning "within"; similarly, *cavern* derived from a root meaning "hollow." In each instance, the general concept was that of shelter: that space within the earth which first served this function would be designated "the cave." Müller's point was that general concepts necessarily preceded those individual names that had constituted humanity's first words.[74]

Yet whence came this ability to formulate general concepts? It existed, Müller said, because human minds were naturally imbued with Kant's categories—in this case the category of spatial extension: "Such a name could not have been given to any individual cave, unless the general idea of being within, or inwardness, had [originally] been present in the mind." Thus, although a name could be based on only one of the many attributes of a thing, in this instance the quality of inwardness, "that attribute . . . is necessarily a general idea."[75] In summary, Müller conceived of naming as a three-step process: "The first thing really known is the general. It is through it that we know *and name afterwards* individual objects of which any general idea can be predicated, and it is only in the third stage that these individual objects, thus known and named, become again the representatives of whole classes."[76] The key was that the actual naming did not occur until the second step in the sequence, a point we will return to below.

How did this process first get started? Müller dismissed the imitative and exclamatory explanations, what he called the "bow-wow" and "pooh-pooh" theories respectively.[77] If the imitation principle had applied anywhere, he said, surely it would have been in the original naming of animals. Yet lengthy etymologies, extending back to the earliest Indo-European roots, offered no evidence of this: "We listen in vain for any similarity between goose [in its root form] and cackling, hen and clucking, duck and quacking, [etc.]" Moreover, recently invented imitative names, like that of the bird *cuckoo,* comprised but a fraction of any language's vocabulary. As for the exclamatory theory, Müller noted that a linguistic expression such as "I suffer" completely replaced an involuntary cry such as "Ouch!"[78] It could not, he said, have developed *out of* that cry.

Müller's own theory of the origin of language ultimately drew from J. G. Herder's famous 1771 essay on that subject. Herder argued that early man must have had "hidden [linguistic] powers dormant in him" and that exposure to the natural environment would have drawn these powers forth.[79] The linguist Karl Wilhelm Heyse of the University of Berlin later elaborated this notion, and Max Müller adopted Heyse's formulation. At the end of his first volume of lectures, Müller suggested that humanity's original root words, or "phonetic types," had arisen as mental responses to surrounding physical stimuli: "There is a law which runs through nearly the whole of nature, that everything which is struck rings. Each substance has its peculiar ring. . . . Gold rings differently from tin, wood rings differently from stone; and different sounds are produced according to the nature of each percussion. It is the same with man. . . . [who was endowed with] the creative faculty which gave to each conception, as it thrilled for the first time through the brain, a phonetic expression." Müller suggested that this special faculty would have died out once the first words had been formed, just as certain instincts in animals die out as the developing individual ceases to need them.[80]

W. D. Whitney favored the imitative theory of speech origins, yet he wanted to buttress that theory with Common Sense epistemological principles. He thus tried to build on the argument in Adam Smith's *Considerations* in a more consistent way than Müller had done. While there is no evidence that Whitney actually read Smith's work, he would have found its essential argument in Dugald Stewart's *Elements of the Philosophy of the Human Mind* (1792) and, in simpler form, in the textbooks by George Campbell and Hugh Blair. (Whitney read Stewart's book on his own during his senior year in college.)[81] All of these writers adopted Smith's theory of linguistic abstraction. Blair emphasized the simplicity of this operation. Even as a child, he said, one was "naturally inclined to call all those [things] which resemble one another, by one common name." This was the Common Sense realist understanding of the abstraction process, which taught that general terms reflected similarities that actually existed in nature.[82]

Still, like Max Müller, Whitney needed to account for the original naming of particular objects. He did not deny that the word *cave* was derived from a root meaning "within," for Whitney and Müller agreed (once again) that general conceptions of this kind had preceded individual names. Their difference came down to this: would a speaker need to signify such a conception verbally before he or she could use it to create a noun? Müller said no: conceptions of general quality—*thus far unnamed*—formed the basis of verbally designating something particular. That is, unnamed quality concepts were converted directly into vocalized proper names. Whitney, on the other hand, answered yes: unnamed quality concepts initially needed to be converted into vocalized quality terms; the latter were the necessary basis for naming some specific attribute of a thing.[83]

Whitney considered the word *dog*. Perceived "synthetically," a dog would be recognizable apart from any attention to its particular attributes or qualities. But it would not yet be nameable. To take that step, one first needed to isolate some attribute—a wag, a bite, or a bark—and *name it*. Hence, *dog* might have begun as "the wagger" or "the barker." Yet before there was any existing language (containing the word *wag* or *bark*), humans could have produced such spoken symbols only by inventing them outright. Whitney thus arrived at the concept of imitation. In no other way, he argued, could a word like *wag* or *bark* have been invented from scratch.

As he said in the Preface to his first book, "At each revision of my views, I have been led to assign a higher and higher efficiency" to the "onomatopoetic principle." This was one of the few ways in which that publication differed substantively from his Smithsonian lectures. Prodding Whitney to make this change were F. W. Farrar's volume of 1865 and especially Hensleigh Wedgwood's of 1866.[84] Wedgwood noted that several new words had been formed in recent times on the basis of imitation, and he argued that this method must have been used in humanity's earliest days as well. He assumed, that is, that a mode of change in effect at present must have operated in the past as well.[85]

Here Wedgwood applied to speech origins the geologists' "uniformitarian" method, a notion widely popularized by Charles Lyell. The subtitle of Lyell's *Principles of Geology* (1830–33) aptly summed up the idea: "An Attempt to Explain the Former Changes of the Earth's Surface, by Reference to Causes Now in Operation."[86] The Whitney brothers, Josiah and William, had embraced uniformitarian thinking long before the latter became a philologist. Thus it was natural for W. D. Whitney to regard Hensleigh Wedgwood as a kindred spirit. Like Lyell, Wedgwood downplayed the influence of exceptional, nonregular, or "catastrophic" events, including supernatural interventions. Whitney put it this way in his lectures: "It is but a shallow philology, as it is a shallow geology, which explains past changes by catastrophes and cataclysms."[87]

This methodology was foundational to Whitney's imitative theory of speech origins. Following Wedgwood, Whitney regarded imitation not only as a normal mode of word coinage at the present time but as a behavioral tendency that could be read back to the beginning of human existence. Taking seriously what Max Müller had made fun of, he said that the expression "bow-wow" was really "a type, a normal example, of the whole genus 'root.' "[88] Müller had objected that names such as "duck" showed no traces of imitative origins. Yet Whitney argued that sound imitation would have been used only for the briefest period at the inception of human speech; the conversion of these utterances into conventionalized signs would have obscured the traces of their imitative origins soon thereafter.[89]

What of the possibility that language arose from exclamations, what Müller called the "pooh-pooh" theory? Whitney always treated this hypothesis as a subset of the imitation theory, although he left this point somewhat vague prior to writing his *Life and Growth of Language* (1875). In that work he suggested that natural cries first awakened humans to the voice's potential. (Thus far he followed *Vestiges of Creation.*) Yet the importance of the cries themselves would have ended almost immediately because the next step would have been to reproduce them intentionally, through imitation. Only the latter utterances would have constituted incipient language. Whitney therefore regarded "*the reproduction,* with intent to signify something, of natural tones and cries, as the positively earliest speech."[90]

Whitney ridiculed Max Müller's idea that the first root words had been produced by a kind of percussive resonance between the mind and its surroundings. He did not fail to mention that Müller's critics had dubbed this the "ding-dong" theory: "He tells us, virtually, that man was at the outset a kind of bell; and that, when an idea struck him, he naturally rang. We wonder it was not added that, like other bells, he naturally rang by the tongue." Whitney especially faulted the only-at-the-outset character of this theory, for it was inadmissible on uniformitarian grounds to posit a special capacity for verbal resonance found only in the mind of primeval man. Why was this capacity not at work today? After all, "new cognitions and deductions still thrill through the brains of men, yet without setting their tongues swinging."[91]

In the future, Max Müller would continue to base his ideas about speech origins on Kantian philosophy. Yet a hail of derision, Whitney's included, forced him to disown the resonance theory. While he still included that theory in later editions of his lectures (attributing it as always to Professor Heyse of Berlin), Müller now said that he was merely offering it for consideration and that he had never actually endorsed it himself. Whitney could not let stand this evasion of responsibility: "Here is either disingenuousness or remarkable self-deception. . . . We defy any person to read the exposition of the theory as given in the first editions, and gain a shadow of an impression that it is not put forward by him as his own."[92] The pattern seen here—deceitfulness on Müller's part and Whitney's exasperated response—would increasingly characterize relations between the two philologists in the coming years.

## The Problem of Positivism

With the publication of his first book, W. D. Whitney finally began to receive recognition—at least in America—as a major linguistic thinker. At the same time, however, his work drew criticism from the nation's mainstream religious intellectuals. Whitney had not set out to pick a fight with the friends of religion: his language theory was not blatantly anti-supernaturalist, nor did it suggest anything close to Horne Tooke's materialist viewpoint. It is true that Whitney wanted to challenge idealist philosophies of language, yet he preferred to do this on strictly "scientific," not ideological, grounds. Hence, he avoided directly questioning the religious worldview embodied in linguistic natural theology. He also avoided taking a stand—at least in his early writings—on the question of Darwinian evolution. Most of all, he preferred to contend with European philologists, not with the theologians who wrote for the American religious journals.

Yet if Whitney tried to ignore the theologians, they did not ignore him. They saw, most glaringly, that his theory of the origin of language dispensed with any need of divine assistance. They also found ominous the entire Common Sense perspective, including the familiar notion of arbitrary and conventional signs. That the general spirit of Whitney's teaching could be regarded as so threatening was largely a matter of the perilous intellectual context in which that teaching appeared. Naturalistic theories of life and human consciousness had been cropping up for decades, and recently they were on the increase. The effect, especially after the appearance of *Vestiges of Creation* (1844), was a perceived reconfiguration of the varieties of nineteenth-century language philosophy. Now, many British and American religious thinkers reduced the three main tendencies to only two. On the one side, they saw the tradition of Herder and Humboldt; on the other side, they conflated the materialist and the Common Sense schools into a single perspective. For in light of the Victorian "war" between science and faith, the moderate Common Sense viewpoint appeared, not as a reassuring antidote to materialist language theory, but rather as something actually akin to it.

The coming decades saw the crisis intensify. In America in the 1850s, the Yale men Noah Porter and Horace Bushnell each condemned the "new infidelity" — not an overt hostility to religion, but rather a naturalistic frame of mind that simply ignored the Deity.[93] The sense of threat deepened in the 1860s. That decade not only brought the rise of Darwinism but also saw a trumpeting of scientific naturalism generally, which increasingly was going under the name of "positivism."

When the Frenchman Auguste Comte coined that term in the 1830s, his goal had been to enjoin intellectual modesty. He urged philosophers to forsake trying to grasp metaphysical reality and to restrict themselves to "positive" knowledge. Comte's writings attracted little attention in the English-speaking world until John Stuart Mill penned an appreciative interpretation in 1866 — just prior to the publication of W. D. Whitney's lectures. The number of articles on the subject burgeoned in the years thereafter. Commenting in the *North American Review,* the scientific writer John Fiske optimistically declared that "the name 'positivism,' after losing its more special connotations, is perhaps destined to become the designation of scientific thought in general."[94]

Yet positivism, like the new infidelity, still sinned by omission. Because it effectively ignored the supernatural, it appeared to be philosophically materialist. It therefore became associated not so much with science-in-general as with the agnostic evolutionism of Herbert Spencer and T. H. Huxley. Especially controversial was the positivist mindset as applied to the study of human psychology. After midcentury, researchers in Europe pioneered psychophysics, the measurement of chemical and motor responses to sensory stimuli, and some writers made explicit what they saw as the naturalistic implications of this research.[95] Such talk alarmed mainstream theological writers. A spokesman for Princeton Seminary denounced the new "positive and semi-positive school" of psychology, charging that it undermined the "fundamental moral and religious convictions of men . . . with weapons claimed to be forged in the laboratories of physical science." Many welcomed Noah Porter's efforts to counter this tendency through his treatise *The Human Intellect* (1868).[96]

W. D. Whitney did not adopt a thoroughgoing positivist outlook, but he did embrace one of Comte's most famous ideas — that human reason had progressed upward through three historical stages: the theological, the metaphysical, and the "positive." And he declared in at least two of his articles that linguistic theory, by and large, had developed no further than the metaphysical stage.[97] Such remarks likely were aimed at the European linguists to whom Whitney sent copies of his work, because they tended to regard the Common Sense viewpoint as superficial. To counter that impression, Whitney identified his own outlook with the scientific vanguard. Still, by adopting even this moderately positivist image when facing Europe, he likely deepened the bad impression he was making at home.

His American critics responded indirectly at first. It was surely no accident that Whitney's relative B. W. Dwight brought out a new edition of his theistically oriented *Modern Philology* in the same year that Whitney gave his Smithsonian lectures. Soon a professor of Old Testament at Princeton Seminary (who, like Dwight, was a member of the American Oriental Society) praised Dwight's volume while reiterating his own institution's position. Language, the writer declared, was an innate human capacity, an aid to abstract reflection, a spontaneous expression of the soul. The Princeton scholar went so far as to commend Humboldt's linguistic relativism, the idea that "every language embodies a particular conception of the universe."[98]

Given this response to Whitney's initial lectures, it is not surprising that his 1867 volume was greeted with dismay. Although some religious writers preferred Whitney's outlook to that of the more mystically inclined German theorists, the opposite response was more adamant.[99] A Princeton theologian protested the "hyper-scientific spirit" of Whitney's book, which struck him as "too 'positive' for our taste, and for our reason and conscience likewise." Far better was the "psychological" (Humboldtian) school, which conveyed "a deep conviction of the permanence and vitality of language that is not found in the old doctrines of the conventionalists." Likewise, a Catholic reviewer judged Whitney's outlook philosophically shallow: "There is a more intimate connection of thought and the word than the professor admits — a deeper significance, a profounder philosophy, a more inscrutable mystery in language, than most philologists dream of."[100]

Whitney told his friends that he was not bothered by these reactions. Concerning the Catholic review, he said that he had "no reason to be otherwise than gratified" by it, "as what it accounts as faults are to every scientific man merits." Again, he boasted that one of his articles of this period had received "the distinguished honor of being denounced for lack of orthodoxy in a religious paper of Boston."[101]

Yet what of the response in Whitney's more immediate neighborhood, among the faculty and friends of Yale? Surely the College leaders saw the published reviews of his book. The frowns emanating from Princeton must have been especially embarrassing. And it could not have helped matters when London's secular-minded *Westminster Review* endorsed Whitney's theory of the origin of speech.[102] Such responses must have made Whitney's foray into general linguistics appear, from Yale's perspective, more of a liability than an asset. True, Whitney was the one scholar among them with an international reputation, and as such he was a credit to the College. Yet he also was accused of positivist leanings, a charge which only deepened his already anomalous position at Yale. He had discovered years earlier that his colleagues could show surprising "liberality" in the face of his unbelief. Even Yale's president, T. D. Woolsey, had seen no reason for Whitney to withdraw from teaching there, "at least at present." Now, however, they had a clearer picture of Whitney's intellectual tendencies.

Events would soon show that a number of the New Haven scholars indeed felt ambivalent about Whitney's presence among them and that the question of his fitness for teaching at a Christian institution was not settled after all. For Whitney's antireligious worldview, his linguistic philosophy now included, would once again provoke a crisis in his official relations with Yale.

Our story thus far has revealed much about W. D. Whitney's devotion to science. His fact-oriented, skeptical, and systematizing spirit have appeared in a variety of contexts — in his Indological research as well as in his general linguistics. We have also seen a flurry of references, from various writers, to the notion that linguistics constituted a "science." Yet for all of this, we still have only begun to see what Whitney himself meant by that term. To unlock this subject further, we must look at what the term *science* was coming to mean to American scientists themselves at this time, and especially at Whitney's firsthand exposure to that new rhetorical trend. It was a small shift in word definition, yet it would deeply influence his efforts to promote linguistics as a high-prestige discipline.

# CHAPTER FIVE

# Organizing a New Science

William Dwight Whitney's linguistic thought represented a gathering of diverse streams. His Orientalist studies prefigured aspects of his scientific ideal; Victorian debates about God, man, and nature set the idealogical context; Scottish Common Sense theory supplied the philosophical framework; and Boppian comparative philology provided the essential research base. Surrounding all of these, however, was an additional set of issues that we have not yet seen, involving the character of linguistics as a scientific profession. The present chapter begins to show why these issues became central to Whitney's theoretical agenda.

Our starting point, once again, lies in the years prior to the Smithsonian lectures, only now focusing on an entirely new sphere of Whitney's activities. These include his involvements with some of the nation's leading scientific institutions, his role in establishing the American Philological Association, and his efforts to enhance language study in American universities. Experiences such as these did much to shape Whitney's thinking about linguistics' status as a bona fide science. As a preliminary to that story, we consider the nineteenth-century redefinition of *science* itself.

## On "Science" and the Naming of Disciplines

W. D. Whitney wanted fervently to see language study achieve parity of status with the most advanced sciences of his day. Indeed, he regarded the vindication of his field's scientific standing as one of his most important tasks as a theorist. This effort, he realized, inevitably included a rhetorical dimension, involving the choice of labels used to name and categorize that field.

Historians of linguistics and other knowledge disciplines could learn a lesson in this area from studies of social class formation, particularly those that focus on the language of class identity and conflict. A similar approach appears in political histories that explore contests to define legitimating "keywords."[1] Like social and political movements, academic disciplines form themselves in competition with their rivals — adjacent fields with which they vie not only for intellectual territory but also for the most potent symbols of status. Nomenclature thus plays an important role in the struggle to achieve standing in the hierarchy of knowledge. And this has been true especially where the word *science* has been involved.

It is well known that "science" enjoyed burgeoning prestige during the nineteenth century. Every group, it seems, wanted their scholarly endeavor — and often their religious or commercial endeavor — to come under that rubric. This aspiration could claim warrant more often than is perhaps realized, since it was based on a legitimate and time-honored definition of the word. We have already seen examples of how the term *science,* as used in W. D. Whitney's day, was not restricted to the investigation of natural or physical phenomena. Rather, it stood for systematic knowledge of any kind.

Accordingly, well into the second half of the nineteenth century, the most basic division of knowledge fell, not between the natural sciences on the one hand, and the humanistic and social fields on the other, but between science and "art." As the dictionaries pointed out, this was essentially a distinction between theoretical knowledge and applied skill: "A science teaches us to know; an art, to do."[2] Even as late as 1875, the American astronomer Simon Newcomb noted the deep divide between "the so-called 'practical men' in our country," and "the investigator in any field which deserves the name science or philosophy."[3] As this remark shows, the latter two terms could almost be used interchangeably.

Disciplinary names based on this broad definition proliferated in the nineteenth century, often applied to fields that are now considered as belonging, at least in part, to the humanities. Examples include moral science, historical science — and, of course, the science of language. F. Max Müller was hardly the first to use this title to designate linguistics. English-speakers had been calling the field by that name at least since the 1830s. Nor was the inclusive definition of *science* in this case a matter of nineteenth-century English-speaking philologists directly borrowing the broad resonance of the German *Sprachwissenschaft*. That sense of the word had been naturalized in English long before. Nor again was it only language scholars themselves who used it in this way. Charles Darwin, for instance, on at least two occasions described philology as a science.[4]

Beginning around midcentury, however, the definition of *science* began to shift toward its more restricted modern meaning. This did not happen by accident; it was an effort to redefine, and thereby gain exclusive possession of, one of post-Enlightenment Europe's most coveted keywords. The trend apparently began among natural scientists, spreading from there to general usage. Many noted the change at that time, and not a few complained about it. Princeton Seminary's top theologian, Charles Hodge, in his book *What is Darwinism?* (1874), said: "The word is becoming more and more restricted to the knowledge of a particular class of facts and of their relations, namely, the facts of nature or of the external world."[5] W. D. Whitney had begun making the same complaint, for reasons of his own, a full fifteen years earlier.

Whitney was committed to preserving the old inclusive definition of *science,* the one still found in the dictionaries. For under that definition, fields such as linguistics could claim full scientific status so long as they were studied in a systematic manner. This would not be the case, however, if the term were allowed to become a shorthand for natural science alone. Whitney's desire to maintain the traditional meaning was therefore quite understandable. Yet it was also deeply ironic. After all, Whitney himself taught that word definitions were subject to continuous change, that the influence of popular usage could not long be resisted, and that prevailing speech practice was the ultimate arbiter of a word's meaning. He also pointed out the routine historical phenomenon in which an unchanged phonetic symbol underwent either an expansion or a contraction of meaning. The word *science* experienced just such a process, specifically involving contraction. This particular redefinition, however, was different from all others, for in this case the change tended to undercut Whitney's efforts to promote the scholarly credentials of his own discipline.

## Threats from the Scientific Associations

W. D. Whitney had been steeped from his youth in botany, ornithology, and geology, and his college years started him toward an impressive layman's knowledge of astronomy. Even after he chose Indic studies as his professional field, he continued to stay involved as much as he could in the affairs of natural science. He did this especially in the years leading up to his lectures on general linguistics. That timing is significant because Whitney's firsthand encounters with the American scientific community in this period would have a profound impact on the content of those lectures—hence on his theoretical system as a whole.

In the six years prior to his Smithsonian and his Lowell Institute series —that is, between 1858 and 1864—Whitney was invited to join nearly all of the nation's leading scientific associations. Each of these bodies already had some philologists among its members, for at least officially, these organizations represented the full range of academic disciplines. Each was divided into three main departments: the physical and mathematical sciences, the earth and life sciences, *and the ethnological, political, and philological fields.* This was the arrangement, for instance, in the American Association for the Advancement of Science, the first such group to elect W. D. Whitney a member.

Whitney looked forward to his initial AAAS meeting. The event was to be held in Baltimore, so it would be his first-ever visit the southern section of the country. As he remarked in a letter to Josiah, he had "never been south of Philadelphia, you know, never breathed the soul-oppressing, disgust-arousing, and purity-contaminating air of a slave state, nor seen the great national beer-garden." (Presumably this last reference indicated Baltimore itself.) More importantly, Whitney was curious to see what the AAAS was like. He especially wanted "to find out by observation whether the department of Ethnology and Philology is likely to be of consequence enough to take hold of."[6]

As it turned out, Whitney thoroughly enjoyed the host city's hospitality, which included a group excursion to the nation's capital. The meeting itself, however, proved disappointing. Whitney gave two papers at poorly attended sessions. (The first was on a proposed phonetic alphabet for the English language, and the second was a description of a twelfth-century Arabic treatise on astronomy.) The other main offering in his own department was from J. Peter Lesley (1819–1903), a prominent Philadelphia geologist and an amateur language scholar. Whitney reported afterwards: "Lesley's philological paper was bosh of the purest and most unmitigated description."[7]

Here Whitney pointed to one of several irritants he discovered in the scientific associations—the problem in this case being natural scientists who dabbled in philology as a sideline. Whitney would later applaud such multiple interests on the part of the Smithsonian geologists George Gibbs (1815–73) and John Wesley Powell (1834–1902), because linguistic fact-gathering among the Native American peoples nicely complemented their geological fieldwork. But it was different with armchair dilettantes like Lesley. For the most part, Whitney wanted each man to stick to his specialty. Having expertise in one field did not give someone the authority to speak in some other area in which he was not trained. By allowing this kind of thing to happen, Whitney complained, the scientific associations were making themselves forums for philological quackery.

Goaded by what he had heard, Whitney resolved to act as a "proper representative" of his field at the next year's association meeting to be held in Springfield, Massachusetts. As he told Josiah, "I mean to get up for the Am. A. [A.] S. a little paper on philology as a science, because I think said science ought to utter a word there, after all the precious nonsense which has been got off in the association, pretending to be philology." The result was his 1859 paper on "The Scope and Method of Linguistic Science," his earliest work on that general subject.[8] Whitney confronted in this paper a further irritant he had discovered in the national associations. Although only in his second year of AAAS membership, he used the occasion to chide his listeners. Philology, he said, was "regarded and treated by many as most nearly allied to metaphysics." To counter this impression, he outlined the field's scientific qualifications, seeking to show that it was "as strictly founded upon observation and deduction as any other natural science."[9] Whitney was hardly the first to make such claims, although he perhaps was the first to address them directly to a group dominated by natural scientists.

Whitney did impress some of the association's leading members, yet this came as a result of a separate paper he presented at the meeting. An early statement of his views on Indian astronomy, this work drew praise from the mathematician Benjamin Peirce and the astronomer Benjamin Apthorp Gould (1824–96).[10] This response was gratifying, yet Whitney failed to gain his larger point about philology as a science. Despite his confident swagger, he sensed that he stood only on the margins of the AAAS. He especially resented the cliquishness of the physical-science big-wigs who dominated that group and the condescension they showed toward those from outside their own fields.[11]

Whitney discovered, moreover, that this condescension could manifest itself in a particularly insidious way. Increasingly, the leaders in the various associations used the term *science* to describe the natural and physical disciplines only. Whitney first observed this practice at meetings of the American Academy of Arts and Sciences, an old and venerable body headquartered in Cambridge, Massachusetts. Like its sister organizations, the American Academy officially embraced the three great domains of academic knowledge. Whitney was elected an "Associate Fellow" in 1860, joining E. E. Salisbury, Theodore Dwight Woolsey, James Hadley, and George Perkins Marsh of Vermont among the group's philologists.[12] To all appearances, this arrangement suggested parity of status among the disciplines.

The spoken word, however, told a different story. After a meeting in 1863, Whitney made a telling complaint against the astronomer B. A. Gould, who, in addition to his prominent role in the AAAS, was also a leading light in the Academy of Arts and Sciences: "Gould was very friendly, but did not think to apologize for monopolizing the name 'science' to the *materialische* branches of knowledge. It is really an outrage to call Academy of Science a body which has to do with only the Physical Sciences."[13] Through this narrow and partisan use—this "monopolizing"—of that all-important word, Gould had implied that a number of fields, philology among them, did not really belong within the charmed circle of the sciences. Naturally, Whitney was offended.

This exclusivist spirit showed itself in yet another organization, the National Academy of Sciences. An elite group of natural scientists had founded this body during the Civil War, ostensibly to advise the government on matters of scientific policy. As with the other associations, the National Academy officially embraced the entire range of scholarly disciplines, including philology and ethnology. W. D. Whitney's election in 1865 as the first member to represent that department augured well for the organization's breadth.

Once again, however, the emphasis remained narrow in practice. Whitney suggested as much to his friend Charles Eliot Norton: "The meeting of the 'National Academy of (Physical and Mathematical) Science' is the attraction which I thought *might* bring you hither [to Northampton] this week. But I knew you were not much given to running after such shows." Although a number of prominent life-scientists had been among the National Academy's founders (Louis Agassiz was perhaps the most famous), they often skipped the meetings, hence Whitney's sneer at the group's "physical and mathematical" leanings. Two months later, in his first full-length article appearing in the *North American Review,* Whitney summed up his experience with the nation's scientific associations: "The votaries of physical science are unreasonably exclusive and recalcitrant; nor have we yet observed that the physicists have hastened to welcome the linguists into their own body, as engaged in pursuing the same end by like means with themselves."[14]

Whitney referred here to the physical scientists in the strict sense, the astronomers and physicists, because by reputation they were the leaders of the American scientific community. As such, they were the worst offenders. Yet in principle his complaint included the other natural scientists as well—those representing biology, geology, and natural history. Ultimately, all of these fields comprised what were commonly called the "physical" sciences, those dealing with either physical *or organic* nature. These were normally distinguished from the "historical" (or "moral") sciences. One sign of that solidarity was that the biologists, geologists, and so on increasingly joined the physicists in monopolizing the unmodified term "science." By implication, this excluded the historical sciences altogether.

Whitney was highly sensitive to this semantic shift, something he encountered, not in the theoretical abstract, but in the face-to-face world of association meetings, arenas in which personal influence and in-group prestige could affect the intellectual standing of entire disciplines. He therefore felt with special intensity the challenge that all linguists of his day came up against— to prove that their field was a true science. For those like Whitney, living in English-speaking countries, that challenge was made more difficult by the new definition of *science* itself.

W. D. Whitney eventually grew disenchanted with the scientific associations. In addition to the annoyances described thus far, he was discouraged by what he regarded as the low intellectual tone of the AAAS and by the decline in attendance at NAS meetings after the Civil War ended.[15] The NAS nearly ceased functioning at this time, yet it was slow to act on the solution Whitney recommended. Based on his experience in the American Oriental Society, he urged the Academy to seek a larger constituency while keeping control in the hands of its original incorporators. With the membership doubled ("and the yearly payment likewise"), the NAS could produce a regular publication which would help it appeal to private citizens for support. Despite the organization's troubles, Whitney's plan was not approved until 1870, when the NAS asked Congress to amend its charter by changing the wording from "not more" to "not less" than fifty members. This change, which rescued the Academy, was credited then as now to Wolcott Gibbs and Joseph Henry.[16]

Most disappointing of all was the way the associations handled a bitter ten-year dispute involving Whitney's brother Josiah. During the 1850s, Josiah had conducted a number of state geological surveys and taught chemistry at the University of Iowa. Then, in 1860, he was made director of the California survey, a position he would hold for the next fourteen years. He continued this work at the same time that he began teaching at Harvard.

The dispute arose from the fact that Benjamin Silliman, Jr. (1816–85), the son of the famous Yale chemist and himself a Yale professor of geology and chemistry, also did fieldwork in California. Operating as an independent consultant, Silliman made upbeat assessments of the new state's oil and mineral potential. In particular, he forecast rich deposits in locations where Josiah had concluded that little wealth would be found. The Whitneys attributed these optimistic reports to venality on Silliman's part, for they brought lucrative fees from mining promoters. Naturally, those reports also embarrassed Josiah and threatened to discredit the official state survey. The Whitneys responded by trying to have Silliman ousted from both the AAAS and the NAS on the grounds of unprofessional conduct. When the organizations demurred, the brothers resigned their memberships in protest.[17]

We will see later how this episode actually affected one of the nineteenth-century's most sensational linguistic disputes. For the Silliman affair came to a head during the most rancorous phase of W. D. Whitney's long-running battle with F. Max Müller.

## The Sheffield Scientific School

Despite these discouraging experiences on the national stage, Whitney enjoyed excellent rapport with his scientific colleagues at Yale—Silliman excepted. Indeed, he made his home base, not in Yale's classical College, the place where one would expect to find a language scholar, but rather in the Scientific School. There Whitney found embodied the inclusive definition of science that he valued so much.

Yale established its Scientific School in 1854 and soon renamed that institution for its chief benefactor, the railroad builder Joseph Earl Sheffield (1793–

1882). By the 1860s the Scientific School had assembled an impressive faculty. The luminaries among its ten or so members were James Dwight Dana (1813–95) in geology and Benjamin Silliman, Jr. in chemistry. Yale's Collegiate Department, meanwhile, looked askance at its scientific counterpart. With no required chapel attendance or morning prayers, the Sheffield School seemed a hotbed of atheism. Neither did the School require the study of classical languages, a policy that sinned against the Yale Report of 1828. In that famous statement, the College had rededicated itself to the notion that rigorous drill in Latin, Greek, and mathematics provided the best "discipline" of a student's mental powers.[18] Departing from this standard gave the Scientific School, in the College's eyes, a look of intellectual shoddiness.

This scornful attitude did have an advantage, for it allowed the Sheffield School to go its own way in molding its curriculum. The result was a remarkable balance between science and letters. The School's three-year course toward a Bachelor of Philosophy required work not only in the natural and experimental sciences but also in history, government, economics, and modern languages. And in 1871 there was added a two-year course in English literature taught by Thomas R. Lounsbury—Yale's first venture in that subject. In these ways, the Sheffield School anticipated the modern "general education" requirement much more closely than did Harvard's open elective system—the famous experiment launched in this period by Charles W. Eliot.[19] Most importantly, in this setting even a linguistic scholar could feel himself an equal partner in the Scientific School's business.

W. D. Whitney developed a strong attachment to the Sheffield School and was proud to play a role in advancing its interests. It must be said that he was not always enthusiastic about his teaching duties there, which consisted mostly of recitations in German and French. But at least he preferred his Sheffield students to what he called the "shirks" in the College. The Sheffield students were more motivated. The teaching itself, moreover, became more interesting with time. While preparing his Smithsonian series, Whitney gave a course of lectures on the "Principles of Linguistic Science"—which became part of his regular Sheffield offerings.[20]

Whitney made his most important contributions to the Scientific School in the area of administration; he served on the School's governing board from 1859 until his death. It was also here that he found his closest associates at Yale other than James Hadley. His particular friends were the metallurgist George Jarvis Brush (1831–1912) and the geographer Daniel Coit Gilman (1831–

1908). D. C. Gilman is of special interest because of the way his and Whitney's careers intertwined. Gilman would later make his reputation as the founding president of The Johns Hopkins University, yet he gained his early experience in academic governance during his seventeen years on the Yale faculty, often working in collaboration with Whitney. During much of that time, Gilmore served as Recording Secretary for the American Oriental Society, which elected him a member on the strength of his geographical interests. Gilman also drew up the Sheffield School's original organizational plan, and he went on to serve that institution as Librarian, as Secretary of the Faculty, and as Professor of Physical and Political Geography.[21]

It was Whitney who presented the obvious choice, however, when it came to defending the Scientific School's lack of a classical language requirement before a tradition-minded public. His colleagues turned to him when they needed a statement describing the appropriate goals and methods of a scientific education for the School's 1868 *Annual Report*. Whitney explained in private: "They put me up to it because I am a college-larnt man and a philologist by trade, and can say some true but disagreeable things about classics and science with more show of authority than the rest of them."[22]

Whitney presented two main themes in his essay for this occasion. First, he set forth an ethical argument in support of specialized higher education. In an environment of rapidly increasing knowledge, each individual was obligated to make a particular contribution to the public good; any kind of training that fit a man for a specific calling was therefore "truly disciplinary." A student still might choose to concentrate on the classical languages, but this would be a subject for advanced study. It could no longer, by itself, be considered the basis of a general education. In making this case, Whitney challenged the most fundamental premise of the Yale Report of 1828.[23]

Secondly, Whitney proclaimed the equal worth of all legitimate academic disciplines. This message, of course, served to elevate the standing of the natural sciences, for it suggested that they should no longer be looked down upon by the guardians of classical learning. Yet Whitney also promoted equality in a broader sense by invoking the old inclusive definition of "science." He said that the Sheffield faculty strove "to make the instruction given in the School thorough, to give it a truly scientific character, *by carrying each study back to the fundamental principles on which it reposes.*"[24] And so, even as he endeavored to situate Yale's Scientific School among the worthy institutions of higher learning, Whitney also made sure to suggest that even historically oriented disciplines such as philology — if rightly pursued — were genuinely and equally scientific.

## The Inauspicious Inception of the American Philological Association

W. D. Whitney's reputation as a scholarly organizer is rightly linked to both the American Oriental Society and the American Philological Association, the two main bodies representing language study in the United States in the nineteenth century. Yet the strength of Whitney's connection to these organizations was by no means equal because he would always be more closely bound to the Orientalists. As for the American Philological Association, Whitney had grave doubts about the idea of even starting such a group. The idea certainly was not his own, and he came very near to skipping the group's inaugural meeting.

The real motivating spirit behind the APA was George Fisk Comfort (1833–1910), a scholarly entrepreneur who taught art history at Cornell and helped to establish New York's Metropolitan Museum of Art. G. F. Comfort had dabbled in a variety of subjects while a visiting student at German universities in the mid-1860s; he also had attended meetings of a regional *Philologische Kongress,* which inspired him to promote a similar, albeit national, organization in the United States. Language study as such had no institutional headquarters in America at that time. (In Britain, by contrast, the London Philological Society had been in operation since 1842.) The American Oriental Society filled the bill to some extent, although it was relatively specialized in its subject matter and its membership was centered in New England.

Seeing the need for something more inclusive, G. F. Comfort submitted his idea to the country's leading philologists in the spring of 1868. He did not, however, receive much encouragement. He thanked W. D. Whitney, for instance, for sending his "calm and candid review of the difficulties to be surmounted." Comfort believed, nonetheless, that there was ample public interest in philology, and as proof he cited the large domestic readership Whitney's lectures had attracted in the year since their publication.[25] He therefore continued to pursue his vision, hoping all along to gain Whitney's support.

Joining Comfort in this effort was the Reverend Howard Crosby (1826–91), a future president of New York University. Together Comfort and Crosby planned an organizational meeting to be held in New York City that November. Again, however, their invitations brought cautious responses. Some feared that a new organization would draw interest away from the American Oriental Society. Another invitee, the Hartford lawyer and philologist James Hammond Trumbull (1821–97), worried for a different reason. Trumbull and Whitney were well acquainted, and they agreed in their view of the matter. As Trumbull said, while an association intended for all American philologists would be a good thing in principle, "it ought to be 'alive and productive,' else it had better not be at all." Whitney concurred, hence he showed little enthusiasm for the New York meeting. As he told Josiah, "I shall perhaps go down, tho' with small hope that anything will come of it."[26]

In the end, Whitney and Trumbull did attend the planning session, and the official record describes them as among the leading discussants. In private Whitney portrayed himself more as a skeptical onlooker. He referred to the event as "Professor Comfort's gathering," and he found it, as such, lacking promise. Despite being well attended, the meeting attracted "few men who could be relied upon to give such a Society character and to keep it alive. What will come of it is very doubtful: the individual at the head of the movement hasn't the brains and character to give it success."[27]

Blessedly ignorant of Whitney's opinion, Comfort forged ahead with preparations for the group's first regular session, slated for Poughkeepsie, New York, that next July. He probably lowered himself in Whitney's estimation even further, however, when he sent Whitney a list of dignitaries promising to attend. Among these were General James Garfield and possibly Massachusetts Senator Charles Sumner, the latter invited to give the opening address. (This did not occur.) As Comfort soberly acknowledged, these figures were " 'nonprofessional' linguists." Still, his plan had its commendable aspects. No one, at least, could accuse Comfort of envisaging an organization of narrow scope. He proposed that it be made up of seven "sections," devoted, respectively, to the Oriental, classical, modern European, English, and American Indian fields; linguistic pedagogy; plus, a field in its own right, "the science of language." He submitted the details for Whitney's approval, still hoping to secure the backing of the country's foremost language scholar.[28]

As the summons to Poughkeepsie went out, however, America's leading philologists once again voiced their doubts. They knew that a national organization could potentially advance their cause. Yet they also knew something else: if the efforts of their humbler colleagues were put on public display, it could harm the reputation of the entire field. Everything depended on whether the numerical majority of philologists was balanced by a sufficient showing of the eminent. And so, like the true believers, the skeptics as well looked toward New Haven to see where Whitney stood. And Whitney stood firm. His hands full with the Oriental Society, he told Josiah in April: "I have entirely declined having any active part in the various philological societies which are now trying to organize."[29]

G. F. Comfort continued to make arrangements for the opening meeting, getting fifty names pledged to attend and twelve papers promised. One of those papers he extracted from G. H. Trumbull, and this single act probably made the launching of the American Philological Association a success. Sometime in the late spring or early summer, Whitney changed his mind about attending the meeting—most likely because Trumbull, who had already committed himself, persuaded him to go. At any rate, Comfort later gave Whitney much of the credit, telling him that without "the timely and efficient cooperation of yourself, and Crosby, and Mr. Trumbull, I fear the meeting would have been nearly a failure."[30]

In July of 1869, the worthies of Poughkeepsie welcomed nearly one hundred philologists, assembled at the city's First Congregational Church, to the "Athens of the Hudson." The meeting began in convention, quickly voted itself the American Philological Association, and immediately elected Whitney its first president. Chosen as vice presidents were Whitney's distant cousin Benjamin Woodbridge Dwight, a clergyman, and Albert Harkness (1822–1907), a Latin professor at Brown University. G. F. Comfort was elected secretary. By Comfort's design, much of this first session was spent discussing the place of language, both classical and modern, in collegiate education. In an evening address, B. W. Dwight urged continuation of the classical curriculum, on the traditional theory that only it could produce sufficient "intellectual power" among the nation's future leaders.

Two of the other papers delivered at the initial meeting concerned American Indian languages, which were J. H. Trumbull's specialty. Trumbull spoke on how best to study these languages, and Joseph Henry of the Smithsonian Institution sent a report to be read at the gathering in which he described the Institution's sponsorship of ethnological fieldwork among Native Americans. Referring to the fact that Henry himself was a physicist, one participant (probably Comfort) described this message as "an olive branch held out by Professor Henry from natural science to language."[31]

Whitney no doubt resented the suggestion that olive branches were needed in this context, and he surely deplored the use of the new association for defending the classical curriculum. (He later complained of Dwight's "interminable" paper on that subject, which "wearied the audience for nearly an hour and a half.")[32] Nevertheless, the former skeptic stepped determinedly into his new role as the APA's standard-bearer. He told Josiah that the first meeting had been "quite a successful affair," although he added: "Not much of matter really new and valuable was offered; more of disquisition and general talk."[33] Intent on making the next year's meeting more substantive, Whitney and his friends began to set the stage.

Whitney managed this campaign quite effectively. In an unsigned "literary note" printed in the New York journal the *Nation,* he heaped shame on the many able philologists who had failed to show up at Poughkeepsie. Although blatantly hypocritical, his remarks were still true enough:

> The friends of the movement have felt from the first the importance of having it controlled by the best men, and in the interests of the highest scholarship. . . . If, after all, it turned out in any degree to be the case that second-rate men obtained the care of the convention and leading places in its counsels, it was not the fault of the convention, but of those scholars of eminence who unfortunately stayed away. For the absence of these men was painfully evident. There were hardly half-a-dozen present who can fairly be considered as standing in the front rank *as philologists.*[34]

Not wanting to embarrass the absent scholars by name, Whitney effectively did as much by listing the colleges and universities that had gone unrepresented—scant mercy for those who had followed too long in his own reluctant footsteps. He solemnly testified, moreover, that unqualified participants would have commandeered the meeting "had not Yale been alive to the importance of the occasion." Still, he wrote, this mere handful of eminent philologists had not been able to prevent all damage, and so those of lesser ability had played an outsized role at the convention.[35] From whence came this philological rank and file? Mostly amateur and clerical, it had its home in the nation's many provincial colleges, local study groups, and sectarian publications. Whitney wanted to wrest control of the field from these lesser types and to promote leadership that was secular and professional. This was the social, as distinct from the theoretical, dimension of his campaign to secure the autonomy of language study.

One week after Whitney's notice in the *Nation* was published, there appeared an anonymous "reply" — again written by Whitney himself. This second piece endorsed the remarks from the original note while adding some specific recommendations. First, the way to keep bad papers from being presented at future APA meetings was to have good papers crowd them out. Yet it was too early, Whitney said, to establish a regular journal, so the Association's annual *Transactions* would have to suffice for the present. (This became the official policy for the next ten years.) Whitney also warned that the APA must face the inevitable comparisons with the better-established scientific societies. Yet such comparisons need not be feared, he said, if philologists would emulate the rigorous spirit of natural-scientific investigation.[36]

Emulating what was best in the natural sciences did not, however, require kowtowing to their representatives: Whitney moved to squash any signs of deference in the APA's dealings with the nation's older scientific organizations. Just after the initial APA session, G. F. Comfort proposed sending an official greeting to the American Association for the Advancement of Science, then holding its annual convention. He drafted a statement calling for mutual respect between the two groups: "We are assured that in the Confederated Republic of the Sciences there will be among the true statesmen no unworthy rivalries and jealousies." Whitney vetoed the idea of issuing this statement, and Comfort dutifully complied. Yet he maintained (speaking to Whitney) that he had had good reason for making his proposal: "It was suggested to me that it would be well for us to disown any unfriendly feelings, at the very outset of our existence, towards science (using this word in its popular and limited sense). Hence I hastily wrote what I did."[37]

Whitney was well aware of the "popular and limited sense" of the word *science,* and of the distance it implied between the natural sciences and philology. Still, he looked for ways of dealing with this problem that did not themselves reinforce that sense of inequity. He demonstrated his own approach a year later in his address as the APA's outgoing president. Rather than play up to the AAAS, he cut it down to size. Warning that the long-term success of the Philological Association was not yet assured, he noted that "the scientists have long had a pleasant and useful organization of the same kind. [But t]he advantage popularly ascribed to them [*sic*] in the range of their subjects and the rapidly progressive character of their methods and results, is wont to be greatly overrated."[38] (Here Whitney used the neologism "scientist," indicating a student of the natural sciences.)

Whitney also used his address to recommend guidelines for the professionalization of American philology. First of all, he wanted the APA to show-case original research: applied subjects such as pedagogy and spelling reform should be kept off the agenda. He also wanted to separate the professional guild from the gallery of onlookers: "The character of the audience we address must be borne in mind, and popular and elementary explanation cut short. General exposition and defense of the merits of philology is also out of place before philologists."[39] These principles, Whitney hoped, would enhance the status of the APA and set it on a productive course.

Subsequent meetings, however, betrayed the signs of a struggling organization. The few substantive papers still came from the acknowledged leaders of the group, these mainly from Harvard and Yale. (The New Haven contingent included Whitney, James Hadley, Thomas R. Lounsbury, and Addison Van Name (1835–1922).)[40] As a commentator (not Whitney) in *The Nation* observed, the voices of these scholars "were always needed to sift the crude lucubrations of the half-learned." Whitney himself confided in 1872 that he hardly expected the APA to continue for another five years.[41] Even so, he did believe that the Association's essential blueprint was sound. For as little faith as he had in G. F. Comfort's leadership, he approved of Comfort's plan for a single institutional forum embracing "philology" in nearly all of its manifestations.

## Philology and the University

Like most scientifically minded academics of his generation, W. D. Whitney was anxious to see America's leading colleges incorporate university-level research and instruction. Yet how best to promote this end? His own idea was to encourage intellectual rivalry among the nation's most prestigious academic institutions, particularly between Harvard and Yale. A healthy competitive relationship between these schools would spur them as well as others toward adopting university standards.

Whitney often alluded to this idea in private, yet he also conveyed its essence on a major public occasion—Harvard's graduation ceremony in June of 1876, during which he received an honorary degree. In an acceptance speech consisting of three sentences, Whitney praised Harvard's achievements and expressed his sincere wish "that Harvard may lead in the race of American education just as long as it is possible." For as long as that situation continued, other colleges would have a visibly high standard to aspire toward. Then, however, Whitney delivered a puckish conclusion: "And I am sure you will all join me in the earnest wish that other institutions shall overtake and pass her [Harvard] just as soon as they are able."[42] In other words, successful emulation should beget genuine competition, which would turn out for the nation's greater good and for Harvard's as well — because Harvard needed strong rivals in order to attain her best. If Whitney perhaps doubted that his audience would entirely accept this logic, he kept those doubts to himself.

Whitney worked to implement his strategy mainly by building up the academic offerings at Yale. Yet on at least two occasions he made efforts to build up Harvard as well, specifically in the area of language study. The first of these, as we saw earlier, was his attempt to get prominent Bostonians to endow a chair in Sanskrit. The second occasion, several years later, brought an even bolder proposal: Whitney urged Harvard to establish the nation's first professorship in American Indian languages. He was led to this idea by an unlikely series of events beginning in the spring in 1866. At that time, Yale's Sheffield Scientific School made a significant addition to its faculty by hiring Othniel C. Marsh (1831–99), a rising star in the field of vertebrate paleontology. Marsh also happened to be a nephew of the financier and philanthropist George Peabody (1795–1869). Soon after his appointment, Marsh proposed that Yale build a museum of natural history to house its growing fossil collection, and for this he secured from his uncle a donation of $150,000.[43]

Even as this project was getting underway, Marsh went to work on a second venture. He was inspired by having recently participated in an archeological fieldtrip, apparently more out of personal than professional interest. The party had excavated an Indian shell-mound near Newark, New Jersey, in search of Native American artifacts. Impressed by this experience, Marsh suggested establishing a second museum, to be dedicated to Americanist ethnology. This, he proposed, should be located at Harvard, which was his uncle's alma mater. Peabody (who resided in London) agreed to finance this institution for the same amount as the one at Yale.[44]

W. D. Whitney heartily approved of these projects, each of them dealing with a subject in which he took considerable interest. What captured his attention the most, however, was a report that the Harvard museum's curatorship was to be combined with a new academic chair. The character of the museum itself was being described somewhat vaguely, in terms of both ethnology and archaeology, and the precise nature of the related professorship was not yet specified. Still, it was Whitney's understanding that the position would emphasize Native American *linguistics*. It is unclear where this idea originated, although O. C. Marsh (as his correspondence suggests) fully agreed with it. In any case, Whitney was confident in his expectation. As he told Josiah, "You will hear more of the Peabody professorship of American language and archaeology in due time, I presume. Mr. P. is in the country, and the doings both there and here [at Harvard and at Yale] will have to be settled in the course of the summer." Whitney warned that the plan was thus far a "great secret," but he said that it was "expected to be put through all right."[45]

As the fall of 1866 arrived, however, there was as yet no announcement of who would fill the new teaching post. Whitney became uneasy, fearing that the position might represent the wrong kind of ethnology. Alerted by Marsh that this was the drift of things, Whitney appealed to one of the museum's leading trustees. He wrote to the Harvard botanist Asa Gray (1810–88), urging that "the place should be filled by one who should be especially a linguist, both because that is the most abundant and promising field for the American archaeologist and because help in the physical departments will always be readily obtainable at Cambridge. It will be a great shame if this is not made a chair for American languages." Asa Gray thanked Whitney for his suggestion but noted that, by the terms of the trust, the founder was likely to name the chair's first incumbent. Moreover, he said, the trust itself appeared "to give rather a natural historical than philological turn to it, in the first instance."[46]

As things turned out, although the Harvard museum and curatorship were founded as planned, the Peabody Professorship of American Archaeology and Ethnology would not be established for another twenty years. (In the interim, the money allocated for that post went toward building up the museum's collection.)[47] Especially bad from Whitney's perspective, the museum's brand of ethnology turned out to be physical rather than cultural. The curator's position went to Jeffries Wyman (1814–74), Harvard's longtime professor of comparative anatomy, whose chief interest was the measurement of human crania. On hearing of this appointment, Whitney declared in disgust: "As if it were to be merely a post for a craniologist!"[48]

When finally established, the Peabody Professorship was filled by Wyman's successor at the museum, Frederic Ward Putnam (1839–1915); Putnam thus served both as curator and professor. Trained under Louis Agassiz, the founding director of Harvard's Museum of Comparative Zoology, Putnam not surprisingly kept up the Peabody Museum's already-established tradition of anatomical studies. Only now this was the emphasis of the professorship as well. As a result, Whitney's efforts notwithstanding, the nation's first academic post bearing the name *ethnology* had nothing to do with language. Even more troubling in Whitney's eyes, ethnology was being claimed as a province of anatomical science. His worries about how this could affect linguistics will be seen in a later chapter.

## A Call to Harvard

Once again, Whitney had failed in an attempt to enhance the philological offerings at the nation's leading college. Even so, he continued to follow developments at Harvard with interest, especially during the years 1869–71, a new epoch at that institution as well as, less famously, at Yale. By that time, Josiah had begun teaching at Harvard (concurrent with his work on the California survey), and the two brothers rejoiced over the selection of Charles W. Eliot as the college's new president. A leading modernizer of the nineteenth-century American academy, Eliot is remembered especially for the curricular reforms he introduced soon after he began his Harvard tenure. Whitney commented: "I have always had a very high opinion of Eliot's ability, both scientific and executive. . . . If we could only get such a man for President here, a new era would begin. Our Prex., I was told, vented at the Club the other evening one of the current sneers at the 'bread and butter sciences.' I am beginning to despair of Yale — only don't tell any one so." Clearly dissatisfied with Yale's Theodore Dwight Woolsey, Whitney congratulated Josiah on Harvard's prospects: "I hope that your *live* President is going to be a vivifying and grow-making power in the institution."[49]

That "live" president soon took one of his characteristically bold steps. Just weeks into his administration, in the summer of 1869, Eliot set out to resuscitate Harvard's University Lectures. First offered several years earlier, then discontinued, these lectures were meant to provide an annual postgraduate course in liberal arts subjects. Although himself a chemist by training, Eliot picked modern languages and literature as the topic for the coming year. He then invited W. D. Whitney to participate. Eliot suggested that, should Whitney agree to come, he could confine his lectures to the three weeks of Yale's spring vacation.[50]

However well-intentioned, this invitation proceeded from a misunderstanding. Seeing that Whitney taught modern European languages, Eliot suggested that Whitney lecture on some aspect of German language and literature. He did not anticipate how this offer would strike Whitney, who responded: "I should look upon the summons as much less imperative than might be one of another character. I am teaching German and French chiefly as bread-work, because I have no other means of support. But it is not my *mission:* that is the study of the old tongues and institutions of the far East and of language itself as one of the oldest and most important of institutions. An invitation to teach in these lines would appear to me a call of duty of a higher character."[51] Whitney therefore begged off, citing in addition his packed schedule: he was conducting eighteen recitations per week and already had little time for his own research.

Soon, however, he changed his mind. He agreed to come, provided he could emphasize the "philological relations and aspects of the modern languages rather than what is ordinarily meant by 'lessons' in them." This was fine with Eliot, who pressed Whitney to name a specific topic. Whitney then asked for more information about the series itself. Eliot sent him the impressive list of names of those who had already signed on — William Dean Howells, James Russell Lowell, and Francis James Child, among others. By now, however, Whitney was having second thoughts about the whole engagement. He told Josiah: "I fear that it will add one more to my list of burdens for the year, with little to show on the other side." That is, his account book would register small gain for the work expended. His regret at having committed himself showed in his further communication with Eliot: although he confirmed his intention to come lecture that next spring, his reluctance was obvious.[52] For his part, Eliot would have had good reason by this point to be fed up with Whitney's vacillation. But if so, events a few months later suggest that he had learned to subordinate such feelings in the pursuit of higher goals.

After enduring in relative silence for fifteen years, Whitney was becoming increasingly vocal about his unbalanced ledger. His salary at Yale had for some time stood at $2600, which, as he told Josiah, was "about two thirds of what it costs a family to live economically." (By then, that family included five children.) With this thought in mind, Whitney wrote to his patron E. E. Salisbury, now retired to his home in Lenox, Massachusetts, and reported on his recent activities. In addition to the heavy teaching load, he was in the midst of preparing a German grammar and reader for classroom use. He had taken on this extra "bread-work," he noted, "as a possible means of making my income meet my expenses."[53]

Only days after dropping this hint, Whitney received stunning news: he was offered a full-time position as a professor of Sanskrit at Harvard. The timing of this event relative to his letter to Salisbury was purely coincidental: he had had no prior knowledge of the offer. Charles Eliot was recruiting new faculty at this time, seeking talent especially in medicine, the applied sciences, and the modern languages. His overriding concern, however, was to attract top scholars, regardless of discipline. Consequently, even though Whitney represented one of the most esoteric of the humanistic fields, he sat near the top of the list of those being sought by Harvard. Eliot extended the offer informally, via Josiah, who was quick to point out its advantages: "You can do such teaching as will be in every way agreeable to you, in the optional course of the senior year in philology, be relieved from all your present drudgery, have plenty of time for scientific research, and be in all respects as pleasantly situated as it is possible to be in this country." Moreover, Harvard would pay $3000, with salaries reportedly set to increase to $4000 shortly. "Indeed," said Josiah, "I cannot see why you should not accept for you certainly cannot stand your present work."[54]

On the heels of this timely offer, Whitney received Salisbury's reply to his letter describing his work load and financial straits. As yet Salisbury knew nothing of the job offer from Harvard. Neither did he respond directly to Whitney's complaints. Rather, he used the occasion to broach a separate concern. He did not, as we will see, describe that concern directly: his *apparent* worry was that he and Whitney were losing their once-friendly relations. This, he implied, was due merely to a difference in temperament: "For myself, I allow that I am too sensitive to those rather sharp expressions of critical judgment which seem natural to you, but behind which is, I know, true geniality of spirit." Whitney accepted these remarks at face value and he replied, at least in part, with thoughtful consideration. He addressed Salisbury for the first time ever as "Dear friend," and he assured him of his own cordial feelings. He blamed himself for the aloofness Salisbury perceived, and in so doing, he sketched a rare self-portrait: "I am myself of a more than usually reserved and unsocial nature: I avoid society as much as I can, and am never quite comfortable in the company of any excepting those with whom I am most nearly bound. My besetting sin is (as my wife could tell you) burying myself in my books and papers, and too much overlooking all that is outside of them — partly from natural tendencies, partly because I feel that in that way I shall on the whole do most good and give most pleasure to others. I have never known any abatement of esteem and affection for you, who were my earliest teacher and patron."[55]

Having confided these intimate thoughts, Whitney abruptly changed the subject. He was obliged to tell Salisbury about the offer from Harvard, and he pulled no punches in describing Yale's relative demerits: "It is the most tempting offer that could, so far as I know, be made to me: for, on the one hand, I have greatly grudged the time which I have had to steal from Oriental and linguistic studies for German and French; and, on the other hand, what I have received for my services to the College has not for a good while paid more than about half my expenses." (Note: he had told Josiah that his pay covered "about two thirds" of his expenses.) Still, he said, he was "simply perplexed" about what to do, and he asked Salisbury for his advice. No doubt he hoped that these declarations would elicit a counter-offer from Yale. All the same, most of what he told Salisbury was the plain truth: he had been surprised by Harvard's offer, was indeed tempted, yet was still undecided.[56]

In private, Whitney made a clear-eyed appraisal of Eliot's offer. He did not, at bottom, want to leave Yale. As he told Josiah, "I have so identified myself in feeling with the College, especially the Sc.[ientific] School, that the thought of tearing myself away is by no means a pleasant one." He doubted that he could find "a more whole-souled and high-toned body of men" than his Sheffield colleagues, particularly George J. Brush. Nor did he suppose that there was "any one in the country who could be to me what Mr. Hadley is." Family ties, too, were strong.

These matters aside, Whitney still had four issues to consider. At the top of the list were the interrelated questions of teaching load and salary: he very much wanted to quit his modern language duties and to become "a real University professor" with commensurate pay. A third issue, at least potentially, was the matter of religious belief. Yet Whitney perceived no change in the surprisingly tolerant spirit he had discovered at Yale years earlier, prior to his engagement to be married: "I have not felt myself constrained here. Many people know, and others have an inkling, how it is with me, and if they can stand it, I can: no one now-a-days ever troubles me upon the subject; and I suppose that I exert some influence toward liberality of belief and sentiment, and so may feel that I am not here for nothing."

The fourth and final issue Whitney had to consider was the prospect of working side by side at the same institution with Josiah. Yet as he tactfully suggested, he could not count on his brother remaining at Harvard permanently without some project calling him elsewhere; hence, Josiah's presence could not be regarded as a major factor. The upshot was that a clear-cut improvement in salary and teaching load would probably induce him to stay.[57]

The Yale community as a whole was rocked by the possibility of Whitney's departure, news of which—somehow—leaked to a local paper. From a certain perspective, of course, public knowledge of the offer was not such a bad thing. Whitney told Charles Eliot that he was mortified by the disclosure, but he said he was now obligated to give his Yale friends a chance to respond. Eliot's reaction was brisk: "Never mind about the unexpected publicity." He urged Whitney to come to Cambridge and talk things over: "Any day will suit me."[58]

Yet how would Yale respond? The answer was not predetermined, for the College's religious "liberality," it turned out, was not really as strong as Whitney thought. At least some faculty members, behind the scenes, had begun to question Whitney's continued presence there. Salisbury was one of these; hence there was more than met the eye in his lament about Whitney's lack of cordiality. Noah Porter was surely another colleague who felt that it might be best to let Harvard have Whitney. Porter, who was a close friend of T. D. Woolsey, was personally a gracious man; yet he was anxious to have theistically oriented teachers on the faculty. That very month (October of 1869), in an article appearing in the *New Englander,* he had called on America's colleges to actively challenge atheism in their classrooms. He warned especially about the kind of atheism that masqueraded as mere neutrality toward religion.[59]

Porter must have been thinking, at least in part, of Whitney. Doubtless he was aware that the publication of *Language and the Study of Language* (1867) had prompted a Princeton theologian to brand Whitney a "positivist." And even more recently, Whitney had written the Sheffield School statement rejecting the old definition of mental discipline—a clear affront to Yale tradition. It is therefore not surprising to find Yale's leadership questioning whether Whitney really supported the College's mission.

Fortunately, Salisbury sought advice on this matter from Daniel Coit Gilman, who urged that Yale do all that it could to convince Whitney to stay. Gilman presented his case masterfully by focusing on the future prospects of Yale's Department of Philosophy and the Arts—which Salisbury himself had helped to organize. From its beginning in 1847, that department had projected an ambitious program of postbaccalaureate offerings in both science and letters. Over the years, however, the natural-scientific side had pulled far ahead. At the time Gilman wrote to Salisbury, the department's thirteen PhDs all had been awarded in the physical sciences. Meanwhile, the section on history, philosophy, and philology attracted only a few students each year, and none of these had taken a degree.[60] Whitney himself was the department's sole outstanding product in that area, this from his brief time at Yale before he proceeded to his studies in Germany. And Whitney's own few students in Sanskrit represented the main hope for the future.

It was with this backdrop in mind that Gilman (writing also for G. J. Brush) appealed to Salisbury. Whitney's departure, he warned, would be fatal to the balanced plan of offerings originally envisaged for the Department of Philosophy and the Arts. That plan, said Gilman, "surely ought to go forward and not backward if there is to be here a *University*." True, the Scientific School would also be hurt were Whitney to leave. But this, Gilman said, would be "quite secondary in comparison with the injury which would be done to other university interests at New Haven." Finally, it was rumored that Whitney was only the first of Harvard's "proposed captures." (Charles Eliot indeed was trying to raid the entire Sheffield School.) Gilman warned that Whitney's influence over the younger faculty was such that his departure alone might spark a stampede. Salisbury was not unmindful of these concerns, for he still hoped for greater things from Yale's graduate department. Even so, he pressed for information on one further point. In response, Gilman supplied what was needed, vouching for his friend's benign moral influence on the undergraduates in the College.[61]

Having received this answer, Salisbury immediately made Whitney a counter-offer. He would increase Whitney's salary, which would allow for a reduced teaching load in French and German. (As a result, he said, Whitney naturally would want to sever his connection with the Scientific School, "where you do not belong except as teacher of modern languages.") Whitney would thus be able to concentrate his instruction in Sanskrit, its literature, and "its Relations to Kindred Languages." Here Salisbury repeated the threefold description of responsibilities that he had used years earlier when Whitney first took the position.

Yet Salisbury now implied—apparently for the first time—that Whitney had neglected to perform all that had been expected of him. He emphasized the several facets of Whitney's appointment, he said, "in order to recall to you, in case it should have escaped your mind, that Comparative Philology is expressly included in your department at Yale"—comparative philology being equivalent to "relations to kindred languages." For several years Whitney had given lectures on "linguistic science" in the Sheffield School, but Salisbury wanted a course in comparative philology per se, and for these to be presented in the College. (Whitney would comply, although he was not enthusiastic about this task.)[62] Finally, Salisbury asked Whitney to name a likely candidate to fill his place in the event of his unexpected death. In a note to his wife, Whitney summed up these proposals: "Mr. S'y offers me $3000 to stay, in a letter which I don't altogether like."[63] Yet most of Salisbury's wishes, in substance if not in tone, fit in with Whitney's own desires.

Unable to comprehend his brother's hesitation, Josiah urged him to accept Harvard's offer. He again pointed to the school's intellectual eminence and suggested that this had been achieved through its commitment to academic freedom. With this thought in mind, Josiah passed along a suggestion from Eliot: Whitney should demand that Yale accept from him a statement of his " 'liberal Christian' ideas; so that at least the principle might be established that a man of liberal ideas can hold a professorship in an Orthodox college and you shall not longer be one *Sub Rosa,* as it were."[64] (The term "liberal Christian," reflecting the Unitarian tradition at Harvard, likely was introduced by either Eliot or Josiah; it was not a label Whitney normally used to describe himself.) Eliot probably was betting that such a proposal would never fly at Yale, and that it would therefore push Whitney his way. On the other hand, if Yale went along, although Harvard would lose Whitney, the precedent thus set would at least help to abolish the tacit orthodoxy-test for American college faculty.

Whitney declined to pursue this scheme, yet he did — in his own fashion — make religious toleration a bargaining point in his negotiations. He expressed interest in Salisbury's offer, while mentioning several items he wanted cleared up. He would be glad to quit teaching French but he would want to continue with German, for he still would need income beyond what his professorship paid. And he would do this teaching, he said, not in the College but in the Sheffield School. There was also the problem of "the wide difference between my views on certain most important subjects and those held by the most of my friends, here and elsewhere." Gilman no doubt had told Whitney that religion was still a sensitive issue on the College's side, and now that Whitney had an offer in hand, he pressed his advantage on this point.

In his reply to Salisbury, he wondered aloud whether "many of those who love the College would not, on the whole, think it as well or better if I retired." By raising this possibility, Whitney moved to force the hand of whatever opposition he still faced on purely religious grounds; the threat of his departure over this issue alone, he calculated, would lay the matter to rest. The response he wanted was quick in coming: Salisbury assured him that, "as much as they [the Yale trustees] regret the difference between your religious opinions and theirs, they are of one mind in desiring that your connection with Yale should not terminate, notwithstanding that difference."[65]

With this roadblock removed, and with the all-important teaching and salary matters settled, Whitney's reconciliation to Yale was complete: by mid-October, he had made his decision. As he told Josiah, "I have a great many roots out in this soil which it will take a great wrench to pull up, and I don't get any help toward the disruption from any quarter here. They are bent on making it worth my while to stay, and I cannot find any one who considered my heterodoxy as any reason for going away, altho' I find that my position is quite well and generally understood. They are much more tolerant here of differences of religious opinion than they have the credit of being; and, as I have not felt hampered in the past, so I see still less reason why I should be so in the future."[66]

Whitney was right: in spite of what Noah Porter and others may have wanted ideally, the religion question would never again affect his position at Yale. Still, he took the opportunity to clear the air further. He waited for two weeks before giving Salisbury his answer, thus leaving the trustees in suspense. And he kept the religion question alive during this time. Addressing Gilman, he again wondered whether, as a matter of conscience, he perhaps should retire from Yale.[67] Gilman no doubt took the hint and ran further interference with the College leadership.

Charles Eliot, meanwhile, still had hopes of retaining Whitney, and Harvard's language professors now joined the effort. Francis Child and James R. Lowell wrote to describe how Harvard's new elective system would free him to teach his favorite subjects. And Ezra Abbot, a co-worker in the American Oriental Society, told Whitney that he "*must* come to Cambridge and do your part towards making this College of ours a real University." But the moment of decision was already past.[68] In accepting the refurbished Yale professorship, Whitney put aside the mistrust of the previous weeks and made a gracious proposal: the chair should be named after Salisbury. The latter agreed on the condition that the change not go into effect until after his death.[69] This eventual renaming of the Yale Sanskrit chair was in a sense quite fitting. The stipulations Salisbury placed on Whitney's continuing in that position could now be met because Salisbury had finally given him the means to do so.

Whitney's attitude as he looked back on his Harvard decision revealed much about his character: especially, it showed once again a considerable degree of scholarly patriotism. Whitney was glad not to have found sufficient cause to leave Yale, for by remaining there he could "do as good work for science and for American scholarship as I could do anywhere—which is the great thing, after all." As usual, he saw the competitive relationship between the nation's top colleges as a primary means to that end. He acknowledged that, apart from the Sheffield School, Yale was "playing a losing game." Yet it was still imperative, "for Harvard's sake as well as her own, that she should not fall into a wholly secondary position, leaving H. without a rival."[70] Yale's traditionalism therefore had a double-edged on Whitney: while it had made Eliot's offer all the more tempting, it also reminded him that New Haven was where he was most needed. Moreover, by staying at Yale he would leverage his influence: not only would he enhance scholarship at that institution, but he would goad Harvard toward greater achievements of its own. Did this thinking betray an inflated sense of his personal significance? Charles Eliot's persistent campaign to hire Whitney suggests that it did not.

Yale itself stood at a crossroads in this period, its future direction to be decided with the choice of a new president upon T. D. Woolsey's retirement. The decision was to be made in the summer of 1871. Writing to Josiah, who was then on a trip to California, Whitney confessed his gloomy view of the prospects: "Mr. Eliot is pushing things on fast at your establishment, that's a fact. As for us, I despair of any new life here: we shall surely have an old fogy for our next President, I think." The candidates for that job were Noah Porter, Timothy Dwight (the grandson and namesake of the past Yale president), and a dark horse, D. C. Gilman. Whitney hoped against hope that his friend would get the job, even though Gilman had a strike against him because of his close ties to the Sheffield School.

Months later, boasting in regard to what might have been, Whitney told Josiah: "If we had Gilman for Pres., you would see things fly." But the reality was otherwise, for by then Gilman had been rejected in favor of Porter. Whitney tried to put the best face on things, remarking that "Mr. Porter will at any rate be much more of a university man than Mr. Woolsey, and things are not quite ripe for a really new start."[71] Noah Porter did become more of a university leader than his predecessors had been—but not "much" more. He famously reaffirmed Yale's commitment to old-fashioned mental discipline, and, as Whitney predicted, he launched no major initiatives in graduate instruction.[72]

Whitney and Gilman, on the other hand, were quietly working on an initiative of their own. Gilman had prepared the ground with the remarks he made to E. E. Salisbury during the crisis over Whitney's offer from Harvard. At that time, Gilman had directed Salisbury's attention to an article Charles Eliot had recently written for the *Atlantic Monthly* in which Eliot praised the outstanding work being done in Yale's Department of Philosophy and the Arts. Through its training of a modest number of graduate students, Eliot said, Yale had shown what steps needed to be taken by America's " 'universities,' which will then better deserve their ambitious title." Certainly this was an encouraging word. Yet as Gilman noted, Yale's graduate department continued to train mostly astronomers and physicists; the original plans for its philological offerings, especially, had thus far gone unrealized.[73] Could not some positive measures be taken to rectify this imbalance — that is, in addition to simply retaining Whitney at Yale?

A brief notice suggesting an answer to this question appeared in the *Nation* a number of months later. Written by an unnamed New Haven alumnus — probably Gilman himself — this piece called for an expansion of Yale's postgraduate offerings in philology: "If courses of lectures by Professors Whitney, Hadley, Porter, and others were established, and the fact widely advertised, so as to be brought to the knowledge of graduates of the other colleges, of teachers, and of the public generally, no one has a right to say that success would not follow. The example of the Sheffield Scientific School shows what may be done where there is faith, and faith attended by works."[74]

This proposal led to the formation of Yale's "School of Philology," which began to accept students in the fall of 1871. The School built on Yale's existing philological strength, augmenting this with several adjunct faculty and combining the whole into an integrated teaching department. Students were offered an impressive range of courses in Sanskrit, Greek, Latin, Anglo-Saxon, Romance languages, Chinese, and Japanese; and soon J. H. Trumbull would add instruction in the Indian languages of the American northeast, particularly the "Algonkin dialects."[75] Whitney benefited especially: he gained five new students in Sanskrit and nearly a dozen for his lectures on linguistic science — all of them, he said, "graduates and men of mark."[76]

This new venture quickly raised Whitney's estimate of Yale's prospects, leading him to boast (in private) that "we have taken a good long step this year toward realizing the University." He went so far as to reverse his opinion about the relative merits of Yale and Harvard: "Our method of making progress in that direction, I am sure, if less showy that Mr. Eliot's, is sounder and more solid." Even some of Harvard's faculty, he reported, "think that we have taken a better start toward a University than they."[77]

These assessments, as the coming years revealed, were far too optimistic. Noah Porter's Yale would continue to give the lion's share of resources to the undergraduate College, while the Department of Philosophy and the Arts still had no funding or faculty of its own. Yet Whitney's estimate of Yale's new potential does suggest a point that has largely been forgotten. In her study of New Haven scholarship, Louise Stevenson shows that nineteenth-century Yale, remembered mainly for its reaffirmation of the old-time curriculum, actually was one of the first American colleges whose faculty believed that they should not only teach but also do original research.[78] What needs to be added as of equal importance is that the emerging university ideal included the recruitment and training of younger scholars. It was this teaching function that made Yale's "School" of philology a significant early embodiment of university aims.

As it turned out, the School's actual product would be meager in terms of fully prepared researchers. Whitney's students were the main exception, and even they usually did their advanced study elsewhere. Moreover, many of these graduates would eventually become instructors of classical languages, since that was still the most likely job for a philologist in America.[79] Still, the very existence of that school, like that of the larger department to which it belonged, must have had a stimulating effect on neighboring institutions. These developments would have presented Yale's academic rivals with the kind of challenge that, as Whitney saw, made them rise to greater efforts.

The span of W. D. Whitney's lifetime saw a growing belief that "science" represented what was of highest value in this-worldly knowledge. Seeking high status for his own field, Whitney naturally argued for its inclusion under the scientific rubric. Yet this aspiration collided with the shrinking definition of the word *science* at that time, a change that Whitney experienced firsthand in the nation's leading scientific organizations. Still to be examined, however, are the more direct kinds of threats that accompanied that new definition, threats coming, not from American physicists and astronomers, but from leading European representatives of language study itself.

# CHAPTER SIX

# Creating a Science of Language

W. D. Whitney and the other language theorists of his era faced a two-part challenge with regard to the fate of their discipline. They also faced a related mystery about language itself. The first part of the challenge is by now familiar: nineteenth-century linguists wanted to assert their field's credentials as a true science. At the same time, however, they needed to show that linguistics was an *autonomous* science, standing, as it were, on its own two feet. This drive for disciplinary autonomy was of special concern to W. D. Whitney.

The mystery about language itself concerned the agency ultimately responsible for long-term linguistic change. Each generation tried to pass its mode of speech on to its children in unchanged form. Yet language changed nonetheless, such that speakers of modern English could not read Chaucer without interpretive aids. Who was responsible for this outcome? No individual or group could possibly have intended it, even though many thousands helped to produce it. Were such transformations beyond human control? Although the connection is not readily apparent, this theoretical conundrum went to the heart of the nineteenth-century debate about how best to promote language study as a genuine science. In turn, the story of that debate begins to point us toward W. D. Whitney's most enduring contributions to linguistic thought.

## The Natural-Historical Tradition

Whitney was clearly a beneficiary of the work of the early comparative philologists, of Franz Bopp's labors in particular. Yet he was also a severe critic of certain aspects of that work. What troubled him especially was the field's conceptual apparatus, consisting of images borrowed from the study of organic and geological nature. We will call this the *natural-historical tradition*. (Here was yet another facet of the German-romantic scientific ethos manifested in language study.) Whitney's critique of that tradition, and the sociology of language he offered in its place, added a further layer of foundation to his theoretical system.

Natural history itself had made great strides in the late eighteenth and early nineteenth centuries, the age of Geothe and Buffon and, a bit later, of Cuvier and Geoffroy Saint-Hillaire. Buffon, in his *Histoire naturelle* (1749–67), described the successive creation of biological forms, each new one bearing structural similarities to related forms that had appeared earlier. Cuvier added detail about the taxonomic links between presently existing and fossilized vertebrate species. The central theme in these writings was that the organic world constantly undergoes change, albeit change that was gradual and continuous with the past. It should be stressed, however, that this vision was pre-Darwinian and, strictly speaking, nonevolutionary. Few naturalists in that period accepted the notion of species transmutation.

A number of thinkers soon drew parallels between this dynamic view of nature and the historical development of society. Geothe and J. G. Herder famously pointed to the life sciences rather than to physics or mathematics as the appropriate models for the study of human institutions. Nations, laws, the arts and sciences — all should be understood as "organic" entities, suffused with a kind of natural growth. Accordingly, Herder described languages as proceeding through stages of germination, budding, and decay.[1]

The pioneers of comparative philology used a similar natural-historical imagery to delineate both the object and the method of their studies. Friedrich Schlegel set the agenda in his 1808 treatise *Über die Sprache und Weisheit der Indier,* where he called on philologists to study "the inner structure of languages, or comparative grammar, which will give us altogether new insights into the genealogy of languages, in a manner similar to that in which comparative anatomy has shed light on the higher natural history."[2] Schlegel's goal was to delimit the field's scope of investigation by isolating what he considered its essential subject matter.

Building on the insight of Sir William Jones, Schlegel noted that the affinity of Sanskrit for ancient Greek and Latin "consists not only in a great number of [word-]roots, which it shared with them, but it extends to the innermost structure and grammar. The agreement is accordingly not one of chance, which might be explained by mixture, but rather an essential one which points to common descent" from an ancestral tongue.[3] What Schlegel called "mixture" of languages resulted from contingent historical processes such as migrations, conquests, and culture contact and mainly produced similar vocabularies. Parallel grammars, on the other hand, pointed to an inherited, genealogical connection. By focusing on comparative grammar, the researcher filtered out mere accidental factors and tested whether a given set of languages had a common ancestor, that is, whether they were related by way of "natural" descent.

The early comparative philologists delimited their field by a further, albeit less direct means. They tended to regard the history of each language as an unfolding of latent form, as in the oak tree emerging from the acorn. Franz Bopp expressed this idea when he declared that "languages should be considered organic natural bodies, which are formed according to fixed laws," and which "develop because they have an inner principle of life." Jacob Grimm made similar remarks.[4] Indeed, the comparativist methodology required that languages be treated as independently evolving entities, almost as if the role of human speakers was irrelevant. "Language itself," rather than speech psychology or linguistic sociology — both of which dealt with actual speakers — was the focus of the comparativist research agenda.

The natural-historical tradition entailed yet another related theme, although one not always made explicit. Again following Herder's lead, the early comparativists tended to regard their field almost as a kind of natural science. Eighteenth- and the early-nineteenth-century European thinkers considered languages, like nations, as part of the larger realm of "nature"; they did not regard such entities as having been humanly constructed, at least not in any conscious sense. This conceptual linkage to the natural sciences had an important practical bearing: it was a way of distinguishing comparative philology from traditional textual philology, which focused on literary history. The inventors of the new mode of language study thus tried to show that their field was a science in its own right, one that had assumed an independent place among the disciplines.

## The Tradition Revitalized

When F. Max Müller delivered his 1861 lectures on "The Science of Language," he pursued two main thematic goals. The first of these we have seen: he offered a sophisticated version of linguistic natural theology as a rebuff to the increasing scientific materialism of that era. At the same time, however, Müller also wanted to establish the new philology's credentials as a bona fide science. He knew that the field did not have the scientific reputation in Britain that *Sprachwissenschaft* enjoyed in the German universities. As an English reviewer of his work lamented, "*Philology* has, to some ears, a slightly *un*scientific association."[5] Müller set out to correct this impression.

He began by saying much the same kinds of things W. D. Whitney had said two years earlier in his paper given at the Springfield meeting of the American Association for the Advancement of Science. Like Whitney, Müller explained how the best modern language study proceeded along lines similar to those used in geology and chemistry. Of languages, he said: "We can collect them, we can classify them, we can reduce them to their constituent elements, and deduce from them some of the laws that determine their origin, govern their growth, necessitate their decay; we can treat them, in fact, in exactly the same spirit in which the geologist treats his stones and petrifactions."[6]

Müller took this comparison with a literalness, however, that Whitney would always avoid. That is, he set out to reestablish the Herderian view of linguistics exclusively as a *natural* science, not a *historical* science akin to traditional philology. His idea was not simply that modern language study used methods analogous to those in the natural sciences (this being Whitney's point), but that it was an actual member of that family of disciplines.[7] The changing definition of science itself in the English-speaking countries no doubt gave Müller an extra incentive to reassert this claim. Living as he did in England, he would have been well aware of the shift in popular usage that was restricting that term to the study of physical and organic nature. He concluded, therefore, that language study must be considered a *natural* science in particular. For only then could it be shown to be truly scientific at all. He therefore made this point the subject of his first two lectures delivered before London's Royal Institution.

Müller knew that it would be difficult to prove this quixotic thesis, especially in a forum dedicated to the physical sciences in the narrow sense.[8] Even so, he set forth an impressive case. His premise was one that most thinkers at that time — including W. D. Whitney — fully agreed with: in order to know what kind of science a particular field represented, whether natural or historical, one first needed to ask what mode of causality normally operated among its phenomena. The common assumption then as now was that the natural sciences had nothing to do with the products of human volition.

"Now it is perfectly true," Müller admitted, that if language were "the work of man, in the same sense in which a statue, or a temple, or a poem, or a law are properly called the works of man, the science of language would have to be classed as an historical science." Müller of course chose these examples precisely to emphasize that language was *not* such a product. Works such as a poem or a statue involved conscious artifice. Changes in language, such as the shift from the Latin *patrem* to the French *père,* occurred "gradually but irresistibly, and, what is most important, they are completely beyond the reach or control of the free will of man." Hence, it was "not in the power of man either to produce or to prevent" such changes.[9]

This notion had been implicit in comparative philology all along, yet Müller gave it a whole new emphasis and theoretical elaboration. He likely drew from Kant's essay "On History" (1784), which described the paradoxical co-existence of subjective free will and law-like patterns in collective behavior. Kant cited country-by-country statistical tables showing annual regularities in the numbers of marriages and childbirths, patterns that none of the participants in these events could have intended to produce.[10] Müller described a similar paradox in the linguistic realm: "The process through which language is settled and unsettled combines in one the two opposite elements of necessity and free will. Though the individual seems to be the prime agent in producing new words and new grammatical forms, he is so only after his individuality has been merged in the common action of the family, tribe, or nation to which he belongs. . . . The individual, as such, is powerless, and the results apparently produced by him depend on laws beyond his control, and on the co-operation of all those who form together with him one class, one body, or one organic whole."[11] Having thus ruled out individual volition, Müller was left with a mystery. Although it was easy to show "that language cannot be changed or moulded by the taste, the fancy, or genius of man, it is very difficult to explain what causes the growth of language."[12]

This argument was provocative in itself, yet its real point, again, was to show that linguistics belonged among the natural/physical rather than the historical sciences. Müller declared at the outset of his second (1862) series of Royal Institution lectures: "*One* thing I feel more strongly than ever — namely, that, without the Science of Language, the circle of the physical sciences, to which this Institution is more specifically dedicated, would be incomplete."[13] That this thesis was hardly convincing does nothing to lessen its ingenuity: it was a clever attempt to endow linguistics with high status at a time of increasing natural-scientific prestige.

Max Müller added a surprising new dimension to this argument toward the end of his second lecture series. Returning to the question of causality in language change, he asked how a new word, such as *to shunt,* or a new pronunciation, such as *gold* instead of *goold,* became accepted as part of common usage, while many other words or pronunciations, even those adopted by well-known writers or speakers, did not. To suggest a solution to this puzzle, he appealed to Charles Darwin's idea of blindly occurring "selection" in nature. There was no inconsistency here, for Müller never abandoned his antipathy for Darwinism itself, especially for Darwin's theory of human origins. Rather, he applied the natural selection idea to language only by analogy. It was a vivid way in which to reemphasize the paradox he had described in his earlier lectures: "We want an idea that is to exclude caprice as well as necessity — that is to include individual exertion as well as general co-operation — an idea applicable neither to the unconscious building of bees nor to the conscious architecture of human beings, yet combining within itself both these operations, and raising them to a new and higher conception. . . . [I]t is the idea of *Natural Selection* that was wanted, and being wanted it was found, and being found it was named. It is a new category — a new engine of thought."[14]

In drawing this analogy, Müller made little actual use of Darwin's biological science. His point, rather, was purely conceptual: the "selection" of rival word forms, like selection in nature, was an undesigned and unconscious process that nonetheless led to patterned outcomes. This itself was a significant insight; it was also probably the earliest application, even if only rhetorical in character, of a Darwinian concept to a sociocultural phenomenon. It suggests, moreover, considerable opportunism on Müller's part. This allusion to Darwinism (and others like it) allowed Müller to update the natural-historical tradition in linguistics and to do so in a way that suggested that field's links to the scientific avant-garde. W. D. Whitney essentially pursued the same goal when he identified his own brand of language theory with the "positive" stage of science. Müller, however, was bolder in his use of this tactic and, it should be said, more au courant. Darwin's new theory promised to establish natural history on a whole new basis, and its adherents multiplied with each passing year after the *Origin of Species* was published. Müller would have seen this trend even in the brief interval between his 1861 and 1862 lectures. He therefore hedged his bets: even as he continued to fight Darwinism's apparent materialist implications, he also portrayed himself as a champion of the new wave, this via his praise of Darwin's "new engine of thought."

Max Müller was not alone in making this kind of argument. The comparative philologist August Schleicher said many of the same things at nearly the same time in his *Deutsche Sprache* (1860) and his *Compendium der vergleichenden Grammatik der indogermanischen Sprachen* (first volume, 1861). Schleicher reiterated the idea of *Sprachwissenschaft* as a science similar to botany, along with the idea that linguistic forms develop according to laws that are "inevitable and determined, from which there is no escape."[15]

When he first said these things, Schleicher had not yet read Darwin's *Origin of Species*. Two years later, however, the zoologist Ernst Haeckel, Schleicher's friend and younger colleague at the University of Jena, gave him a copy of that work. Haeckel knew that Schleicher was an enthusiastic amateur plant scientist, and it was in this connection that he thought Darwin's book would interest him. Yet what impressed Schleicher the most was the way the new bio-evolutionary theory suggested analogies with the development of language. And like Max Müller, he saw an opportunity to update philology's natural-historical tradition by clothing it in Darwinian dress. Schleicher therefore produced a pamphlet entitled *Die Darwinsche Theorie und die Sprachwissenschaft* (1863), in which he drew an elaborate parallelism showing how languages, like living species, undergo continuous development, gradually diversify, and can be classified genealogically. Pushing the comparison to an extreme, Schleicher proclaimed that languages were actually "organisms of nature."[16]

Responding to Schleicher in the published (1863) version of his second lecture series, Max Müller was careful to distance himself from this last point. It was "sheer mythology," he said, to regard language as having "a life of its own" like an organism. Even so, the two philologists agreed in their main ideas. Like Müller, Schleicher declared that languages "*have never been directed by the will of man;* they rose, and developed themselves according to definite laws; they grew old, and died out." Then came the corollary: "*The science of language is consequently a natural science.*"[17] It was the same connection Müller had drawn a year earlier: the kind of science, whether natural or historical, depended on the kind of causality involved. Again, the practical point was to bolster both the status and the autonomy of language study.

Some observers warned, however, that this strong attachment to the natural sciences could produce the very opposite of its intended effect. Instead of suggesting that linguistics was a science in its own right, Müller's and Schleicher's arguments threatened to make linguistics a mere appendage of nature study. What had been meant to liberate could therefore turn into a prison. Foremost among those who issued this warning was W. D. Whitney.

## A Sociology of Language

In their discussion of language change, Max Müller and August Schleicher presupposed a distinctly German-idealist sociological tradition. Whitney, by contrast, embraced a familiar Anglo-Scottish explanation of collective behavior, one that focused on the freely chosen actions of individuals—albeit individuals in constant *interaction* with one another.

Applying this perspective to language, Whitney said that all linguistic innovation derived from those slight peculiarities that distinguished one person's characteristic speech behavior from another's. Not only did each class and region have its distinct dialect, but each speaker produced a distinct *idiolect*— to use the modern term. That is to say that no two individuals pronounced a word exactly the same way or gave it precisely the same meaning.[18] The gradual accumulation of these small variations eventually resulted in dramatic change, such as the transition from Chaucerian to modern English. Likewise, the divergence of a single language into multiple daughter dialects, and then into entirely new languages, was only the extension, given the right conditions, of simple idiolect variation. Here again Whitney applied the geologists' uniformitarian principle to language. Earlier we saw this idea used in his imitative theory of speech origins, yet it pervaded his entire theoretical system. According to this outlook, the minute changes that occur at the present moment are responsible for cumulative effects produced over long stretches of time.

What, then, gave language its relative stability, so that idiolect innovations did not pile up and eventually create a babble of confused tongues? Whitney said this in his published lectures: Even though language "tends toward diversity, circumstances connected with its employment check, annul, and even reverse this tendency, preserving unity, or producing it where it did not before exist." These stability-promoting factors came in two variations. The first to appear was *self-inhibition,* arising from the need simply to make oneself understood: "I may alter the sign as I please, and to any extent, even to that of substituting for it some other wholly new sign; only, if by so doing I shock the sense of those about me, or make myself unintelligible to them, I defeat the very end for which I speak at all. This is the consideration which restrains me from arbitrariness and license in the modification of my speech, and which makes me exert my individual influence upon it only through and by the community of which I am a member."[19] Excessive innovation was thereby inhibited at its very source, for personal idiosyncrasy willingly gave way to the demands of mutual intelligibility.

The second stability-inducing factor was *group constraint,* the requirement that those innovations which individuals did produce needed to be taken up by others. The vast majority of idiolect peculiarities went no further than the lips of the person who spoke them, for the originator usually lacked sufficient influence, on his own, to make those novelties part of common speech. Whitney accordingly described the speech community as a "republic," whose "general suffrage" determined which innovations would be approved for collective use.[20] This was a picture of constant interplay between the individual innovator and all others with whom he dealt: "Every single item of alteration, of whatever kind, and of whatever degree of importance, goes back to some individual or individuals, who set it in circulation, from whose example it gained a wider and wider currency, until it finally won that general assent which is alone required in order to make anything in language proper and authoritative."[21]

Responding to Max Müller and August Schleicher, Whitney acknowledged the irresistible constraint exercised by the community as a whole: "It is indeed true that the individual has no power to change language. But it is not true in any sense which excludes his agency, but only so far as that agency is confessed to be inoperative except as it is ratified by those about him." Thus, while Whitney conceded that language change was in a sense the work of the community, he insisted that the community could not act "except through the initiative of its individual members, which it follows or rejects."[22]

Still addressing the likely objections to this theory, Whitney acknowledged that language *seemed* to change of its own accord. The process appeared, he said, to be "as little the work of man as is the form of his skull, the outlines of his face, or the construction of his arm and hand." As a result, "the linguistic student feels that he is not dealing with the artful creation of individuals." Whitney also conceded that in modifying language "the work of each individual is done unpremeditatedly, or as it were, unconsciously." These factors made it seem as if the process went untouched by human will: "Now it is this absence of reflection and conscious intent which takes away from the facts of language the subjective character that would otherwise belong to them as products of voluntary action."[23]

As far as initial changes were concerned, this meant that speakers normally were unaware of their own idiolect peculiarities. Could volition still be considered operative even in the case of innovations that sprang, not from any conscious intent, but from "a lazy habit of the mouth"? Whitney answered yes, based on the mental philosophy he had learned in college. The Scotsman Dugald Stewart taught that even habitual behavior, characterized by a lack of conscious intent, nevertheless entailed volition. The burden of proof, Stewart said, fell on those who denied the will's influence in this realm, because free will was known to explain all other, *nonhabitual* forms of human action. Using a similar argument, Mark Hopkins of Williams College affirmed that habitual action could "never wholly escape from the control of will."[24] Whitney applied this principle to his own subject, concluding that even the most automatic aspects of speech behavior were freely chosen.

What still needed to be explained, however, was the ultimately volitional character of long-term and large-scale linguistic changes. Speakers did not normally set out to invent new verbal forms. Rather, such changes resulted from a "gradual and unreflective" process. As Whitney noted, "It is impossible to suppose, for instance, that, in converting the adjective *like* into the adverbial suffix *-ly,* there was anything like intention or premeditation, any looking forward, even, to the final result. One step simply prepared the way for and led to another." Yet this did not lessen the role of individual speakers: "Such phonetic changes, we are accustomed to say, are inevitable, and creep in of themselves. But that is only another way of saying that we know not who in particular to blame for them." Although the responsible parties could not be named, one still had to acknowledge the agents behind the event.[25] For Whitney, then, there could be no such thing as a group mind or social will that guided individual behavior, for society was not a self-existing entity, standing above its constituent members.[26]

We are now at a point where we can see how closely interconnected were the various components of Whitney's language theory. Following the Common

Sense theorists, Whitney taught that words were arbitrary and conventional signs. This meant that word definitions were variable rather than fixed for all time. It also suggested that definitions consisted of tacitly made agreements that a community of speakers entered into voluntarily. These agreements, moreover, were the product of a communicative context: through their reciprocal influence on one another speakers created and modified conventional signs. This continuous interaction produced a paradox: language change, a diachronic process, was created by behavior in the ever-present *synchronic* moment. And this led finally to the notion of *semantic presentism*. Because the mental association between a sign and its meaning was constantly being reestablished and frequently revised, a word's historical derivation often had little bearing on its current definition. To summarize: interaction among individuals in the ongoing present provided the social medium in which conventionalized speech behavior arose and was continually reshaped.

The sources of Whitney's ideas on these subjects are not hard to find. They appear in eighteenth-century British social and economic theory, most basically in the Utilitarian principle that self-interest forms the main spring of human behavior—even socially beneficial behavior. Tacitly adopting this principle, Whitney emphasized the way speakers voluntarily conform to the speech of those around them in order to be understood. Building on this Utilitarian foundation, the classical economists described society as a collection of autonomous and self-seeking individuals. Adam Smith famously summed up this outlook in his *Inquiry into the Nature and Causes of the Wealth of Nations* (1776), which included the following portrayal of the economic actor: "He generally, indeed, neither intends to promote the public interest, nor knows how much he is promoting it. . . . [H]e intends only his own security; and by directing that industry in such a manner as its produce may be of the greatest value, he intends only his own gain, and he is in this, as in many other cases, led by *an invisible hand* to promote an end which was not part of his intention."[27]

At first blush, the "invisible hand" metaphor gives the impression that society somehow directs the behavior of its individual members. As used by Adam Smith, however, the image conveyed precisely the opposite point. It suggested that the voluntary actions of individuals, in the aggregate, made up the larger social pattern. More specifically, Smith pictured an arrangement whereby each individual caters to the needs of others in order to receive reciprocal rewards. Self-regarding behavior thereby produced unintended benefits for the entire community via the medium of market exchange.

W. D. Whitney probably never read *Wealth of Nations,* and he apparently never invoked the "invisible hand" image itself. Yet he clearly was familiar with this kind of explanation. (Note, for instance, the striking similarity between his description of the members of a speech community and the passage from Adam Smith quoted above: "Each is intent only on using the common possession for his own benefit, serving therewith his private ends; but each is thus at the same time an actor in the great work of perpetuating and of shaping the general speech.")[28]

Whitney could have been exposed to this brand of social theory in any number of ways. As a college senior, for instance, he read William Paley's *Principles of Moral and Political Philosophy* (1785). Although not a text on economics per se, Paley's book, like Smith's, set out to justify the emerging market-oriented society. The point was to show how the new masterless men of that era, possessing a degree of social freedom previously unknown in the world, could become responsible moral agents. Seeking to discourage excessive individualism, Paley showed how keeping promises, honoring contracts, and otherwise engaging in voluntary self-restraint served to advance the individual's own interests through the law of social reciprocity.[29] Again, W. D. Whitney absorbed this principle and made it his own.

An additional source likely reinforced Whitney's sociological vision, particularly his idea that all linguistic innovation stems from the miniscule idiosyncrasies of individual speech. Remarks scattered throughout his lectures show that Whitney was conversant with Darwin's *Origin of Species* (1859), which taught that no two members of the same species are exactly alike — the basic condition that allowed some individuals to beat others in the struggle for existence. This aspect of Darwin's theory fit neatly with Whitney's belief that idiolect variation was the only raw material (other than time) needed to bring about major long-term language change. A further analogy could be found in Darwin's notion that biological "species" were really ideal types constructed from the similarities found among various related breeding populations. Whitney likewise noted that a given language, such as "modern English," could be found nowhere in its ideal state. It was always a construct based on the average usage of all of its speakers at a certain time.[30] These analogies between Darwinism and Whitney's language theory were of course completely different from those offered by Max Müller and August Schleicher.

Whitney did not, however, get his original inspiration on these points from

Darwin. The real basis of his outlook was the longstanding British sociological tradition from which Darwin apparently drew much of his own perspective as well. Still, the appearance of the *Origin* just as Whitney was turning his thoughts toward linguistic questions would have buttressed his preexisting affinity for this school of sociological explanation.

## The "Moral Science" Imperative

A surprisingly useful introduction to Whitney's deeper theoretical agenda can be found in an embarrassing incident that took place at the end of his first year on the Yale faculty. The occasion ought to have been triumphant, for Whitney was presenting a formal address to a gathering of colleagues and local alumni at the home of Yale's president, T. D. Woolsey. And his topic, East Indian antiquities, filled him with more interest than anything else at that time. Other conditions, however, were not in his favor. The crowded room was stifling that summer night, and Whitney was weak from a recent bout of illness. As a result (he reported) he "broke down." He fainted in the middle of his speech, and his friend James Hadley was obliged to finish delivering it for him.[31]

The significance of this episode lies in a comment Whitney made several days later. Writing to his sister Elizabeth, he tried to put the best face on what had happened: "It was rather disagreeable and somewhat mortifying, but I couldn't fairly be ashamed of myself, as the evening was warm and the rooms most oppressively close; *and one is not morally responsible for physical weakness.*"[32] Here Whitney alluded to a cardinal principle of the moral philosophy he had learned in college: the degree of responsibility one held in a situation depended, at bottom, on the kind of causality involved, whether the impelling agency was "physical" or "moral" in character.

According to the philosophers, a person could be held accountable only for those events that he or she had brought about by a free act of the will. This characteristic quality of moral action was well understood in Whitney's day: the 1869 edition of Webster's dictionary defined *moral,* in part, as "voluntary; implying conscience and free will; that which admits of a choice between doing and not doing."[33] As a college senior, Whitney would have read in Francis Wayland's *Elements of Moral Science* (1842) that "[moral] action is never affirmed, but of beings possessed of a will; that is, of those in whom the putting forth of power is immediately consequent upon their determination to put it forth." In other words, moral action manifests the impelling force, as it were, of the unfettered will.

By contrast, "physical" causes appeared at work in the impersonal forces of nature, where no volitional element was involved. Accordingly, their outcomes were exempt from moral judgment. A fainting spell, for instance, an event brought on not by an act of the will but by external heat, high atmospheric pressure, and bodily infirmity, was to be classed in the physical, not the "moral" realm. As such, Whitney consoled himself, it was not something about which he needed to feel ashamed.

The important point for our purpose is the distinction between moral and physical *causation*—wholly apart from issues of moral responsibility. The Anglophone writers with whom Whitney was most familiar emphasized individual free will as something basic to the human condition. In his *Philosophy of Rhetoric,* for instance, George Campbell pointed to an awareness of one's own volition as a fundamental datum perceived by "common sense." Similarly, Mark Hopkins told his seniors that the "mind knows itself as acting voluntarily, and as a proper [that is, an originating] cause."[34]

While not all Continental thinkers agreed with this latter thesis, they did concur with the Anglophone writers in distinguishing between the two essential kinds of causation; Max Müller, August Schleicher, and W. D. Whitney were at one in this regard. Whitney also agreed that the kind of agency considered to have caused a phenomenon determined which kind of *science* was appropriate to that phenomenon's investigation. Hence, as he was preparing his Smithsonian lectures, he said that he was especially anxious to address two interrelated issues: "What is the nature of the force which produces and modifies language, and what the nature, *accordingly,* of the science, physical or moral." These were topics he had to speak out on, he said, "or I shall burst."[35]

As we saw earlier, Müller and Schleicher taught that language generally was *not* under the control of human volition, so they concluded that linguistics ought to be classed among the natural or "physical" sciences. Whitney believed the opposite on both counts. He told his Smithsonian audience that "in language, the ultimate atoms are not dead matter, but intelligent beings, acting for a purpose."[36] The implication for linguistics' place among the sciences was clear: Whitney sided with the "general opinion" that "classes the linguistic student with the philologist, the archeologist, the historian, the mental philosopher." That is, he believed that language study belonged with the "moral" (historical or social) sciences, those that dealt with phenomena caused by freely choosing agents.[37] This coupling of the terms *moral* and *science* was not something unique to Whitney. Webster's 1869 definition of *moral* included: "Relating to mind and not to matter; not physical; *as in 'Moral Science.'* " Corresponding themes appeared in the definitions of *physical* and of *science* itself.[38]

Whitney believed that it was crucially important for linguistics to be classed as a moral science, so much so that he made this issue the subject of the first full-length article he wrote for the *North American Review*. As he told the *North American*'s editor C. E. Norton, this piece (entitled "Is the Study of Language a Physical Science?") presented "a tolerably full exhibition of the ground-work of my system of linguistic philosophy." He added: "I think I have demolished the view of Müller and Schleicher, beyond all restoration."[39] What was at stake, Whitney believed, was disciplinary self-preservation. Of course, he wanted to show that linguistics was genuinely scientific, having parity of status with the long-established sciences. Yet it was just as important for linguistics to be considered free of any implied subordination to its disciplinary neighbors. And on the latter score, Whitney found that Müller's and Schleicher's argument undermined its professed intent. The supposed achievement of high status that would come from linking language study to the natural sciences would never be realized, he argued, because the linkage itself spelled a loss of autonomy. For what enhancement of status could accrue if there were no longer an independent discipline to which it could attach? As Whitney saw things, Müller and Schleicher had struck a singularly bad bargain.

This tactical disagreement reflected two distinct phases commonly found in the development of an intellectual discipline. As the nineteenth-century French sociologist Gabriel Tarde once noted, spokesmen for a new field typically emphasize the similarities between their own activities and those pursued by workers in the older and more prestigious sciences. Yet they do this only for a short while before declaring their field's independence.[40] Müller and Schleicher represented a belated instance of the first of these moves, the bid for an advantageous alliance. Whitney made sure to include the second step as well: he pursued scientific status, yet never at the expense of autonomy. His insistence that language change was the product of free agency thus had two sources. Not only did he believe that this explanation made sense, but he also regarded it as a key to the future viability of linguistics.

Of Whitney's main adversaries, Schleicher represented the lesser popular threat, especially in Britain and America. Yet philologists everywhere held him in high regard, and when he died prematurely in 1868, even Whitney deemed it "no small loss." Still, he hoped that Schleicher would be remembered more for his technical work than for his theoretical pronouncements. In this he was disappointed, however, for just after Schleicher's death, an English translation of his *Darwinsche Theorie* pamphlet was published in London. The mere fact that the piece had been translated was enough to upset Whitney, for he described that essay as Schleicher's "very worst and absurdest production." Moreover, the English version carried a bold new title — "Darwinism Proved by the Science of Language" — the implication of which (for reasons we will see later) Whitney thought wholly unjustified. The crowning blow came two years later when Whitney found a copy of the translated pamphlet in the Yale College library — where, he complained, "it could only do unmixed harm."[41] No doubt he was thinking of the bad influence Schleicher's work could have on the graduate students in Yale's "School of Philology," which was set to begin operations that next fall.

Whitney (he confessed) got "rather riled up" by this discovery, and he responded by immediately composing a new essay reiterating his position against Schleicher. He presented this at the 1871 meeting of the American Philological Association. Here Whitney set forth an uncompromising restatement of his voluntarist outlook, even to the point of echoing the convoluted prose of his old moral philosophy textbook: "That congeries of changes which makes up the so-called growth or life of language is produced solely by human action; and that, since human action depends on human will, languages, instead of being undeterminable by the will of man, are determinable by that will, and by nothing else." From this basis, Whitney reaffirmed his belief that linguistics constituted a moral rather than a physical science.[42]

## The Conceptual Refounding of a Discipline

The physical-science thesis derived much of its seeming plausibility from its links to three broader intellectual tendencies. These consisted of *monopolizing,* the use of the term "science" to indicate the natural sciences only; *analogizing,* the representation of linguistic phenomena via comparisons with nature; and *materializing,* the resort to purely physical determinants in explaining humanity's mental and linguistic capacities. W. D. Whitney devoted considerable effort to combating these tendencies, all of which had become part of the surrounding intellectual landscape by the early 1860s. His treatment of these subjects drew upon many of the threads we have seen in our story thus far; hence, in surveying those arguments we recapitulate some of Whitney's key experiences and ideas. At the same time, we encounter two significant ironies. First, Whitney actually agreed to a surprising extent with the linguistic idealists of his day. Second, his own arguments often were bound up with problems of linguistic representation itself.

The original promoter of the American Philological Association, George F. Comfort, gave an apt description of the *monopolizing* tendency. Just after the APA's founding, he expressed the hope that there would be mutual respect between philologists and men of "science" — using the term, he hastened to add, in its "popular and limited sense." Whitney was already touchy about this new definition, something he had heard coming from the mouths of the country's leading physicists and astronomers. These men, he complained, were guilty of "monopolizing the name 'science' to the *materialische* branches of knowledge." He elaborated the point in his lectures: "There is a growing disposition on the part of the devotees of physical studies — a class greatly and rapidly increasing in importance and influence — to restrict the honourable title of science to those departments of knowledge which are founded on the unvarying laws of material nature, and to deny the possibility of scientific method and scientific results where the main element of action is the varying and capricious will of man."[43]

Refusing to accept the new definition, Whitney declared that "the name 'science' admits no such limitation."[44] This was a deeply ironic position for a philologist who usually taught that changes in definition such as the word *science* was undergoing were all but inevitable. Whitney even analyzed the particular kind of change involved in this instance, the move from a general to a more specific meaning. His favorite example was the word *planet:* a term that originally had applied to any "wanderer" in the heavens eventually became restricted to bodies orbiting a specific star. The process with *science* was much the same, except that in this case it was shifting the ground under Whitney's own feet.

Max Müller saw the futility of clinging to the old definition, so he argued that linguistics was a physical science specifically. As Whitney (and others) rightly surmised, Müller and like-minded writers did this out of "an apprehension lest otherwise they should be unable to prove it entitled to the rank of a science at all."[45] By contrast, Whitney counted himself among those traditionalists "who still hold to the grand distinction of moral and physical sciences," thus implying that the two domains were equally scientific.[46] He was convinced, moreover, that this old sense of equality could be maintained. He was strengthened in this belief by his experience at Yale's Sheffield Scientific School, with its balance between the social, natural, and applied sciences. From this perspective there was no disadvantage to classing linguistics among the "moral sciences" only.

The second reinforcement of the physical-science thesis was the *analogizing* tendency, the longstanding use of organic and geological imagery in linguistics. Whitney did not object to this practice per se. He could appreciate, for instance, the "noteworthy and often-remarked similarity [that] exists between the facts and methods of geology and those of linguistic study," especially since geology was "the most historical of the physical sciences." He even found such analogies useful himself, particularly for illustrating the gradual building up and wearing down of words and grammatical forms. Whitney also saw the aptness of organic imagery. Obviously, he felt no qualm about entitling one of his own books *The Life and Growth of Language* (1875); he also said that linguistic processes were "like" the "birth, increase, decay, and death of a living creature."[47]

As Whitney noted in his 1867 volume, there was a "yet closer parallelism" between a language and an entire species, inspired by Darwinian evolution theory. He admired the series of language-species analogies included in Charles Lyell's *Geological Evidences of the Antiquity of Man* (1863). And he particularly affirmed the similarity between Darwin's theory and his own explanatory schema founded on idiolect variation: "The speech of each person is, as it were, an individual of a species, with its general inherited conformity to the specific type, but also with its individual peculiarities, its tendency to variation and the formation of a new species. The dialects, languages, groups, families, [and] stocks, set up by the linguistic student, correspond with the varieties, species, genera, and so on, of the zoologist." To top this off, Whitney all but repeated August Schleicher's claim that philology supplied an independent illustration of the evolutionary process: "Transmutation of species in the kingdom of speech is no hypothesis, but a patent fact, one of the fundamental and determining principles of linguistic study."[48]

Even so, having said all of this, Whitney's main point was to warn that such images were potentially misleading. They were harmless if treated as "analogies only, instructive as illustrations." Lyell, to his credit, had taken this approach. Yet comparisons of this kind became "fruitful of error when, letting our fancy run away with our reason, we allow them to determine our fundamental views respecting the nature of language and the method of its study."[49] Here Whitney borrowed from a long rhetorical tradition that regarded figurative language as a source of intellectual mischief. John Locke had warned about this, and the eighteenth-century Scots did too. Whitney would have found this theme in Kames's *Elements of Criticism* (1761).[50] Accordingly, in the Preface to his first book, Whitney promised to avoid letting "terms founded on analogies" take the place of the plain truths they represented. With Schleicher in mind, he especially derided the "personification of language itself as an independent existence, an organism."[51]

The founders of comparative philology had used bio-organic imagery as a way to distinguish their own field from traditional philology and to suggest its independent status. Yet as Whitney realized, while such imagery may have served that purpose originally, in the long run it produced the opposite affect: it conveyed the impression that linguistics had become a wholly-owned subsidiary of natural science. Hence, he insisted, the right use of rhetoric was "of essential consequence in linguistic philosophy."[52]

The last of the three threats Whitney confronted was the *materializing* tendency, which attributed humanity's mental functions to purely physical determinants. Here Whitney agreed with his religious critics more than they perhaps realized. It is true that he moved to purge linguistics of theological influences. And his own religious beliefs were decidedly secular; he embraced positivism and he had once even described himself as "an avowed materialist." Yet Whitney was by no means a materialist in his mental philosophy. The hyperpositivist stance taken by some writers in that field which so disturbed Whitney's religiously oriented peers actually disturbed Whitney too. His fear was that the notion of mind as a product of nonconscious causes would absorb language as well, making it too part of the *materialische* realm. He described this danger in a crucial passage in his lectures:

> There is a school of modern philosophers who are trying to materialize all science, to eliminate the distinction between the physical and the intellectual and moral, to declare for naught the free action of the human will, and to resolve the whole story of the fates of mankind into a series of purely material effects, produced by assignable physical causes, and explainable in the past, or determinable for the future, by an intimate knowledge of those causes, by a recognition of the action of compulsory motives upon the passively obedient nature of man.

*With such [modern thinkers], language will naturally pass, along with the rest, for a physical product, and its study for a physical science.*[53]

As this last remark indicates, although Whitney made the same kind of analysis as did the theological writers, he drew a different conclusion. He was not worried about the modern intellect's spiritual vulnerability or about the moral implications of materialism. He worried, rather, that linguistics could lose its autonomy and authority, for his was the agenda of a scholarly professionalizer.

Part of the problem came from advances in linguistics itself, particularly in the study of phonetics and speech physiology. Whitney acknowledged the contributions these subfields were making, yet he feared that as a result of the attention they were receiving, important areas of linguistic investigation would become annexed to physicalist agendas and assumptions.[54] Whitney's antidote was to cleave to the Common Sense philosophy of mind. Human action, he said, was "fundamentally and essentially different from that of atoms moved by gravity, chemical affinity, and the other immutable forces of nature, as we call them." While vocal physiology certainly helped shape language, language was more than "articulated sound alone, which might, in a certain sense, be regarded as a physical product." For the speech apparatus would be nothing without the speaker's active consciousness: "Between all determining causes and their results" there intervened, "as middle term, the human mind, seeking and choosing expression for human thought."[55]

Finally, a significant share of the materializing tendency in linguistics was not literal but figurative—thus overlapping with the analogizing phenomenon. Indeed, Whitney's complaints about analogies drawn from nature focused largely on their materialistic implications. This was the main shortcoming, for instance, of the comparison with geology: "In the formation of geological strata, the ultimate cognizable agencies are the laws of matter. In language, on the other hand, the ultimate agencies are intelligent beings."[56]

Here again, Whitney joined to a surprising degree with his idealist neighbors, especially those at Yale. Noah Porter, following his teacher Josiah Gibbs, embraced the standard Lockean teaching about physical metaphors at the base of conceptual terms; he then used this insight to critique the rhetoric employed by his fellow mental theorists. For instance, Porter faulted an 1854 psychology textbook for its careless use of "physical analogies." This did not mean that the text's writer knowingly advocated materialism, especially since the writer in this case was Francis Wayland, the Baptist president of Brown College. Yet

danger arose nonetheless, Porter warned, "from the fact that the language employed to describe mental phenomena, is necessarily borrowed from the world
of sense." Even if readers were aware that certain terms consisted of "faded
metaphors, we do not always observe, nor do we always guard against the insidious influence of the image from which the metaphor was taken. . . . [T]he
student of psychology should place himself ever on his guard against the influence of the images and associations which are continually put into his mouth
by the language which the necessities of his being force him to use."[57]

W. D. Whitney made precisely the same analysis in his own area of study.
First, he affirmed the basic Lockean insight: "All, as the historical study of language distinctly shows, has been won through the transfer to an ideal use of
words and phrases which had before designated something physical and sensible."[58] And Whitney's application of this insight was also the same as Porter's,
for Whitney too assumed that the language a person used to describe a phenomenon affected the community's mental conception of it. Hence, his concern about beguiling figures of speech, which could predispose readers "to
deny the agency of man in the production and change of language, and to pronounce it an organic growth, governed by organic laws."[59] To this extent, like
the idealists he often opposed, Whitney believed in the power of words over
thought.

What, then, were the long-term effects of W. D. Whitney's battle against the
physical-science thesis? It will be useful to adopt an attitude of skepticism at
this point and to question whether his polemics were actually necessary. Writing in the 1920s, the Danish linguist Otto Jespersen recalled that "Schleicher
and Max Müller in their own day had few followers in defining linguistics as
a natural or physical science."[60] And the German linguist Hugo Schuchardt
had said, as early as 1885: "Our day ascribes to linguistics the character of an
historical science. It does not view language as a natural organism, but as a social product."[61] Do these affirmations serve as proof that Whitney's arguments
had quickly won the day, or do they suggest that such thinking was "in the
air" already and that Whitney's arguments had not really been needed in the
first place? After all, the outlook Schuchardt described could well have been
inspired by other sources. Wilhelm Dilthey's *Einleitung in die Geisteswissen-
schaften* (1883), for instance, clarified the distinction between the natural and
human-social sciences for many European thinkers.

Yet even if Whitney's contribution was but one among many, it alone was still significant. The German Neogrammarians, the most influential school of linguists in late-nineteenth-century Europe, spoke clearly on this point. We will examine Whitney's relationship to this group in detail later, yet it will be useful here to take a preliminary measure of their opinions. In a memorial tribute composed shortly after Whitney's death, the linguist Karl Brugmann said:

> The most important thing Whitney taught was the following. If we ascribe to language an independent existence, certain activities, certain inclinations or moods, a capability for adaptation to the requirements of mankind, and other similar things—then these are only figurative expressions. They do not signify the thing itself, and one should not permit oneself to be deluded by them. In reality, language lives only in the minds and on the lips of those who speak it.

Brugmann did not mention the bio-organic analogy per se, yet one of his colleagues, August Leskien, did do this in his memorial statement: "Whitney taught above all that language is not an independent organism, but that it can be comprehended only as an intrinsic part of the living environment of man. This is the fundamental view found in Whitney's discussions of language."[62]

As these passages suggest, Whitney's contribution lay in his attack on the entire "organic" view of language—something larger and more deeply ingrained than the physical-science thesis. Moreover, Otto Jespersen said that this natural-historical tradition was a real problem that had needed to be addressed, as we can see by placing his above-quoted comment in its full context:

> *Though* Schleicher and Max Müller in their own day had few followers in defining linguistics as a natural or physical science . . . there can be no doubt that the naturalistic point of view practically, though perhaps chiefly unconsciously, had wide-reaching effects on the history of linguistic science. It was intimately connected with the problems chiefly investigated and the way in which they were treated.[63]

Here, then, was the more fundamental issue at stake in the theoretical debates of the 1860s. Had the "naturalistic" viewpoint not been met with convincing argument, the other, more social approaches to language study might not have been as effective in making their claims to legitimacy in the early twentieth century. Whitney's battle against Müller and Schleicher on this subject has not been fully appreciated because it consisted in error prevention; it was an effort to keep linguistics from taking a wrong path. This kind of work, by its very nature, hides its own success. Because the feared outcome is averted, the preventive effort seems not to have been needed much in the first place. Still, the successful outcome was not inevitable; it only appears inevitable in retrospect because polemics have done their work. Hence, the negative side of Whitney's theoretical labors, although preliminary to the task of building, was still thoroughly necessary. On the positive side, Whitney entwined his polemics with expositions of his interactionist sociology of language. The latter, in the long run, was his main contribution to his field. He was, in fact, the earliest guide, as well as the most consistent among the other early guides, to a genuinely social understanding of language.

# CHAPTER SEVEN

# Forging an Alliance with Anthropology

In the early 1870s, only a few years after the publication of his first book, W. D. Whitney added a subtle new element to his linguistic writings. Although he continued to teach that linguistics belonged with the "moral" sciences as a whole, he now emphasized the field's special kinship with anthropology. Whitney drew this connection partly as a way to underscore themes that had been present in his work all along. He also used anthropology as a reference point as he elaborated his views on a number of important topics. Among these were race and ethnology, culture and human nature, myth and religion, and the idea of scientific "law" as applied to language. A further issue linked to anthropology was Darwinian evolution. Where exactly did Whitney stand on this crucial question? Did he accept an evolutionary explanation of human origins, and if so, what was his response to Darwin's ideas about the origin of language specifically? By exploring these various themes, we further situate Whitney in relation to the human sciences in that day. At the same time, we lay the groundwork for a fuller assessment of his ties to Continental linguistics.

## Linguistic Ethnology

W. D. Whitney made no original contributions to ethnological research, yet he did take a keen interest in ethnological theory. This interest on his part was all but inevitable. In the early nineteenth century, ethnologists often used linguistic data to aid them in their main task—tracing the ties of blood kinship among the earth's peoples. The field's overarching question was this: Did humanity's racial groupings all share a common ancestry, as the Bible apparently taught, or had they each emerged from a separate act of creation? The two sides in this debate were known as "monogenesis" and "polygenesis," respectively.[1]

The expectation that linguistic evidence would decide this issue was based on two long-held assumptions. First, traditional ethnology taught that the family tree of nations and the family tree of languages were essentially one and the same. Language therefore provided a reliable index of blood community. The second assumption was that human history spanned a relatively short period of time. The estimate as of midcentury stood at a little less than 10,000 years—only a modest extension of the 6,000 years suggested by a literal reading of Genesis. This brief time scale gave ethnological researchers the confidence they needed. With such a short period to cover, it seemed probable that research would eventually show whether or not the world's languages, hence peoples, had derived from a single tongue and tribe. In this way the biblical affirmation of human unity would be confirmed or denied by "scientific" language study.

By the end of the 1850s, however, this heroic quest had to be abandoned because of the collapse of its founding assumptions. First, the language-race identification came under attack; a majority of thinkers now agreed that a person's mode of speech did not necessarily indicate his or her ethnological descent.[2] Soon the brief human time frame was overthrown as well. Excavations in England's Brixham cave and elsewhere revealed manmade implements commingled with the fossil remains of extinct animals, proving that humanity had existed far longer than was previously thought. This revolution in ethnological time, it should be noted, was separate from the revolution in geological time publicized most famously in Charles Lyell's writings in the 1830s.

Even by itself, the new chronology proved fatal to traditional language-based ethnology. For while the length of humanity's existence was now vastly extended, the linguistic data still went back only so far. The common ancestor languages such as proto-Indo-European were revealed to have originated far more recently than the period of human origins. (Linguists have long held that proto-Indo-European emerged around 4000 B.C.E.) Accordingly, researchers gave up hope of tracing the ultimate historical source—or sources—of language. And this conclusion led them to abandon the expectation that linguistic evidence could ever uncover the origins of ethnic diversity.

W. D. Whitney's conversion to this new perspective was absolute. In 1856, near the beginning of his career, Whitney declared that scholars looked to the ancient Oriental texts in order "to read the early history of the human race." The assumption was that humanity had appeared on the scene not much earlier than the oldest Eastern writings. When he gave his Smithsonian lectures eight years later, he remarked on the change that had taken place: "Recent discoveries are proving that man's antiquity is much greater than has hitherto been usually supposed." The implication for the monogenesis debate was clear: "The evidence of language can never guide us to any positive conclusion respecting the specific unity or diversity of the human races."[3]

Especially important is the way Whitney deployed the other half of the new ethnological thinking—the formal distinction between language and race—in a way that served the interests of his own discipline. His aim was to head off a challenge from anatomically based ethnology, which constituted a further threat from the "physical sciences." Linguistic ethnology and physical ethnology had coexisted for decades, yet the latter began assuming an increased prominence around midcentury. Its most extreme advocates were members of the "American school"—researchers who compared cranial types in order to champion polygenism and teach racial inequality. Not surprisingly, this school of ethnology became popular among the southern slaveholding aristocracy in the 1850s, the decade prior to the Civil War. Yet it also had representatives in the northern states, chief among them Louis Agassiz, director of the Museum of Comparative Zoology at Harvard.[4]

Like most educated New Englanders, W. D. Whitney was dismayed at this racialist use of ethnology by a celebrated Harvard naturalist. In part, no doubt, he regretted the comfort it gave to the southern regime. Yet the moral issue of slavery was not what provoked Whitney in his capacity as a language theorist. Rather, he deplored the way racialist thought suggested a further encroachment by physical science on his discipline. We saw this concern earlier in Whitney's disgust with the emphasis on craniology at Harvard's Peabody Museum of American Ethnology and Archaeology.[5] Significantly, he expressed that opinion at the time of the Museum's founding in the fall of 1866 — *after* the Civil War and the Thirteenth Amendment had put an end to American slavery. However momentous, that development did not stop Whitney's worries about physicalist ethnology.

Whitney never named Louis Agassiz in this connection, although he hardly needed to. Clearly he was referring to the famous zoologist in his 1867 book when he deplored the idea "put forth and defended by certain authorities, . . . that language is the immediate and necessary product of physical organization, and varies as this varies; that an Englishman, a Frenchman, and a Chinaman talk unlike one another because their brains and organs of articulation are unlike." Whitney recoiled from this kind of explanation. He did so, moreover, for what to him was the most important of all possible reasons: "Doctrines akin with these are more or less distinctly and consciously implied in the views of those who hold that language is beyond the reach of the free-agency of men, and can be neither made nor changed by human effort. *All who think thus virtually deny the existence of such a thing as linguistic science, or reduce it to the position of a subordinate branch of physiology.*"[6] For Whitney, then, the racialist theory of language was problematic mainly because it compromised the autonomy of linguistics as a discipline.

Yet what were his ideas about "race" itself? Like many nineteenth-century thinkers, Whitney understood racial phenomena to be a blend of biological, historical, and cultural factors, with considerable ambiguity as to the relative importance of each. He apparently believed in a quasi-Lamarckian combination of inherited and acquired characteristics — a commonplace viewpoint at that time and one that left unclear the extent to which biological inheritance figured in the mix. He also followed prevailing practice by using the terms "race" and "nation" nearly interchangeably.

Whitney did share the prejudices of most Euro-Americans of his day: he held that there were "differences in the mental endowment of races" and that some races were "exceptionally endowed." He specifically believed that dark-skinned Africans were, on average, cognitively inferior to northern Europeans. But at least he thought that the median capabilities of these groups were not very far apart. As he once declared, "There are plenty of English blockheads who fall below the average African, and whose store of ideas and signs for them no average African need envy." Whitney thus denied that race invariably determined an *individual's* mental rank relative to the members of other ethnic groups. He suggested, rather, that the particular community in which a person was brought up played the larger role in shaping that outcome. In sum, Whitney's ideas about race, although manifesting prejudice, were nevertheless cautious and were only in part reductionistic.[7]

Whitney was especially against the idea that the structural complexity of a language mirrored the mental capacity of the nation that spoke it. Although he held that the "present state of perfection" of language was "greatly different in different races," he attributed this phenomenon to a complex blend of historico-cultural factors; it was by no means a measure of cerebral inheritance. As he said late in his career, "To account for the great and striking differences of structure among human languages is beyond the power of the linguistic student, and will doubtless always continue so. We are not likely to be able even to demonstrate a correlation of capacities, saying that a race which has done this and that in other departments of human activity might have been expected to form such and such a language." In short, Whitney concluded that "mental power is not measured by language-structure."[8] Again, the point was to separate language and race as causal variables.

And yet, having said these things, Whitney added a twist. Although he joined others in rejecting speech type as an indication of *ethnos,* he distinguished between the *formal separation* of those variables and their general *historical correlation.* In the formal sense, the identification of language type with blood inheritance led to obvious absurdities. It would mean that orphaned infants from Shanghai, even if raised in Paris, would show an inborn propensity to speak Mandarin.[9] Even so, Whitney noted, history did tend to keep language and ethnicity together: over the centuries, most languages had been spoken by the peoples with whom they were historically identified. In this sense, he said, "upon the whole, language is a tolerably sure indication of race."[10]

Whitney thus showed that the formal distinction between language and race was fully compatible with the historical tendency of these factors to coincide. Indeed, he argued, the lengthened human chronology suggested that the identification of language and race became increasingly the norm the further back in time one looked, especially in the period before empires began to bring entire peoples under new linguistic regimes. The implication was that linguistic evidence continued to make a unique contribution to our understanding of the distant past, even taking precedence over paleontological evidence. For even after the revolution in ethnological time, the oldest linguistic data still predated the known anatomical or other physical remains of ancient peoples. Whitney therefore urged the continued use of linguistic research for "tracing out . . . the actual connection and genealogical history of human races."[11]

Did this mean that he accepted traditional ethnology's boldest claim, that historical linguistics could resolve the dispute about monogenesis? He did not believe that it could do this directly, for linguistic evidence could no longer be regarded as reaching back far enough. Yet he did not, like some, abandon the question itself. Quite the contrary, Whitney argued that the discovery of prehistoric time actually tipped the balance in favor of original human unity. This was because, henceforth, while there could never be conclusive evidence *proving* polygenesis, it also would never be possible to *disprove* monogenesis. Moreover, the addition of abundant time only increased the possibility of gradual divergence from a common ancestor. As Whitney said, "We cannot presume to set any limits to the extent to which languages once the same may have grown apart from one another."[12]

And so, even as he embraced the formal separation of language and race as well as the lengthened human chronology, Whitney came close to reviving the traditional ethnological paradigm those new ideas had undermined. He reaffirmed not only the paradigm's monogenetic conclusion but also its language-centered methodology. These arguments probably had little influence on actual ethnological research, yet they are significant for what they tell us about Whitney's own agenda. The point, again, was to bolster the standing of his discipline within the ethnological household, yet another effort to keep the rising tide of physical science from engulfing language study. Whitney thus tailored his linguistic ethnology, like other aspects of his linguistic theory, to fit a professional disciplinary agenda.

It is important to see, however, that he pursued this goal with arguments that could stand on their own merits. As with his voluntarist theory of language change, Whitney's ethnological opinions were motivated by partisan interest, yet at the same time they served as a convincing "scientific" interpretation of the available evidence. (That combination is, after all, a possibility one must always admit.) Later we will note the dogmatism of certain other aspects of Whitney's "anthropological" language theory. Yet his views on ethnology, like most of his other arguments for the autonomy of linguistics, consisted of ideas that, although self-serving, were generally compelling in themselves.

## Problems of Indo-European Ethnology

In addition to the monogenesis debate, nineteenth-century ethnology also addressed a number of issues concerning the Indo-European peoples. Here again, researchers traditionally assumed that these nations were identified historically with a distinct set of languages. In fact, the whole idea of an Indo-European linguistic family was ethnological in character.[13] August Schleicher codified this outlook in the late 1850s when he began depicting the relationships among the Indo-European languages on the model of a *Stammbaum*, or "family tree." According to this theory, as the once-unified Indo-European community subdivided via successive out-migrations, the original common tongue would have subdivided as well, thus producing new dialects and eventually whole new languages.

W. D. Whitney heartily endorsed this traditional theory. He declared that the similarities among languages of the same family "constitute an identity which can only be explained by supposing those who founded those tongues to have been members together of the same community." Accordingly, Whitney believed in "the *Stammbaum*-connection of Indo-European races." He also affirmed, along with Schleicher, the primacy of classifying languages genealogically, that is, according to common historical descent.[14]

The main rival to genealogical classification was the grammatico-structural scheme of classification formulated by Wilhelm von Humboldt in the early nineteenth century. Humboldt had discerned four basic types of languages—isolating, agglutinative, inflective, and polysynthetic—each having its characteristic type of word construction. In *isolating* languages, such as Chinese, words were compiled from indissoluble roots: the Chinese word for "twenty," for example, was a juxtaposition of the words "two-ten." *Agglutinative* languages, such as those of the Semitic family, added a distinctive class of words that fused their constituent elements more closely. *Inflective* languages, found mostly in the Indo-European family, contained many words of which no part remained in its original root-form. The fourth type, *polysynthetic,* consisted mainly of American Indian languages, in which "words" expressive of a cluster of ideas were formed from strings of dependent syllables.

Whitney thought that this morphological scheme of classification had been overrated and that it ought to be kept subordinate to the genealogical approach. This stance amounted to a de facto privileging of the Indo-European family, for which genealogical investigation had proved especially fruitful. Still, Whitney conceded that the Humboldtian taxonomy was useful for those classifying families of languages about which little historical information was available due to a scarcity or absence of written records.[15]

Along with Schleicher and many others, Whitney was convinced that there once had been a single Indo-European (or "Aryan") tribe. And like most writers on the subject, he held that a series of out-migrations from the Aryan homeland accounted for the peopling of India, Iran, and Europe. Could linguistic evidence reveal anything about these matters? Whitney conceded that it was of no help in locating the Indo-European homeland, whether in Europe or Asia. Nor could it determine the time of the tribe's origin.[16] Yet Whitney suggested that linguistics was still valuable in other ways. He endorsed the work of the Frenchman Adolphe Pictet, who was piecing together a description of life among the Aryan mother-tribe by reconstructing the Indo-European proto-lexicon, especially the names of plants and animals. Already Pictet and his followers had shown that the first Indo-Europeans engaged in agriculture, organized themselves into clans, and practiced a simple polytheistic religion.

So while acknowledging the "imperfection of speech as an historical record," Whitney argued that linguistic evidence still was as good as any other kind for investigating the prehistoric Indo-Europeans.[17] In this way he again pushed the explanatory efficacy of his own field as far as he could, continuing his campaign to show that linguistic ethnology was at least equal, and in many ways superior, to physical ethnology.

## Americanist Ethnology

Ethnology in North America mainly concerned the origin and kinship of the Native American peoples, the key question being whether the migrations that first populated the continent had come from Europe or from Asia. In his *Notes on the State of Virginia* (1787), Thomas Jefferson had called on investigators to compile vocabulary lists from the various American Indian languages and then to compare these with similar lists from other parts of the globe.[18] (This followed the model set by Catherine the Great, who sponsored research of this kind on the nearly two hundred languages spoken within the Russian empire.) A handful of scholars in the early national period pursued Jefferson's

project under the auspices of the American Philosophical Society in Philadelphia; many of those who came later were connected with the Smithsonian
Institution.

As a Sanskrit specialist, W. D. Whitney moved in a different world, Europe-
centered and collegiate, from that of Americanist researchers such as Lewis
Henry Morgan and John Wesley Powell. Still, Whitney did have links to these
figures. He supplied Morgan's request for Sanskrit terms to be used in comparing vocabularies gathered from North America and the Indian subcontinent.[19]
He also helped prepare a standardized phonetic alphabet for an ethnology
handbook published by the Smithsonian. That work, written by the geologist George Gibbs, came out in 1863.[20] (Thus was the way paved for Whitney's
Smithsonian lectures on linguistic science the following year.) Ideally, construction of an alphabet involved a partnership between trained philologists
and amateur ethnological field-workers, the explorers, soldiers, and missionaries who had routine contact with American Indians and needed a system for
observing and recording their unwritten languages.

Whitney's efforts in this line proved abortive, however, as shown by his subsequent collaboration with the geologist-explorer J. W. Powell. Whitney and
Powell first met when the latter visited New Haven in 1876. The two men spent
several days together discussing American Indian languages and mythology.
Whitney reported afterward: "I liked him much. It is astonishing how many
geologists take to collecting language, etc., and what a good fit they make of
it." Whitney then helped devise a new phonetic alphabet (a revision of the
one for the Gibbs volume) for the first edition of Powell's *Introduction to the
Study of Indian Languages* (1877). Yet his schema did not work well in practice,
for laymen needed something that could be learned and remembered more
easily. Whitney bowed out of the project, at the same time affirming his commitment to the pragmatic orthography the task demanded. He told Powell:
"You have no good reason for regarding and treating me as an authority on
these matters. . . . Questions of alphabetizing are questions of expediency and
compromise." Whitney did not contribute to the new alphabet included in the
second (1880) edition of Powell's *Introduction*.[21]

Despite this occasional involvement in Smithsonian work, Whitney had
long criticized the Institution's approach to Americanist ethnology. Joined by
his Hartford friend J. H. Trumbull, he called on the Smithsonian to shelve its
plans for a general treatise on the subject. Trumbull and Whitney wanted more
data, arguing that it would be premature to address the ethnological issues be-

fore the internal genealogical relationships among the languages themselves had been worked out. As Whitney said in his published lectures, "What we have to do at present . . . is simply to learn all that we possibly can of the Indian languages themselves. . . . If our studies shall at length put us in a position to deal with the question of their Asiatic derivation, we will rejoice at it. I do not myself expect that valuable light will ever be shed upon the subject by linguistic evidence: others may be more sanguine; but all must at any rate agree that, as things are, the subject is in no position to be taken up and discussed with profit."[22]

This pessimism arose from the view—standard at the time—that unwritten languages had a propensity for rapid change. As Max Müller once put it, the languages of most Native American and African peoples were in a state of "continual combustion." This meant that any traces of a proto-lexicon bearing witness to the original unity of those languages would be long past recovery. Whitney urged that, instead of gathering word lists, the Smithsonian should sponsor detailed studies of Indian grammars, since grammar was presumably more stable over time.[23] Nevertheless, the "salvage" method prevailed. The Institution wanted at least a compilation of vocabularies before the native populations were much further reduced.

In practice, then, Whitney operated only at the periphery of Americanist linguistics. Still, he did what he could to promote that field: he tried to encourage research in the American Philological Association, chiefly by showcasing J. H. Trumbull's work in the annual *Transactions*. And as the APA's first president, he declared that "the philology of the American aboriginal languages . . . demands, as it has already begun to receive, the most hearty encouragement. Circumstances, and our duty toward the races whom we are dispossessing and destroying, make American philology and archaeology our especial responsibility, and it is our disgrace as a nation that we have been unfaithful to it."[24]

This last comment suggests Whitney's attitude toward the native peoples themselves. Apparently he had no sense of the colossal irony of invoking a scholarly "duty" toward peoples whom Euro-Americans were "dispossessing and destroying." The implication was that a scientific interest in the native American languages would demonstrate the white man's regard for Indian culture and that this would afford a kind of compensation to people who were being robbed of their land and often their lives. Beyond this, Whitney showed no particular concern for the fate of the Indians. This attitude was typical of American ethnological writers of that era. From Jefferson to J. W. Powell, all were resigned to the ultimate necessity of Indian removal—something they regarded as tragic yet inevitable. Still, they worried about the scholarly loss this process would entail.[25]

In his first book, Whitney lamented that no academic institution in the United States had taken up the investigation of the native languages. Yet he did anticipate a change: "This reproach, at least, is about to be removed, by the establishment of a chair of American archaeology at Cambridge."[26] Whitney wrote this in the early days of Harvard's Peabody Museum of American Archaeology and Ethnology, still under the impression that the related professorship would soon be initiated and that the position would go to a language specialist. (Or perhaps by mentioning this expectation in print, Whitney hoped to prod Harvard into making it a reality.) As it turned out, American Indian linguistics became a university subject only after the anthropologists made it one of their main subfields in the 1890s.

## Darwinian Nature versus Social Nurture

Despite his strong interest in ethnology, Whitney had a much greater theoretical affinity for "evolutionist" anthropology. The differences between those fields will become apparent as we proceed. As a preliminary, however, we need to examine Whitney's views on the related question—or rather questions—of actual biological evolution. There were four distinct issues in this regard.

First of all, some have suggested that Whitney owed much of his linguistic theory to influence from bio-evolutionary writings. Stephen Jay Gould, for instance, described Whitney's *Language and the Study of Language* as "a standard nineteenth-century work inspired by the Darwinian revolution."[27] This impression is understandable enough, although it fails to take into account the way philology as a whole in that era emphasized language's gradual historical unfolding—an idea not at all dependent on Darwinism. As Whitney himself pointed out in 1883, Darwin's writings merely reinforced the notion of civilizational progress that had been current for some time: "That every successive phase of a historical institution is the outgrowth of a preceding phase, and differs little from it, is a truth long coming to clear recognition and fruitful application in every department of historic research, prior to and in complete independence of any doctrine of evolution in the natural world. Only error and confusion have come of the attempts made to connect Darwinism and philologic science."[28]

Besides this matter of evolutionary thinking in the broad historicist sense, there were three other issues that Whitney considered: Charles Darwin's theory as such; Darwin's views on the origin of humanity; and the question, specifically, of the origin of speech. Whitney first addressed these questions, not in his published lectures, but in a review he wrote for the *Nation* two years later. This 1869 article considered the origin-of-language theory recently set forth by W. H. J. Bleek, a respected German linguist and a cousin of the pro-evolutionary zoologist Ernst Haeckel. Here for the first time Whitney spoke directly to the question of species evolution. Not surprisingly, he affirmed his "great faith in the substantial truth of the central Darwinian idea." Whitney was still not ready to commit himself, however; and indeed, his main point was to urge caution: "We cannot think the [Darwinian] theory yet converted into a scientific fact; and those are perhaps the worst foes to its success who are overhasty to take it and use it as a proved fact." He reprimanded those "headlong Darwinians" — Haeckel being the chief culprit — who treated the theory as "already proved and unquestionable."²⁹

Whitney would remain circumspect in public, but he must have become increasingly convinced in his own mind. An essential component of Darwin's theory was the notion of branching descent from common ancestors, and a mere stroll across Yale's campus would have shown the latest evidence of this. In 1870 the Peabody Museum of Natural History began displaying fossils from the American West collected by O. C. Marsh. The most talked-about discovery was the remains of an extinct species of bird having teeth and other reptilian features — suggesting an ancestral link between two long-separated biological genera. Such vivid evidence likely informed private remarks Whitney made in 1874. The occasion was the passing of Louis Agassiz, the most vocal opponent of Darwinism among America's professional naturalists: "Yes, Agassiz's death is a sad loss — less, so far as science is concerned, than if he had not concentrated all his powers in a fruitless fight with the evolution theories. We shan't soon see another such grand personality in this country."³⁰

Whitney's 1869 review article also touched on the two remaining issues — the all-important question of human origins, and the related problem of the origin of speech. More than a year would pass before Darwin stated his own views on these subjects in *The Descent of Man* (1871), yet Whitney, like most observers, saw where he was headed. Whitney again urged caution, faulting those (such as Haeckel) who rushed to draw up detailed genealogies of man's prehuman ancestry. Still, he gave a strong indication as to his own leanings:

"Now we, for one, must confess that we have not a particle of prejudice against such kindred." For if it were asked whether humans had originated "by a long and tedious climb upward from a miserable semi-simious state, or by a briefer slide downward from a condition of paradisiacal purity and intuitive wisdom," he would respond without hesitation that "the former account of our position is the more flattering and gratifying of the two."[31]

Did Whitney also follow Darwin's thinking concerning the origin of language? At least one writer thought so. A review of Whitney's first book appearing in *Bibliotheca Sacra* criticized its "theory that we came up into the possession of language out of a mute state." According to the reviewer, that theory made "a weighty contribution to Mr. Darwin's doctrine"; indeed, he said, Whitney "scarcely disguises his leaning to Darwinism."[32] This no doubt was the impression many readers came away with, especially those who faulted Whitney's philosophical "positivism." Whether this charge was accurate, however, is another matter. Did Whitney in fact believe that the first glimmerings of language had been produced by some ape-like being from which humanity later evolved?

The answer is a clear-cut *no.* This is surprising on the face of it, because Whitney obviously accepted the idea of human evolution; he also taught that language had developed gradually, beginning with the imitation of sounds in nature. One would think that he ought to have concluded that these two processes occurred in tandem. Yet this was precisely what he denied. Even before Darwin published his own views on the subject, Whitney had rejected the notion that speech emerged in the course of humanity's evolution from lower animals. In his 1869 article, he insisted that only humans as such, possessing a fully evolved brain capacity, could have invented language:

> If the first man had not had a power of analytic apprehension, and a mastery over consciousness, very different from those of other beings, neither hearing nor imitation [of sounds in nature or instinctive cries] would have led him to anything. This power is man's characteristic, and where he received it, at whatever time and in whatever way, he became man. We object entirely to having his conversion into man treated as the result, rather than the cause, of his cultural development as man. When the process of language-making began, man was man *in esse* as well as *in posse,* ready to have his powers drawn out and educated—just as is every human being nowadays at the commencement of its existence.[33]

In sum, Whitney kept his belief in humanity's evolutionary emergence entirely separate from his belief in gradual and naturalistic speech origins. This stance was demanded by the way he interpreted two widely held principles, each of them fundamental to the emerging human sciences. First, he called for a strict separation between inherited biological nature and sociocultural nurture. By keeping language in the latter category only, Whitney reflected the growing tendency among anthropologists to regard "culture" as an autonomous realm, unaffected by biological influence.

Second, Whitney's *non*-Darwinian view of speech origins expressed what he regarded as a consistent uniformitarian methodology, the idea that the explanation of events in the distant past must refer to the kinds of causal forces found operating at present. There was considerable irony in Whitney's conclusion on this point because Darwin is usually considered one of the early champions of uniformitarian methodology. It is even more ironic in light of who had done the most to inspire Whitney's uniformitarian-based imitative theory of speech origins. As we have seen, that inspiration came from Hensleigh Wedgwood, Charles Darwin's cousin and brother-in-law.

Wedgwood put the argument as follows in his *Origin of Language* (1866): "The investigator of speech must accept as his starting-ground the existence of man as yet without knowledge of language but endowed with intellectual powers and command of his bodily frame, such as we ourselves are conscious of possessing, in the same way that the geologist takes his stand on the fact of a globe composed of lands and seas subjected as at the present day to the influence of rains and tides, tempests, frosts, earth-quakes, and subterranean fires."[34] Wedgwood wanted to emphasize that language was not, even in part, a divine gift to man. It had developed, he insisted, from human powers only. Yet this also meant that language had been invented by full-fledged humans, beings endowed with capacities (as Wedgwood said) "such as we ourselves are conscious of possessing."

There was, then, a fundamental difference between the way Wedgwood and Whitney, on the one hand, and Darwin, on the other, applied the uniformitarian principle to language. Darwin assumed that, essentially, *nothing more* could have existed in the distant past than exists at present—whether unknown causal factors within nature or special interventions from outside nature. Taking this logic a step further, Wedgwood and Whitney argued that, if in the past there could have existed nothing more than at present, then there also could have existed *nothing less*. A human faculty such as speech must have begun under conditions that lacked none of the basic structures that support language use today, the key elements being the human vocal apparatus and a fully evolved *homo sapiens* brain. On the face of it, it is surprising to find this dissenting viewpoint coming from Wedgwood and Whitney, two pro-Darwinian thinkers who were fully committed to the uniformitarian principle. They ought, one might suppose, to have agreed with Darwin on this point as well. Yet the reality was not as simple as that.

Darwin apparently did not discuss with his cousin the full extent of his bio-evolutionary thinking about the origin of speech, at least not prior to the appearance of *The Descent of Man* (1871). Wedgwood presumably was not aware, writing several years earlier, that his own views on the subject differed significantly from Darwin's. In *Descent,* Darwin made respectful mention of Wedgwood and a number of other writers who suggested that articulate speech had evolved from a combination of instinctive cries, such as mating calls, and the imitation of these and other sounds from nature.[35] Yet Darwin worded these remarks carefully so as not to suggest that he necessarily agreed with everything Wedgwood said. Then, on the following pages, he argued that the imitative rudiments of speech must have been uttered by man's prehuman ancestors. Said Darwin: "It does not appear altogether incredible, that some unusually wise ape-like animal should have thought of imitating the growl of a beast of prey, so as to indicate to his fellow monkeys the nature of the expected danger. And this would have been a first step in the formation of a language."[36] Continued use of this expedient would have made the final stages of humanity's mental evolution simultaneous and interdependent with the origin of speech.

Darwin's new book did nothing to change W. D. Whitney's essential position. Less than a year after the publication of *Descent,* Whitney reaffirmed his opinion that "the rise of language had nothing to do with the growth of man out of an apish stock, but only with his rise out of savagery and barbarism." He said again, somewhat later: "No steps between the wholly instinctive expression of the animals and the wholly (so far as articulate words are concerned) conventional expression of man will ever be discovered."[37] The same message would continue to appear in Whitney's writings in the years following.[38] There was, however, a particular occasion on which he hedged. This once, Whitney made a special point of declaring himself *generally in agreement* with Darwin's theory of speech origins. Why he did this, and the surprising results that followed, we will see in our next chapter.

## The Template of Cultural Evolution

Writing to his brother Josiah in the spring of 1872, W. D. Whitney offered a revealing glimpse of his home life. At the same time he suggested his growing attraction to anthropology. He reported the following: "I am reading Tylor's 'Primitive Culture' aloud to the girls, with great interest. He is far the soundest and ablest English writer on this general class of subjects, I think: clear-headed, logical, and with no hobbies at all. Lubbock can't compare with him." In referring to "the girls," Whitney presumably indicated all three of his young daughters. This would mean that he read the Englishman Edward B. Tylor's newly published anthropological treatise not only to his eldest, Marian, who had just celebrated her eleventh birthday, but also to Emily and Margaret, who were seven and five, respectively.[39] (Whitney's sons, Edward and Roger, were fourteen and nine at this time.) To say the least, this was ambitious reading material for children of their ages. Still, it suggests an aspect of daily life around the Whitney fireside.

E. B. Tylor's *Primitive Culture* (1871) was the latest product of the evolutionist school of anthropology. Closest in spirit were Tylor's previous book, his *Researches into the Early Condition of Man* (1865), and two books by John Lubbock: *Prehistoric Times* (1865) and *The Origin of Civilization and the Primitive Condition of Man* (1870). Other works in this vein had been written by J. F. McLennan, Herbert Spencer, and the American Lewis Henry Morgan. Whitney favored Tylor, however, because he found Tylor's approach to anthropology an especially fitting complement to his own outlook in linguistics. This is not to suggest that Whitney borrowed any of his essential views from Tylor: those were all in place before the appearance of Tylor's *Researches*.[40] Rather, the agreement between these writers came from the fact that both drew from the same source: British Enlightenment social thought.[41] We have seen a number of the ideas Whitney borrowed from that tradition, yet there were others as well, ones that reveal even deeper assumptions underlying his theoretical system.

The Whitney-Tylor connection centered on the notion of *cultural evolution*. Eighteenth-century writers had already described human institutions, language included, as developing from simple beginnings and growing more elaborate over time.[42] By contrast, the romantic generation of the early nineteenth century had offered a vision of historical and linguistic decline.[43] The comparative philologists approximated the older view with their theory that rudimentary monosyllables had supplied all of the basic materials used to form the inflective languages. The anthropological writings of the 1860s then brought an even greater resurgence of progressivism. This move was inspired not so much by Darwinism as by the lengthened human chronology: the new abundance of time made more plausible a scenario of gradual upward development.[44]

Reflecting this progressive view of history, W. D. Whitney regarded the "utterly savage state" as humanity's original condition; he also affirmed that the "wealth" of even the most complex languages had developed from an original "poverty." The development of words thus paralleled the development of tools and weapons. As anthropologists had recently shown, stones and clubs necessarily preceded hammers, hatchets, and spears. This "law of simplicity of beginnings," said Whitney, surely had applied to language as well.[45]

Whitney also embraced the idea of *cultural* evolution—an emphasis on sociocultural nurture as opposed to inherited biological nature.[46] In his 1871 book, E. B. Tylor famously defined culture as "that complex whole which includes knowledge, belief, art, morals, law, custom, and any other capabilities and habits *acquired by man as a member of society*." Already in his published lectures, Whitney had described language as "an institution, as much so as any other body of usages which goes to make up the sum of *acquired knowledge and culture*." And when he elaborated this point in 1871, he clearly took his cue from Tylor's formulation of that same year: "Under the name 'culture' we mean all that knowledge and training which comes to each individual from his being born a member of society, who acquires what those about him are able to impart."[47]

This theme of acquired behavior has been the enduring hallmark of cultural anthropology—linking E. B. Tylor to all who came after him in that field. More significant for our purpose, however, is the way evolutionists like Tylor and Whitney differed from the relativists who came later. Tylor and Whitney always spoke of *culture* rather than *cultures*, suggesting development along a single timeline. Although the world's peoples all were traveling the same path, different societies had made different amounts of progress thus far. All were capable of advance, yet there was still a single standard of civilization by which their different degrees of progress were to be measured.[48]

Especially important to Whitney was the linguistic version of this outlook. Like many other nineteenth-century philologists, Whitney believed that the three main morphological types — isolating, agglutinative, and inflective (here omitting polysynthetic) — represented three successive stages in the universal history of language. This meant that the earliest human speech had consisted entirely of isolating (that is, monosyllabic) root-words. Some languages had then progressed to the agglutinative stage, and some of these had gone on to the inflective. Every inflective language, therefore, had emerged from an agglutinative ancestor, and every agglutinative language had been built on a monosyllabic foundation.[49] As noted earlier, Whitney considered these morphological types as unreliable for classificatory purposes because many languages did not neatly fit into one or another type. Yet this blurring of categories only made the three-stage developmentalist schema all the more plausible, for it confirmed the notion of one type of language gradually evolving into the next.[50]

This evolutionist scenario led Whitney to an all-important conclusion: Indo-European structural principles supplied the interpretive key to language history globally. Many mid-nineteenth-century linguists more or less held this view, but Whitney made it one of his guiding principles. This did not mean that he cared about the Indo-European tongues only. He urged the study of "every existing and recorded dialect, without rejection of any," and he also disclaimed any "reprehensible partiality for the tongues of our own kindred."[51] Yet as a practical matter, Whitney assumed that all of the world's languages could be analyzed via Franz Bopp's combinatory morphology. Because the inflective tongues appeared at the top of the evolutionary ladder, the principles used in their analysis seemed to enjoy universal validity.

Whitney had been enamored with this universalist quest from his earliest days of philological study, when he had affirmed his interest in "language not languages." Hence, when he came to formulate his general linguistic principles, he drew these not only from Boppian morphology, but more fundamentally, from Enlightenment social science. Specifically, he drew upon the idea that an essential and unchanging human nature provided the ultimate explanatory factor in human affairs. The classical economists had set the pace by positing an abstract "economic man," whose propensities with regard to production and exchange applied irrespective of time and place. In this same mode, E. B. Tylor explained similarities between widely dispersed cultural practices by appealing to the "psychic unity" of humankind.[52] Thus we see why Whitney ultimately was attracted less to ethnology, the study of diverse nations, than to anthropology, the study of universal "man."

Whitney did *not,* however, anticipate the idea of "linguistic universals," as proposed by Joseph H. Greenberg in the 1950s. For Whitney did not actually believe that such principles adhered in language itself. He made this clear in *The Life and Growth of Language* (1875) when he declared that the "general laws or general tendencies of language, well enough called by that name if we do not let ourselves be deceived by the terms we use, are really the laws of human action, under the joint guidance of habit and circumstance." A genuine linguistic "law," therefore, needed to take into account "the known and re-corded facts of human language, *in combination with the known and observable characteristics of human nature.*" [53]

What were those characteristics? One was simply the desire to communi-cate, something that applied to "every human being, in every stage of culture." In addition, Whitney pointed to "economy of effort" as the fundamental mo-tive behind nearly all changes in linguistic behavior. This idea of conserving effort was grounded in the Utilitarians' hedonist psychology, the notion that people generally are guided by the pursuit of pleasure and the avoidance of pain. Whitney likely absorbed this principle from Francis Wayland's *Elements of Political Economy* (fourth edition, 1841), which taught that one of the eco-nomic actor's universal tendencies was to minimize exertion.[54] Ease of physi-cal utterance was another idea to which most nineteenth-century philologists accorded at least some importance yet that Whitney made central to his theo-rizing. As he flatly declared, "The science of language has not succeeded in bringing to light any more fundamental law than this." [55]

Coupled with Whitney's universalism was the uniformitarian principle of continuity between past and present, which Whitney employed not only in his discussion of the origin of language but throughout his theoretical sys-tem. (That principle, we should add, was rooted as much in Enlightenment social science as in Lyellian geology.) Accordingly, like his theory of linguis-tic "law," Whitney's uniformitarianism actually applied, not to language itself, but rather to something more basic: "The scientific method requires that no assumption of a different *human nature* from that which we see and know [today] be made a factor in the inquiry." [56]

The most telling manifestation of Whitney's anthropological outlook ap-peared in his treatment of so-called sound laws — arguably the most significant results of nineteenth-century linguistic investigation. Especially famous was Jacob Grimm's discovery (published in 1819) of a set of correspondences between the initial consonants of cognate words in Latin, Greek, Sanskrit, and early Germanic. For instance, the stem words for *foot* in Greek and Latin were *pod-* and *ped-*, respectively, while the Gothic equivalent was *fotus.* The words for *heart* in these languages were *kardia, kor,* and *hairto.*[57] The regularity of these patterns suggested that a general shift from *p*-sounds to *f*-sounds, and from *k*-sounds to *h*-sounds (among other combinations) had accompanied the emergence of the Germanic tongues from their Indo-European antecedents. This pattern, which became known as "Grimm's Law," set a standard for future research in comparative phonological behavior.

As Whitney pointed out, however, this "law" applied only during a particular historical period and in only a portion of the Indo-European language-family. In this sense, it really was not a law at all. Patterns of this kind, Whitney said, resulted from the "more recondite . . . influences which are deep-seated in the individual character of different tongues and the qualities of the people who speak them."[58] Yet Whitney rejected any notion of a national *Sprach-gefühl,* a linguistic "feel" particular to an entire people that leads them to conform their speech behavior to some unseen design. He therefore characterized Grimm's discovery as "that greatest of phonetic mysteries," and as "one of the most remarkable and difficult phenomena of its class which the linguistic student finds anywhere offered him for explanation. Nor has any satisfactory explanation of it been yet devised." The best a philologist could do, he said, was to "take the differences in national [linguistic] character as ultimate facts, content with setting them forth clearly, [but] not claiming to explain them."[59]

In sum, Whitney treated phonological correspondences with extreme caution and gave them but a small place in his theoretical system. Boppian morphology he found much more intelligible: truncating, recycling, and recombining bits of lexical material—all expressed the universal tendency to take ad hoc steps toward more efficient behavior.

Constructed on this basis, Whitney's theoretical system showed impressive coherence and consistency. Yet it also had major shortcomings. Whitney's purported universalism actually masked an Indo-Eurocentric outlook, in which non-Indo-European languages appeared to be in some sense less developed. For instance, Whitney considered inflective grammar to be the most subtle means for the expression of ideas. Chinese and Japanese forms of word structure, by contrast, he judged as limited in their expressive capability. He also faulted certain languages for their "less elaborate and complete" systems of color distinctions and enumeration as compared with those used in the Indo-European family. (He was careful to reemphasize, however, that these limitations had nothing to do with a group's inherent mental ability.)[60]

Over the years, Whitney would become increasingly dogmatic in his commitment to the Boppian view that all purely grammatical (that is, "formal") elements, such as the -*ly* in *quickly*, had derived from a previously independent word (that is, a "material" element). He maintained this view even in the face of mounting historical evidence to the contrary. Similarly, Whitney grappled late in his career with the discovery that some reputedly monosyllabic languages actually had evolved from bi-syllabic roots. Wanting to accommodate this new research with the least departure from Boppian orthodoxy, he insisted that the two parts of any such roots at least must have been grammatically undifferentiated. As he said, to hold that a linguistic family's initial words had *combined* material and formal elements was like claiming that man's most primitive tools had been invented with handles attached. The grammarlessness of roots was thus a "theoretical necessity" on the principle of simple beginnings.[61]

Already at the end of his 1875 book, Whitney had declared that comparative-philological data must be "made to fit" with a right understanding of human nature and cultural development, what he now called "general anthropology."[62] This cast of mind showed even more clearly in an article he wrote ten years later: "It is evident that what is true of this [Indo-European] family of speech, one of the most highly organized that exist, may also be true of the rest—must be true of them, unless some valid evidence be found to the contrary. The unity of human nature makes human speech alike in the character of its beginnings and in the general features of its after-history."[63] Here again, Whitney projected Indo-European morphology onto a worldwide canvas by insisting that the rudimentary components of inflective word construction "must," of necessity, be found in the agglutinative and isolating languages.

Whitney's embrace of such a rigidly deductive approach was ironic in light of his vaunted empiricism. It was indeed a major blind spot. It can said by way of partial explanation that the use of deduction per se accorded with the best social-scientific thinking of that era. John Stuart Mill had argued in the 1840s that empirically discovered regularities in behavior could form the basis of a genuinely scientific sociology—but only as long as they conformed to what might be deduced rationally, from the universal principles of human motivation. E. B. Tylor made the corollary point: "When a general law can be inferred from a group of facts, the use of detailed history is very much superceded."[64]

Even so, Whitney's reliance on this kind of procedure could not always withstand the empirical test.

We can now take a more comprehensive view of W. D. Whitney's thought within the development of the modern human sciences—with perhaps surprising results. During most of the nineteenth century, the human or social sciences were torn between two competing methodological models. On the one side stood the universalizing field of political economy, along with its theoretical successor, late-Victorian anthropology. On the other side stood philology, its defining trait being historical particularity. This trait was of course a chief characteristic of traditional philology, which elucidated old writings, in part by relating them to their unique national and literary contexts. Yet comparative philology too dealt with the particular: although it often revealed the unities underlying large and diverse groups of languages, it still grouped these into specific clusters.[65] Other fields based on this model also manifested this quality. The comparative-historical jurisprudence set forth in Henry Sumner Maine's *Ancient Law* (1861), for instance, traced the legal traditions of specific nations, an approach developed in contrast to the ahistorical abstractions of Utilitarian legal theory.[66]

By keeping in mind philology's particularizing impulse, we highlight an important thread of continuity in the history of the cultural sciences. This thread began with the Herderian emphasis on the distinct literary consciousness of each *Volk*, and it continued in the relativist anthropology of Franz Boas and his students in the early twentieth century. The characteristic throughout was an essentially *philological* approach to cultural analysis. This continuity is easy to overlook because post-Boasian anthropology has emphasized firsthand fieldwork and cultural praxis—thus downplaying old texts. The underlying spirit showed itself, however, when the anthropologist Clifford Geertz famously spoke of "reading" a culture as if it were a complex "manuscript." Through such readings, each culture-group would yield up its distinctive worldview.[67]

Tylorian anthropology—and W. D. Whitney's linguistics along with it— thus formed a distinct interlude between two Herderian moments in the development of the human sciences. That interlude saw a resurgence of the Enlightenment's classical-economic model; it did not follow the philological model. Although himself a practicing philologist, Whitney tried to fit philology (especially comparative philology) into a larger conceptual harness. For this he looked to a cluster of post-Enlightenment mental and social philosophies, including those that had filtered down into evolutionist anthropology.

## A Curious Analogy with Myth and Religion

Whitney always took an interest in the historical study of myth and religion, a rising field in the nineteenth century that was closely connected to ethnology and anthropology. He approved of much of the recent research on the original "Aryan" religion. The idea was to glean traces of that belief system from the Vedas on the assumption that the Indians of the Vedic period had been more or less direct descendants of the prehistoric Aryans. Scholars such as Alolphe Pictet concluded that the Aryan religion had been a simple form of nature worship, for there was nothing in the Vedas to suggest the complex Brahmanism that came later. With this much Whitney agreed. He grew skeptical, however, when Pictet, Ernest Renan, and F. Max Müller, extrapolated from this basis and argued that a pristine revelation, akin to monotheism, could be found in the dim Indo-European past. In taking this stand, they continued the similar speculations of the early Orientalists, including William Jones and Friedrich Schlegel.[68]

Max Müller did the most to develop this idea and to popularize it among English-language readers. He taught that the polytheistic myths and religions scattered throughout the ancient Indo-European world represented a falling away from the original God-consciousness. He also argued that the multiple gods of myth had been invented only by accident. What began as mere verbal personifications of natural forces—giving names, for instance, to wind, water, and fire—had lapsed over time into deification. Myth-making was thus a kind of forgetfulness as to what certain words really meant. It was, Müller said, a "disease of language."[69]

W. D. Whitney acknowledged Max Müller's preeminent qualifications for pioneering the comparative study of religion. Müller was, after all, the Western world's foremost expert on the Ṛg Veda. Whitney also was willing to emphasize the solid aspects of the work Müller had done in this area. When Müller brought out his *Chips from a German Workshop: Essays in the Science of Religion* (1867), Whitney pronounced it "a capital thing." He praised the work in print and told Charles Eliot Norton of the *North American Review* that it gave him "real hearty pleasure to be able to speak almost unqualifiedly well of it."[70]

This magnanimous spirit, however, was short-lived, for Whitney soon learned that one of the essays reprinted in *Chips* had read differently in its original version. As first published, the piece had derided the St. Petersburg *Sanskrit Lexicon,* charging that the work's editors (including Rudolph von Roth) and contributors (including Whitney) together constituted a mutual admiration society. (Müller had called them an "International Sanskrit Insurance Company.") In response, Whitney wrote a second review of *Chips,* now taking a tough new line against Müller's mythological theories.[71] It was the same duality that had appeared earlier in Whitney's criticism of Müller's views on Indian astronomy. While personal animus motivated him, there was still substance to what he said.

Whitney had various complaints, but the main one concerned Müller's view of myth as a declension from an originally exalted state of religious consciousness. Whitney commented: "Doubtless he [Müller] believes in a general upward progress of mankind since the earliest ages. . . . But his phraseology does not fairly imply this; it seems hardly accordant with any other theory than that of an original paradisiac condition of man, as a being with powers miraculously developed and knowledge stored up by superhuman means."[72]

There was more at stake here than at first meets the eye, for the religious question actually mirrored a major debate in late-nineteenth-century linguistics. As Whitney pointed out, there was a "curious analogy" between Müller's theory of myth and religion and his teachings about the history of language: both found "disease," "degeneration," and "decay" taking place over time. Whitney was careful to praise Müller to the extent that Müller consistently taught that language underwent "a continuous process of development from elements the most simple and formless." Yet Müller did this, said Whitney, only "until he gets back to the very beginning: there he assumes a miracle — not precisely a scriptural, but a kind of natural or materialistic miracle; namely, an original instinct, different from anything which men have nowadays, vouchsafed for the express purpose of setting in motion the process of linguistic development, and withdrawn when it had answered that purpose."[73] Müller had thus offended against the uniformitarian principle.

Later we will return to this notion of separate phases in the universal history of language, a notion that, as we will see, was an intrinsic feature of early comparative philology. Whitney's puzzlement over this idea, and his severe criticism of it, would soon exert a deep influence on the emerging Neogrammarian movement — and would thereby help shape Western language study down to the present.

## A Theoretical Readjustment

When his first book was published in 1867, Whitney had hoped that this event would immediately involve him in debate with the most eminent European linguists of that day. His chief targets were Max Müller, August Schleicher, and Heymann Steinthal; the last of these figures taught at the University of Berlin and was a philosophical disciple of Wilhelm von Humboldt. The direct kind of debate Whitney had wanted, however, did not occur. Schleicher died a year later, and although Müller and Steinthal each wrote reviews of Whitney's book, neither deigned to acknowledge its critiques of their own theories. Steinthal did predict that Whitney's volume would prove popular in its own country since it was "easily accessible to the common mind." And after all, he said, one should not expect from this sort of book the same depth of treatment one would find in a work written for a German audience.[74]

Whitney saw an opportunity to fight back several years later when Steinthal published his *Einleitung in die Psychologie und Sprachwissenschaft* (1871), a summary statement of his linguistic psychology. What especially caught Whitney's attention was a chapter dealing with the mental process by which speakers continually generate new utterances. Using Humboldtian terminology, Steinthal taught that language was not *ergon*, an object external to the psyche, but *energeia*, a creative ability inherent in the speaker's mind. In private, Whitney characterized this as "just metaphysical bosh and nonsense, nothing better; a complete flying-in-the-face of sound science and common-sense throughout."[75]

Still, he hesitated before launching a critique. He had begun to feel that this kind of writing was self-indulgent, and he had promised himself to stop "showing up" other linguists after his recent foray against Schleicher. Yet at the same time, he found compelling reasons to give in to his real inclination. Although Steinthal was not a popular figure like Max Müller, he was held in high esteem by his professional peers in Europe. And as in Schleicher's case, Whitney complained, Steinthal's eminence as a technical scholar led many to accept his theoretical views as "pure gospel." The doctrines Steinthal taught were those of an entire school, "the largest and most influential body of writers on the theory of language." This group, moreover, regarded Common Sense linguistic theory as full of "superficiality and philisterism [*sic*]." Finally, and not surprisingly, Steinthal's sarcastic response to his own book still rankled. For all of these reasons, Whitney could not resist "this one temptation more."[76]

Remarks made to Josiah as he prepared this new article suggest a growing obsession: "I think I shall make as utter a demolition of him and the metaphysical theory of language as ever was made of anything, and shall perhaps succeed in compelling some attention to the views put forth in my volume of Lectures, which the philologists have hitherto contented themselves with simply ignoring.... I haven't for some time enjoyed anything so much as showing him up and arguing him down." Whitney added a month later: "I shall, I think, give his bones something of a rattling, and shall possibly induce sundry of these stuck-up fellows who despise the common-sense view of language as too low for philosophers to revise their opinions."[77] This agitated state of mind was reflected in the finished article, which was notably caustic in tone. Later we will see the indignant response that article elicited among philologists in Europe.

The important point for now, however, is the article's substance, which reflected a subtle shift in Whitney's theoretical emphasis. Whitney now saw more clearly what he must have suspected all along, that Steinthal's psychological approach to language was something distinct from Schleicher's bio-organic perspective. He noted that distinction while preparing the article: "I think it my especial mission to prove, and force people into seeing, that language is *not an emanation of the soul, nor a physical organism,* but an institution, or part of human culture."[78] The challenge now was to readjust his own theory so as to address Steinthal's special emphasis.

Whitney accordingly gave new prominence to three interlocking themes. First, he stressed the limitations of philosophical psychology as an ally of linguistics. "The psychologic method," he said, relied too much on introspection and tended to ignore "all that has been done by anthropology, in tracing out the history of other departments of human culture."[79]

Second, Whitney put greater stress on the notion that language is an object that exists independently of speech activity. Here he responded to Steinthal's declaration that language was "not a something, like [gun] powder, but an occurrence, like the explosion; it is not an organ, like the eye and ear, but a capacity and activity, like seeing and hearing." In response, Whitney said that language was "an actual concrete possession" of the human community—again, analogous to human-made instruments.[80] Although produced *by* human minds, language itself was a phenomenon external to the mind's workings.

Third, Whitney now qualified his voluntarist theory of language change. He said that changes came about "both consciously and unconsciously: consciously, as regards the immediate end to be attained; unconsciously, as regards the further consequences of the act."[81] As we have seen, Whitney had previously acknowledged that the long-term evolution of language was not something foreseen or intended. Yet he now laid particular emphasis on this point, as in the following illustration:

> The first man who, on being attacked by a wolf, seized a club or a stone and with it crushed his adversary's head, was not conscious that he was commencing a series of acts which would lead finally to rifles and engines. . . . [A]ll that he himself knew was that he was defending himself in a sudden emergency. We are not loath to admit that all the later advances in mechanics have been made in a similar way, to meet some felt necessity.

Could not the same be admitted in the linguistic arena? Whitney concluded that "all the . . . uses and values of language come as unforeseen consequences of its use as a means of communication."[82] By making this theme of unintended long-term consequences more prominent, he sought to compensate for the rhetorical overkill that sometimes accompanied his insistence on voluntary agency.

We can combine these ideas from Whitney's Steinthal article with those found in his earlier writings and attempt to synthesize them. This would mean taking his picture of language as an evolving cultural product and superimposing it on his picture of moment-by-moment interpersonal behavior. By offering both of these perspectives in his writings, Whitney attempted to bridge the gap between two fundamentally different ways of analyzing sociocultural change. The first of these (reversing the order just used) focuses on the social interactions from which cultural products arise, while the second focuses on the externalized products themselves — whether tools, artwork, or languages. The first mode of analysis is synchronic in outlook; the second is diachronic, concerned with development over time.[83]

Whitney did his best to balance these perspectives. Yet the history of social theory suggests that these do not blend well in practice, and writers usually find it difficult to give close attention to the one while doing justice to the other. Efforts at synthesis therefore tend to produce an unstable compound in which one side assumes explanatory predominance. Over the whole of his career, Whitney gave synchronic interaction the more fundamental role in his system, and it was on this basis, ultimately, that he attempted to explain even the phenomenon of long-term and unintended change. As we will see, it was the best solution he could have chosen.

During the period highlighted in this chapter, Whitney and his family experienced two personal tragedies. First, in 1872, came the untimely death of Yale's James Hadley, Whitney's closest friend apart from his own relations. Whitney regarded Hadley's passing not only as a loss personally but as a major blow to American scholarship.

Much worse was to come. Just over a year later, the Whitneys' eleven-year-old son Roger drowned in an ice-skating accident. They had already lost one child, Willy, in infancy. But this was immeasurably harder.[84] In the aftermath, Whitney sought solace in private. As he later told his friend Albrecht Weber, "In my great grief, I turned to the continuation of my work as a relief." It is the kind of response one might expect from Whitney. Although a conscientious husband and father, he tended, as he confessed, to bury himself in his books. The result, in any case, within a mere month after the tragedy, was a substantial new piece of polemical writing. This was an article (passages from which we have seen already) dealing with the relationship between language and Darwinian evolution. It was, in fact, the most comprehensive statement on that subject that Whitney ever produced. It would also, as he ruefully noted, serve as "the proximate cause of all this fuss."[85] That is, the new article would precipitate what had been so long in coming—a major showdown between himself and Max Müller.

# CHAPTER EIGHT

# The Battle with Max Müller

In the mid-1870s the long-simmering antagonism between William Dwight Whitney and F. Max Müller finally boiled over into a sensational public quarrel. The substance of the affair was nothing new: the two philologists again aired their opposing views on the origin of language and the explanation of language change. What was special about this period was the level of rancor now openly expressed, something for which both parties were responsible. Whitney had criticized Müller's work for years, and when Müller finally fought back, he did so through increasingly devious means. These tactics, and the outrage they elicited from Whitney, eventually converted the philologists' dispute into an international cause célèbre. In the process, the linguistic questions themselves were all but obscured.

Even so, the period of heightened controversy did bring forth two new features of substantive interest. First, it produced surprising repositionings on each of the main issues: Max Müller now appeared to accept elements of Whitney's voluntarist theory of language change, and Whitney now gave the impression that he actually agreed with Charles Darwin's explanation of the origin of speech. The second new feature was the forging of an alliance between

Whitney and Darwin himself. The Whitney-Müller controversy thus brought to a dramatic climax the Victorian era's interweaving of linguistics and natural science.

## A Mixed Reception in the Old World

W. D. Whitney had long sought scholarly recognition in Europe, and in pursuing that goal, he inevitably made himself obnoxious to Max Müller. This effect derived in part from Whitney's increasing stature in the Orientalist world. First, the Royal Asiatic Society elected Whitney a member in recognition of one of his papers on Indian astronomy—a work critical of Müller's views on that subject.[1] Then the Russian Imperial Academy awarded him one hundred rubles for his contributions to the St. Petersburg Sanskrit Lexicon. Next, in 1870, the Berlin Academy of Sciences made Whitney the first-ever recipient of the Bopp prize, given in honor of the most significant contribution to Sanskrit studies made during the previous three years. The work selected was Whitney's translation of an Indian phonetic treatise, the *Tāittirīya-Prātiśākhya*.[2] Finally, a London publisher commissioned Whitney to prepare an annotated edition of H. T. Colebrooke's essay *On the Vedas* (1805), a classic of British Indology. Whitney thus took precedence over Britain's best-known Sanskritist-in-residence.[3]

The bad blood between the two men also had more direct sources. Whitney wrote reviews faulting the slow progress of Müller's *Ṛg Veda* edition. Although its first volume had appeared in 1849, the work would not be completed until 1874. Whitney also noted that Müller's assistant, Theodor Aufrecht, had done much of the actual labor.[4] Of course, Whitney antagonized his rival on general linguistic matters as well. In his first book, he belittled Müller by describing him as a "recent popular writer" on language. And throughout that work, as he privately admitted, he took every opportunity to discredit Müller's ideas.[5]

C. E. Norton had encouraged Whitney to compose shorter writings in this same critical spirit, and Norton's successor at the *North American Review* urged this even more. That successor was Henry Adams, the historian, cultural critic, and descendent of the country's greatest political dynasty. As the *North American*'s new editor, Adams requested from Whitney a review of the sixth edition (1871) of Müller's *Science of Language*. Here Whitney repeated familiar themes, pointing out Müller's illogic, his failure to reply to his critics, and his frequent use of arcane examples. Referring to one of Müller's lengthy etymologies, he remarked: "Very interesting, doubtless, but what has it to do with the argument? It seems almost as if the author were afraid of the latter, and wanted to break up the concentration of our attention upon it by a little harmless by-play."[6]

Although he wrote for American journals, Whitney intended his review articles mainly for overseas consumption. He always requested extra offprints to distribute among scholars in Europe—except for Max Müller. Some of his correspondents found these writings overly combative.[7] Yet Whitney felt that he had little choice but to go on the attack. Lopsided sales figures for his first book testified to the problem. It had done well in the United States—Charles Scribner sold almost 900 copies in the first year and soon issued a new printing. Yet in thrice the amount of time, the house of Trübner had sold fewer than half that number in England. Indeed, by that point Trübner had sold more copies of the Roth-Whitney edition of the *Atharva Veda*.[8]

The overseas reviews of his book also brought disappointment on the whole. Although the classicist Wilhelm Clemm praised the work for its "thoroughly sensible judgment," the more prominent German reviewer, Heymann Steinthal, did not (as we saw) deign to acknowledge Whitney's critiques of his own views.[9] In Britain the initial response was more positive. The *Westminster Review* gave his book a strong commendation: "If the Americans go on writing so many excellent treatises on philology, we shall soon have to call English the American language." Favorable reviews also appeared in the Edinburgh *Scotsman* and the London *Atheneum,* the latter even including an anti-Müller slant.[10] The only other response, however, was distinctly hostile, albeit indirectly. This unsigned piece, written by Max Müller himself, ostensibly was about a new book by a French linguist: of this work, Müller approved. Yet he contrasted this with other recent (unnamed) works, one of which included superficial denials of linguistics' true status as a "physical science." In private, Whitney dismissed this attack as "highly naive and Müllerish." Still, it confirmed what his friends in Britain had warned of: although Müller rarely engaged in open controversy, he was still a dangerous opponent.[11]

After this the British reviewers fell silent, prompting Whitney to complain that his book "could not be more generally and completely ignored if it were written in Russian." Was there some impediment? His friends in London thought so. The expatriate American Sanskritist Fitzedward Hall reported in 1872: "You have no notion of the attempts I have made to get a favorable notice of your Lectures into print. Wherever I have applied, I have been rebuffed by worshippers of M. M.—Minimus Maximus being in the field."[12]

Whitney saw his worst fears confirmed a year later, after he republished a number of his shorter writings as a volume entitled *Oriental and Linguistic Studies* (1873). He presented a copy of this work to the London Philological Society, and the organization's secretary, Frederick J. Furnivall (1825–1910), sent his hearty thanks. He added, however, an unfortunate postscript: "But we shouldn't be content with your producing essays only: some day you must give us a solid big book. You lead America, and have responsibilities accordingly." Whitney's response was swift, and Furnivall soon corrected himself: "Your reproach to us about neglect of your book is too well deserved." Happily, he was able to report that one of the Society's members had read Whitney's lectures and had found them superior to Max Müller's. Furnivall added: "As to M.M., at our Society he is not set very high. All along, Goldstücker [Professor of Sanskrit at the University of London] took care to prevent that, and used to quiz [mock] him and his works, and stick pins into him in the most refreshing manner. But M. has a nice style, and writes books that young ladies and easy-going people read with pleasure, fancying themselves thereby enlightened, and so they are, which results in M.M. being greatly glorified in society. But behind the scenes he's not much thought of."[13]

The London philologists did what they could for Whitney: they elected him to their Society in 1874, and that same year, their old stalwart, Thomas Hewitt Key, publicly rated Whitney's origin-of-language theory above Müller's.[14] This was welcome recognition. Moreover, the publication in Britain of *Oriental and Linguistic Studies* would likely increase Whitney's visibility even more. These shorter writings could appeal to a British readership in a way that Whitney's big book could not—competing as it did with Müller's hugely popular volumes of lectures. The change showed when a London literary weekly, the *Academy*, printed a review of Whitney's new book.

The review's author was the respected Leipzig Sanskritist Bertholdt Delbrück, a professional friend of Whitney's. Delbrück had only good things to say about the essays on Orientalist topics. Like others (such as the French linguist Michel Bréal), however, Delbrück found the items on general linguistic topics needlessly abrasive.[15] (The collection included not only Whitney's reviews of Max Müller's lectures but also his articles on Schleicher and Steinthal.) Delbrück surmised, rightly enough, that Whitney's truculence sprang from a desire to capture some of the limelight these famous European scholars enjoyed. Yet Delbrück was even-handed, for he also noted that many of Max Müller's theoretical views were idiosyncratic — even though Müller had implied, and his readers apparently believed, that they reflected the scholarly consensus.[16]

In sum, while Delbrück had only partial praise for Whitney, he was even less favorable toward Müller. Also, the mere fact that the *Academy* reviewed Whitney's new volume served to advertise the existence of Whitney's anti-Müller writings: *Oriental and Linguistic Studies* included no less than six essays that were critical of Müller's efforts either as a Sanskritist or as a language theorist. It was the kind of publicity Max Müller could not leave unchallenged, and he quickly moved to counteract it.

His purpose was well served by the fact that *Oriental and Linguistic Studies* reprinted Whitney's attack on Steinthal. The tone of that essay had been unusually caustic. For instance, Whitney said near the article's conclusion: "Here, for the first time, Professor Steinthal is seized with a slight misgiving. May not his conclusions strike some persons as paradoxical?. . . . We seem to hear from his readers one universal cry of assent. But it does not reach his ears; and he proceeds to reason down his misgiving, after his peculiar fashion."[17]

When the *North American Review* first printed this piece, Whitney sent copies to nearly thirty correspondents in Europe, hoping, he said, "for some effect from it." This he got, although not the kind he wanted. It provoked bad feeling in Germany, especially among younger scholars who greatly admired Steinthal. Whitney admitted that the review had not received "as many good words as usual; indeed, I hardly know of any." Even Josiah said that he had gone too far. Writing to Albrecht Weber, Whitney defended himself: "In judging my Steinthal article, you must remember that I do not deny the great ability of much that he has done and does (any more than of Schleicher's work), but hold that his fundamental philosophy of language is false, and irreconcilable with the historical work that he does."[18]

Whitney's intentions notwithstanding, once reprinted in *Oriental and Linguistic Studies,* the article drew a response from Steinthal himself in the form of a scorching pamphlet published in Berlin. (Henry Adams told Whitney: "I wish I could get someone to write a pamphlet against me, but that, I suppose, is the last and highest crown of science.")[19] What mainly concerns us is not Steinthal's response itself but rather the unsigned reviews of that work that appeared in London's *Academy* and *Atheneum*. A number of Max Müller's supporters were connected with these periodicals, both of which now did an about-face. They took Müller's side against Whitney, who thus got a taste of the danger his friends had warned him about.

As a first step, the London papers deplored the fierceness of Steinthal's rebuttal. At the same time, however, they also suggested that such a reply was just what the occasion called for. After all, said the *Atheneum,* "Prof. Steinthal is not the only scholar whom Mr. Whitney, presuming too much on the ignorance of his American audiences, has either misrepresented or abused." The *Academy* took up the thought:

> For years it has been a matter of surprise to many people that Mr. Whitney should have been allowed to pursue his extraordinary course with impunity. He evidently imagined that the easiest means of gaining a reputation was to attack other scholars, and to challenge them to a pugilistic combat. He apparently did not understand why they shrank from an encounter with the American champion. He became more defiant and offensive with every year, and he has now at last obtained his heart's desire. We do not defend the tone which Professor Steinthal has adopted in his reply, though there seems to be but one opinion among unprejudiced persons, that the extraordinary behavior of the young American scholar would have been an excuse for almost any reprisals.[20]

Counseling a more high-minded engagement, the *Academy* suggested that Steinthal might have satisfied himself merely with demonstrating the "shallowness" of Whitney's views. And as examples of the kind of thing that ought never to appear in print, the *Academy* quoted Steinthal's descriptions of Whitney himself: "the scolding flirt," "the tricky attorney," "the man who barks against the spirit of our [German] classics in poetry, philosophy, and philology. What he writes, we are told, are empty bubbles, jesuitic insinuations, full of impudence, deserving a flagellation. A climax is reached in the following sentence: 'Everywhere when I read him, hollow vacuity yawns in my face, arrogant vanity grins at me.'" Again, the *Academy* could only deplore such attacks.[21]

But of course, putting Steinthal's remarks on display was a way to undercut Whitney by proxy and to do so without calling attention to Whitney's *other* reprinted articles, the ones critical of Max Müller's work. Devious and malicious, the *Academy* notice made it nonetheless clear that Whitney had left himself vulnerable. Even a writer in the *North American Review* warned that his attacks on foreign scholars were "possibly too sharp and too likely to pro-voke animosity, rather than to correct errors."[22] Whitney finally got the point, and he resolved to be more tactful in the future.

At this juncture, European discussion of Whitney's views subsided, and the first phase of the Whitney-Müller controversy came to a close. Two more phases would follow, although first there would be an interlude of nearly a year. During the interlude, Whitney found time for a much-needed vacation, albeit a strenuous one. In the summer of 1873, the forty-seven-year-old philologist explored the wilds of Colorado as part of a geological expedition led by Ferdi-nand V. Hayden. Whitney later summed up the trip: "It has all been one of the greatest frolics I ever had in my life; it will help to enliven my memory until my dying day."[23]

Unlikely though it would seem, this kind of activity — the scientific explo-ration of the American West — played an important role in the dispute be-tween Whitney and Max Müller. The first half of the 1870s brought to a climax the Whitney brothers' bitter ten-year campaign against the Yale geochemist Benjamin Silliman, Jr. At issue were Silliman's optimistic reports on Califor-nia's oil and mineral wealth, which differed significantly from the assessments made by Josiah, who was director of the state geological survey. The Whit-neys charged Silliman with purposely inflating these reports, which earned him substantial consulting fees. Still, W. D. Whitney had advised his brother to avoid a public quarrel over the matter. Then he changed his mind and led the effort that forced Silliman to quit his post at the Sheffield Scientific School in 1869. (Silliman stayed on at Yale's Medical School until his death in 1885.) Whitney also spearheaded an attempt to have Silliman ejected from the National Academy of Sciences, although in this he found himself repeatedly thwarted.[24]

In part the result of the Academy's reluctance to take sides, this outcome owed as much to Josiah's failure to send his brother sufficient documentation to back his charges. Said Whitney in a typical plea: "You had better be getting your own evidence at least on some one case (say the Bodie Bluff mine) into detailed readiness, and let it be here when his [Silliman's] answer is handed in."[25] But Josiah, who was then in California, failed to supply what was needed. When the NAS dismissed the dispute in 1874, the embittered Whitneys quit that organization, and for several more years they pursued other efforts to have Silliman censured by the American scientific community.

These events affected the quarrel with Max Müller in three ways. First there was a coincidence in timing: both episodes built slowly during the second half of the 1860s and reached a climax toward the middle of the next decade. Second, Whitney found Silliman and Müller to be of similar character. Both, he believed, had sold themselves to gain popular success and had thereby overshadowed scholars of greater integrity—such as the Whitneys. The remaining connection between the two situations was more complex. Josiah's delinquency in pressing his case left W. D. Whitney exposed—and no doubt embarrassed—in his dealings with the nation's most prominent scientists. Yet Whitney appears never to have blamed Josiah. Rather, the solidarity he maintained with his brother was paid for through psychological displacement: he directed his frustration elsewhere. Mainly he demonized Silliman, yet Max Müller made a useful secondary target. Indeed, Whitney used almost exactly the same language in describing the two men.[26] Coming when it did, the Müller controversy thus provided Whitney with an additional means by which to vent his sense of aggrievement and to vindicate, as he saw it, the honor of disinterested scholarship.

## Darwinism Reassessed

The second phase of the Whitney-Müller controversy centered around the philologists' contrasting responses to Darwinism. As we have seen, those responses did not divide along simple lines of support versus opposition; the situation was more complex—and more interesting—than that. Max Müller had fashioned a two-sided argument, and he emphasized one side or the other according to the need of the moment. After the *Origin of Species* appeared, he rejected that book's implications concerning human ancestry. He also denied that natural selection could have converted the cries of animals into meaningful speech.

At nearly that same time, however, Müller enthusiastically applied the idea of blindly occurring selection to the problem of language change. He reaffirmed this outlook in 1870, describing how Darwin's theory offered a useful model by which to understand the classic antinomy between individual freedom and social constraint: "It is by supplying a new point of view for the consideration of these world-old problems, that Darwin's book 'On the Origin of Species' has exercised an influence far beyond the sphere for which it was originally intended. The two technical terms of 'Natural Selection' and 'Struggle for Life,' which are in reality but two aspects of the same process, are the very categories which were wanted to enable us to grasp . . . the inevitable limitation of spontaneous action by the controlling influences of social life."[27]

Müller never gave up this notion of a conceptual parallelism between Darwinian evolution and the long-term "evolution" of language. He did shift his priorities, however, after the appearance of Darwin's *Descent of Man* (1871). Now he placed his emphasis back on the antimaterialist theme. In a new set of lectures in 1873, delivered under the title "Mr. Darwin's Philosophy of Language," Müller again drew on Herderian linguistic theory and Kantian epistemology to argue for the transcendent origins of human consciousness. Language, he said, was the outward sign of humanity's unique ability to engage in abstract thought — which suggested that the difference between animal and human mental life was one of kind, not just of degree. Again pushing this argument to an extreme, Müller concluded: "If the Science of Language has proved anything, it has proved that conceptual or discursive thought can be carried on in words only. *There is no thought without words, as little as there are words without thought.*"[28]

There was little new in all of this, except that Müller now directed his argument specifically against Darwin's theory of mental evolution set forth in *Descent*. That fact made these lectures of particular interest to science-oriented readers: a respectful review, for instance, appeared in the journal *Nature*.[29] This intertwining of linguistics and the question of human evolution would soon grow even stronger because of the unlikely events that followed: within the year, Max Müller, Charles Darwin, and W. D. Whitney entered into a complicated three-sided debate.

"Mr. Darwin's Philosophy of Language," soon published as a series in *Frazer's Magazine,* struck Whitney as providential: it gave him a new excuse to try to push his own views into notice.[30] He did not act on this impulse immediately. It was the death of his son Roger a number of months later and the need to distract his mind afterward that led him to put pen to work. The result was his article "Darwinism and Language," which appeared in the *North American Review* in the summer of 1874.

Whitney struck a pose of official neutrality on this subject. As he said, "So far, linguistic science has not been shown to have any bearing on Darwinism, either in the way of support or of refutation." Whitney concentrated, however, on the latter error, devoting all but a few pages of his new article to picking apart Müller's argument. Müller had said that even the simplest nouns actually represented general ideas and that language therefore demonstrated a highly sophisticated mental capacity that never could have evolved from animal brains. Whitney countered by denying that general ideas depended on the use of language. People — and the higher animals too, apparently — formed such ideas routinely, through abstracting and then generalizing from an object's distinctive qualities. Müller's fallacy, Whitney added, was "the assumption that, if general ideas were formed, they could not help finding expression in words; and that I can see no good ground for."[31]

We have already seen Whitney's views on the trickiest question of all — the issue of evolution in relation to the origin of language. In *Descent,* Darwin suggested that the rudiments of speech began among humanity's ape-like ancestors. Whitney had already rejected this idea and he reiterated his case in his 1874 article. Even assuming human descent from an animal ancestor, he said, the beginnings of speech could have taken place only *after* humanity's full mental stature had been reached. That stature could not have evolved "through and by means of" the invention of language because "speech, like the other elements of our civilization, is the result of our human capacities, not their cause. . . . Man was man in *esse* and in *posse,* when the development of speech began."[32] This was Whitney's essential position, and it would remain so in the future.

Still, on this one occasion, Whitney gave this viewpoint a distinctive twist. First, he faulted Max Müller alone for trying to bring linguistics to bear on the evolution question. Second, when he spoke against the idea that language and the human mind had evolved in tandem, Whitney avoided acknowledging the fact that Darwin himself had been the chief purveyor of that idea. Indeed, he mentioned the famous naturalist by name only in the final paragraph of his article, and there he made only the vaguest reference to what Darwin had written about the origin of speech. Choosing his words carefully, Whitney said that Darwin had shown "a remarkable moderation and soundness of judgment in his treatment of the element of language. . . . *Very little exception* is to be taken by a linguistic scholar to any of his statements."[33] Here Whitney not only downplayed his substantial disagreement with Darwin on the issue of speech origins, but he also left the impression that he *generally approved* of Darwin's views on that subject. To a degree this was fitting, because in *Descent* Darwin had hinted at his own respect for the imitation theory taught by Hensleigh Wedgwood and F. W. Farrar, writers Whitney admired. Whitney could therefore conclude his article by declaring that Darwin's views were "far truer" than Max Müller's. He thus suggested solidarity with Darwin against their mutual opponent.[34]

## A Hearing in England

After completing "Darwinism and Language," Whitney said that he felt "almost ashamed" to have produced yet another polemical work.[35] This did not stop him from engaging in a bit of self-promotion, however, for he immediately sent a copy of the article to Charles Darwin himself. What Whitney did not then know was that Darwin was already making use of his *Oriental and Linguistic Studies* in preparing a revision of *Descent.* (Darwin used a copy of that work that Whitney had sent him the previous year.)[36] Darwin wanted to rebut Max Müller's recent lectures, and to accomplish this, he quoted from Whitney's critique of the linguist W. H. J. Bleek's teaching—similar to Müller's— about the interdependence of thought and speech. Said Whitney: "He would fain make thought absolutely impossible without speech, identifying the faculty with its instrument. He might just as reasonably assert that the human hand cannot act without a tool. With such a doctrine to start from, he cannot stop short of Müller's worst paradoxes, that an infant (*in fans,* not speaking) is not a human being, and that deaf-mutes do not become possessed of reason until they learn to twist their fingers in imitation of spoken words."

After quoting these remarks, Darwin appended Max Müller's aphorism, "There is no thought without words, as little as there are words without thought," to which he added a comment: "What a strange definition must here be given to the word thought!" (Darwin chose to ignore the fact that Whitney's piece was chiefly a refutation of Bleek's bio-evolutionary explanation of the origin of speech.)[37] Darwin quoted this passage as well as another passage from Whitney's essays in two newly added footnotes in *Descent,* thereby including the American among his acknowledged authorities on language.[38]

Whitney was not aware of this use of his earlier writings when he mailed his latest article to Darwin's home in England. Hence, he was still trying to spark Darwin's interest in his ideas. A public acknowledgment from the famous naturalist, even if only mildly approving, would be one sure way to match Max Müller's influence in that country. And such help appeared to be needed more than ever. Fresh proof arrived in letters from F. J. Furnivall of the

London Philological Society. Furnivall liked the way Whitney's "Darwinism" article cut Müller down to size, but he warned that Müller enjoyed strong public support. He noted that the Society's president, Richard Morris, held Müller to be "at bottom a hearty good fellow, not cocky." And Furnivall himself declined to confront the Oxford scholar: "I can't answer M. M. for you: and, as I said, all our men are too busy for that, and no doubt too ignorant. You must chaff him yourself, or cut him up. He must be pretty open to attack, as you've already shown." Finally, Furnivall admitted that Müller's past kindnesses to himself and his friends made them reluctant to challenge him.[39]

Darwin, however, would not be bound by such constraints. And Darwin showed real interest in the new article Whitney sent. Rather than reply with a perfunctory note of thanks, he first penned a request to James Knowles, editor of London's *Contemporary Review:* "I fear that you never republish articles which have appeared in foreign journals. But one on Language has just been published in the *North American Review* for July, by a distinguished philologist, Prof. Whitney, who has sent it to me. In this he answers in a very able manner, as it appears to me, Max Müller's views which were published [illegible]. As a writer in the July number of our Quarterly has abused me in strong words, 'amazing ignorance' etc. for what little I have said on the development of language, I much desire to see Whitney's article republished in England."[40] Darwin even offered to pay for the printing. Yet Knowles sent his regrets, for editorial policy (and "a considerable American circulation") made it impossible to republish. He quickly added, however, that an article on the same subject by Darwin would be more than welcome. And he suggested that Darwin might quote from Whitney to any extent he pleased. Darwin graciously accepted Knowles' refusal to republish. At the same time, he turned down Knowles' counteroffer: he would write no article on language or on any other subject, as he was on vacation and was badly in need of rest. He added: "I am also at all times very unwilling to enter on any controversy."[41]

Having made this effort, Darwin then wrote to thank Whitney for sending his article:

> It seems to me most clearly reasoned, and by far the best argument against Max Müller's views which has ever appeared. I heartily wish I had read it two or three months ago, as I'd have quoted several passages with great advantage in a new ed. of my Descent of Man; but the part in question has been printed off. I have however quoted from one of your previous works, your judgment on the main

question, and have added a few remarks of my own, but they are quite feeble compared with yours. I have been the more gratified by your article, as in the July number of our Quarterly there is an abusive attack on my short discussion on language; and your essay is so splendid an answer to it, that I have tried to get it reprinted in the Contemporary, but the Ed. is unwilling to break through his decided rule of not republishing anything.[42]

Two things should be said about these remarks. First, Darwin valued Whitney's "judgment on the main question," the notion that language and rational thought were inseparable. Hence, Darwin did not suggest that he agreed with everything Whitney had said in his article; obviously, he did not accept the idea that only fully evolved humans could have developed language. Second, the source of the "abusive" essay Darwin mentioned was not Max Müller but rather the English zoologist St. George Mivart (1827–1900). Still, Mivart's piece had included an attack on Darwin's account of the origin of speech, and against this, Whitney's comments aimed at Müller would have served as a useful rebuttal.[43] Darwin was sorry, therefore, that Whitney's article could not receive wider exposure in England. Yet he had tried and had failed, and there the matter would have to rest.

Or rather, it would have but for the intervention of one of Darwin's sons, George H. Darwin, who was an instructor in mathematics at Cambridge University. Without asking Whitney's permission, although doubtless with his father's, George Darwin paraphrased material from Whitney's latest article in his own published refutation of both Müller and St. George Mivart. His essay, entitled "Professor Whitney on the Origin of Language," appeared in the November 1874 *Contemporary Review*—thus bringing the linguistic debate into that journal after all. This was the beginning of a three-part exchange, with follow-ups from Max Müller and from Whitney himself.

George Darwin applauded Whitney's critique of Müller's position, thereby treating Whitney as an ally in a common cause. Yet he also saw that Whitney's own views were not in keeping with his father's, and he spent the final pages of his article airing that difference. Whitney had argued that linguists would never be able to discover the steps leading from "the wholly instinctive expression of the animals" to "the wholly conventional expression of man." The younger Darwin respectfully disagreed. "Does Professor Whitney mean that it is impossible to track the Aryan languages higher [that is, earlier] than their roots, or to discover the imitational and interjectional sources of those roots?"[44] Whitney would have answered yes: as far as tracing the historical origins of specific roots, he did mean that.

Yet George Darwin considered this conclusion overly pessimistic. Like his father, he heard what he thought were echoes of the transition from instinctive to conventionalized vocal behavior. He knew, for example, of a terrier that had "a particular bark, like 'wuff!' " — used only when it wanted the door opened. Certain animals, he reasoned, could thus select from a range of instinctive sounds — in this case, various kinds of barks — to produce a signal having a specific meaning. George Darwin scolded Whitney for not seeing the force of such evidence — even as he used Whitney's arguments to club Max Müller and St. George Mivart. The result pleased his father. With both of these battles in mind, Charles Darwin told his son: "You have defended me nobly."[45]

It was surely no accident that the Darwins singled out Whitney for censure on this point, even though their cousin Hensleigh Wedgwood had held virtually the same view concerning the origin of language. Indeed, Wedgwood had been the teacher and Whitney the student. As we have seen, it was Wedgwood who first argued that speech could have been developed only by beings with the same inborn mental capacities found in modern *homo sapiens.* The senior Darwin had kept silent about this difference between his cousin's outlook and his own, especially since his own views were not yet on record when Wedgwood's *On the Origin of Language* (1866) appeared. But when Whitney made the same case in 1874, *after* the publication of *The Descent of Man,* the Darwins saw both the need and the opportunity to make a response. Using Whitney as a distant target, they could state their objections without embarrassing a close family member.

Yet at the same time, the Darwins also were willing to treat Whitney as a valued friend. They accepted his *North American* article chiefly for what it was — a blow against their mutual enemies. Indeed, as we have seen, Charles Darwin was so pleased with that article that he strongly desired to see it reprinted in its entirety in England. Whitney adopted a similar attitude. He knew that George Darwin's *Contemporary Review* essay, despite its criticisms, was mainly an endorsement of his own position, and he therefore gave that piece his post hoc blessing.[46] It was, after all, by far the most conspicuous appreciation his ideas had received anywhere abroad up to that point. Whitney and the Darwins were thus sincere allies; yet it was an alliance based on convenience. Each party pursuing its own agenda, they downplayed their differences and jointly fought against the linguistic doctrines they both rejected. It was, by its very nature, a temporary arrangement.

For years Max Müller had avoided direct confrontation with Whitney—that is, as long as the latter's challenges attracted only limited notice in England. Even after the publication of *Oriental and Linguistic Studies* (1873), he thought it safest to let his friends at the *Academy* respond to that work. Yet how could he ignore this latest eruption of Whitneyism, linked as it was to the name of Charles Darwin's son? Müller now presented an open rebuttal in the *Contemporary Review,* under the attention-getting yet strictly accurate title, "My Reply to Mr. Darwin."

He began with a characteristic blend of flattery and sarcasm. Although he described George Darwin's article as a "defense of Mr. Darwin's philosophy, so ably and chivalrously conducted by his son," he added that it came from "one who writes if not in, at least with, Mr. Darwin's name."[47] This last phrase contained an intentional ambiguity: did "Mr. Darwin" here refer to Charles or George? That is, was Müller accusing the younger Darwin of using his father's name in order to get a hearing, or was he accusing Whitney of doing essentially this same thing, only using George Darwin as his representative? In any case, Müller then turned to Whitney directly. First of all, he declared that his labors on the Ṛg Veda edition had thus far kept him from reading Whitney's published lectures. (According to Whitney's friends in England, Müller actually had finished that work twenty-one months prior to writing his "Reply to Mr. Darwin.")[48] Müller therefore thanked George Darwin for having brought Whitney's work to his notice, "for I have seldom perused a book with greater interest and pleasure—I might almost say amusement." Entire passages in Whitney's volume, said Müller, presented the "*ipsissima verba*" of his own 1861 lectures, "though immediately after they seemed to be changed into an inverted fugue."[49] Even though Whitney had acknowledged in his book's Preface that he had borrowed illustrations from Müller, here he stood accused of stealing (and then distorting) Müller's essential ideas.

Müller then appealed to his British readers in time-honored fashion: "Of course, we must not expect in Professor Whitney's lectures, anything like a systematic or exhaustive treatment. They touch on points which were most likely to interest large audiences at Washington, and other towns in America. They were meant to be popular, and nothing would be more unfair than to blame an author for not giving what he did not mean to give." Indeed, said

Müller, he had discovered in Whitney's book "whole chapters where by keeping more on the surface of his subject, he has succeeded in making it far more attractive and popular than I could have hoped to do."[50] Müller followed up these backhanded jabs by charging that Whitney had claimed himself superior to the leading German language scholars and by asking why other American philologists, such as George Perkins Marsh and Francis Andrew March, felt no need to resort to invective as Whitney did.

Next Müller rehashed the Steinthal affair. He allowed that Steinthal had gone too far in his pamphlet against Whitney, and to prove this, he paraded once again Steinthal's epithets ("that tricky attorney," etc.). His commentary on these remarks, moreover, was filled with calculated obfuscation: "Surely, mere words can go no further—we must expect to hear of tomahawk and bowie-knife. Scholars who object to the use of such weapons, whether for offensive or defensive purposes, can do nothing but what I have done—remain silent, select what is good in Professor Whitney's writings, and try to forget the rest." Here Müller was supposedly lamenting Steinthal's overreaction, yet what stood out in this passage were the tomahawk and bowie-knife, the archetypal weapons of the violent American. Müller also tried to exploit the disagreement between Whitney and the Darwins. He said, accurately enough: "If I may judge from Professor Whitney's lectures, . . . I doubt whether he would prove a real ally of Mr. Darwin in his views on the origin of language. Towards the end of his article, even Mr. Darwin, jun., becomes suspicious."[51]

In the most inventive part in his "Reply," Müller pointed to the complaint in Whitney's first book about the attempt by some modern thinkers to "materialize all science." Whitney had warned of the recent tendency to eliminate the distinction between the physical and "moral" realms, explain away human volition, and "resolve the whole story of the fates of mankind into a series of purely material effects." Müller described this passage as a "sermon," in which Whitney's "theological bias, long kept back, breaks through at last."[52] It was true that Whitney agreed with those religious thinkers who worried about materialist encroachment in the human sciences. Yet as Müller was fully aware, Whitney's point had been to defend linguistics' disciplinary autonomy—hardly a "theological" agenda. Even so, he cynically portrayed Whitney as an advocate of religious idealism. It was another attempt to discredit him with the Darwins.

Müller then turned to the question of human agency in the production of language change. He reiterated his own position by quoting from his second (1863) series of Royal Institution lectures: "The process through which language is settled and unsettled combines in one the two opposite elements of necessity and free will. . . . The individual, as such, is powerless, and the results, apparently produced by him, depend on laws beyond his control."[53] Müller elaborated this thesis in his *Contemporary Review* article, however, by incorporating a distinctly Whitneyesque theme. He said that, in the process of language change, "the individual does not act freely, but under reciprocal restraint." Müller actually had used a similar formulation several years earlier when he referred to the "implied co-operation" between speakers.[54] He thereby narrowed the distance between his and Whitney's formulations, and he did this by using phrases suspiciously reminiscent of Whitney's own.

Continuing this campaign of trimming, Müller took an even more surprising tack. He claimed in the *Contemporary Review* that he and Whitney had fundamentally agreed all along in their views about language change. He suggested, however, that he knew this to be the case, while Whitney did not: "Sometimes, amidst all the loud assertion of difference of opinion on Professor Whitney's part, not only the substantial, but the verbal agreement between his and my Second Lecture is startling. I had said: — 'The first impulse to a new formation in language, though given by an individual, is mostly, if not always, given without *premeditation,* nay, *unconsciously.*' My antagonist says: — 'The work of each individual is done *unpremeditately,* or as it were *unconsciously.*' " Müller therefore asked: "What is the difference between us?"[55]

In posing this apparently reasonable question, Müller brought the debate about language change itself to an impasse. From here onward, this aspect of the quarrel turned on a separate issue: had Müller kept his position constant over time, or had he adjusted his formulation in an attempt to incorporate Whitney's best insights? As Whitney would soon point out, some of Müller's self-quotations actually came from a revised edition of his lectures, where Müller had modified his original wording. Moreover, Müller likely made this change under the influence of Whitney's lectures — which he claimed not to have read until the latter part of 1874. The result was that Max Müller's duplicitous dealings, not his ideas about language change itself, became an issue in the dispute.

Whitney received a copy of "My Reply to Mr. Darwin" soon after its publication in January of 1875, and he immediately went to work on a rebuttal.

Communicating via George Darwin, he asked permission to respond in the *Contemporary Review*.[56] James Knowles replied to the elder Darwin, assuring him of his willingness to receive a "substantive paper" from Whitney. Yet with a publicist's eye, Knowles added a wistful postscript: "I need hardly say that should you yourself be at all persuadable to write a few introductory pages — or even paragraphs. . . ." Darwin forwarded Knowles' letter to Whitney, with a penciled comment beside its final lines: "This is nonsense. C. D."[57] Charles Darwin would not presume to steal Whitney's thunder — which also meant that he would not risk his own reputation by involving it in the philologists' quarrel.

In any event, Whitney at last had a platform from which to present his views to the British public. As he prepared his rejoinder, he submitted drafts to his friends, who assured him that he was exercising due restraint.[58] In the first two-thirds of this article, "Are Languages Institutions?" Whitney calmly outlined his own system of ideas while mentioning neither Müller nor the Darwins. The final, more polemical section was equally calm in tone. Whitney did defend his practice of critiquing famous linguists whenever they made what he thought were untenable arguments. And he admitted that he had spoken too bluntly on occasion. Yet he maintained — unconvincingly — that he judged arguments rather than men. More on-target with respect to Müller was his remark that "the plainest of plain speaking is far less really injurious than misrepresentation and detraction under the mask of extreme courtesy."[59]

Whitney's main challenge was to deal with the balderdash about his holding a "theological bias." He responded to this charge by revising his categories. Rather than warn about the "materializing" of the human sciences, he now divided linguistic opinion between his own "positive" and "common-sense" viewpoint, and his opponents' "sentimental" and "metaphysical" outlook.[60] Here Whitney reverted to a simple opposition between his own perspective and that of his adversaries — the latter representing the sentimental-metaphysical camp. Only a few years earlier, he had portrayed himself as fighting a two-front war, against both Humboldtian psychology and the natural-historical ("organic") tradition — the one represented by Heymann Steinthal and the other by August Schleicher. Now he lumped these together. This was perhaps allowable, because Whitney regarded the extreme version of the organic analogy as more metaphysical than physical. It also made sense because Max Müller, with his genius for synthesis, combined elements of

Schleicherian organicism and Humboldtian psychologism. Still, the fact that Whitney had been forced to use such varying terminology suggests the difficulty he sometimes faced in characterizing the things he was against.

If he did not achieve theoretical precision on this point, Whitney at least had had the final word in the *Contemporary Review* series. Even better, he had been able at last to defend his views in a prominent British forum. After this, he must have felt a burden lifted, confident that his foothold in the Old World would soon be made secure and his enemies put to rout. Events just ahead appeared to confirm those expectations.

## A Cause Célèbre

The spring of 1875 was fruitful for Whitney. In addition to writing his *Contemporary Review* article, he prepared an abridgment of his original lectures for the British market. Richard Morris of the London Philological Society contributed an Introduction to this volume, which would appear under the title *Language and its Study* (1876). Whitney also finished writing his *Life and Growth of Language* (1875), a more complete condensation of his linguistic thought. That book had been commissioned for the prestigious International Scientific Series, which brought simultaneous publication in New York and in cities throughout Europe. It also meant that Whitney's linguistics (like his Indology) was coming into heady company. Among the works that had appeared in the series already were Walter Bagehot's *Physics and Politics* (1872), Herbert Spencer's *Study of Sociology* (1874), and John William Draper's *History of the Conflict between Religion and Science* (1875).[61]

These projects behind him, Whitney departed for a long-anticipated trip to Europe, his first visit there since the journey he made with his wife and sister in 1856, soon after his wedding. This time, however, he went alone. The main purpose of the trip was to do research for the second volume of the Roth-Whitney *Atharva Veda* edition. Whitney wanted to examine additional copies of the text obtained by German universities since the first volume's appearance twenty years earlier. He also looked forward to renewing old ties and to widening his European acquaintance. First he spent several days in London, staying with Reinhold Rost, librarian of the East India Company Office. (Rost had been appointed to that position on the retirement of Fitzedward Hall.) A highlight of this part of the journey was to have been a visit with Charles Darwin, although this never took place. Whitney received Darwin's invitation to dinner at his home in Kent, only to see it revoked the next day by the re-nowned invalid's wife. Mrs. Darwin apologized, yet she remarked pointedly that her husband had been ill the previous night "after the exertion of having some friends in the house." She hoped, she said, that the American professor would be able to call if ever he was again in England.[62]

Still, there were other things to do: Whitney visited the zoological gardens and the Kensington Museum; he had lunch on one day with the Oxford Assyriologist Archibald Henry Sayce (1845–1933) and dinner the following evening with the Unitarian religious writer Moncure Conway (1832–1907). Conway was an expatriate American with an interest in philology and a knack for cultivating Europe's famous scholars. After dinner Whitney went as Conway's guest to a meeting of the London Anthropological Institute. The program included a paper by Conway on the history of mythology, leading, as Whitney described it, to a "most stupid debate."[63]

Next, Whitney enjoyed several weeks of triumphal procession through Germany. He visited Berlin, Jena, Leipzig, Munich, and Tübingen, retracing his steps of student days. In Berlin, his old friend Albrecht Weber hosted a reception in his honor. Among the guests were his former teacher Karl Lepsius, plus the eminent classicist Georg Curtius, who was visiting from Leipzig. At Jena, Whitney stayed with Otto Böhtlingk, a co-editor of the Sanskrit *Wörterbuch,* and he again was honored at a gathering of philologists. As he bragged to his wife, he had been the second person toasted at dinner, "and with a very handsome speech by Delbrück." In short, he said, "the journey has been quite a festival all the way."[64]

Proceeding to Leipzig, Whitney again saw Georg Curtius and met a number of his students from the university there. He also met August Leskien, an influential young member of the philological faculty. Along with Bertholdt Delbrück, Leskien would become a particular friend of Whitney's. During this visit, Leskien asked permission to do a German translation of *The Life and Growth of Language,* to which Whitney readily agreed. As we will see later, this event reflected the quiet influence Whitney had already begun to exert on Leskien and other like-minded young scholars, many of whom would join the rebellious Neogrammarian movement. What mattered to Whitney at the time, however, was the ready interest shown in his new book.[65] Leskien's translation would come out only a year after the English original, a pleasing contrast to the long gap between the publication of *Language and the Study of Language* (1867) and its German translation in 1874.[66]

Whitney's visit to Leipzig also brought an even greater honor, and one that was equally unexpected. The publishing house of Breitkopf and Härtel was planning a series of major grammatical studies of the Indo-European languages to be prepared by some of Germany's brightest up-and-coming scholars. For the volume on Sanskrit, however, they enlisted an American. Immensely gratified by this commission, Whitney told his wife, "What most pleases me in the matter is to see that I am fairly taken into the ranks of the German scholars, as if no outsider or stranger."[67] A capstone to his earlier successes, this distinction would silence any remaining question as to Whitney's eminence among European Orientalists.

Unfortunately, this warm season in Germany was clouded by the reception Whitney's *Life and Growth of Language* was receiving in England. Writing under his own name in the journal *Nature*, Max Müller suggested that Whitney had borrowed, without attribution, all of that book's best material:

> But who were the first to conceive a Science of Language as different from Comparative Philology, though beholden to it for its most valuable materials? Who first drew the outlines of that science, collected the facts required for its illustration, and established the leading principles of its study? Prof. Whitney could have answered all these questions better than anybody else, whereas, by his reticence, he may now leave on many of his readers the impression, though no doubt very much against his own will, that the science of language had its cradle in America, and that German, English and French scholars have added nothing to it, except "incongruities and absurdities."[68]

Another effort to kindle European grievance against the American upstart, Müller's statement ignored the fact that Whitney had long before acknowledged his debt to other linguists. Still, Whitney said that this signed review at least brought a refreshing openness to the conflict.[69]

Meanwhile, Whitney had settled down to his *Atharva* labors, which took up July and most of August. He also rewrote his *Contemporary Review* article to prepare it for translation in the *Deutsche Rundschau*. (G. H. Darwin's and Max Müller's articles were reprinted as well.)[70] By the time Whitney completed these tasks and departed from Germany, the European vacation season had begun. He was therefore disappointed when he passed through England en route home; many on whom he had wished to call, including the Darwins and Hensleigh Wedgwood, were unavailable. Another letdown came on the day Whitney sailed from Liverpool: the London *Academy* published a second hostile review of his new book. Whitney now stood accused of having shifted his position on certain issues. For example, "animals are now admitted to possess no language in the proper sense of the word. . . . What will Mr. Darwin, jun., say to this?"[71] The anonymous writer had a familiar style.

Whitney composed a short statement while on shipboard, which was duly printed in the next week's *Academy*. He calmly explained that he had not knowingly changed any of his views and that he certainly had never suggested that animals possess language. There was, at any rate, little doubt as to the source of this latest jab. Arriving home in New Haven, Whitney found a postcard from Furnivall: "You must fight M. Skin him." His friend Reinhold Rost was similarly enraged by the "insidious remarks" in the *Academy*. "Your temperate reply, keeping strictly to the point—what a contrast!"[72] Whitney would struggle to maintain this dignity of tone, at least in public, even as the controversy entered its most antagonistic phase.

That fall there appeared a new installment of Max Müller's *Chips from a German Workshop*. Composed mostly of Orientalist studies, *Chips*, volume four, also included two essays aimed at Whitney: an expanded version of "My Reply to Mr. Darwin," and a new seventy-five-page essay entitled "In Self-defence." The latter, the final item in the collection, caught the attention of the literary press throughout Europe. Here Müller gave a detailed recital of his grievances, both scholarly and personal, against Whitney. He alleged, among other things, that Whitney had had the effrontery to pay him a visit at Oxford a number of years previously and to ask him for favors—this after having repeatedly abused him in print: "It was because I thought Professor Whitney capable of rendering useful service to the science of language in America that I forbore so long, that I never for years noticed his intentional rudeness and arrogance, that I received him, when he called on me at Oxford, with perfect civility, that I assisted him when he wanted my help in procuring copies of MSS. at Oxford. I could well afford to forget what had happened."[73] Müller said that he had wanted to avoid a quarrel but had been dragged into it. He accused Whitney of instigating the series in the *Contemporary Review* by getting "possession of the pen of the son [George Darwin], fondly trusting it would carry the weight of the father." By this means, Müller said, Whitney had hoped to gain the "*aura popularis* of Darwinism."[74]

Müller's "Self-defence" ended with a proposal: a tribunal of arbitration should be set up to judge twenty "principal bones of contention" between himself and Whitney. "In order, therefore, to satisfy Mr. Darwin, Professor Haeckel, and others whose good opinion I highly value, because I know that they care for truth far more than for victory, I now appeal to Professor Whitney to choose from among his best friends, three who are *Professores ordinarii* in any university of England, France, Germany, or Italy, and by their verdict I promise to abide." (Müller named the zoologist Ernst Haeckel because Haeckel was a cousin of the linguist W. H. J. Bleek.) A number of Müller's disputed points were either trivial or obscure: for instance, "Whether E. Burnouf has written two or three bulky volumes on the Avesta, or only one," and "Whether the grammatical blunder, with regard to the Sanskrit *pari tasthushas* as a nominative plur. was mine or his." Yet several of the items had more substance. In particular, were there not "verbatim coincidences" between his and Whitney's published lectures? And had he, Müller, "ever denied that language was made through the instrumentality of man"?[75]

Müller still hoped Whitney would do valuable work in the future. A scholar could be in no more useful place than America, he said, for the study of "languages but little known, and rapidly disappearing"—thus suggesting that Whitney really should be investigating the American Indian tongues, not Sanskrit. Yet to this Müller added a caveat: "I admit that America has also its temptations." In that undeveloped society, he explained, there were few intellectual authorities qualified to gainsay Whitney's opinions, "and by his command of a number of American papers, he can easily secure to himself a temporary triumph."[76]

Müller, of course, commanded sources of his own, as the *Academy*'s announcement of his new *Chips* volume showed. According to that statement, "the piquant justice of the last essay, 'In Self-defence' will be thoroughly appreciated by every class of readers." A. H. Sayce, Müller's protégé at Oxford, wrote an additional review that likewise recommended the book's final article. (Whitney learned that Sayce had not wanted to write this but had been obliged to "knuckle under.")[77] The result was that Whitney's reputation in England now hung by a thread. Despite his many triumphs, especially in the Orientalist world, he still could not feel that his victory was complete.

Coming after the warm springtime and summer, the exasperating charges included in Müller's new article blighted the winter of 1875–76. Indological projects went by the boards as Whitney spent nearly all of his spare time preparing his case. By December he had drafted a letter of response to the *Academy.* He also consulted with friends about writing on his behalf in American journals. Several of those journal's editors also pledged to stand by Whitney, and from these most of the local newspapers took their cues.[78]

Whitney's friends in England reported that many there were on his side: members of London's Atheneum Club, for instance, thought badly of Müller's "Self-defence."[79] Yet this was only part of the picture. Reinhold Rost said that Müller, although an outsider to the English social elite, had secured a strong following among the royal family, among a clique connected with the *Academy*, and among a large readership. Under these conditions, even those who disliked Müller thought it best not to cross him. Rost claimed that there was "not a paper in the whole kingdom that would dare to insert an article in any way damaging to him."[80] So although many British scholars sympathized with Whitney, this did him little good in public.

As Whitney prepared his response to Müller's "Self-defence," friends offered him tactical advice. In a chastened mood after having been burned by Müller in the *Contemporary Review*, George Darwin counseled a cease-fire: "One does not see the end of this kind of polemic." (He added a post-script: "My father dictates to you as follows: 'There is a sentence in the Chips in which M. M. expresses great satisfaction at having received a letter from me, and which seems to imply that I had said that I thought that you were wrong in the controversy and he Max Müller right, whereas there was nothing whatever in the letter which could bear any interpretation of this kind.' ")[81]

Unlike George Darwin, Charles Eliot Norton felt that Whitney needed to respond. Yet he recommended that this be done through "a measured, calm and colourless historic rehearsal of the controversy."[82] Norton's influence showed in Whitney's "Rejoinder," which appeared in the *Academy* on New Year's Day, 1876. Whitney dealt with a variety of points, including the matter of his visit to Oxford. Müller had said that Whitney came to see him and asked for favors, even after having attacked him on linguistic matters. Yet that visit, Whitney noted, had occurred in 1856, which was years "before either of us had ever written a word on the 'Science of Language.' " Whitney also recalled various favors he had done for Müller. He had "supported heartily" Müller's candidacy for the Boden Professorship at Oxford, and he had brokered the original agreement between Müller and his American publisher. Imprudently, however, Whitney tried to establish these facts by quoting from Müller's letters of request, all of which he had kept. The *Academy*'s editor Charles Appleton properly excised this passage from Whitney's printed "Rejoinder." (Explaining his action, Appleton chided Whitney: "This is our code of journalistic morals:

isn't it so in America too?")[83] The result was that Müller could continue to accuse Whitney on this matter with impunity.

As to what Müller had written about language change, Whitney cried foul. He showed in his "Rejoinder" that Müller had subtly shifted his stance over the years and then had quoted from a revised edition of his own lectures while claiming that this represented his original views. In his *Chips* article, Müller quoted himself as saying: "Though it is easy to show that language cannot be changed or moulded by the taste, the fancy, or genius of man, *it is neverthe-less through the instrumentality of man alone that language can be changed.*" Here Müller tried to show that he had always acknowledged the human role in language change; the implication was that Whitney had attacked him need-lessly. Yet as Whitney pointed out, the italicized passage represented, "so far as I know, the nearest approach to be found in Mr. Müller's works to the doctrine which I have always held and defended, that language is made and changed, not only through the instrumentality, but by the actual agency, of men; but those words do not stand in the edition of the Lectures which I criticized: in-stead of them we read '*it is very difficult to explain what causes the growth of language.*'"[84] In short, this "bone of contention" arose purely from Müller having declared that he had never changed his view.

Last of all, Whitney responded to Müller's arbitration proposal: he said that he was willing to go along but would not take responsibility for setting up the tribunal. Instead, Müller would have to pick his own friends as judges.[85]

In reply, Müller ignored the bulk of Whitney's "Rejoinder" and seized on this last point only: twisting Whitney's meaning, he charged Whitney with re-fusing to submit to arbitration. This forced Whitney to send a second letter to the *Academy,* denying this charge. The *Academy,* however, refused to print the letter. Instead, Charles Appleton published a statement urging Whitney to ac-cept a tribunal's judgment rather than write more letters full of "angry recrimi-nation." Thanks to the intervention of friends, the London *Examiner* offered itself as an alternative venue. Here Whitney repeated his earlier points while admitting that he had little faith in arbitration as a means of settling scholarly disputes. He reaffirmed his willingness to accept an independent judgment, yet he said that his own role would be purely that of a respondent.[86]

What turned all of this into a international cause célèbre were the reports of the affair that ran in Continental periodicals. One of these, appearing in Florence's *Rivista Europa*, clearly sided with Müller. Whitney responded by sending an irate letter of protest to the *Rivista*'s editor, Angelo de Gubernatis.

This was but one of several such letters he wrote during this period, and it would have remained like all the others except for the fact that de Gubernatis published it. Here Whitney mainly repeated what he had said in the *Academy* and the *Examiner*. What stunned European readers, however, were remarks he added at the conclusion: "In the whole history of religions, I do not think there is a stranger form of idolatry, than Müller-worship. I venture to predict that it will prove transitory, and that the next generation will look back upon it only with wondering curiosity. It is, I am sure, already fast waning; and probably an uneasy consciousness of the fact has led to this last furious but ill-judged outbreak on the divinity's part."[87] Whitney told his friends overseas that he had intended this letter for de Gubernatis only, noting that it was "decidedly more plain-spoken" than anything he would have written for publication. "If I am criticized for its plainness anywhere within your reach," he implored, "I wish you would kindly make this explanation on my behalf." Still, even some of his supporters were taken aback.[88]

At this point, a would-be mediator stepped forward. Moncure Conway must have seemed perfect for the job. An American familiar with British scholarly circles, he was acquainted with both antagonists — although more so with Müller. He had visited the United States that January and had been Whitney's guest at a meeting of the New Haven Philological Society. Later that evening, during a long private conversation, Conway had urged Whitney to go through with the arbitration scheme and had offered his services as a go-between.[89] Back in England that spring, he solicited from Müller a response to Whitney's complaints. Müller therefore addressed himself to Conway in five extraordinary letters, written during five consecutive days in May.

For the most part, Müller tried to substantiate his charge about Whitney's presumptuous visit to Oxford. Conway had passed along Whitney's contention that Müller had got the date wrong, and Müller finally admitted that he might have made a mistake: "How should I remember the exact year? I still believe that his rudeness had begun before he called, for though forgetting the date, I remember a certain feeling of suspicion at receiving his friendly visit. But how does that affect the questions between him and me? Add the date, and yet every word may remain as I wrote it. Besides, if he called on me today, I should receive him, I hope, as a gentleman."[90]

Müller said that he could still prove that Whitney had sought and accepted favors from him "long *after*" attacking him in print. But he was evasive about the favors he himself had requested: "Can you remember what position I wished to be recommended to by Whitney? I ransack my memory in vain. I never stood for anything but the Sanskrit Professorship." Two days later, Müller grudgingly acknowledged that Whitney had supported him for precisely that post: "No no, these are not the points at issue, nor his testimonial which he gave me when I stood for the Boden Professorship, and which with about fifty others I pursued at the time."[91]

Müller then returned to his earlier point:

> With regard to his visit in 1856, though I had completely forgotten the date, I had the distinct impression that it surprised me and that I was pleased by it. But why was I surprised? Because in several articles on the Veda which W. had published in 1853, he had, while blowing the trumpet for Roth, Weber and others, carefully avoided any mention of my name. When he could not help mentioning my edition of the Rig Veda, all he says is: a new edition of the Rig, too, with accented text and the native commentary is now in progress at *London* (J.A.O.S. vol. III, p. 293). I mention this simply as showing his animus at the time, in 1853.[92]

Here, finally, Müller divulged what for him, at least in retrospect, was the original source of the quarrel. His charge was accurate: one of Whitney's earliest publications, an 1853 article surveying modern Vedic scholarship, had omitted Müller's name from its reference to the Oxford *Ṛg Veda* edition. Whitney later (in 1872) admitted that he had intentionally snubbed Müller on this occasion, although he did not explain why.[93] The 1853 article appeared nearly ten years before Whitney's falling out with Müller during the Indian astronomy controversy. Hence, his slighting of Müller at that early date likely was an expression of partisanship for Albrecht Weber in his own long-running dispute with Müller. In any case, Müller's explanation to Moncure Conway did not at all fit with the charge made in *Chips,* that Whitney had attacked him on matters of linguistic science prior to his Oxford visit. Müller concluded his letters to Conway on a note of unintended irony: "I must only repeat again that all this is far far away from the real point at issue."[94]

Later that month, Whitney wrote his own final letter to Moncure Conway. The latter had appealed for peace and harmony, but Whitney would have these only on the following terms: "Let Müller publicly withdraw his last article, 'In Self-defence,' confessing that it is wrong from beginning to end, and the thing will be put well in train." Whitney also betrayed his growing irritation with Conway himself: "I think you mistake the aspect of the case, as it now stands. I am not aware of having done anything which I need to retract or to apologize for. . . . I have no 'personal matters to brush away' (to use your expression)." This last point was, to say the least, not quite convincing, along with Whitney's frequent declarations that he cared only for scientific truth. Still, his conclusion about Müller was accurate enough: "He has now at last answered me [via Conway], but it is with simple misrepresentation and abuse. . . . To me he is simply, with all his ability, one of the great humbugs of the century; he has long shown himself to be as much intellectually; now he has exposed himself as being the same thing morally."[95]

In his own parting words on the affair, Conway wrote an equivocal paragraph for the London *Palladium*. He wrung his hands and vouched for the honor of both parties. He also said that Müller still was willing to accept a tribunal made up of any three German scholars known to be Whitney's friends, "and there is every reason to credit him with good faith, because he is himself by no means a favorite with the Germans."[96] Considering the ineptness of this remark, Müller must have regretted ever attempting to use Conway as a mouthpiece. Needless to say, the tribunal never was constituted.

The Whitney-Müller controversy had lost steam by midsummer: the principle combatants had had their say, and neither backed down. One unfortunate outcome was the end of Whitney's once-cordial relationship with the *North American Review*. Henry Adams felt that the dispute had played itself out, so he discouraged any more contributions on the subject. As he told Whitney's Sheffield School colleague T. R. Lounsbury, "The *odium philologicum* is not a pleasant matter to keep alive." Adams did finally agree to publish a review of the affair that Lounsbury had written—which set forth probably the best summation of Whitney's case.[97] But he put off Whitney himself, who had prepared an article on the long-awaited final volume of Müller's *Ṛg Veda* edition. Whitney claimed that he judged this work purely on its "scientific" merits, but Adams and C. E. Norton sensed otherwise from the tone of the piece. As Norton told Whitney, "Anything—any word, any turn of phrase—savoring of sarcasm or indignation, is consequently, in your position, of bad policy and questionable taste."[98] In the last letter he would ever write to Norton, Whitney said that he would not allow his article to be bowdlerized. It therefore appeared in full in the *New Englander*.[99]

As it turned out, this piece presented a masterful survey of European Vedic scholarship in the mid-nineteenth century. It also contained, as Adams and Norton realized, a devastating portrait of Max Müller's Indological career.

Others would eventually confirm this judgment. The eminent British phoneticist Henry Sweet later told Whitney: "I am no admirer of Müller (except in as far as I consider him an excellent type of the 'Graeculus eswiens'—the successful humbug), and consider his influence on English scientific work to be an unmixedly bad one." A knowledgeable observer from Oxford corroborated this assessment in an article written after Müller's death in 1901.[100]

## The Virtues of the Invisible Hand

In terms of intellectual content, the one new feature of the Whitney-Müller controversy was the apparent convergence of the two philologists' views on the role of agency in language change. Müller's claim that he and Whitney had basically agreed on that subject all along was of course deceptive: in reality, Müller had revised his own formulation. Yet this still leaves the question of whether, in the end, these verbal changes produced a convergence of outlook. Did the adjustments Müller introduced in the later editions of his lectures amount to an actual shift in explanation, such that he indeed came closer to Whitney's position? The answer proposed here is that Whitney's and Müller's theories were neither convergent nor complementary, but rather were fundamentally at odds; it will also be argued that Whitney's viewpoint was clearly superior.

In his second (1863) series of Royal Institution lectures, Müller showed that his own perspective was essentially dualistic. The phenomenon of language change, he said, "combined" in unresolved tension the "two opposite elements of necessity and free will."[101] This perspective did suggest a distinguished intellectual pedigree: Müller often said that the problem of language change mirrored the old theological conundrum of apparent human freedom coexisting with divine sovereignty. For this reason, the Calvinists at Princeton Seminary and at *Bibliotheca Sacra* sided with Müller against Whitney.[102] Yet this viewpoint, while it suggested the mystery and complexity of language change, did no more than restate the explanatory problem.

Max Müller appeared to moderate his position during the main years of controversy, when he spoke of "implied cooperation" and "reciprocal restraint" among individual speakers. He thereby conveyed superficial agreement with Whitney's outlook, leading some observers to conclude that the difference between the two philologists' views was "not so profound as the public is led to imagine."[103] That difference, however, becomes clear when one looks at their writings as a whole. While Müller left the matter unresolved, Whitney supplied an intelligible explanatory framework via his voluntary-interactionist sociology, which, as we have seen, elaborated Adam Smith's "invisible hand" concept.[104] It will be useful to reemphasize three interlocking characteristics of this Smithian mode of explanation, all of which would be central to Whitney's enduring legacy.[105]

First, unlike the dualist outlook, a genuine invisible-hand schema explains the whole in terms of its constituent parts. Whitney made precisely this point in *The Life and Growth of Language* (1875): "It is manifestly absurd to recognize one force in action in the items and another in their sum. If we refuse to examine the items when forming an estimate of the [causal] force, and only gaze with admiration at the great whole, there is no theory so false that we may not for a time rest in it with satisfaction." Rather, like Adam Smith, Whitney explained concerted social behavior in terms of the freely chosen actions of individuals.[106]

Second, an invisible-hand schema entails not only individual action but also social interaction. It involves mutual influence among a collection of independent selves, each of whom orients his behavior to the behavior of those around him. Individuals act in this manner even as they pursue their own interests — indeed, as the necessary means to achieving those interests. Because of the intrinsically communal nature of speech, the introduction of linguistic innovations was always being counterbalanced by self-restraint and conformity to group practice.

Finally, the emphasis on social interaction necessarily involves a synchronic perspective. When Adam Smith used his "hand" metaphor to explain how the free market induces autonomous individuals to interact, he pictured this taking place more or less at a given point in time; it was only by appeal to this present interaction that he accounted for eventual change. In the same way, Whitney tied the long-term evolution of language back to the constant interface among speakers. Here again, he collapsed two levels into one, not only reducing society to a collection of individuals but also linking the diachronic process to the synchronic moment.

Whitney added nuance to this schema midway through his career, largely in response to critiques of his voluntarist position. These came, not from Max Müller, but rather from various (often American) reviewers of his published lectures as well as his *Oriental and Linguistic Studies* (1873). One reviewer noted, with some sympathy, the difficulty caused by the inherent imprecision of words such as "unconscious," "intention," and "will": "The want of fit terms probably explains why Professor Whitney describes the same thing as [both] conscious and unconscious."[107] Two other writers, however, were more critical on this score. The Pennsylvania philologist Francis Andrew March agreed that individual speakers were the source of all changes in language; that much, he said, was obvious. Yet he questioned whether speakers consciously intended to produce those changes.[108]

The philosopher Chauncey Wright (1830–75) pushed this argument further, producing probably the most incisive criticism of Whitney's voluntary-agency thesis ever made. A member of the Boston-Cambridge "Metaphysical Club" and a mentor to the American pragmatists, Wright pointed out that speakers normally intend, not to change their language, but rather to conform to customary usage. One could hardly say, therefore, that speakers change their language voluntarily, "for the same wills cannot act from contradictory intentions."[109] Wright included this argument, along with references to Whitney's essay on August Schleicher, in an 1873 article on humanity's mental evolution that appeared in the *North American Review*.

Whitney did not directly acknowledge his detractors, but he did respond to them. Actually, he had already begun grappling with the problem of unconscious action in his anti-Steinthal essay published the previous year. There, as we have seen, he conceded that the long-term modification of language did involve an element of non-intent. A caveman using a stone to defend himself against a wolf "was not conscious that he was commencing a series of acts which would lead finally to rifles and engines." Similarly, changes in language were "unforeseen consequences of its use as a means of communication."[110]

Whitney expanded this thesis in *The Life and Growth of Language* (1875), no doubt in order to address his recent critics. Every time a speaker took even the smallest articulatory "short cut," Whitney said, that person "commits thus an addition to language without ever being aware of it; any more than the parents who name their son reflect that they are thus virtually making an addition to the city directory. If he will well understand it to be in this sense, everyone is welcome to hold that alternations of speech are not made by the human will; *there is no will to alter speech; there is only will to use* [existing] *speech in a way which is new; and the alteration comes of itself as a result*."[111] Here Whitney was probably responding to Chauncey Wright's argument. To reinforce his point, he added a further illustration: "So it was not by the exertion of his will that the reptile, creeping over the muddy surface of a Permian or Jurassic shore, made a record of himself for the human geologist to study, a few million years later; and yet, if he had not voluntarily taken the steps, under sufficient inducement, there would have been no record."[112]

These analogies — involving the caveman, the new parents, and the prehistoric reptile — were limited in the sense that they failed to convey the dimension of social interaction that remained fundamental to Whitney's theory. Still, they did suggest the crucial distinction between initially voluntary (even if only half-conscious) speech behavior and the long-term outcomes of that behavior, which most speakers never intend or live to see produced. That distinction was represented, for instance, by the gap between the reptile's movements and the fossilized record those movements left behind. Whitney emphasized this gulf between intent and outcome yet again in an article he wrote in 1880. After affirming that language change lay "wholly within the domain of voluntary human action," he added the now-familiar qualification: "This does not by any means imply that the will is exerted directly toward the change of language, any more than the will of the fugitive is directed toward his own discovery when by voluntary action he leaves the tracks by which he is followed."[113]

Yet how could a *synchronic* sociology of language bridge this chasm between the immediate and the long-term? Whitney's ability to remain untroubled by this problem likely stemmed from a lifelong familiarity with the notion of geological gradualism. One could thus imagine miniscule speech innovations acting like wind erosion or silt deposition, that is, accumulating over long periods and eventually resulting in large developments such as the splitting of a single language into a number of distinct dialects. Seen in this light, the long-term aspect took care of itself, and the theorist could legitimately focus on the motivating impulses close at hand. Whitney is therefore to be commended for not falling into his own version of dualism — in this case, an unresolved tension between the synchronic and the diachronic. Keeping within the Smithian tradition, he collapsed the two perspectives into synchronic explanation alone.

Linguists would largely abandon questions about the role of intent in language change by the end of the nineteenth century, and it would be nearly a century more before they again became attracted to Adam Smith's invisible-hand perspective.[114] The latter occurred only after the field of sociolinguistics became established in the late twentieth century. Then came the realization that Smithian theory provided one of that school's central intellectual underpinnings. What has not been recognized, however, is the extent to which W. D. Whitney's sociological perspective has accordingly been put into practice. This we will see better in our final chapter, when we examine Whitney's legacy in the sociolinguistic school itself.

# CHAPTER NINE

# The Elder Statesman and the *Junggrammatiker*

As the smoke cleared from the Müller controversy, W. D. Whitney dusted himself off, grieved the time lost, and returned to the projects he had laid aside. Most of those projects were Indological: he had fallen behind, for instance, in his *Prātiśākhya* editing.[1] Whitney also renewed his efforts to develop American philology's institutional structures, particularly in the nation's new research universities. This return to normal routine, however, did not spell an end to Whitney's involvement with general linguistics. Indeed, his most significant impact on that field was beginning to manifest itself only now in connection with the advent of the Neogrammarian movement.

An understanding of Whitney's contribution to the Neogrammarians is crucial for a right appraisal of his personal legacy. More than that, it is essential for an accurate account of the development of modern linguistics. Still, this has proved to be an elusive topic. Historians of the Neogrammarian phenomenon routinely rank Whitney among the group's predecessors. Some have even identified Whitney himself as a *Junggrammatiker*—if not an actual member of that school, then at least a strong sympathizer.[2] Yet Whitney's relation to the Neogrammarian program was ambiguous. He did in fact exert a deep influence on the group's fundamental assumptions. However, it was a different story when it came to the doctrines for which the school would become best known. Those, it turned out, were not at all what Whitney had wanted to encourage. Eventually, therefore, he became one of the movement's most uncompromising critics.

## A Philological Statesman at Home and Abroad

By the late 1870s W. D. Whitney had emerged as America's guiding voice in the academic professionalization of philology. His efforts in that line manifested themselves most dramatically, although not always effectually, through his friendship with Daniel Coit Gilman. After being passed over for the Yale presidency in 1870, Gilman had accepted the top post at the University of California. He presided there until 1875, when he was called to head the newly established Johns Hopkins University, to be located in Baltimore. That institution would launch American postgraduate education by becoming the nation's first thoroughgoing research-oriented university.

On the day that he accepted the offer from Johns Hopkins, in virtually his first acts on behalf of that institution, Gilman wrote to two of his former colleagues at Yale's Sheffield Scientific School. Here he followed the example of Charles W. Eliot, from the beginning of *his* presidency at Harvard, by attempting a raid on the Sheffield faculty. Gilman told the geologist George Jarvis Brush that he wanted to enlist, early on, a few key advisors "with whom I can confer in the intimacy of long-tried friendship. You will not think it strange that I turn to Whitney and you." Writing to Whitney himself, Gilman asked a specific question: What would Whitney do if he were to head up the department of languages at the new university? Gilman added: "If we can capture you for Baltimore your name will be a tower of strength." Although he could not extend an offer without the trustees' approval, Gilman assured Whitney that, at the very least, "you are the one man of all men whose counsel I shall seek on the philological side."[3]

Here once again, a leading architect of the American university courted W. D. Whitney. Once again, however, Whitney responded with caution. It would be hard, he said, to uproot and transplant; he also needed to hear more specifically what Gilman had to offer. Meanwhile, he answered the immediate question. To begin with, Whitney replied, Gilman should recruit a core of three professors: one in general Indo-European; one in Semitics; and, for the time being, one sufficing for Europe's classical languages. Next should be added chairs in the Germanic and the Romanic branches: "I should incline to do that earlier than divide Latin and Greek." "Then," said Whitney, "I should *crave* an Am. Indian department; and a Chinese and E. Asiatic (Japanese and Scythian); and if it ever came to an Egyptian, so much the better."[4]

This was a vision of breathtaking scope. Although it began with the familiar Indo-European and Semitic families, it went on to embrace many of the major language groups then recognized by European scholars.[5] If realized in practice, this plan would have produced, perhaps as early as 1880, a significant departure from American academe's focus on the Western literary dialects. And it would have included what Whitney still "craved" to see established: an academic chair in the American Indian languages. As it turned out, however, Gilman did not find himself able to follow much of Whitney's advice.

Gilman did continue to consult his old friend during the university's early years. Whitney approved the selection of Basil L. Gildersleeve (1831–1924), an acquaintance from their student days in Berlin, as professor of Greek. He also secured a teaching fellowship in Sanskrit for one of his own former students, Charles Rockwell Lanman (1850–1941). Lanman had been among the crop of college graduates (the "men of mark") who trained under Whitney in the early days of Yale's graduate program in philology. After receiving his Yale doctorate in 1873, Lanman had studied with Whitney's former teachers at Berlin and Tübingen. He then proceeded to Johns Hopkins, where his initial fellowship year led to a regular teaching appointment.[6]

Charles Lanman would play a major role in Whitney's later life and career. Once Lanman assumed his teaching post at Johns Hopkins, Whitney began treating him as a protégé in running the American Oriental Society. Even before that, while Lanman was abroad as a student, Whitney had expressed his hope that the younger man would become "an active help to us when you come back, and of my not continuing always quite so lonely as I have been."[7] Lanman would not achieve Whitney's eminence as a scholar, yet he was a consistent and conscientious worker — qualities that suggest themselves in photographs from the period. Square-jawed and poised, Lanman appears a model of Victorian manhood. His loyalty and his tact, moreover, stood him well in his dealings with Whitney, who proved to be a demanding mentor. Eventually, Whitney would make Lanman a personal confidant nearly equal to his brother Josiah.

Whitney quickly decided against joining the resident faculty at Baltimore, yet as he told Gilman, he was willing to come and lecture on an occasional basis and on a particular topic: "I should rather represent the Science of Language than anything else." He performed this service during Johns Hopkins' first two years of operation, then severed all official connection with that school. At first pleading schedule restrictions, Whitney finally confessed to Gilman the real reason for his decision: "I have not face enough, nor adaptability enough, for such work. It seems to me too much like 'starring it in the provinces' — an occupation which I cannot possibly relish." This was a telling remark, suggestive not only of Whitney's personal temperament but also his professional ethos. Even at the academically precocious new university, he still found the role of visiting lecturer redolent of the lyceum circuit. Gilman was able to retain him for the second season only by barring the general public from the audience.[8]

Charles Lanman taught for several years at Johns Hopkins, then joined the faculty at Harvard, where he would remain for the rest of his long career. Whitney approved of this decision, judging that Harvard still offered the better stage for professional advancement. He also thought that Yale's philology department had pulled ahead of Harvard's of late, and that Lanman's presence there would help restore the competitive balance.[9]

Unfortunately, the opening at Baltimore created by Lanman's departure led to a disagreement between Whitney and D. C. Gilman. To fill the vacant spot, Whitney recommended Edward Washburn Hopkins (1857–1932), an aspiring Sanskritist who had just completed his doctorate at Leipzig. Although not a student of Whitney's (he had attended Columbia College in New York City), Hopkins was the son of a family friend in Northampton. Whitney suggested that Gilman give the young man a one-year fellowship as a trial. Gilman, however, was considering someone who *had* been a student of Whitney's, Maurice Bloomfield (1855–1928).[10] A childhood émigré from Austria, Bloomfield had done a year of graduate work at Yale, after which Whitney had sent him on to Johns Hopkins. There he completed his doctorate under Lanman. Bloomfield then proceeded to Europe for further study. Having finished this phase of his training, he was available to fill Lanman's newly vacated position.

Lanman himself agreed with Whitney in favoring E. W. Hopkins, and he confided to his former teacher his prejudicial reasons. Although, he said, he had nothing against Bloomfield, "I do think that Hopkins is personally a vastly superior man, and a genuine *American* — whereas B. is an Austrian Jew — born in Austria." (Lanman added: "Please, however, to be careful about the contents of this letter. Perhaps you'd better burn these two pages.") Writing to Gilman, Whitney too declared that he had nothing against Bloomfield, although in saying this he took with one hand what he gave with the other: "Mr. B. may turn out to be the most advisable choice, and to have capacities of sound work corresponding to his forwardness and self-reliance, which at first is [*sic*] a little repelling." With this thought in mind, Whitney again pressed the case of E. W. Hopkins. He admitted that Hopkins was young and untried, yet suggested that he was a scholar of "uncommon promise."[11]

This question of who to hire created an awkward situation between Whitney and Gilman. More importantly, it raised the issue of the standards by which academic appointments should be judged. Gilman's criterion was simple: "We only want the best."[12] In the end, therefore, Maurice Bloomfield became Johns Hopkins' Professor of Sanskrit and Comparative Philology, the position he would hold until his retirement. Adding Bloomfield alongside B. L. Gildersleeve was a significant step: Johns Hopkins was beginning to build one of the world's finest philology departments. Still, it would not approach the breadth of Whitney's ideal.

As it turned out, Whitney soon revised his opinion of Bloomfield. Heedless of any inconsistency, he sent Gilman a congratulatory note after the next meeting of the AOS: "We had a *first-class* paper from Mr. Bloomfield yesterday, and I have no doubt that he is going to do you admirable service, and bring credit to American scholarship. You could have made no other so good appointment, and you mustn't load him with work that will take away his leisure for investigation." In fact, Whitney and Lanman both went on to become Bloomfield's warm admirers.[13] E. W. Hopkins, meanwhile, took a job teaching Greek at Bryn Mawr College and became active as a Sanskritist in the AOS. Eventually he would succeed Whitney at Yale.

At the same time that the Johns Hopkins Sanskrit position became vacant (1880), so did the university's Semitics post. Whitney tried to have a hand in this decision as well. He urged Gilman to hire his one-time student William Rainey Harper (1856–1906), a young Hebraist who later became famous as the founding president of the University of Chicago.[14] When Gilman demurred, Whitney tried to apply pressure, even to the point of hinting that relations between Johns Hopkins and the AOS hung in the balance: "There is a sad change at Baltimore since you seemed to be promising soon to become almost the head-centre of Oriental as well as other philology for the country, and I was hoping we should soon have an Or. Soc'y meeting under your auspices. I think, from all I hear, that Mr. Harper is worth considering as a Semiticist; I do not at present know of anyone more promising in the country."[15]

Whitney's mean-spirited threat did little good, for in the end, Daniel Coit Gilman declined to hire William Rainey Harper. Harper went on to teach at Yale for a number of years before proceeding to the presidency at Chicago. Johns Hopkins eventually filled its Semitics chair with a German scholar, Paul Haupt (1858–1926).

These efforts to shape appointments at John Hopkins met with clear-cut failure, recalling Whitney's earlier failed attempts to get philological chairs established at Harvard. Yet these were the conspicuous exceptions, for by the time of the Hopkins decisions, Whitney had become the country's most sought-after advisor on matters related to academic language study. Requests arrived, for instance, from the presidents of Harvard, Columbia, and Princeton—the latter asking for information about Yale's postgraduate philology offerings.[16] Whitney received a constant flow of such queries for the remainder of his career.

W. D. Whitney's role as a leader of his profession also showed in his relations with the American Philological Association, at least from its founding in 1869 through the early 1880s. He retained much of his influence in that body even after his tenure as its first president ended. He continued to serve on the board of directors and got C. R. Lanman to become the Association's secretary. The latter move was typical. Whitney knew that routine service of this kind would purchase leverage, helping them to combat, as he put it, "the forces of philological folly" within the Association itself.[17] Whitney took courage for the fight from a cohort of gifted young APA allies led by Lanman, Maurice Bloomfield, and E. W. Hopkins.

For years Whitney would present papers at APA meetings, often in response to imploring requests from the meetings' organizers. Following his advice, however, the Association held back from establishing a regular journal. They produced only an annual *Transactions* containing a handful of articles along with abstracts of the papers delivered.[18] Outlets for the publication of original philological research in America were therefore limited. Until the end of the 1870s, the *Journal of the American Oriental Society* provided the nation's only other forum for this purpose.[19]

This situation, meanwhile, created an undercurrent of dissatisfaction, prompting B. L. Gildersleeve to lead a revolt against Whitney's policies. He began this with his address as the Association's outgoing president in 1878 — which took place while Whitney was in Europe preparing his *Sanskrit Grammar*. First of all, Gildersleeve said that the nation's younger philologists needed to be given increased opportunities to publish their work. When the APA refused to oblige him on this matter, Gildersleeve responded by establishing the *American Journal of Philology* the following year. He had help from D. C. Gilman, who would encourage a number of such projects under Johns Hopkins University auspices. Whitney too gave the new journal his blessing, showing a remarkably unruffled demeanor in the face of Gildersleeve's obvious criticism of his APA leadership.[20]

Gildersleeve also charged in his presidential address that the subject matter presented at APA meetings was too miscellaneous in character.[21] The group's founders, Whitney included, had envisaged a forum for "philology" in the widest sense. Yet Gildersleeve wanted the Association to specialize, the growing trend at that time throughout the academic world. The effect of that trend on language study manifested itself in the founding of new, more narrowly focused associations such as the Society of Biblical Literature and Exegesis (1881), the Modern Language Association of America (1883), and, an important promoter of fieldwork in the native American languages, the American Anthropological Association (1888).

Following suit, by the middle of the 1880s the APA had shifted its emphasis to the languages of classical Greece and Rome, the format it has kept ever since. In at least this aspect, Basil Gildersleeve's imprint on the Association long outlasted Whitney's. Whitney continued to contribute papers to be read at the meetings, a number of which would address the Neogrammarian controversy. Yet he retreated from his leadership role as the APA became less relevant to his own interests.

W. D. Whitney made two trips to Europe in the 1870s, the first preparing the way for the second. He had visited in the summer of 1875 to do research on the *Atharva Veda,* yet the trip produced other benefits as well. As we have seen, Whitney made the acquaintance of a number of eminent philologists at this time — including Georg Curtius of Leipzig as well as several of his protégés. One of the latter figures, August Leskien, would soon translate Whitney's *Life and Growth of Language* (1875). Also during that trip, Whitney was commissioned to prepare what would become his *Sanskrit Grammar* (1879). As he proudly noted, this invitation placed him among "some of the best of the younger generation of scholars here."[22]

Whitney returned to Germany three years later in order to produce that work, now accompanied by his wife and his daughters. His passport described a man of fifty-one years and of medium height, with gray eyes, a "high fore-head," sandy hair, and a white beard.[23] It was the beginning of a fifteen-month sojourn. Whitney spent most of this time conferring with his editors, com-posing the Sanskrit grammar, and correcting proof sheets as they emerged from the press. For the task of writing itself, he retired to the quiet city of Gotha. There were also side-trips to Tübingen, Jena, and of course Leipzig, where he again visited Curtius and became acquainted with Hermann Osthoff, Eduard Sievers, and other members of the nascent *Junggrammatiker*. He was already friends with two members of that group, Leskien and Bertholdt Delbrück. As he boasted in private, Delbrück "thinks well of my grammar: we have gone over a good deal of it together." Whitney also worked closely with the Berlin Sanskritist Heinrich Zimmer, who prepared a German edition of the grammar to be published simultaneously with the English version.[24]

It was likely Zimmer who introduced Whitney to yet another young scholar, one who would produce major innovations in linguistic theory. During a visit to Berlin, Whitney met one of Zimmer's young doctoral students, Ferdinand de Saussure. We will see later how Saussure drew inspiration from Whitney's writings as he prepared his celebrated lectures on general linguistics.[25]

Although productive and in many ways pleasant, Whitney's stay in Europe was marred by physical discomfort. Just before leaving the United States, he began experiencing pain in his right arm—an initial warning that he suffered from heart disease. He made few extra excursions during his first months abroad: he skipped, for instance, a Congress of Orientalists in Florence to which his friends tried to lure him. Soon he was seeing a doctor in Heidelberg and was taking extra rest.[26] By thus conserving his strength and carefully regu-lating his work schedule, he brought his *Sanskrit Grammar* to completion. His illness, however, would plague him intermittently to the end of his days.

A final irrelevant note: some events in a life defy categorization because of their palpable incongruity yet invite mention for that very reason. Writing from New Haven several years after his stay in Germany, Whitney reported the fol-lowing to C. R. Lanman: "Oscar W. lunched with us today: a perfectly pleasant fellow, full of interesting talk, and with no affectations that showed." Lanman penciled in the margin: "Oscar Wilde." The visit to the Whitney household occurred during Wilde's American lecture tour in 1882.[27]

## Clearing Ground for the Neogrammarians

Of the various assessments of W. D. Whitney's impact on linguistics, the most intriguing appears in Ferdinand de Saussure's *Cours de linguistique général* (1916). That work would become famous for presenting a new synchronic-structuralist mode of language analysis. Yet this did not mean that Saussure turned his back on historical perspectives, for he always regarded the historically oriented Neogrammarian school as a milestone in the development of modern linguistics. Indeed, he placed that school at the culmination of the brief historical survey of the field with which he opened his lectures. It was in this context that he described Whitney's importance.

According to Saussure, the early comparative philologists had regarded languages in the same way that a botanist regards plants: "Languages were looked upon as belonging to a province of their own, a fourth realm of nature."[28] August Schleicher had pushed this view to its furthest extreme by teaching that closely related languages, like plants of the same genus, necessarily undergo parallel kinds of development. Schleicher had thus been blinded (Saussure said) to the actual histories of various languages. It was therefore a crucial turning point when linguists began to reject this organic-growth schema. Saussure described the beginning of that transition: "Some first steps in the right direction were taken by the American scholar Whitney, the author of *The Life and Growth of Language* (1875). Shortly afterwards a new school arose, the Neogrammarians (*Junggrammatiker*)." That school, Saussure explained, "no longer looked upon a language as an organism developing of its own accord, but saw it as a product of the collective mind of a linguistic community."[29]

Although these remarks were terse, their meaning was clear: Saussure was saying that Whitney had prepared the way for a key aspect of Neogrammarian teaching. The connection was made more explicit in the student notes on which the published *Cours* was based. There, after declaring that the *Junggrammatiker* pointed the field in a "new direction," Saussure added: "The [1875] book by Whitney. . . gave the [or 'an'] impetus."[30] Obviously, Saussure regarded Whitney's *Life and Growth of Language* as a major break with the natural-historical tradition of language study, particularly with the tendency to view languages as developing according to their own internal dynamic. Usually the Neogrammarians themselves receive credit for overthrowing the old biologistic reasoning. Yet as Saussure indicated, they actually followed a path blazed by Whitney. In the pages that follow, I will flesh out this brief allusion to Whitney's "first steps" and show what those steps meant to the Neogrammarians.

Prior to the beginning of the Neogrammarian school, most comparative philologists believed that there had been a long period of degeneration in the universal history of language. Finding higher degrees of linguistic "perfection" the farther back they looked, philologists concluded that the modern European languages had declined from an original state of grammatical completeness and regularity. There was, to be sure, a kind of evidence supporting this thesis, for many latter-day Indo-European languages had in fact lost much of the inflectional apparatus that had characterized their ancestors. Scholars had discovered this pattern during the Renaissance, when they compared the modern Romance languages with the Latin found in ancient texts. It showed itself on a still larger scale when they later compared the Romance, Germanic, and Indic languages with Sanskrit. Few realized at the time that these conclusions were based on limited evidence — those few famous writings that preserved the learned dialect rather than common speech. It therefore seemed reasonable to conclude that the entire Indo-European family had undergone a loss of morphological structure over time. This was the view not only of the first generation of comparative philologists — led by Friedrich Schlegel, Franz Bopp, and Jacob Grimm — but also of their midcentury counterparts, including Ernest Renan, Georg Curtius, August Schleicher, and Max Müller. Curtius reaffirmed the idea as late as 1871: "That the full forms are prior to the weaker forms is the basic, hardly disputable assumption underlying all of comparative grammar."[31]

This downward trend, it was believed, formed part of a two-stage schema in the universal history of language, with loss of structure characterizing only the latter stage. It is important to see that this theory rested on the traditionally short human chronology, the view held prior to the discoveries at Brixham cave and elsewhere in the 1850s. For if humanity had appeared on the scene only shortly before the age that exhibited the fullest linguistic structure, then an initial burst of creativity would have been needed to bring language so quickly to that high state of development. Franz Bopp accordingly believed in a rapid transition from monosyllabic roots to inflectional grammar, a process he described in typically botanical terms: "The grammatical forms and collective organism of the languages are the production of their earliest period of life, when they blossomed forth with the whole strength of youth, like blossoms and fruits from a young stalk." Only afterwards came the era of slow grammatical decay.[32]

August Schleicher did the most to perpetuate this schema after midcentury, despite the fact that he adopted a longer chronology and described the earlier phase as one of gradual development. In the Introduction to his *Die Deutsche Sprache* (1859) and also in his *Compendium der vergleichenden Grammatik der indogermanischen Sprachen* (1861–62), Schleicher posited an initial "prehistoric" phase in each linguistic family's development that saw the production of both a superabundance of root words and a complete regularity of grammatical apparatus. Thereafter, he said, "language declines both in sound and in form."[33] To this Schleicher added the bio-evolutionary framework found in his 1863 *Darwinsche Theorie* pamphlet, but that did not change the essential schema.

More than just a theoretical construct, the life-cycle thesis had practical research implications. Comparative philologists could not be certain of either their methods or results as long as they assumed that linguistic regularity could be found only in the earliest stage of development. That assumption deeply affected each of the two main models of early comparativist study. Franz Bopp's version focused on similarities of word construction as evidence that various languages were genealogically related. In a typical instance, Bopp listed for comparison the singular nominative pronouns ("I"): *ahan* (Sanskrit), *azem* (Zend), *ego* (Latin), *ik* (Gothic), *asz* (Lithuanian), and *az* (Old Sclavonic).[34] Jacob Grimm's version focused on phonological correspondences, particularly in the pronunciation of cognate words or word-parts in various languages. The earliest and most famous discovery of the latter kind was of course Grimm's "Law" of sound shift, which showed how initial *k*'s in Latin and Greek had converted to *h*'s (and so forth) as the Germanic tongues emerged.

It was unclear as of midcentury which of these two research methods was more productive. Bopp's approach still could explain a greater number of linguistic phenomena, while few really consistent patterns of phonological change had yet been discovered other than Grimm's Law or the Great Vowel Shift in early English. On the other hand, Bopp's method had led to a host of improvised, patchwork etymologies. When researchers ran into morphological anomalies the origins of which were difficult to account for on Boppian principles, the convenient solution was to posit an intervening phonological change to supply the missing piece of the etymological puzzle.

This *ad hoc* appeal to sound change raised a fundamental question: Should or should not such changes be expected to manifest law-like regularity, affecting every phonetically similar word in the relevant languages? When employed in makeshift fashion to shore up a difficult etymology, phonological changes appeared, not rule-governed, but rather arbitrary and sporadic. Applied only to a particular situation, they lacked the consistency required to prove a genealogical connection among the affected languages. But then even Jacob Grimm had not regarded phonological correspondences as unfailing "laws." He saw the Germanic consonant shift only as a general tendency that allowed for some exceptions. And Schleicher and Curtius, both of whom called for stricter adherence than Grimm did to the sound law principle, still taught that the known rules did not apply in all cases.[35]

In sum, neither the morphological nor the phonological method of proving kinship-filiation between languages was entirely satisfactory. This state of affairs would continue as long as philologists in both camps distinguished between the primeval "growth" of languages and their subsequent "decay." Again, that schema assumed that complete regularity in both grammar and phonology was to be found only in the earliest period. The subsequent loss of grammatical fullness, it was believed, had been accompanied by phonological changes, bringing a loss of regularity. The early comparativists considered those changes as "disruptive," albeit natural, occurring normally in the course of linguistic history. Hence, it was thought that *any new regularities, introduced later, could not be considered "natural" to a language.* These assumptions about linguistic growth and decay created difficulties for comparativist research pursued in either of its two main modes.

Where did W. D. Whitney stand on these issues? First of all, he vigorously opposed the organic life-cycle thesis. He complained especially about Schleicher's "very peculiar" notion "that language-making and historical activity necessarily belong to different and successive stages in the life of a race or nation."[36] Whitney remonstrated (in a private letter) with his friend Georg Curtius for adopting a similar viewpoint: "What should lead us to suppose the earlier and less cultivated representatives of mankind to have possessed an exceptionally creative mental power? Or that, if they possessed it, they would employ it in inventing a superabundance of words and forms? I do not see that during the historical periods men produce any more language than what they require for the expression of their mental wealth. . . . A paradisiac condition of primitive humanity, in which our ancestors should have been engaged in laying up ideas and words for future use is to me unsupported, even opposed by all evidence."[37]

Here Whitney likened Curtius's viewpoint to Max Müller's belief in an original Eden-like era of spontaneous linguistic (and in Müller's view, religious) creativity.[38] Whitney, of course, based his critique on the uniformitarian principle. As he had always argued, current processes could be projected back to the earliest times, making it superfluous to invoke unknown causes: "The nature and uses of speech, and the forces which act upon it and produce its changes, cannot but have been essentially the same during all the periods of its history, amid all its changing circumstances, in all its varying phases; and there is no way in which its unknown past can be investigated, except by the careful study of its living present and its recorded past, and the extension and application to remote conditions of laws and principles deduced by that study." In short, Whitney stressed the essential unity of linguistic history, "without a break, being of one piece."[39]

Whitney did acknowledge that the Indo-European languages had lost much of their inflectional apparatus since the time of ancient Sanskrit, Greek, and Latin. Even so, he found the larger trend to have been one of increasing complexification. He thus reframed Franz Bopp's combinatory morphology, detaching it from any association with separate historical stages and construing it as a timeless mechanism in accordance with the uniformitarian principle. He did see a kind of growth and decay taking place, yet chiefly at the micro-level, commingled in the continual breaking down of words and recombination of word-parts.

This outlook is best termed *gradualistic* uniformitarianism, for it presupposed not only continuity between past and present but also an abundance of time during which change could occur.[40] The outlook appeared most famously in Lyellian geology; it then entered the study of human history with the revolution in ethnological time. As we have seen, Whitney adopted this backward extension of human time right when he was producing his first writings on general linguistics — and this was what made possible his vision of gradual, straight-line linguistic development from primitive beginnings.

Adopting this same perspective, a younger generation of German philologists found that it was no longer necessary to invoke an initial flowering of language followed by a long period of decline. Like Whitney, they too replaced the ascending and descending arc with a single upward gradient. The group that would employ this new vision of language history most consistently would be the Neogrammarians.

Whitney must have heard rumblings of discontent when he visited Leipzig in the summer of 1875. That next year, August Leskien presented an initial statement of Neogrammarian teaching in his university lectures on Slavic languages.[41] Here Leskien called for a rigorous new approach to comparative-philological investigation, one that would emphasize the absolute regularity of phonological laws. Recently, the Danish linguist Karl Verner had shown that a well-known exception to the Germanic consonant shift was itself systematic in character, and Herman Grassmann had made a similar discovery in 1863. These developments suggested the possibility that *all* of the apparent exceptions to known sound rules actually followed some additional rule of their own. Leskien therefore insisted that any bona fide law of phonological change must apply in its appropriate situation "without exception." In other words, every newly discovered phonological pattern must either be shown to conform to an already-known law or be attributed to a yet-to-be-discovered qualifying condition that itself exhibited law-like regularity.

In this context, Leskien placed new emphasis on the principle of grammatical "analogy." Philologists had long noted the tendency of languages to smooth out irregularities in their inflectional systems. For example, the past tense of the verb *fare* in Middle English had originally been *fōr*, yet later was changed to *fared*, thus bringing it into line with the dominant pattern in modern English.[42] Such extensions of prevailing morphological tendencies promoted greater regularity within a language.

The pioneers of comparative philology had made only sparing use of this principle. They saw analogy as something that occurred only sporadically, and they regarded its regularizing influence as an attempt to artificially repair the grammatical damage that occurred inevitably in the more recent phase of language history. The early comparativists therefore spoke of "false" analogy, because they saw this kind of change as a deceitful guide to the etymological researcher; it obscured, they said, a language's natural path of decay. Even less did the comparativists invoke analogy to explain changes that had occurred in the *early* phase of language development. In that era of grammatical fullness, the theory ran, new regularities would hardly have been needed.

August Leskien, however, insisted that more phenomena could be attributed to the workings of analogy than philologists were accustomed to admitting. Specifically, he recommended analogic analysis as a means of explaining at least some of the so-called exceptions to phonological rules. He regarded analogy as only a secondary means to this end, that is, secondary to invoking subordinate phonological rules—such as "Verner's Law" as a supplement to Grimm's Law. This meant that the use of analogic explanation was permissible only after explanation in terms of sound laws had been exhausted. Still, Leskien argued, analogy added an important element to the total picture: phonological change and analogy were complementary, accounting between themselves for most patterned linguistic changes.[43]

For present purposes, the main question is whether W. D. Whitney's ideas had any impact on Leskien's argument. On one hand, Whitney exerted no influence whatsoever on the strict new conception of sound law. As we have seen, he treated that entire subject quite gingerly, regarding Grimm's Law in particular as "that greatest of phonetic mysteries."[44] He also clung to the traditional view that sound correspondences allowed for exceptions. As he declared in 1874, "every student of phonetic history knows that the tendencies of phonetic change work most irregularly."[45]

Yet while Whitney contributed nothing to the exceptionless sound law doctrine, the situation was different with respect to Leskien's other main point, the revised estimate of grammatical analogy. In an earlier chapter we saw Whitney's own ambivalence on this subject: in both of his major books he said that the creation of new forms via analogy often amounted to "blunders." This was true especially when unschooled adults perpetuated the common errors of children, as in saying "badder" instead of *worse*.[46]

At the same time, however, Whitney also taught that the production of new forms via analogy was a completely normal mode of linguistic development. Not surprisingly, he regarded this as "a case of mental economy: an avoidance of the effort of memory involved in remembering exceptions and observing them accurately in practice." As he flatly concluded in *The Life and Growth of Language* (1875), "The force of analogy is, in fact, one of the most potent in all language-history."[47] This understanding of analogy as a historically normal kind of language change was an outworking of Whitney's uniformitarian principle, especially the notion of continuity throughout the phases of a language's development. Even in its earliest phase, speakers naturally would have extended already-prevailing grammatical paradigms so as to eliminate remaining irregularities.

Most important, Whitney pointed to analogy as a normal method by which regularity is reintroduced into a language in the wake of phonological shifts. He said this clearly in his 1875 book: "When phonetic corruption has disguised too much, or has swept away, the characteristics of a form, so that it becomes an exceptional or anomalous case, there is an inclination to remodel it on a prevailing [grammatical] norm. The greater mass of cases exerts an assimilative influence upon the smaller."[48] Whitney thus brought the analogy principle right to the point at which August Leskien took it up. Leskien, moreover, was doing the German translation of Whitney's book at the same time that he was lecturing on analogy in relation to sound law—a fact that reinforces the case for Whitneyan influence.

Whitney did not receive credit, however, when Karl Brugmann (writing also for Hermann Osthoff) drew up a distinctly polemical statement of Neogrammarian principles two years later, in 1878. This "official" charter of the movement created a sense of generational rebellion, for, like Leskien, Brugmann and Osthoff were implicitly critical of the senior philologists of that era, including their mentor Georg Curtius. Even though Curtius, along with August Schleicher and others, had called for increased attention to grammatical analogy, Brugmann charged that they had not gone far enough. They had failed to recommend analogy as an explanation for apparent exceptions to sound laws—at bottom because they did not consistently apply the uniformitarian method. Brugmann pointed to two philologists who *had* paved the way for this new set of investigative principles: Heymann Steinthal and Wilhelm Scherer (1841–1886), both writing in the 1860s. W. D. Whitney, however, was not mentioned.[49] This neglect probably came in response to Whitney's scathing criticism of Steinthal, whom the Neogrammarians admired. Indeed, some of them—Hermann Paul and Bertholdt Delbrück—were Steinthal's former students.

Another Neogrammarian writer, Eduard Sievers, tried to set the record straight several years later. In an article on comparative philology appearing in the 1885 *Encyclopedia Britannica,* Sievers made up for Brugmann's silence about Whitney's role: "Amongst those who have recently contributed most towards a more correct evaluation of analogy as a motive-power in language, Professor Whitney must be mentioned in the first place." In this area, said Sievers, Wilhelm Scherer actually deserved secondary credit. Still, as Sievers rightly added, Leskien had been the first to envisage analogy and phonological change as "co-ordinate factors" that between themselves explained nearly the whole of linguistic development.[50] Even so, Sievers here suggested that Leskien, hence the Neogrammarians as a group, had built on Whitney's foundations.

Although true as far as it goes, this interpretation actually gives only a partial view of Whitney's contribution to the Neogrammarians. More fundamental was the uniformitarian outlook in which his reassessment of analogy came embedded. The linguist and historian Craig Christy points to a crucial piece of testimony in this regard. The source was Wilhelm Scherer—ironically, one of Karl Brugmann's heroes. In 1875 Scherer wrote a review of the German edition of Whitney's *first* book, that edition having appeared the previous year. Rather than focus on what Whitney had said about analogy, however, Scherer placed his emphasis elsewhere. Important above all was the notion of uniformitarianism, which Scherer described as "this methodological principle of Whitney's." As he noted, Whitney had suggested that the nature and development of language could be studied "really with greater clarity in the most recent periods of language than in the older." And this idea, said Scherer, had been well-known among German linguists for a number of years already: *they had picked it up from reading the original English edition of Whitney's lectures published in 1867.* Scherer recalled having applied the idea himself in a work he wrote the following year.[51]

These remarks are critical for our understanding of Whitney's influence on the Neogrammarians—actually more so than what Eduard Sievers said ten years later in *Encyclopedia Britannica.* Wilhelm Scherer's comments suggest that Whitney's impact did not have to await the publication of his second book and that it involved something deeper than the analogy principle itself. The discussion in Whitney's 1875 volume did probably help confirm August Leskien in his strong emphasis on analogy. But what was conceptually more foundational was the entire uniformitarian view of linguistic development— that, after all, gave the new view of analogy its explanatory power. The idea of essential continuity in the kinds of forces that shape language throughout its history supplied the basic underpinning of the Neogrammarian program: that is, historical continuity was what made phonological change systematic and regularizing rather than piecemeal and disruptive. Furthermore, according to Scherer, German linguists had learned this perspective from Whitney's first book—the work Whitney for years believed was going unappreciated in Europe.

Karl Brugmann actually confirmed this view of Whitney's contribution, beginning, at least implicitly, in his 1878 manifesto. Although he did not mention

Whitney by name in that statement, he did declare that the new relationship between sound law and analogy was "based on a two-fold concept, whose truth is immediately obvious." First, everything in language proceeded from the free activity of speakers: language was "not a thing which leads a life of its own outside of and above human beings." The second idea was the uniformitarian principle.[52]

Brugmann then applied these two themes specifically to the phenomenon of analogy in a passage that shows perhaps better than any other how Whitney cleared a path for the Neogrammarians. Here Brugmann took aim at the organic life-cycle thesis:

> Many believe that analogical formations arise principally in those stages of a language in which the "feeling for the language" has "degenerated" or, as one also says, in which "the awareness of language has grown dim"; and thus they believe that one cannot expect analogical formations in the older periods of a language to the same extent as in the later. A strange way of looking at things! This point of view arose among those who think that a language and the forms of a language lead a life to themselves, apart from the individual speakers, and who permit themselves to be governed to such an extent by terminology that they continually regard metaphorical expressions as reality itself. . . . If someone could once and for all manage to get rid of these generally harmful expressions "youth" and "old age" of languages![53]

Years later, Brugmann finally attached Whitney's name to precisely the two themes just outlined. In his memorial statement after Whitney's death, his praise was somewhat diffuse, yet the main points come through. As we have seen, Brugmann commended Whitney for warning linguists not to "ascribe to language an independent existence"; he also affirmed Whitney's uniformitarian understanding of the "forces" responsible for language change.[54] He enlarged on this latter point in an address he gave at Princeton University in 1897: "Among the many valuable contributions of William Dwight Whitney to linguistic science is one especially important and fundamental principle. It may be stated in these words. In explaining prehistoric phenomena of language we must assume no other factors than those which we are able to observe and estimate in the historical period of language development. The factors that produced changes in human speech five thousand or ten thousand years ago cannot have been essentially different from those which are now operating to transform living languages."[55] It was the same thing Brugmann had said in his manifesto twenty years earlier, only now naming Whitney as a seminal thinker in this area.

A final note on the revolution in human time. Although most historians of the Neogrammarian movement have overlooked the significance of this development, this is not surprising.[56] The *Junggrammatiker* themselves apparently never remarked on it. And it has not been obvious in retrospect for at least two interconnected reasons. First, by the time the younger generation began their careers, historically oriented scholars were presupposing the new chronology without thinking about it. Second, it was treated in most discussions as a component of uniformitarianism, the latter idea being more often recognized and remembered. Hence, uniformitarianism both subsumed and obscured the time revolution. Nevertheless, it was actually here that W. D. Whitney made his most fundamental contribution to the Neogrammarian program — by consistently working out the implications of the new chronology. An abundance of historical time was even more basic than the stress on uniform change, because in order for linguistic change to be uniform, it needs to be extremely gradual.

All that we have seen here helps to unlock the meaning of Ferdinand de Saussure's remark, in his *Cours de linguistique générale,* that the American Whitney had taken "some first steps in the right direction."[57] That reorientation of comparative-historical linguistics actually began nearly a decade prior to the official 1878 advent of the Neogrammarian movement.[58] By then, Whitney's criticisms were already discouraging any return to the notion of a natural linguistic life-cycle. That, at least, would not be the way forward. More positively, Whitney supplied the theory of essential continuity ("without a break, being of one piece") on which Neogrammarian doctrine would be based and on which historical linguistics has been based ever since. These deep connections, however, were not readily apparent at the time, and Whitney found himself perplexed by the way the young Germans were elaborating his principles.

## Seeking an Independent Judgment

Whitney did not respond immediately to the statements about exceptionless sound law issued by August Leskien and Karl Brugmann; in fact, it would be several years before he expressed his opinion on that issue. He did, however, go straight to what he regarded as the real heart of the matter. In a new paper he prepared for the APA in 1877, Whitney gave a discreet rebuttal to Leskien's treatise of the previous year. (He distributed copies of this paper among his German acquaintances via Georg Curtius.) Here Whitney addressed the theoretical problem of what constituted a genuine linguistic "law." He objected to the application of that term to describe phenomena such as the Germanic consonant shift, which occurred only in particular languages or language groups; rather, he said, the term should be reserved for universal and permanent human traits. The chief instance of such a trait was of course the tendency to conserve effort. Whitney judged it unlikely "that any other law of phonetic growth will be established in any degree whatever comparable with it."[59]

Although confident that the least-effort principle furnished the motive underlying almost all forms of language change, Whitney conceded that "the details of this working are . . . not a little obscure." Many such changes were "national idiosyncrasies, results of such subtle differences of organization, influences of circumstances and habit, whim and accident even, that . . . will ever baffle the study of the investigator." Hence, what was easy to enunciate or sounded euphonious to one language group often was not so to another. The tendency to conserve effort thus assumed a bewildering variety of guises. All the same, Whitney argued, these considerations did not rule out its universality. A right-minded researcher "will not think of ascribing them [sound changes] in his perplexity to any other agency than that which brings about such phonetic changes as are most obviously a relief to the human organs."[60]

It was in the next year that Karl Brugmann and Hermann Osthoff published their manifesto. Here, in addition to the Whitneyesque themes we have seen already, Brugmann stressed Leskien's new teaching: "Only he who adheres strictly to the principle of sound laws [*Lautgesetze*], this mainstay of our whole science, has firm ground under his feet in his investigations." To continue to admit unaccounted-for exceptions, as philologists had been accustomed to doing, was to perpetuate "subjectivism and arbitrariness."[61] The younger scholars conceded that they were far from being able to explain all exceptions. Yet Brugmann saw this as no reason to deny the existence of "mechanical sound laws." He also joined Leskien in calling for a more careful coordination between phonological change and morphological analogy; heretofore, he charged, researchers had employed the analogy principle too sporadically. Finally, Brugmann urged linguists to strictly separate these phenomena according to their two underlying causes — speech physiology seen as explaining sound change, and mental assimilation (a psychological process) explaining analogic leveling.[62]

W. D. Whitney no doubt saw a number of things to agree with in Brugmann's manifesto: its uniformitarianism, its rejection of biological imagery, and its acknowledgment that individual speakers were the real source of linguistic events. He also would have appreciated the emphasis on coordinating analogy and phonological change. Yet he was still skeptical. Especially problematic was Brugmann's mechanistic view of phonological activity, with its exclusive appeal to physical-articulatory factors. In a sympathetic letter to Curtius the next year, Whitney admitted that he was not fully conversant with the new theories, but he said that thus far they struck him "very strangely." Preoccupied of late with his *Sanskrit Grammar,* he looked forward to a time when he could form "an independent and competent judgment" on the matter.[63]

Further statements from the Neogrammarians solved some of the problems in their theoretical outlook, even while adding new ones. The years 1880 and 1881 saw the appearance of two major treatises, in which Hermann Paul and Bertoldt Delbrück (respectively) tried to meet the objections raised thus far in Europe. Delbrück, for instance, acknowledged that the idea of exceptionless sound rules was dogmatic and said its real value lay in promoting investigative rigor. He also conceded that so-called phonological laws really were "nothing but uniformities which appear in a certain language and period, for which alone they are valid. Whether the expression 'law' is really applicable here is doubtful." Still, he said, the term should be retained because it had already become fixed in scholarly usage.[64]

The most intriguing aspect of these statements concerned the role of the individual in producing language change. To a degree the Neogrammarians said many of the same things Whitney did. Brugmann, as we saw, began in this direction; and both Delbrück and Paul went further. Delbrück affirmed that every language was a collection of idiolects, and he and Paul each sketched out the basics of an interactionist linguistic sociology.[65] Delbrück, however, went on to confront a special challenge. According to the Neogrammarians, the strict operation of sound laws meant that a language's phonological system was absolutely regular at any point in time.[66] Yet as critics noted, phonological changes usually had to work their way through a speech community, a process of *populational diffusion.* The implication was that changes did not affect the speech of an entire community all at once, and in this sense "a language" was never homogeneously regular.

Delbrück contrived to skirt this problem by adding a bold qualification to the original Neogrammarian principle: "We must therefore confess at the outset that a homogeneous language in its strictest sense can only exist in the individual." He was obliged, therefore, to reformulate the question concerning exceptionless sound laws. He now put the matter thus: "Can it be expected, *in the case of the single individual,* that phonetic change will take place in a perfectly uniform and regular manner?" Even with the issue restricted in this way, an affirmative answer could be given only after making a further stipulation: "If we wish to be quite exact," said Delbrück, perfectly regular phonological patterns could be found "only in the average speech of an individual *at any one moment.*"[67]

This was an ingenious yet problematic pair of expedients. First, Delbrück had created an abstract, isolated individual. His theory therefore had little relevance for the investigation of actual speech situations. Second, he narrowed the case down to a single moment in time. Yet even after adding this further qualification, Delbrück still could not rule out the phenomenon of *lexical diffusion* — the slow spread of phonological changes, not through a population but through an individual speaker's word inventory. Hence, a speaker often gave noticeably different pronunciations, *at the same time,* to two morphologically similar words, such as *bone* and *stone.* (The issue in this case would be different vowel pronunciations.) As a result, Delbrück's proposed restriction of sound laws to single individuals, even at only a moment in time, still could not fully satisfy the criterion of exceptionlessness.

W. D. Whitney must have felt ambivalent about Delbrück's new book, his *Einleitung in das Sprachstudium* (1881). He arranged for a favorable review to appear in the *American Journal of Philology,* a sign of at least guarded acceptance.[68] After all, Delbrück's trimmed-down Neogrammarianism reflected his own outlook to some extent. Yet Whitney was still not ready to give a full assessment of the new movement. Writing to Georg Curtius again in the fall of 1881, he assured him of his continued respect, "and this whether there shall finally prove to be more or less of truth in the new doctrines which are now attracting attention. I have been for some years past so absorbed in special Sanskrit work that I do not feel myself competent really to criticize and judge those doctrines; at present they rather confound and in part repel me."[69]

Once again, therefore, Whitney fell back on what he sure of: he came out with another discussion of economy-of-effort. For their part, the Neogrammarians doubted that this principle could account for all phonological changes. As proof, they cited cases of apparent strengthening rather than weakening of articulation. Delbrück, Osthoff, and especially Eduard Sievers, in his *Grundzüge der Phonetik* (1881), looked specifically at the relationship between *sonants* and *surds,* voiced and unvoiced consonants. Historical instances of sound shift from the sonant *b* to the surd *p* appeared to demonstrate an increase in effort because of the latter's more forceful aspiration.

Replying to Sievers in a new article, Whitney declared that sonants and surds could not be differentiated in terms of the effort expended because the *p* really was no more difficult to enunciate than the *b.* The voiced *b,* he argued, required the same amount of energy, only instead of being directed toward an explosive aspiration, it was used to activate the vocal chords. Also, the relative strength accorded the two types of sound could be affected by syllabic accent: in the word *biped,* for instance, the *b* actually was stronger than the *p.* Whitney concluded that the universal ease-of-effort principle still held if applied the way in which sounds were combined in continuous speech.[70]

Reports from Leipzig during this period kept Whitney apprised of the situation there. One informant was his sister Maria, who had come to Germany to pursue her own linguistic studies while Whitney was there preparing his *Sanskrit Grammar.* She stayed behind when he and his family returned home. Maria Whitney roomed in the Curtius household during part of this time, thereby gaining a unique perspective on the Neogrammarian revolt. She witnessed especially the personal strain it placed on her host: "Mrs. C. tells me that he has taken the defection of some of his best pupils greatly to heart, and their attacks upon him seem to him directed against him personally as much as against the views he represents." Another of Whitney's correspondents, a former student, reported in 1882 that the *Junggrammatiker* were "gaining slowly but surely on the old school."[71] Whitney, however, was not swayed, and he continued to ponder what shape his "judgment on the main question" should assume.

## The *Lautgesetz* Controversy in America

The new teachings from Germany eventually touched off debate in America, centered around the question of exceptionless sound laws. Some writers, such as Maurice Bloomfield, sought to balance doubts about the Neogrammarians as theorists with admiration for their practical accomplishments. (This eventually became the majority response among linguists.) Bloomfield noted in 1884 that the exceptionlessness principle constituted "a dogma which from the nature of the case will never be proved." Still, he said, that dogma had stiffened the backs of researchers. Similarly, F. A. March described the exceptionlessness principle as a "working hypothesis" which, by being insisted upon in practice, had "led to great results."[72]

W. D. Whitney, however, could not agree with this tolerant stance. Not surprisingly, he had come to regard the exceptionlessness principle as yet another rejection of the idea that human volition lay at the root of all linguistic behavior. The Neogrammarians themselves denied this: they disowned the Schleicherian view of language as an organism of nature, and they affirmed that language was a social institution. Yet at the same time they talked of "mechanical" sound laws, and of phonological behavior as being governed by vocal physiology. In this light, their declarations about language's social character, at least for Whitney, were devoid of real meaning. Whitney had little interest, however, in another public fight with European linguists. Besides, the Neogrammarians were scholars he knew and in large part respected, and two of them — Delbrück and Leskien — were his personal friends. He therefore continued to work indirectly, only now recruiting two young allies to help handle the polemics.

The first of these was Morton W. Easton, a former graduate student of Whitney's and a professor of classical languages at a college in Tennessee. Easton wrote an 1884 article on the sound law question, in which he made two especially important points. First, he charged the Neogrammarians with viewing sound change as "a phonetic epidemic seizing the entire community at once" — thus keeping alive the issue that Bertoldt Delbrück had tried to put to rest. Second, Easton said that it was arbitrary to draw a bright line between sound laws based on purely phonetic (physical) causes and grammatical analogy based on purely psychological causes. In practice, every case of analogy had a phonetic manifestation, and every phonological change had its psychological motive — even if the latter was hidden from the observer's view.[73]

Two years after Easton's article appeared, Whitney teamed up with his other young ally, Frank B. Tarbell, to mount a coordinated assault. A former student like Easton, Tarbell was a professor of logic and classical languages at Yale.[74] We should picture the two men colluding together at Whitney's home in New Haven — since Whitney's health was poor at this time. The result was two articles, appearing in tandem in the 1886 *Transactions of the American Philological Association*.

Whitney took the lead, although he still wanted to appear above the fray.

Hence, he made no mention of the Neogrammarians, either individually or as a group. And in large part he reaffirmed familiar themes. With sage-like patience, he insisted once again on the voluntary character of language change. He acknowledged that articulatory factors played a role in shaping speech behavior, yet he said that these were not its main determinants: "There can be no question here, as among things purely physical, of such a law as 'like causes produce like effects'; because we have not to do with physical causes, but with causers, human beings, no one of whom is like any other, in any such manner and degree as should compel accordant action in changing the uttered signs of a language or their meanings." Whitney, of course, believed that uniform human nature gave language certain general tendencies, but he denied that these were the same as deterministic laws. Phonological behavior therefore had a dimension of contingency and free play: "To introduce any element of necessity into such processes, like the necessities that connect cause and effect in the physical world, is a regrettable error."[75]

The argument here was familiar, but the application was new. Gone was the concern about linguistics being regarded as a physical science: that issue had mostly been put to rest. The problem at this point with a doctrine of necessity (even if only implied) was its incompatibility with a genuinely social approach. Accordingly, Whitney now emphasized certain on-the-ground implications of his sociology of language. Like M. W. Easton he opposed the idea that phonological changes proceed like an "epidemic" that suddenly seizes every member of a community. This, he believed, failed to take into account the reality of communicative interaction. Because of that reality, speech innovations had to spread gradually through the mass of speakers:

> Since change of uttered form, like changes of significance, consists in a modification of habit on the part of a whole community, it can obviously take place only by degrees. There is no conceivable inducement that can move simultaneously and uniformly all the members of a community. At any given time, while certain changes of recent origin have established themselves in general usage, there must be others which have only partially won acceptance, and yet others which are [only] beginning to show themselves as candidates for acceptance. Even in the most homogeneous communities, the diversities of pronunciation are endless.[76]

By invoking this phenomenon of populational diffusion (involving "all the members of a community"), Whitney countered at least one of the shortcomings of the Neogrammarians' uniformity doctrine.

Then he blended in the second kind of diffusion. Here he responded to Bertoldt Delbrück's contention that invariable sound laws applied at least in the speech of an individual at a given point in time: "The [so-called] invariability of a given change of utterance of an alphabetic element, in the mouth of an individual and then of a community, means only that such a shift of pronunciation is pretty sure, and the surer according to its importance and conspicuousness, to spread finally through the whole body of occurrences of the element in question."[77] With these final words ("the whole body of occurrences of the element in question"), Whitney added the phenomenon of lexical diffusion — the gradual spread of an innovation, not just person-to-person but also word-to-word within the speech behavior of both an individual and a group.

Whitney's colleague Frank Tarbell took up the discussion at this point, specifically naming Delbrück as his target. He framed the issue thus: "The discussion as to the uniformity of phonetic law leads to an important question touching the origin and propagation of phonetic change. The question is this: Do changes begin with individual words, and spread from these until whole classes of words are affected, or do they attack simultaneously all words in which the same essential phonetic conditions occur? The latter alternative must almost necessarily be adopted by the believers in strict phonetic uniformity."[78]

Tarbell's main contribution was to offer actual evidence for the first of these positions: this he found in New England dialect. He pointed to the inconsistency with which individual speakers employed "the peculiar New England *o*." This short vowel sound appeared in words such as *stone, most,* and *toad*—but not invariably. The striking fact, Tarbell noted, was that "in hardly any two localities do we find this *o* pronounced in the same list of words."[79] His conclusion: "Differences such as this strongly suggest that the reduction of *o* to New England *o* has not, in the speech of any individual, attacked simultaneously a number of words constituting a single class by virtue of the presence of identical phonetic conditions, but has progressed, differently in different places, from word to word."[80] With these remarks, Frank Tarbell set forth perhaps the earliest description of the lexical diffusion concept by an English-language writer.

Tarbell, however, clearly had help from W. D. Whitney. As early as 1867, Whitney had solicited data on the pronunciation of words such as *home, whole,* and *stone* in Philadelphia as compared with New England, showing that he had long been interested in this phenomenon.[81] He would later use these same examples in an article of his own, once again in order to confront the Neogrammarians. As it turned out, this would be his final published work in general linguistics.

## Between Two Conceptions of Science

As he responded to the new teaching about phonological laws, Whitney also weighed the idea of scientific law as such, particularly as applied to society. He actually stood astride two competing versions of that idea, these marking the two poles of a crucial transition in modern thought. Like the word *science* itself, the concept of scientific *law* was undergoing a change of definition during Whitney's lifetime. In the seventeenth century, European thinkers had figuratively banished arbitrary power from the universe, thus converting nature's ruler into a constitutional monarch. Most still believed in the divine governance of the natural order, yet they now saw this as *government by law*.[82] By the mid-nineteenth century, however, the law trope was losing its substance. The new tendency was to regard laws, not as extensions of divine power ordained prior to the events they affected, but as patterns discovered only after the fact.[83] The governmental aspect increasingly became merely rhetorical, and the term *law,* in this context, was reduced to a faded metaphor.

We may sum up the transition thus: in their understanding of nature, the spokesmen for the scientific revolution had replaced arbitrary *government without law* with *government by law;* the nineteenth century then saw a shift toward *law without government.* This last phase excluded the notion of divine superintendence — or at least it relegated the divine to the private realm of a scientist's conscience. In addition, and especially important for our purpose, this view suggested that causal agency itself was no longer necessary — indeed, was a hindrance — to the idea of a truly "scientific" law.

The point is that W. D. Whitney stood poised between two worlds. On the one hand he actually retained the essence of the traditional government-by-law idea. (As with the word *science,* he again held fast to an old and weakening definition.) Of course Whitney made no appeal to divine providence as the causer of linguistic events, yet he did regard "human nature" as performing essentially this same function. That is, he kept to the old-fashioned view of human nature as an ultimate and irreducible motive force, as the causal agency behind linguistic "laws" such as ease-of-utterance. This he still considered to be legitimate scientific procedure. Reasoning of this kind would appear quaint

SCALE AND RATE OF FREQUENCY OF ENGLISH SOUNDS.

| Con-sonant. | Vowel. | Per Cent. | Per Cent. | Minimum. | | Maximum. | |
|---|---|---|---|---|---|---|---|
| r | .. | 7.44 | .. | VI. | 5.4 | VIII. | 9.3 |
| n | .. | 6.76 | .. | III. | 5.7 | IX. | 7.9 |
| t | .. | 5.93 | .. | VI. | 4.6 | II. | 8.9 |
| .. | i | .. | 5.90 | VI. | 4.7 | VII. | 7.4 |
| .. | ə | .. | 5.66 | II. | 4.3 | I., VII. | 6.9 |
| d | .. | 4.94 | .. | I. | 4.0 | V. | 5.8 |
| s | .. | 4.69 | .. | III., VIII. | 3.7 | I., II. | 5.8 |
| l | .. | 3.84 | .. | I., VII. | 2.5 | III. | 6.2 |
| dh | .. | 3.83 | .. | VIII. | 2.4 | III. | 5.1 |
| .. | ĕ | .. | 3.34 | I.–III. | 2.6 | IX. | 4.7 |
| .. | æ | .. | 3.32 | III. | 2.4 | VIII. | 4.0 |
| m | .. | 3.06 | .. | VIII. | 1.8 | I. | 4.1 |
| z | .. | 2.92 | .. | VI. | 2.2 | I. | 4.3 |
| .. | i | .. | 2.80 | VII., IX. | 1.5 | VI. | 4.8 |
| .. | ă | .. | 2.59 | IV., IX. | 1.8 | VII. | 4.2 |
| v | .. | 2.37 | .. | I. | 1.4 | I. | 3.5 |
| h | .. | 2.34 | .. | IX. | 1.2 | V. | 3.1 |
| w | .. | 2.31 | .. | III. | 1.6 | VIII. | 3.0 |
| k | .. | 2.17 | .. | II. | 1.1 | X. | 3.1 |
| f | .. | 2.06 | .. | IV., VII. | 1.2 | II. | 2.8 |
| .. | ŭ | .. | 2.00 | VI. | 1.1 | I. | 3.5 |
| .. | ai | .. | 1.91 | IX. | .9 | VI. | 4.8 |
| .. | æ | .. | 1.85 | I. | .9 | VIII. | 2.5 |
| .. | ŏ | .. | 1.76 | X. | .9 | III. | 2.6 |
| p | .. | 1.71 | .. | V. | 1.0 | VII. | 2.6 |
| b | .. | 1.64 | .. | IX. | 1.0 | I. | 3.4 |
| .. | ē | .. | 1.61 | I. | .5 | X. | 2.7 |
| .. | ʌ | .. | 1.54 | X. | .8 | II. | 2.2 |
| sh | .. | .86 | .. | II. | .1 | IV. | 1.8 |
| .. | au | .. | .83 | X. | .3 | III., IV. | 1.3 |
| g | .. | .79 | .. | VII., IX. | .3 | VIII. | 1.6 |
| ng | .. | .79 | .. | I. | .1 | III., VIII. | 1.4 |
| y | .. | .66 | .. | IX. | .3 | IV. | 1.1 |
| ih | .. | .58 | .. | VIII. | .2 | IV. | 1.0 |
| .. | a | .. | .56 | VIII., X. | .1 | IX. | 1.2 |
| ch | .. | .53 | .. | I., II. | .1 | VIII. | 1.2 |
| .. | Æ | .. | .47 | VII. | .0 | III. | 1.4 |
| j | .. | .47 | .. | VI. | .1 | IX. | .9 |
| .. | ŭ | .. | .44 | IX., X. | .2 | VIII. | 1.2 |
| .. | ḷ | .. | .35 | VII. | .1 | I. | .7 |
| .. | ṇ | .. | .16 | I., III., X. | .0 | II., VII., IX. | .3 |
| .. | ȧi | .. | .12 | I., II., VIII. | .0 | III.–VI., IX. | .2 |
| .. | ŏ | .. | .08 | II., IV., VI., VII. | .0 | I., III. | .2 |
| zh | .. | .02 | .. | I.–VIII. | .0 | IX., X. | .1 |
| | | 62.71 | 37.29 | | | | |

Table from Whitney's "Proportional Elements of English Utterance," published in *Proceedings of the American Philological Association* (1874).

at best by the standards of twentieth-century-style positivism. From that viewpoint, it would hardly be considered valid to explain social phenomena by appeal to some innate human proclivity.[84]

On the other hand, Whitney also hinted at the newer view of *law* in his efforts to quantify grammatical and phonological patterns. He did this mainly through statistically oriented Indological investigations, including sections of his *Sanskrit Grammar*.[85] Similarly, in a long 1874 essay on "The Proportional Elements of English Utterance," Whitney tabulated the average frequency of each sound in that language's "spoken alphabet" with data he gathered by conducting his own recitations of passages from modern English literature.[86]

Through these projects, Whitney reflected the trend toward quantification in the social sciences as a whole—a trend which in turn reflected the new understanding of scientific "law." By the end of the century, laws of society were construed in this descriptive sense only, avoiding any appeal to the innate characteristics of man or society.[87] Whitney, however, still believed in the human essence behind the numbers. Even as he experimented with the new methods, he did not abandon the Common-Sense appeal to human nature as the motivating force behind—hence the ultimate explanation of—law-like speech patterns. In spite of himself, he thereby retained vestiges of an older "metaphysical" spirit.

# CHAPTER TEN

# Enduring Legacies

The kind of complexity seen in W. D. Whitney's relationship with the Neo-grammarian movement appeared as well in the other main facets of his legacy. The similarity in the case of Ferdinand de Saussure was especially strikingly. Here again, Whitney laid essential foundations, even though the better-known features of Saussurean doctrine represented a denial of his viewpoint. This turning away from Whitney's ideas was widespread: it occurred in structuralist linguistics as a whole and also in twentieth-century cultural and anthropological theory. Eventually, however, a major revival of Whitneyan outlook accompanied the rise of sociolinguistics. A further, albeit more diffuse legacy appeared, not in any school of linguistic thought, but in the research orientation of the modern American university. There Whitney's influence ran deep, so much so that it has remained largely hidden from later view.

## Final Projects

W. D. Whitney continued in his later years to produce scholarship in a variety of fields. He had long done creditable work as a writer of modern language textbooks, although much of this was a burden borne of necessity. He had described his German grammar and reader of 1870 as "bread work"; similarly, his *Practical French Grammar* (1886) was purely "a money affair." He said while preparing the latter volume: "I detest the job. It is going to keep me in hot water for some time to come."[1] Far more welcoming was Whitney's attitude toward projects dealing with the English language. He felt that he had made a significant intellectual contribution in this area with his *Essentials of English Grammar* (1877), in which he jettisoned many of the traditional Latin-based grammatical categories. He was also interested in English lexicography. Inspired by the St. Petersburg Sanskrit *Wörterbuch,* he dreamed of giving his own language a similarly thorough treatment.[2]

His chance to do this came in 1884 when the Century Publishing Company undertook the first major advance in American dictionary-making since the 1869 edition of Webster's. The result was the seven-volume *Century Dictionary* (1889–91), prepared under Whitney's general oversight. Whitney and the company's directors agreed that their guiding principle should be inclusiveness according to current American usage. With a word total of about 200,000, the *Century Dictionary* contained an unprecedented number of provincial and colloquial words as well as many new technical and scientific terms. (For this reason, early editions of the *Oxford English Dictionary* cited the work some 2,100 times.) All of this called for a prodigious effort on Whitney's part. His health broke soon after he took on the project, obliging him to lean heavily on his managing editor, Benjamin Eli Smith (1857–1913). Even so, associates testified that Whitney read all 21,138 columns of page proof.[3]

The definitions for the *Century Dictionary* were written by a corps of some thirty scholars and scientists, probably the most eminent group assembled for such a purpose in nineteenth-century America. Among these, Josiah Whitney did the words related to geology, mining, and metallurgy; and W. D. Whitney himself wrote on philology, ethnology, and anthropology. What interests us especially is the contribution of Charles Sanders Peirce (1839–1914) of the U.S. Coast and Geodetic Survey, who was responsible for definitions in logic, metaphysics, mathematics, and astronomy as well as weights and measures. The erratic genius Peirce was perhaps the country's most original thinker of that era. He is remembered especially as a member of the Boston-Cambridge "Metaphysical Club" and as a formulator, along with William James, of pragmatist philosophy. Peirce was also America's leading writer on "semiotics," or sign theory, a field with implications for the symbolic nature of language.

As the initial volumes of the *Century Dictionary* appeared, so did criticism: the Johns Hopkins astronomer Simon Newcomb (1835–1909) charged that a number of the definitions in the physical sciences were either inaccurate or confusing. Whitney was distressed to hear this, although as he told Benjamin E. Smith, some reviewers, and even some of their own contributors, held overly exacting standards: "Prof. Peirce would, if we had let him, have swamped the book with the rarest and unknown star-names." Yet as Whitney soon learned, it was Peirce himself who had written the impugned definitions.[4] Josiah Whitney looked into the matter and confirmed Newcomb's judgment. He told his brother that the descriptions of astronomical instruments and weights and measures "have been bad and sometimes ludicrously so." Peirce blamed the editors, claiming that he had not been given sufficient time to revise all of his proof sheets. W. D. Whitney accepted final responsibility and lamented that corrections would have to await the dictionary's second edition.[5] Thus ended what was apparently the only collaboration between Whitney and C. S. Peirce, having no reference to sign theory and disagreeable to both parties.

Comparatively little needs to be said about Whitney's later writings on general linguistics. His most important contribution in this period was the essay "Philology: The Science of Language in General," prepared for the ninth (1885) edition of *Encyclopedia Britannica.* This work not only gave a thorough summation of Whitney's theoretical system, but it represented the clear-cut triumph of his views among the English-speaking arbiters of knowledge. Even London's *Atheneum* now abandoned Max Müller and swung solidly behind Whitney, hailing him as "certainly the highest living authority" on linguistic science. The *Britannica* would reprint Whitney's article up until its fourteenth edition, in 1929.[6]

The *Britannica* essay also contributed to the ongoing debate about language and human origins. Charles Darwin had died in 1882, but his disciple George John Romanes continued to battle Max Müller on that subject. In his book *Mental Evolution in Man* (1888), Romanes cited Whitney's imitative theory of speech origins as well as his refutation of Müller's belief that rational thought could not have developed without speech — taking as his source Whitney's encyclopedia essay.[7] The Romanes book, however, represented the high-water mark of Whitney's influence on the origin-of-language question. The imitative theory received mixed reviews in the years thereafter, and it generally fell out of favor in the early twentieth century.[8]

Whitney added a final chapter to his own long-running battle with Mül-ler when he published, at his own expense, an eighty-page response to a new (1892) reprint of Müller's *Lectures on the Science of Language.* Whitney's views had not changed one iota. As he told Josiah, this latest rebuttal allowed him to "inculcate once more certain cardinal principles which I have greatly at heart, and was seeking fit opportunity for stating anew." He made sure, moreover, that his voice would be heard: he sent copies of the new work to over 200 corre-spondents in Europe and the United States. One of the recipients, his old APA colleague and occasional disputant F. A. March, thanked Whitney and gave the new essay a guarded yet fitting assessment: "I feel sure that it will do a good part towards keeping clear the orthodox views of the Science of Language."[9]

Indological projects claimed the greatest share of Whitney's attention in these years. Here too, he stayed in character: there was no change in his gener-ally low opinion of traditional Indian literature, grammatical scholarship, and textual exegesis.[10] Most philologists were beginning to reject these negative judgments, especially of Indian linguistic science. Yet they could not discount Whitney's own technical accomplishments; the reception given his *Sanskrit Grammar* was especially favorable.[11] Describing that work as his "daily com-panion," the British phoneticist Henry Sweet told Whitney that he considered it "one of the greatest boons that have ever been conferred on the comparative philologist as well as the Sanskrit specialist."[12] Indeed, the *Grammar* led to the highest public recognition Whitney would ever receive, his election as a For-eign Knight of the Prussian Order *Pour le Mérite* in the Arts and Sciences. (Karl Lepsius of the University of Berlin had first made the nomination years earlier, but a vacancy was needed. This was supplied by the death of the British histo-rian Thomas Carlyle in 1881.) Whitney revised his *Sanskrit Grammar* in 1882, and in this form it would long do service. It was reprinted, without additional changes, in 1975.[13]

Once his labors on the *Grammar* were behind him, Whitney longed to com-plete the *Atharva Veda* edition, the work he had begun decades earlier in col-laboration with Rudolph von Roth. The plan all along had been to add a vol-ume of critical and explanatory material to accompany the text published in 1855. Whitney wanted to begin this task immediately, yet Roth, who had finally completed his own duties with the St. Petersburg lexicon, became distracted (once again) by other projects.[14] Reluctant to press his old teacher, and com-plaining in private of Roth's "awfully *hochmütig* [arrogant] and obstinate" manner, Whitney decided to go it alone. He was in hopes of finishing the work within a few years. Poor health dragged him down, however, and then he became sidetracked himself by the *Century Dictionary.*[15] As a result, he made little progress on the *Atharva* until the early 1890s.

## Triumph and Decline

In 1884 the American Oriental Society elected W. D. Whitney as its president, an office he would hold for the next six years. As his old patron E. E. Salisbury noted, this honor would have been conferred much earlier but for the importance of Whitney's work as the Society's corresponding secretary. That post, which included responsibility for AOS publications, now went to Charles Lanman.[16] Whitney was pleased with this arrangement since it allowed him to retain personal control over the Society's main business.

As it turned out, Lanman's help would be needed more than ever, for it was just after Whitney became AOS president that his health began to fail. At first only on crutches, he soon was confined to bed and for a considerable period was obliged to have his right foot suspended above the level of his heart. (It was from this position that he did much of the editing of the *Century Dictionary.*) Time and rest brought improvement: he was able to work half-days in the spring of 1887, and he resumed teaching the next fall, holding classes in his home. Still, the most debilitating effect of the illness remained: Whitney was obliged to absent himself from AOS meetings during the whole of his presidency. Prior to this, he had not missed a meeting in thirty-two years, except during periods when he was abroad. After his doctor refused him permission to attend the fall of '89 session in New York, his response was poignant: "Now I shall begin to hope about next May."[17]

Under these conditions, Whitney's dependence on C. R. Lanman was nearly total. The two men conferred on AOS matters at least once a week for over a decade, their letters shuttling between New Haven and Cambridge. Sometimes Whitney grew petulant. He knew just how he wanted the *Proceedings* handled, and he once berated Lanman: "I wish you had been a little freer about consulting me this time *before* printing. I have thirty-one years of experience in dealing with such things." Usually more patient, he was always exacting: he cast a frugal eye, for instance, on all expenses.[18]

Such details aside, Whitney's main goal as AOS president was to bring the Society's thematic content more into line with what he considered to be genuinely "Oriental." That term was being used to cover an increasing range of scholarly territory in this period, a result of the burgeoning knowledge of ancient and non-Western cultures in the wake of resurgent European imperialism. The Near East attracted particular interest. Yet Whitney wanted to keep Indology at the forefront of Orientalist studies, especially within the AOS. A look at the Society's *Proceedings* from this period suggests the challenge he faced. There were five types of papers delivered in the years between 1880 and 1900. Those dealing with Sanskrit and Zend-Avestan continued to be, by far, the largest in number. There were also a smattering of contributions on Chinese and Tibetan Buddhist subjects, a number touching on biblical Hebrew, and another handful on archaeological discoveries related to classical antiquity.

Whitney did not object to a degree of topical breadth in the Society: he encouraged, for instance, the addition of Buddhist studies. Yet a problem rose because of papers in the fifth category, which had been increasing in number and now were second only to those having to do with Sanskrit. These dealt with the ancient Assyrian and Babylonian languages, a relatively new branch of Semitic studies. Representing this field was a small but dedicated cohort, among them Whitney's friend William Hayes Ward (1835–1916), who labored by day as editor of the New York *Independent*. Others included the German immigrant Paul Haupt and Haupt's student Cyrus Adler (1863–1940), both professors at Johns Hopkins University, and Morris Jastrow (1861–1921), who taught at the University of Pennsylvania. An additional Semitics field was the study of rabbinical literature, represented by Richard J. H. Gottheil (1862–1936) of Columbia University. These last four scholars all began their careers in the mid-1880s and (along with W. H. Ward) frequently presented their research at AOS meetings. As a result, out of 263 papers presented in that decade, 101 — well over a third — were in some sense Semitic, dealing with Assyrian, Babylonian, or Hebrew language and literature. It was this situation that made Whitney want to tighten the definition of "Oriental" scholarship.

A preliminary task was to restrict the number of general-interest biblical papers — a survival of earlier days when the Society's membership included a large number of clergymen. Whitney had already used his position as corresponding secretary to keep such papers out of the *Proceedings,* and after he became president, he excluded them from the meetings themselves. In a typical instance, he instructed C. R. Lanman to advise a Society member of "the brevity, the non-Biblical, and the scientific character" of the material being sought for presentation. If a paper on a biblical subject was of high quality, Whitney would sometimes recommend that it be abstracted in the *Proceedings* and sent to William Rainey Harper's journal *Hebraica* for full publication. More commonly, he wanted Hebrew-related papers excluded altogether: most of them, he said, were "Biblical rather than Oriental."[19]

Whitney's larger goal was to reduce the Society's involvement with Semitics topics as a whole. There was an invidious aspect to this campaign, for in private Whitney used terms related to "Semitic" equivocally, to describe not only a family of languages but also an ethnic identity. Following the Society's semi-annual meeting in 1888, for instance, he complained that "the Semites are piling in hot and heavy; more than half the papers were by them." He soon learned, moreover, that an issue of the *Proceedings* was appearing without a single item bearing on Sanskrit. Writing to Lanman, who was then on a visit to Europe, Whitney sounded the alarm: "The Soc'y has pretty much turned into a Semitic club. But that is our fault, or misfortune; you will have to go to work when you get home to help keep up our end of the load."[20]

The Semitics scholars saw their papers duly abstracted in the *Proceedings,* but what they really wanted was full publication in the *Journal:* that was the sticking point. They chafed at the fact that the *Journal* came out only once per year, not often enough, they said, to meet the publication needs of the entire organization. It was the same problem Basil Gildersleeve had noted over a decade earlier when he urged the American Philological Association to provide more publication opportunities for rising scholars. Since then the pressure had only increased for faculty in the emerging research universities. Even with the new specialized journals being created in this period, many found that they were not able to get their work into print. And in this environment of growing need, W. D. Whitney's narrow definition of the Orientalist field was actively restricting opportunity within the AOS. Speaking for the group's Assyriologists, Cyrus Adler suggested that that specialty deserved greater visibility than the Society was giving it.[21] Yet Adler surely was aware that not everyone in the field felt this restraint. W. H. Ward, especially, had no difficulty getting *his* work into the *Journal.*

These tensions (at least in part) finally became public, beginning at the Society's annual meeting in 1890. The timing was not accidental. It was announced on that occasion that Whitney would decline re-election as AOS president. As he told Lanman, "I see no chance of my ever getting to another meeting."[22] In his place the members elected W. H. Ward, who was Whitney's choice of successor, and for vice president they picked Daniel Coit Gilman, an old AOS stalwart and a well-respected name. They returned Lanman to his post as corresponding secretary and consoled Whitney by giving him the powerful chairmanship of the Publication Committee.

These matters settled, Cyrus Adler rose to speak. He moved that the AOS seek a new corporate charter, to be granted by the United States rather than the Massachusetts government. The reasons for this proposal were two. First, under its 1842 charter the Society was required to hold its annual business meeting in Boston. That stipulation had kept control of the organization in the hands of its New England members, putting at a disadvantage those from the rising Semitics strongholds at Johns Hopkins and the University of Pennsylvania. Second, a new "national" charter would allow the Society's papers to be printed at government expense, bringing an increase in the amount of work published. (The model for this idea was the recently established American Historical Association, whose scholarly papers came out in the form of government reports.) The AOS members agreed to consider this recommendation and to put it to a vote at its next meeting, to be held at Princeton in October.[23]

What followed shows the considerable influence W. D. Whitney still wielded, even though confined to his home in New Haven. He agreed with Lanman that the proposed reform was unnecessary: "I too do not see any need of a change of charter: we can do what we please as things are." He also continued to believe that an increase in the quantity of published work by American philologists would significantly lower its aggregate quality. Neither did he want to see the Society grow accustomed to government funding. No doubt Whitney recalled the sad experience of the National Academy of Sciences, which had been crippled in its early years in part because of its financial dependence on Congress. Whitney's verdict: the proposal for a new AOS charter should be "well mutilated, and then voted down." Of this outcome he was hopeful. In addition to his usual allies among the Sanskritists, Whitney expected the backing of someone who had particular influence over the younger members. Lanman had already lined up the support of D. C. Gilman, who agreed to come to Princeton to oppose the change. Said Whitney: "I should think that would be almost equivalent to its squelchment." He was willing, however, that the annual meeting be held in locations other than Boston.[24]

At the meeting that fall, Cyrus Adler reiterated his main concern. Society members were producing no lack of "suitable scientific material"; what was lacking was the funds to print all of it. Adler might have added that the axe tended to fall in predictable places. Several years earlier, the *Journal* had declined to publish an article by Morris Jastrow on the Hebrew prophet Haggai. A similar refusal had led the rabbinics scholar Richard Gottheil to complain of unfairness. After all, as he told Whitney, it was "hard to draw the line between that which is Hebrew and that which is Oriental."[25]

The growth of Semitic studies was indeed the real source of the charter controversy. Charles Lanman said as much, thereby confirming Whitney's suspicion that the insurgency consisted of a particular group: "I know absolutely of no one in favor of the change of the AOS status save Adler (who is a good fellow), Haupt (who is improving immensely), Jastrow, and Gottheil, the very four you mention." Gilman seconded this report, observing that "the Oriental revolutionists" were "chiefly Semites supported perhaps by those who are more familiar with Teutonic than with American ways." This last reference was to Paul Haupt, a German-born gentile and the chair of Gilman's own Semitics department.[26]

When it came to a vote, few were willing to go against the Society's long-standing leadership. The members agreed to allow the annual meeting to be held in places other than Boston, but they rejected the proposal to seek federal funding. How all of this would be reported in the *Proceedings* was a stickier question. Whitney wanted the entire controversy to be kept out of print, for he considered it purely an in-house affair. Lanman warned, however, that "the discussion will have to be put in with some little fullness, as that I believe was expressly voted." Whitney still got his way, at least in part. In the published minutes, Lanman identified the insurgents by name but hid the fact that Whitney and Gilman had done so much to shape the outcome.[27]

Once the charter dispute had been put to rest, Whitney quietly responded to the grievances behind it. As an immediate gesture to the non-New Englanders, he recommended a more southerly location for the next annual meeting. His further action was far-reaching as well as remarkably unselfish. Whitney, never a wealthy man, contributed $1000 to the Society's publication fund, stipulating that the source not be made public until after his death. The *Journal* could thus accommodate more articles, which went to the source of the complaint.[28] Ironically, Whitney thus aided the increased publication of Near Eastern Semitic studies, which would claim a growing share of the Oriental Society's agenda over the next several decades.

By addressing the Society's problems in his own fashion, Whitney could preserve the sense that he was acting according to the dictates of conscience, not under pressure from others. Yet at the same time, he saw his influence slipping. Even Lanman did not always act strictly according to his wishes but responded increasingly to the younger members with whom he sympathized.

A case in point occurred in 1893 when W. H. Ward decided to step down as AOS president. Lanman privately urged D. C. Gilman to consent to fill the post. On hearing of this, Whitney complained that Gilman was "no Orientalist at all" and said that he would be useful for the job only if he were to exert his influence to really promote the Society, "and for that I imagine he is too busy." But by then it was too late: the Society elected Gilman president only a few days later.[29] Lanman tried to placate his old teacher with a glowing report of that meeting: "How I wished that you, dear Mr. Whitney, could have been there, to see these men, so many of them young and full of promise, with their earnest, interested faces. Be sure, you were not forgotten on these memorable days."[30] Inadvertently, Lanman's words signified a passing of the torch.

Whatever his frustrations with the AOS, Whitney at least was making progress toward completing the second volume of the *Atharva Veda* edition. Just as he announced that the end was in sight, however, a new bout of cardiac trouble brought his efforts to a halt. That took place toward the end of 1892. Whitney's condition subsequently improved, and by the spring of 1894 he was ready to resume. He decided at this point to enlist Lanman's aid in making the final revisions. As he reported to Rudolph von Roth, "The work will begin as soon as I come back from our country vacation, at the beginning of October."[31]

The hopefulness with which Whitney began the summer is suggested by the recollection of a former student, A. V. W. Jackson, who visited him at that time. The younger man, a professor at Columbia College in New York City, spent part of an afternoon at Whitney's home before going abroad on a research trip. "Bright, cheerful, and happy, he was in his study and at work," Jackson recalled. "I shall never forget the charming talk that I then had with him. He took down from the shelves his album of photographs of friends and distinguished scholars; they were German, French, English, Italian, and American; and as he turned the pages he would have some pleasant word to say or some kind greeting to send to this one or to that, in case I should meet them during the summer in Europe."[32]

Whitney no doubt recalled journeys of his own, those extended European tours that had set milestones to his career. And soon, he thought, he would see the conclusion of that first large project he had begun so many years be-fore while a student at Tübingen. By now Whitney had over 2,400 manuscript pages of *Atharva Veda* text and commentary, nearly complete but unrevised. He intended that the final phase of that work would get underway as soon as he returned from vacation in the fall. Yet as things turned out, this schedule could not be followed. Long before autumn arrived, Charles Lanman would hold sole responsibility for the revision.[33]

In his final letter to his protégé, Whitney not only discussed *Atharva* matters but also reasserted his long-held views on key subjects. He cast his vote against a paper submitted to the AOS by the University of Pennsylvania ethnologist Daniel Garrison Brinton (1837–99), a specialist in American Indian languages and a philosophical disciple of Humboldt and Steinthal. "The Brinton article I haven't read, but I am quite sure in advance that we cannot publish it; it is not at all 'Oriental,' and we ought, I think, to refuse such matter on principle; nor do I think it will prove good; in matters of general philology he is not to be praised."[34] To the end, Whitney was anxious to guard the purity of doctrine he had worked so long to establish in general linguistic theory. William Dwight Whitney died of heart failure on the seventh of June, 1894.

He managed, however, to speak once more. Just after his death there came a parting shot at the German *Junggrammatiker* — appearing, of all places, in Karl Brugmann and Wilhelm Streitburg's *Indogermanische Forschungen,* a leading Neogrammarian journal. Here Whitney pronounced his final verdict on the notion of exceptionless sound laws, which he again described as a "dogma." As evidence, he presented examples of "sporadic and partial phonetic change" that he had gathered over the years from rural New England dialects. It was the same material his Yale colleague Frank Tarbell had used earlier in the *Laut-gesetz* debate. Once again, the point was to show a transitional phase of sound change in which some New Englanders used a short vowel in pronouncing words such as *stone,* while using a long *o* in similar words such as *bone.*[35] This discrepancy proved that phonological change did not necessarily affect every eligible word in a speaker's lexicon, or at least not all at once. Rather, changes could appear in only a portion of the lexicon at any given moment. In the speech of an individual, this inconsistency suggested lexical diffusion.

There was also, however, an inconsistency in the speech of the entire com-munity. While some inhabitants of the American northeast still pronounced *stone* with a short *o,* most speakers had adopted the long vowel. Whitney thus hinted that lexical diffusion normally blended with populational diffusion.

That is, a new pronunciation would spread from word to word in the individual's lexicon partly under the influence of person-to-person contact. For Whitney had never conceived of a speaker in isolation. Individuals did not take up new pronunciations suddenly and mechanically, but rather through a process of social interaction.

Whitney concluded that, *in both its individual and collective manifestations,* "a language" could be "honey-combed with inconsistencies and anomalies, while yet doubtless the leading tendencies are working themselves out to ultimate uniformity."[36] In other words, the uniformity of language was something that was always emerging yet never complete, because new traits were constantly being spread through a population. This conclusion had been anathema to the original Neogrammarians. Brugmann and his colleagues had tried to discover, and had insisted upon finding, clockwork regularity in phonological change and strict homogeneity within dialects. Whitney had been willing to acknowledge such regularities to the extent that investigation revealed them. Yet his presumption lay in the opposite direction unless empirical evidence proved him wrong.

## Pathways to Saussurean Theory

Whitney's death set off an unlikely chain of events that eventually would help produce a revolution in Western linguistic thought. The initial step came when the sobering news reached the leaders of the American Philological Association, who were laying plans at that time for the first American Congress of Philologists. That event, a joint gathering of seven scholarly organizations, was to be held in Philadelphia late that year.[37] On hearing of Whitney's passing, the host committee set aside a plenary session to commemorate his life and work; this became the Whitney Memorial Meeting. Charles Lanman worked hard to prepare for the occasion, one of his jobs being to contact a list of prominent scholars, requesting statements assessing Whitney's contributions to language study.

He received in return some twenty-three letters of tribute, parts of which were read at the Philadelphia meeting. (They were later published in full.) Some of these were written in French or Italian, but most were in German: the *Junggrammatiker* (now not so young) were especially well represented. In earlier chapters we noted the admiration the Neogrammarians expressed for Whitney at this time. They sincerely praised his critique of the organic analogy as well as his uniformitarian thinking. They also wrote in a properly eulogistic mode, which required that they overlook the fact that Whitney had become a strong critic of their own teaching. Karl Brugmann thus spoke of Whitney's wholesome early influence: "For me as for other young scholars, Whitney was a guide in the conflict of opinions between linguistic philosophy and specialized research, whose . . . hints one always followed with rich profit." In this same spirit, Bertholdt Delbrück testified to Whitney's thoroughness of research, clearness of thinking, and solid common sense. He concluded: "In a real sense we all are his students."[38] If such passages were generous and somewhat vague, they were not insincere and were fit for the occasion.

Later we will do a final summing up of the Neogrammarians' assessment of Whitney. Our larger task, however, is to examine what was by far the single most important statement composed for the Whitney Memorial Meeting. That piece of writing, strange to say, was never completed, and for this reason it was never sent to America. Its author was Ferdinand de Saussure.

The only known meeting between Whitney and Saussure took place in Berlin in the spring of 1879 when Whitney was preparing his *Sanskrit Grammar*. Saussure was completing his doctoral work at that time. A linguistic prodigy, Saussure had just produced, at age twenty-one, a 300-page dissertation on early Indo-European phonology.[39] This project no doubt dominated the conversation between the two scholars; it is not likely that their discussion dealt with general linguistics. Yet it is also clear that, sometime before Whitney's death in 1894, Saussure read Whitney's two main books on language. He especially admired the 1875 volume, which he probably had at least heard about before he met Whitney. Prior to transferring to the University of Berlin, Saussure had studied at Leipzig with August Leskien, who had recently translated *The Life and Growth of Language* into German. Whether Saussure read that book in Leskien's version, or in the English or the French version, will probably remain a mystery.

After finishing his Berlin doctorate, Saussure taught in Paris for a number of years and then returned to his native city to teach at the University of Geneva. There he became Professor of Sanskrit and Comparative Grammar, the post he would occupy for the remainder of his career.

Saussure must have fallen near the bottom of the list of names to be contacted about the Whitney Memorial Meeting. He received his request only six weeks before the event, too short a time for someone as meticulous as he was to organize his thoughts on paper.[40] As a result, Saussure never completed his memorial statement. He did, however, produce a lengthy set of preliminary notes, in which he did much more than had been asked. He quickly strayed from considering Whitney's accomplishments and set down on paper, apparently for the first time, his own thoughts on the principles of general linguistics.[41] This failure to fulfill the request from America would have momentous consequences. Over a decade later, owing to the retirement of a colleague, Saussure was obliged to give courses of lectures on general linguistics: this he did in 1907, 1909, and 1911. Although these were wide-ranging in the topics they covered, their theoretical portions contained much that Saussure had worked out in his 1894 "Notes pour un article sur Whitney."

Saussure died prematurely in 1913 without having put his lectures into publishable form. Two of his colleagues set out to do this work themselves by editing several sets of notes taken by students who had attended Saussure's courses. To supplement this basic text, however, they added material from Saussure's private papers, and much of this they took from the "Notes sur Whitney." This material from the "Notes," moreover, would be of the highest importance in shaping the finished product — the *Cours de linguistique générale* (1916).[42] Some of the most celebrated passages in that work were thus the unintended outcome of preparations for the Whitney Memorial Meeting.

Saussure told his students in Geneva that Whitney's 1875 book pointed linguistics "in the right direction." This, however, was a subdued version of what he had written in his "Notes," where he accorded both of Whitney's books superlative praise. In the process of beginning several drafts of that statement, Saussure said repeatedly that Whitney's books had been the best available at the time they were published. He went on to suggest that those volumes had not been surpassed since that time. This meant that Saussure rated Whitney's works above even the two main surveys by Neogrammarian writers, Hermann Paul's *Prinzipien* and Bertholdt Delbrück's *Einleitung*.[43]

After this, however, Saussure weighed Whitney's achievement more critically. He went on to declare himself "in agreement with no school in general, no more with the reasonable doctrine of Whitney than with the unreasonable doctrines that he victoriously [fought]. And this disagreement is such that it admits of no compromise or shading, under penalty of finding myself obliged to write things that make no sense to me."[44] These remarks epitomized Saussure's evaluation: even if Whitney's linguistic thought was unsurpassed to date, an entirely fresh approach was needed.

A parallel passage in the *Cours* hinted at the reason for this strong dissent.

Here Saussure began with the usual words of praise: "In order to emphasize that a language is nothing other than a social institution, Whitney quite rightly insisted upon the arbitrary character of linguistic signs. In so doing, he pointed linguistics in the right direction." Then came the qualification: "But he did not go far enough. For he failed to see that this arbitrary character fundamentally distinguishes language from all other institutions." Language was different, for example, from other semiotic devices, such as pictographic writing or performed rituals. As Saussure explained in his draft "Notes," this was because language had "no manner of connection with the thing designated."[45]

Saussure's point was that language entailed a more thoroughgoing arbitrariness than had been allowed by the Common Sense theory of the linguistic sign. And for the purpose of making this case, Whitney presented a useful foil. Western thinkers had traditionally regarded a "sign" as something distinct from its referent, the latter consisting of some preexisting concept that needed to be signified. As Whitney himself said in his 1875 book, "In common phrase, we first have our idea, and then get a name for it."[46] Saussure, however, argued that no element of language could be regarded as "simple" in this way; hence, he declared that "common sense is not enough." His alternative was to have the sign embrace *both* the signifier *and* the signified, the point being that even the latter was a conventional construct. The *Cours* gave as an example the difference between the French *mouton* and the English *sheep. Mouton* indicated both a kind of animal and a kind of meat to be served as a meal; *sheep* indicated only the animal. English added the word *mutton* to designate the edible aspect, thus betraying a different construction of the link between word and object. For Saussure, then, the arbitrariness of the sign encompassed the *entire relationship* between signifier and signified — a departure from what Whitney and the Scottish Common Sense theorists had taught.[47]

Saussure's other main idea was that language consisted of an interdependent *system* of signs, this being the heart of linguistic structuralism. He said in his "Notes sur Whitney": "The altogether ultimate law of language is . . . that there is never anything which can consist in one item (as a direct consequence of the fact that linguistic symbols are without connection to what they must designate), thus that two such [symbols] have their value only by their reciprocal *difference,* or that none has any value . . . other than by this same network of eternally negative differences." A genuinely isolated word could therefore have no meaning, for each word derived its semantic "value" only by standing in opposition to a contrasting word. The merely positive form of a sign, Saussure declared, was "irrelevant" and "tantamount to zero."[48]

This notion of a system of signs demanded a synchronic perspective. To illustrate this point in his 1894 "Notes," Saussure drew his famous analogy distinguishing between the two dimensions of a game of chess. A chess player needs to see not only the movement of each piece in its temporal sequence but also the positions of all the pieces in relation to one another at a given moment—the latter analogous to the structuralist view of language.[49] Saussure apparently omitted this illustration from the lectures he gave between 1907 and 1911, since it does not appear in the student notes. It came to be included in the *Cours* only because the editors of that work borrowed from his draft statement on Whitney.

Here again, the contrast to Whitney's own teaching is instructive. Whitney introduced a *kind* of synchronic perspective when he argued that the linguistic sign got its meaning only in the present moment—what we have called *semantic presentism*. Yet Whitney's viewpoint here was generally atomistic rather than structuralist. As he said in his first book, "Language is made up of signs for thought, which though in one sense parts of a whole, are in another and more essential sense isolated and independent entities." He also said that speakers "establish a direct mental association between the idea and the sign," suggesting simple word-object representation.[50]

There is, however, a countertheme to this story. Whitney presented in subsequent writings a nearly opposite perspective—indeed, a striking anticipation of Saussure's outlook. He did this by offering, especially in his 1875 book, a new interpretation of the familiar distinction between "material" and "formal" elements in language. In his first book, he set forth the standard view that material elements (such as the *full* in *fully*) had descended from a language family's root words, and so had retained their independent significance. Formal elements, the theory ran, had emerged with the development of inflective grammar and expressed grammatical elaboration only; they had no independent meaning.[51]

Although he never explicitly abandoned this orthodox Boppian theory, Whitney introduced in his mid-career writings the idea that the material and formal aspects of language actually exist in a reciprocal relationship on a strictly synchronic plane. He also expanded the realm of the "formal," even to the point of implying that no truly independent "material" elements exist.

He gave as examples paired terms such as *brook:brooks* and *man:men.* The semantic difference between the members of these pairs, he said, was generated purely "by contrast." Even the primary term, *brook,* was itself "formed," because it received its ability to express singleness of number "not by a [positive] sign, but by the absence of an otherwise necessary sign to the contrary."[52]

Here we enter a realm of speculation, going beyond — and indeed against — Ferdinand de Saussure's actual remarks about W. D. Whitney's linguistic thought. It appears, nonetheless, that Saussure took more from Whitney than he himself realized. In light of what he later taught, it seems hardly possible that he had not been impressed, at some level of awareness, by the highly "structuralist" teaching presented in *The Life and Growth of Language,* the work by Whitney that he particularly admired.[53] One indication of this impression can be seen in Saussure's own use of paired terms, similar to Whitney's, in his discussion of the chess game in the 1894 "Notes."[54] Here, then, we have a wholly contrasting side of the Whitney-Saussure relationship than what we saw above, suggesting that the intellectual connection between these thinkers, like Saussure's theory of the sign, was not at all "simple."

Still, it cannot be said that Whitney became a structuralist. For even as he explored the idea that meaning was generated by word-oppositions, he also continued to teach that meaning was imposed by social convention. Even in the 1875 volume he said that "the reason why he [the speaker] calls a certain idea by a certain name is simply that the community in which he lives so call it, and will understand him when he does the same."[55] Whitney was in this sense — a rare thing for him — logically inconsistent. For the most part, he persisted in grounding conventional word meanings, not in the abstract system of signs, but in the relationship between individual signs and the speech community that attributed to them their significance.[56]

The source of Whitney's thinking on this subject was, once again, his college textbooks, particularly the associationist psychology outlined in George Campbell's *Philosophy of Rhetoric* (1838). Campbell described three interlocking relationships: between things and things, between things and words, and between words and words. Experience revealed various "original and natural" links between actual things. And although the link between things and words was a matter of "the conventions of men," the psychological impression produced paralleled the natural relations between things themselves. The last of these connections, between words and words, therefore reflected the relationship between actual things, albeit through the medium of mental association.

In short, languages displayed a systematic quality because they were mirrors of an ordered reality.[57]

The heart of Whitney's thinking was thus at odds with Saussure's insight into the self-referential nature of language. Whitney did produce some striking anticipations of Saussurean themes, yet Saussure needed to recontextualize these in order to formulate his distinctive outlook. Saussure reaffirmed this need for a substantially new framework in a notebook entry he jotted in 1908, after he had given his first course of lectures on general linguistics: "The American Whitney, whom I revere, never said a single word on . . . [these] subjects which was not right; but like all the others, he does not dream that language needs a systematics."[58] Rightly enough, Saussure judged Whitney as representing a pre-structuralist version of language theory.

Thus far we have seen how direct contact with Whitney's ideas stimulated Saussure's thinking, mostly *via negativa* but in a positive sense as well. There was also, however, an indirect way in which Whitneyan influence came to Saussure — through the intermediary of Neogrammarian doctrine. This would seem unlikely, on the face of it, because the Neogrammarians worked in the tradition of historically oriented comparative philology, the antithesis of a structuralist treatment. Still, there was a distinct thread running from Whitney to the Neogrammarians and then from the Neogrammarians to Saussure. We can see this clearly if we juxtapose two passages that are widely separated in the published *Cours* but that appear in connected sequence in the student notes.

The first passage we have seen already. In the book's opening pages, Saussure briefly summed up the Neogrammarians' achievement and pointed to Whitney's preparatory role. Significantly, Saussure said nothing here about the exceptionless sound-law principle. Rather, he suggested that the Neogrammarians' important legacies were precisely those that built on Whitneyan thought: the rejection of the organic life-cycle thesis, and the new emphasis on grammatical analogy.[59]

In the second passage, Saussure described how the Neogrammarians had regarded analogy as a primary means by which language was resystematized in the wake of phonological change. According to this view, entire languages thus "*pass from one state of organization to another.*"[60] Here Saussure probably was referring to Hermann Paul, who hinted that analogy was a source of ongoing synchronic regularity-production. Although applied to a diachronic phenomenon (sound change), Paul's use of the analogy principle suggested, for explanatory purposes, that regularity itself was a matter of successive language "states"—an approximation of Saussurean doctrine.[61] These two passages appear in completely different sections of the *Cours,* but in the student notes they follow immediately. There, in the space of a few pages, Saussure described Whitney's preparation for the *Junggrammatiker,* the Neogrammarian revolution itself, and then the Neogrammarians' use of analogy. Originally, then, these topics had formed a single chain running from Whitney to Saussure.

This does not mean that the Neogrammarians themselves were structuralists. They assumed, as Whitney did, that historical and synchronic perspectives were *not* fundamentally opposed. Indeed, they subsumed the latter in the former.[62] Saussure, by contrast, made the separation between synchronic and historical perspectives foundational to his theoretical system. Still, he likely had been brought to this realization by his exposure, while a student, to Paul's emphasis on internally regularizing linguistic "states."

What ultimately linked these figures—Whitney, the Neogrammarians, and Saussure—was the grand reorientation of language theory according to the progressive-uniformitarian principle. It is worth quoting the linguist Paul Kiparsky's sweeping summary of that transition, especially because it assigns Whitney his rightful place. Like Saussure, Kiparsky downplays the importance of the exceptionless sound-law principle per se:

> A more important change in the field was surely the acceptance of the new paradigm of historical explanation. This far exceeds the sound change debate in productivity and concrete consequences. . . . As long as the morphologies of the attested Indo-European languages were seen as nothing more than pitiful, jumbled remnants of an earlier stage, there was no way of supposing that these morphologies could undergo any sort of systematic modification. . . . Analogy only became a conceivable form of change when it was admitted that the morphology of the daughter languages could be described as a system in its own terms. It is no accident that the linguists who first began to use proportional analogy as a principle of explanation were [Wilhelm] Scherer, Whitney, and the other linguists who headed the rejection of the Bopp [life-cycle] paradigm in the 1860s. It can also be argued that the concept of a synchronic system is ultimately connected with these changes in the prevailing views about [the history of] language. At the very beginning of the reaction against Bopp, the objection was already being raised that his theory, which saw all change as [phonologi-

cal] decay, could make no sense out of the fact that the daughter languages had system and structure too.[63]

Seen in this light, the Neogrammarians continued building a bridge toward Saussurean theory that W. D. Whitney had already begun.

In their statements for the Whitney Memorial Meeting, the Neogrammarians confronted a paradox: Whitney's contribution to linguistic theory consisted in making a case for principles so convincing that they ought to have been obvious already. As it happened, both his uniformitarian method and his rejection of the "organic" view of language-history quickly became part of the common wisdom. Hence, they also quickly acquired an apparent banality. Yet as Karl Brugmann suggested, this did not lessen their significance: "At first these views appear perhaps too prosaic, if not indeed too commonplace. Yet here Whitney proceeds no differently from other thinkers who have not been honored enough for having clothed known truths in simple and understandable words."[64]

Similarly, August Leskien sought to explain why Whitney's contributions had not been given the recognition they deserved: "Whitney's viewpoint, particularly most recently, has worked itself into linguistics far more than one perceives at first glance. The work of a linguistic researcher consists for the most part in detailed investigation, in which there is little opportunity to refer directly to Whitney. But in recent decades, even in specialized studies, and more naturally in questions of general principles, a methodological pathway has been cleared [*eine Behandlungsweise Bahn gebrochen*] that seeks to approach the essential nature of things, in this case the real makeup of language; and certainly a large portion of this has been inspired directly or indirectly by Whitney."[65]

Hence, in 1894 the Neogrammarians pinpointed both the nature of Whitney's influence on their discipline and the source of its elusive quality. By clearly and cogently asserting principles that were so sensible, and in retrospect so basic, Whitney had accomplished much—largely because his principles were not yet self-evident to many philologists, especially to those of the older generation, when he first stated them. It was a matter of his having said what needed to be said at the historical moment in which he lived. By doing this he served the linguistic community far into the future.

## A Mixed Legacy

We have seen how W. D. Whitney built essential foundations both for the Neogrammarian movement and for Saussurean theory. Either of these achievements alone would have been enough to establish his historical importance. Still, there is more to be said about Whitney's legacy, for there were further ways in which he influenced, or at least anticipated, modern linguistics. This part of our story will unfold in three stages. First, Whitney provided the theoretical framework adopted by most American linguists for roughly twenty-five years after his death. Then came a period of eclipse from the 1920s through the 1960s as structuralist approaches predominated. Finally, the Whitneyan spirit returned with the rise of sociolinguistics and lexical-diffusion research. Contrary themes that add nuance to this outline will be noted along the way.

Three writers took the lead in maintaining Whitneyan linguistics in the early decades of the twentieth century. The first to appear was Whitney's student Hanns Oertel, who became Professor of Comparative Philology at Yale. Next was Leonard Bloomfield (1887–1949), a nephew of the Sanskritist Maurice Bloomfield and a specialist in North American Indian languages. Although he would emerge as the preeminent American linguist of the first half of the twentieth century, Leonard Bloomfield was not the most important representative of the Whitneyan tradition. That was the role of a third figure, the classicist Edgar H. Sturtevant. Sturtevant did his advanced training at the University of Chicago under Carl Darling Buck, who was a student of Whitney's; he later cited Buck's classroom lectures as an important source of his own general theory. In 1927 when Sturtevant attended Buck's class in comparative philology, the main text was still Whitney's *Life and Growth of Language*.[66]

Books by these writers — Oertel's *Lectures on the Study of Language* (1901), Bloomfield's *Introduction to the Study of Language* (1914), and Sturtevant's *Linguistic Change* (1917) — were standard in their time.[67] All three followed tradition by emphasizing historical rather than synchronic or "descriptive" approaches. Moreover, they taught many of the specific concepts found in Whitney's writings. All, for instance, said that words were "arbitrary and conventional signs" — showing that this idea had actually been absorbed into mainstream American linguistics before Saussure's *Cours* appeared.[68] Most important, these writers maintained Whitney's sociological vision: they pointed to individual peculiarities of speech and subsequent communicative inter-action as the sources of both diversification and cohesion in language.

There were differences, however, in the degree to which these writers em-braced that sociological schema; and here we find the key distinction between Whitney and Bloomfield. On one hand, Bloomfield declared his allegiance to Whitneyan tradition. He affirmed in his 1914 *Introduction* that he had taken Whitney's texts as his model; he praised the "remarkable clearness of truth and comprehensiveness" of Whitney's theoretical views; and he recommended that beginning students in linguistics read Whitney's books first of all.[69] On the other hand, Bloomfield qualified these remarks in two important ways. First, although he considered Whitney's views to be correct as far as they went, he also said that they were "incomplete" and that they applied mainly to the "historic phase" of language study. Second, Bloomfield said that Whitney's chief contribution had been to challenge the "mystic vagueness and haphaz-ard theory" prevalent in his own day.[70] As important as that achievement was, he implied, the time had come to move on.

Bloomfield especially wanted linguists to benefit from the advances in psy-chology made since the time Whitney and Heymann Steinthal wrote their main works. Oertel and Sturtevant each did this to some extent by drawing on Wilhelm Wundt's notion of "assimilative habit." Yet Bloomfield made the greater use of that concept. In order for a speech innovation to spread through-out a community, he argued, it needed "to fall in readily with the other habits and associations" already characteristic of that group of speakers—the key factor being the "psychic predisposition" of the entire group.[71]

Its merits notwithstanding, this early Bloomfieldian emphasis on collec-tive mental habit effectively downplayed the element of interaction between speakers. By contrast, Oertel and Sturtevant were more faithful to Whitney's vision. In addition to Wundtian psychology, Oertel adopted the sociologist Gabriel Tarde's Whitneyesque principle of interpersonal emulation.[72] More importantly, both Oertel and Sturtevant made an essentially Whitneyan dis-tinction between "primary" and "secondary" changes in language. Primary change occurred when an individual first produced a speech innovation; sec-ondary change occurred when the other members of the community adopted it. (The Neogrammarian Hermann Paul had taught the same idea.)[73] This dis-tinction was implicit in Bloomfield's book as well, yet Bloomfield mainly em-phasized tendencies at work in the group mind—that is, the identical "psychic predisposition" of every individual in that group. Oertel and Sturtevant, however, focused on the diffusion of new traits via interactions among diverse individuals.

The most telling applications of this social-diffusion thinking came in response to Neogrammarian doctrine. Like most linguists of that day and since, Whitney's successors embraced the idea of exceptionless sound rules, even while rejecting what they considered the more dogmatic aspects of Neogrammarian doctrine. Accordingly, Sturtevant argued that the regularity principle was truer to reality when taken with certain qualifications. Echoing the early criticisms of Neogrammarian teachings (Whitney's included), he rejected the purely physiological explanation of linguistic regularity as well as the related assumption that all members of a community changed their phonological behavior simultaneously.[74] Instead, he stressed the gradual diffusion of innovations.

This emphasis made Sturtevant's works—his 1917 book and a similar volume published in 1947—serve as the major reminders of Whitney's outlook. Hanns Oertel's book soon fell into oblivion, and Bloomfield's *Introduction* did not stress social diffusion. It was Sturtevant's writings, with their pronounced Whitneyan themes, that sociolinguistic researchers would later remember.

## The Structuralist Turn in American Linguistics

A turning away from Whitneyan theory came with the ascendancy of linguistic structuralism. Saussure's ideas contributed to that movement internationally in the 1920s, yet the impulse had gotten an early start in America in the form of "descriptive" linguistics. Franz Boas first developed this kind of approach in his work on American Indian languages during the 1890s; his students, especially Edward Sapir (1884–1939), later carried that work forward. The point was that descriptive rather than historical modes of analysis worked best for native American languages, most of which lacked written traditions. This did not mean that historical linguistics faded away in this period, however. Historically oriented papers would still make up the majority of those presented to the Linguistic Society of America for over a decade after the founding of that organization in 1924.[75] During the 1930s, however, and especially by the 1940s, linguists from various countries were giving increasing attention to the analysis of structure. They converged on the idea that each language was composed of a unique set of meaningful sound units they called phonemes, and that by examining this set of sounds, the researcher could produce a distinct structural profile of a given language.[76]

A counter-theme in our story is that W. D. Whitney actually anticipated the phonemic concept, albeit in a rudimentary way. As he said in his 1874 study of the "Proportional Elements of English Utterance," "If we are rightly to estimate the phonetic character of a language, it is necessary for us to know not only the sounds which compose its spoken alphabet, but also the comparative frequency of their occurrence." Whitney therefore constructed a list of the consonant phonemes found in English, with a frequency percentage for each. (He did the same for Sanskrit in a subsequent article.)[77] The resulting table of percentages is strikingly similar to one that Bloomfield included in his book *Language* (1933), although the numbers themselves differ slightly. Echoing Whitney (apparently unknowingly), Bloomfield said that discovering the "relative frequencies" of basic consonant sounds was a useful first step in phonemic analysis.[78]

Whitney also foreshadowed the distributionalist method developed by the post-1945 "Bloomfieldian" linguists. Those researchers sought to produce a strictly formal (not semantic) analysis of the distribution of grammatical elements in a language, according to an exhaustive review of the linguistic environments in which each element occurred.[79] Whitney had pursued a similar goal in his *Sanskrit Grammar* by converting at least some of his data into statistical form; he again said that this would enable the student to appreciate the special "character" of that language.[80]

Whitney never really explained what he meant by either phonological or grammatical character. Still, his comparison of consonant frequencies did imply the description of a language state, with each element set in relation to other contemporaneous elements rather than to its historical antecedents. He also tried to show all of the different synchronic contexts in which a grammatical element of Sanskrit had appeared in the various periods of Indian literature, along with its frequency of usage. These approximations of descriptivist ideas again suggest that, in certain limited contexts, Whitney thought in structuralist terms.

The more characteristic Whitneyan perspectives, however, were being left behind in the decades after about 1920. That trend occurred not only in structuralist theory but in other ways as well. One of these was a ratcheting up of the longstanding impulse to restrict the scope of linguistic study to "language itself." Saussure contributed by famously distinguishing between *langue*, the language system shared by a community, and *parole,* the voluntary speech-acts of individuals. Although he said that both dimensions came within the province of linguistic study, his *Cours* focused mainly on the former. In practice, then, Saussure treated language as something unaffected by actual speech behavior.

Surely the most thoroughgoing effort of this kind appeared in Leonard Bloomfield's writings. In the late 1920s, Bloomfield abandoned the habit psychology of his 1914 *Introduction* and adopted a strict stimulus-response behaviorism. Now he regarded both mental activity and social context as theoretically irrelevant to the investigation of speech acts.[81] Bloomfield's goal was to further delimit the realm of purely "linguistic" phenomena, to separate the field not only from the natural sciences but from the human and social sciences as well, producing complete independence.[82] This of course suggested a much more radical kind of disciplinary autonomy than W. D. Whitney had envisaged. Whitney had wanted to prevent linguistics from being dominated by any other field, yet he still saw it as part of the "moral" or human/social sciences, because he saw language itself as the work of free and responsible agents. He would not have accepted the dehumanized world suggested by Bloomfield's later position.

## The Diffusionist Idea and Sociolinguistics

A clear-cut reaffirmation of Whitneyan perspective came with lexical diffusion study and sociolinguistics, both of these movements beginning in the late 1960s. In order to show this connection, however, we must first look at Whitney's relationship with early-twentieth-century dialectology, which prepared the way for these later developments. Whitney was not a profound student of dialects, yet he did share the early dialectologists' main insight: he saw linguistic diversity as something that is always present within a speech community. The key is to see how Whitney applied this insight to August Schleicher's *Stammbaum* ("family tree") theory of linguistic kinship. Whitney actually held an idiosyncratic version of that theory, and this allowed him to cling to it even after the dialectologists had shown its limitations.

The *Stammbaum* implied genealogical descent from a common ancestor-tongue; it therefore explained structural similarities among languages as the result of their common origin. Thus far, Whitney agreed.[83] Yet Schleicher also suggested that a parent-tongue remains homogeneous up until such time that it subdivides into separate daughter dialects. This aspect of the theory had become untenable by around 1870 as mounting evidence showed that dialect variation already existed within any geographically extensive speech community.

Whitney accepted this new evidence even while continuing to hold the essential family-tree idea. As he told C. R. Lanman, "In my view, those who think . . . that they are putting down the *Stammbaum* system of relationship are only exposing their ignorance of the forces which control the life of language."[84] Whitney could still affirm the *Stammbaum* because he had never believed in the first place that a "parent" language was homogeneous throughout the territory in which it was spoken. He assumed that such languages were uniform only in a relative sense, in contrast to the more conspicuous diversity that marked off their daughter dialects one from the other. (As he noted during the Neogrammarian controversy, "Even in the most homogeneous communities, the diversities of pronunciation are endless.")[85] Whitney regarded dialectal diversity within a parent-tongue as but the normal extension of idiolect diversity, especially when a sizable population and geographic area were involved. Hence any out-migration and consequent splitting of a parent community (as the *Stammbaum* hypothesized) only magnified a condition that already existed while the community was still unified.[86] In short, Whitney believed that speech communities were inherently multidialectal.

Here once again, Whitney stood poised between old and new perspectives. He was stand-pat in his loyalty to the *Stammbaum* as far as attributing linguistic similarities to common descent. Yet he construed that theory in a way that put him into fundamental agreement with the dialectologists—who were among the *Stammbaum*'s original critics. He thereby anticipated the dialectologists' critique of the Neogrammarian dogma that each language or dialect manifests complete phonological and grammatical regularity at a given point in time. For instance, in a classic 1904 study, the Romanic specialist L. Gauchat showed how even the dialect of an isolated Swiss village, relatively untouched by outside influence, was not homogeneously regular.[87]

Whitney had little or no influence on the actual practice of dialect geography. Although a founding member of the American Dialect Society (est. 1889), his involvement in that group would be limited. Others pursued the large research projects, the national speech atlases published in the twentieth century. Yet Whitney's armchair data collection, which appeared in his 1894 article on "partial and sporadic sound change," showed at least a desire to investigate dialectal variation. As we have seen, it also showed his tactic of using that data to challenge the Neogrammarian doctrine of strict regularity.

Whitney had replied to the Neogrammarians by asserting his interactionist sociology of language, which (among other things) envisaged the diffusion of new traits within a speech community. Edgar Sturtevant elaborated this outlook in his 1917 book, supported by what the dialectologists had thus far discovered about the spread of phonological changes. Sturtevant used those discoveries to overturn a two-part thesis taught by the early Neogrammarians. First, Hermann Paul and Eduard Sievers had argued that sound changes are *phonologically gradual:* a given phoneme changes so slowly and incrementally that even the speaker himself fails to notice the transition. (Leonard Bloomfield reaffirmed this idea in his 1914 *Introduction.*)[88] Secondly, the Neogrammarians held that sound change was an autonomously phonetic (that is, physical) process, and that a given change therefore touches all eligible speakers and words in just the same way and at roughly the same time. A sound change was thus *populationally and lexically abrupt.*

Sturtevant reversed these axioms. First, he noted that at least some initial changes are *phonologically abrupt,* for they are large enough to be noticeable. More importantly, he found that changes tend to spread gradually and unevenly: they are "irregular when they first appear." Like Whitney, moreover, Sturtevant saw populational diffusion (changes spreading from speaker to speaker) and lexical diffusion (changes spreading through each speaker's vocabulary) as interlocking processes. This meant that, at any given moment, not only would different individuals speak differently, but that changed and unchanged word forms would coexist in the speech of a single individual. Sturtevant summarized: "The two processes of spread from word to word and spread from speaker to speaker progress side by side until the new sound has extended to all the words of the language which contained the old sound in the same surroundings." He repeated these points in his 1947 textbook, noting that it was "impossible to draw a sharp line" between the two kinds of diffusion.[89]

Later, however, the University of California linguist William S.-Y. Wang did draw that line. In an influential 1969 article, Wang described how lexical diffusion (here Wang coined that term) could be isolated as a significant variable in phonological change. He concluded that, even in the speech of an individual, linguistic regularity is always a work in progress: "Many types of change are phonologically abrupt and [yet] require long spans of time to diffuse across the lexicon. . . . Since living languages are constantly undergoing change, we should expect to find many seeming exceptions to changes which have not completed their course. These forms are not true residues [that is, exceptions to a sound law], . . . since in time the appropriate phonological changes will reach them and make them regular."[90]

Here Wang confirmed one of the main points found in Whitney's 1894 article; it had appeared also in Whitney's critique of Bertholdt Delbrück's scaled-back version of the regularity doctrine. That doctrine, Delbrück argued, applied at least in the speech of an individual at a given moment. But according to the lexical diffusion principle, even an individual's synchronic speech pattern manifests inconsistency. Like Wang, Whitney did not say that such inconsistencies were actual exceptions to the regularity of phonological changes. He said only that regularizing tendencies were always in the process of working themselves out.

Wang arrived at his conclusions through his research on sound change in Chinese dialects. He made no mention of Whitney on this subject, and although he did cite Sturtevant's remarks about phonological abruptness, he did not refer to those passages in which Sturtevant anticipated the lexical diffusion idea.[91] Even so, research done since 1969 has confirmed the Whitney-Sturtevant outlook. Even though Wang started out investigating lexical diffusion alone, he and his co-workers broadened their research in subsequent decades to incorporate populational diffusion as an intersecting variable.[92]

At the same time that William Wang was beginning to analyze lexical diffusion, William Labov and his associates at Columbia University were launching sociolinguistics. Workers in this field call for the study of actual speaker activity as opposed to the study of abstract language systems. From their perspective, the other main schools of modern linguistics—Neogrammarian, structuralist, and generativist—have all been guilty of neglecting speech behavior.[93] Labov has, however, pointed to a number of intellectual predecessors. These he finds in a series of forward-looking, socially oriented linguists, among whom he names W. D. Whitney as the earliest. Following Whitney in this line are Hugo Schuchardt, Antoine Miellet, Jules Vendres, Otto Jespersen, and, most recently, Edward Sturtevant.[94]

Labov mounts a compelling critique of the "asocial" outlook that dominated linguistics, in various guises, from the 1920s through much of the 1960s. Downplaying the usual distinctions between historical, structuralist, and generativist approaches, he shows how an asocial tendency has pervaded all of these. It appeared, of course, in early comparative philology's focus on language in isolation, apart from the activity of speakers. It also appeared in Neogrammarian theory. While rejecting the old idea of language as an independent organism, the Neogrammarians retained the essence of that view by teaching that language behaved according to "mechanical" rules.[95]

Ferdinand de Saussure claimed to be launching a more social approach when he said that language was the possession of the speech community. Yet as the linguist John Joseph points out, Saussure construed the "social" as a realm of unconscious speech behavior so that it took over many of the functions that had previously been assigned to "nature." Hence, he too preserved the essential outlook (if not the rhetoric) of the old natural-historical tradition. Moreover, as Labov notes, Saussure's focus on *langue* rather than *parole* suggested an ideal language state, ignoring speech as behavior. Noam Chomsky produced his own influential version of this dichotomy when he distinguished between linguistic *competence* and linguistic *performance;* again, the emphasis fell squarely on the first of these.[96]

A further manifestation of asocial linguistics has been the tendency, from the Neogrammarians onward, to generalize from the speech of "the individual." We have seen how Bertholdt Delbrück did this in the abstract sense. Leonard Bloomfield did the same thing, albeit concretely by analyzing his own speech into thirty-two phonemes. Bloomfield's goal was to represent the "standard English" of Chicago circa 1933. Implicit here was the old assumption that language is homogeneous throughout a community, an ignoring of both dialect and idiolect variation. Chomsky added his own version of this theme when he declared that the subject of his studies would be the "ideal speaker-listener in a completely homogeneous speech community."[97] This isolation of the individual, in its various manifestations, clearly has been at odds with W. D. Whitney's sociological perspective.

As in the case of William Wang and his colleagues, Labov and the other sociolinguists rediscovered Whitneyan themes apparently without any direct input from Whitney's writings. Indirect influence could have been involved, however, to the extent that Labov and others learned from Sturtevant's two books on general linguistics, which were reprinted in 1960 and 1961, respectively. In any case, the main point is that the sociolinguistic program has vindicated Whitney's leading ideas. Labov readily acknowledges this as far as Whitney's pioneering articulation of the uniformitarian principle: that principle, he notes, is essential to the sociolinguistic investigation of ongoing language change.[98] What should be added is that sociolinguistics actually presupposes Whitney's entire sociological vision, including its emphasis on synchronic interaction. By focusing on change-in-process, the sociolinguists adopt an *atemporal approach to the diachronic*—something implicit throughout Whitney's system. For according to Whitney's uniformitarian outlook, an understanding of the present moment of exchange between speakers is the key to an understanding of all aspects of language change.

Whitney also anticipated sociolinguistics through his attention, at least theoretically, to the "actuation" of change by individual speakers. Labov, Wang, and others have been interested in incipient change as a subject of research. To help conceptualize this project, the British linguist James Milroy distinguishes between those innovations that remain as mere idiolect features and those that are admitted to the internal grammar of a language. In this context, Milroy invokes E. H. Sturtevant's distinction between primary and secondary change, a direct elaboration of Whitneyan theory.[99]

We may summarize Whitney's legacy with a final set of ironies. On the one hand, Whitney helped lay the foundations of both the Neogrammarian movement and Saussurean structuralism, especially of the progressive-uniformitarian assumption these two schools shared. These comprise Whitney's major legacy as far as his actual influence is concerned. On the other hand, it was Whitney's *criticisms* of the Neogrammarian program and the *non*-Saussurean aspects of his thought that anticipated, in the most specific ways, the outlook of the diffusionist and sociolinguistic schools. And it has been these more recent approaches to language study, on which Whitney apparently exerted no direct influence, that have brought the most unalloyed affirmation of his ideas.

Not the least of that affirmation is that sociolinguistics has fulfilled Whitney's main disciplinary goal by keeping a large share of language study within the sphere of the social or human sciences. As the chief alternative to the Chomskyan approaches developed since the 1950s and to cognitive science more recently, sociolinguistics has ensured that linguistics as a whole will not be annexed by, or dispersed among, the natural sciences.

## Reversals in Cultural Theory

Whitney's outlook has been vindicated within an important domain of linguistics, yet within sociocultural thought as a whole, the result has been ambiguous. Whitney did anticipate the individual-oriented and interactionist perspective that came to dominate early-twentieth-century American sociology.[100] Ironically, however, while he anticipated American sociology's voluntarist orientation, Whitney apparently likely helped to actually stimulate a well-known dissent from that viewpoint. The latter appeared in William Graham Sumner's classic *Folkways* (1906), the book that made famous the concept of social "mores." A graduate of Yale, W. G. Sumner returned there in 1872 to become Professor of Political and Social Science. We can infer that he and his older colleague Whitney developed a strong mutual respect: both men valued their independence of mind and were impatient with old dogmas. They were also welcome in one another's homes, and Sumner eventually served as a pallbearer at Whitney's funeral.[101]

Whitney perhaps helped Sumner free himself of an early commitment to Herbert Spencer's cosmic evolutionism. By the 1880s, Sumner had replaced this theory of preordained biosocial development with the notion of culture as an independent variable. Later, however, Sumner departed from Whitney's outlook by portraying culture as something that overrides individual volition. As he said in *Folkways*, "The authority of traditional custom . . . exerts a strain on every individual within its range."[102] Then, in a height of unintended irony, Sumner pointed to illustrations of this thesis in the work of a well-remembered colleague: "Whitney said that language is an institution. He meant that it is in the folkways, or in the mores." Here Sumner quoted passages in which Whitney acknowledged the "absence of reflection and intention" on the part of speakers to bring about changes in their language, and where he said that "no one ever set himself deliberately at work to invent or improve language." Sumner commented: "These statements might be applied to any of the folkways [and] . . . would serve to define and describe the mores," practices that "are imperceptibly modified and unconsciously handed down through the generations."[103]

The fact that Sumner was able to reinterpret Whitney in this way suggests an important truth — that the idea of social conventions contains a built-in ambiguity. It can convey the plasticity of institutions over time, or it can suggest how institutions place constraints on individual thought and action. Sumner, of course, chose the latter emphasis. Clearly, then, the notion of conventionality need not imply a voluntarist outlook as it did in the old Scottish sociological tradition embraced by Whitney. W. G. Sumner had turned a corner, anticipating the perspective that would soon dominate American anthropological theory.

It was, of course, in anthropology that Whitney's viewpoint especially lost out. Although he was an early champion of the culture concept, that idea would be recast in a relativist mould — a rejection of the universalistic evolutionism and the deductive appeals to "human nature" of the kind Whitney had espoused. Even though Whitney stressed the historical and conventional aspects of language, his outlook was never deeply *historicist*. Rather, in his hands, these themes were fully compatible with the notion of language as a product of the unchanging and universal human mind.

Following a pattern we have seen before, however, Whitney did make at least one striking remark suggesting linguistic relativism. At the beginning of his 1875 volume, he noted that "every single language has . . . its own peculiar framework of established distinctions, its shapes and forms of thought, into which, for the human being who learns that language as his 'mother-tongue,' is cast the content and product of his mind."[104] Yet Whitney made this comment prefatory to the main body of the book, where he routinely distinguished between thought and language, between ideas and the getting of names for them. Hence, he did not in any consistent way anticipate the famous Sapir-Whorf hypothesis, which taught that different languages produce different constructions of reality. Steeped as he was in Common Sense realism and old-style scientific positivism, Whitney did not consider "consciousness" as something problematic. Theorists at the turn of the twentieth century revolted against this kind of epistemology, considering it part of a naïvely universalist and deductivist view of human science.[105]

## Toward a University Ideal

We conclude with a last look at W. D. Whitney's impact on American academe. This did not arise from anything unique to Whitney's identity as a philologist. As the queen of the interpretive sciences, philology would have a profound influence on the American university, especially in making a place in the curriculum for humanistic subjects such as literature and art history.

Yet unlike his one-time friend Charles Eliot Norton, a celebrated translator of Dante, Whitney was not a great humanist. That is, he did not conduct his own investigations in a philological spirit.[106] His method can perhaps best be seen in his final project, the second volume of the *Atharva Veda* edition. That work consisted of historico-linguistic commentary, based on carefully collected data about grammatical and lexical usage. It was intended as an aid for other scholars who would translate — that is, interpret — the text for modern readers.[107]

Whitney's significance in the university context derived not from his philological specialty but from his drive to make himself a model of the academic research scientist. With his emphasis on precise methodology, he intended to demonstrate just how generically "scientific" a philological field could become, thus setting a standard that would be applicable across the disciplinary spectrum. Whitney largely achieved his goal, for he became one of only a small number of American academics of his generation, natural scientists included, who made an original contribution to knowledge. This is why his name appeared near the top of the recruitment lists when two of the nation's earliest university-builders, Charles Eliot and D. C. Gilman, began their presidencies at Harvard and Johns Hopkins. These figures ranked Whitney's accomplishments alongside those of the other research scientists they hoped to hire.

Whitney's work on behalf of Yale's Department of Philosophy and the Arts was similarly important. That Department did not train many eminent scientists or scholars, but it did have significant effects elsewhere. Charles Eliot saw it as a hint of what was needed, hence as a goad to other schools that were considering forming their own graduate programs. This, of course, was precisely the outcome Whitney had aimed for.[108]

A further aspect of higher education likely was affected by Whitney's leadership in the Sheffield School. This and other scientific institutes dispensed with required chapel attendance as well as other rules reflecting the old collegiate ideal of *en loco parentis*. In this way, they spearheaded the secularization of the American academy. The emerging graduate schools soon followed suit, and the university undergraduate programs eventually did too.[109]

Whitney's greatest impact on academe likely came through his leadership in scholarly associations, especially in preparing those organizations for their partnership with the universities. Faculty members increasingly sought distinction within the discipline-based associations; likewise, university administrators looked to these groups to establish professional standards for their various academic departments. The associations thus helped the emerging universities chart their course as research institutions. It is true that W. D. Whitney met some signal defeats in this arena: the American Oriental Society and the American Philological Association each veered away from the kinds of topics he favored. Yet he won in a deeper sense through the policies he established in procedural matters. He directed both the AOS and the APA in the path of research, and he limited the amount of material they published to ensure that it would be of the highest quality. Thus by the end of the 1870s, these language-oriented bodies were ready to serve as models for the newly established associations in a variety of other fields.

Much of Whitney's influence on these trends came in a very specific personal context, through his long friendship with Daniel Coit Gilman. The Whitney-Gilman collaboration has been little remembered, yet it was immensely important. Their later disagreements notwithstanding, the two men had built a close working relationship during Gilman's seventeen formative years on the Yale faculty. They served their administrative apprenticeships in this period, often working side by side in the AOS and in the Sheffield School.[110] Together, they laid the foundation of experience that Gilman later built upon when he became president of the University of California and then of Johns Hopkins University. Significantly, Gilman made Johns Hopkins the nation's leading sponsor of new disciplinary journals and organizations: examples of the latter were the American Economic Association (est. 1885) and the American Political Science Association (est. 1889). Once again, William Dwight Whitney had helped prepare the way. Yet, as with other aspects of his legacy, most traces of his influence on academic institutions soon became hidden beneath the new growth he had done so much to make possible.

# W. D. Whitney Chronology

1827 Born 9 February, Northampton, Massachusetts.

1842 Begins three years at Williams College, Williamstown, Massachusetts. Founding of the American Oriental Society (AOS) in Boston. Brother Josiah Dwight Whitney, Jr., begins advanced study in geology and chemistry at Berlin and Geissen.

1845 January: Josiah visits home for eleven months and brings books purchased in Europe. WDW reads Robert Chambers' *Vestiges of the Natural History of Creation* (1844); graduates from Williams College, as valedictorian, at eighteen years of age. Begins to clerk at Northampton bank, where he remains for three years. Begins serious language study.

December: Josiah returns to Europe for year and a half.

1846 By January, WDW has decided on a vocation in philology.

1847 Josiah returns from Europe in May, bringing Franz Bopp's *Sanskrit Grammar*, becomes director of the Lake Superior Survey.

1848 WDW begins study of Sanskrit.

1849 Summer: Joins the geological survey in Michigan. Fall: Begins one year studying Sanskrit and other languages at Yale under E. E. Salisbury.

1850 Sails to Germany for three years of study at the Universities of Berlin and Tübingen. Elected a member of the American Oriental Society (AOS).

1853 Spends four months in Paris, Oxford, and London gathering materials for *Atharva Veda* edition. August: Returns to United States. Spends a year in various employments.

1854 Begins teaching at Yale at age twenty-seven.

1856 Publication of Roth-Whitney edition of *Atharva Veda*, vol. 1. Spring: Crisis surrounding Whitney's marriage engagement. August: Married to Elizabeth Baldwin of New Haven. Visit to Italy and France, accompanied by wife and sister, November 1856 to July 1857.

1857 Elected Corresponding Secretary of AOS, a post held until 1884.

1858 Gives first paper on a general linguistic subject: "On the Origin of Language."

1859 Gives paper on "The Scope and Method of Linguistic Science." Charles Darwin's *Origin of Species* published.

1860 Beginning of debates on the history of Indian astronomy.

1861–62 Max Müller delivers two series of lectures on "The Science of Language" at London's Royal Institution.

1864 March: WDW delivers six lectures on "The Principles of Linguistic Science" at the Smithsonian Institution, Washington, D.C. December through January 1865: Delivers twelve lectures on same subject at the Lowell Institute, Boston.

1865 Josiah becomes professor of mineralogy at Harvard, a post held until 1896. WDW's first articles for the *North American Review*.

1867 Lectures published as first book: *Language and the Study of Language*.

1868 Composes statement of purpose for the annual report of Yale's Sheffield Scientific School.

1869 Charles W. Eliot becomes president of Harvard University, offers WDW a teaching post. WDW declines and assumes the newly endowed Salisbury Chair at Yale. Founding of the American Philological Association (APA); WDW elected first APA president.

1871 Charles Darwin's *Descent of Man* published. WDW reads Edward B. Tylor's *Primitive Culture* (1871). Critique of August Schleicher's linguistic views.

1872 Critique of Heymann Steinthal's linguistic views.

1873 Accompanies Hayden scientific expedition to Colorado. Publication of *Oriental and Linguistic Studies* (two volumes: 1873–74).

1874 Second edition of Darwin's *Descent of Man,* citing WDW's writings on language. Writes "Darwinism and Language"; sends copy to Charles Darwin.

1874–75 Three-part series on language in London's *Contemporary Review:* George H. Darwin, "Professor Whitney on the Origin of Language"; Max Müller, "My Reply to Mr. Darwin"; and WDW, "Are Languages Institutions?"

1875 Publication of *The Life and Growth of Language* as part of the International Scientific Series. Trip to England and Germany for work on the second volume of *Atharva Veda* edition. Publication of Max Müller's *Chips from a German Workshop,* vol. 4, including article "In Self-Defence."

1876 Winter-spring: Whitney-Müller controversy. *The Life and Growth of Language* translated into German.

1878–79  Fifteen months in Germany to prepare *Sanskrit Grammar,* accompanied by wife and daughters. Illness begins. Beginning of Neogrammarian movement in Leipzig.

1879  *Sanskrit Grammar* published in Leipzig.

1881–85  Neogrammarian controversy plays out in America.

1881  Elected a Foreign Knight of the Prussian Order of Merit.

1884  Elected president of AOS. Begins work as editor-in-chief of the *Century Dictionary.*

1885  Article on "Philology: The Science of Language in General" appears in the *Encyclopedia Britannica.*

1886  End of teaching career because of heart ailment.

1890  Resigns presidency of AOS.

1889–91  Publication of the first edition of the *Century Dictionary* (6 vols.).

1892  Publishes *Max Müller and the Science of Language: A Critique.*

1894  Dies on 7 June at age 67. Whitney Memorial Meeting held at the First American Congress of Orientalists in Philadelphia.

1905  Roth-Whitney *Atharva Veda* edition, second volume, completed by Charles R. Lanman, published in the Harvard Oriental Series.

# Notes

## Abbreviations

| | |
|---|---|
| AOS | American Oriental Society, Sterling Memorial Library, Yale University |
| AJP | *American Journal of Philology* |
| DAB | *Dictionary of American Biography* |
| DNB | *Dictionary of National Biography* |
| JAOS | *Journal of the American Oriental Society* |
| JDW | Josiah Dwight Whitney, Jr. |
| LGL | *The Life and Growth of Language* (1875) |
| LP | Charles Rockwell Lanman Papers, Harvard University Archives, Pusey Library, Harvard University |
| LSL | *Language and the Study of Language* (1867) |
| NAR | *North American Review* |
| OLS | *Oriental and Linguistic Studies* |
| PAOS | *Proceedings of the American Oriental Society* |
| PAPA | *Proceedings of the American Philological Association* |
| SP | Edward Elbridge Salisbury Papers, Sterling Memorial Library, Yale University |
| TAPA | *Transactions of the American Philological Association* |
| WDW | William Dwight Whitney |
| WP | Whitney Family Papers, Sterling Library, Yale University |

## Introduction

1. Thomas Trautmann pointed out the need for a Whitney biography in *Lewis Henry Morgan and the Invention of Kinship* (Berkeley: University of California Press, 1987), vii.

2. B. L. Gildersleeve, "Oscillations and Nutations of Philological Studies," in *The Selected Classical Papers of Basil Lanneau Gildersleeve,* ed. Ward W. Briggs, Jr. (Atlanta: Scholars Press, 1992), 80–92, on p. 80.

3. Charles R. Lanman, ed., *The Whitney Memorial Meeting* (Boston: Ginn and Co., 1897), 78, 94.

4. Ferdinand de Saussure, *Course in General Linguistics,* trans. and annotated by Roy Harris (1916; La Salle, Ill.: Open Court, 1983), 110; see also p. 26.

5. William Labov, *Sociolinguistic Patterns* (Philadelphia: University of Pennsylvania Press, 1972), 261, 264.

6. Leonard Bloomfield, *Introduction to the Study of Language* (New York: Henry Holt, 1914), vi, 312, 308 n; idem, *Language* (New York: Henry Holt, 1933), 16; Charles F. Hockett, "Introduction to the Dover Edition," in William Dwight Whitney, *The Life and Growth of Language* (1875; New York: Dover Publications, 1979), xvii.

7. Benvenuto Terracini, "Le origini della linguistica generale: Whitney," in *Guida allo studio della linguistica storica* (Roma: Edizioni dell'ateneo, 1949), 73–121, on p. 109, author's translation.

8. Saussure, *Course in General Linguistics*, 76; Bloomfield, *Introduction*, 312. Also in this vein: B. I. Wheeler, "The Progress of the History of Language during the Last Century," in *The International Congress of Arts and Sciences*, ed., Howard J. Rogers (New York: Houghton-Mifflin, 1906), 3:17–28, on p. 24.

9. Saussure said later, in reference to Whitney's work: "Mais un éloge de ce genre qui ne serait peut-être pas banal devient extraordinaire dans la linguistique proprement dite" (*Écrits de linguistique générale*, ed., Simon Bouquet and Rudolf Engler, with the collaboration of d'Antoinette Weil [Paris: Gallimard, 2002], 203–22, on p. 222).

10. Randy Allen Harris, *The Linguistic Wars* (New York: Oxford University Press, 1993), 16.

11. Henry Adams to Albert Stanburrough Cook, 16 October 1910, in *The Letters of Henry Adams*, ed. J. C. Levenson et al., 6 vols. (Cambridge, Mass.: Belknap Press, 1982–88), 6:377.

12. Lanman, *Whitney Memorial Meeting*, 75, 94, author's translation. Others have noted the image of Whitney "clearing the ground" for later linguists: E. F. Konrad Koerner, "L'Importance de William Dwight Whitney pour les jeunes linguistes de Leipzig," *Etudes saussuriennes* (Geneva: Editions Slatkine, 1988), 1–16, on pp. 7–8; and John E. Joseph, Review of *Saussurean Studies* by Konrad Koerner, in *Language* 65:3 (1989): 595–602, on p. 598.

13. Craig Christy, *Uniformitarianism in Linguistics* (Philadelphia: John Benjamins, 1983), 78–89. For a full list of works on Whitney, see the Essay on Sources at the end of this volume.

O N E : An American Orientalist

1. WDW, "Autobiography," October 1856, WP.

2. Whitney's mother was Sarah Williston Whitney (1800–33). *DAB*, s.v. "Whitney, William Dwight." JDW, Sr., to WDW, 25 September 1856, WP. The description of Whitney Sr., appears in James Hadley, *Diary of James Hadley*, ed., Laura Hadley Moseley (New Haven, Conn.: Yale University Press, 1951), 32. Justice of the Peace documents, Hampshire County, 1 February 1842, 30 January 1856, WP. Other information on Whitney Sr. comes from WDW, "The Elements of English Pronunciation," *OLS*, 2:2 n.

3. Solomon Clark, *Historical Catalogue of the Northampton First Church* (Northampton, Mass.: Gazette Printing Co., 1891), 147; Charles C. Gillispie, ed., *Dictionary of Scientific Biography* (New York: Scribner, 1970), s.v. "Whitney, Josiah Dwight." *DAB*, s.v. "Cogswell, Joseph Green."

4. WDW, "Autobiography"; James Russell Trumbull, *History of Northampton, Massachusetts*, 2 vols. (Northampton, Mass.: Gazette Printing Co., 1898–1902), 2:47–48; Solomon Clark, *Antiquities, Historicals and Graduates of Northampton* (Northampton, Mass.: Gazette Printing Co., 1882), 360–61. For W. D. Whitney's genealogy, see

Benjamin W. Dwight, *The History of the Descendants of John Dwight of Dedham, Massachusetts*, 2 vols. (New York: John F. Trow and Son, Printers, 1874), 2:828–29, 832–33, 836. Whitney advised the researcher: "If you want to know more, you know that Dr. Benj. W. D.[wight] of Clinton, N. Y., is the official all-knower about all Dwights." WDW to JDW, 2 March 1882, WP.

5. Folder of Architectural Drawings; WDW to JDW, 18 January, 1 March 1842, WP.

6. Insights into Whitney's "secularized Calvinist sensibility" appear in Carl Diehl, *Americans and German Scholarship: 1770–1870* (New Haven, Conn.: Yale University Press, 1978), 125–26, 128, 130.

7. Charles Gillispie, ed., *Dictionary of Scientific Biography*, s.v. "Whitney, Josiah Dwight."

8. WDW to Elizabeth Whitney Putnam, 16 March 1854, WP, emphasis in the original.

9. WDW, *LGL*, 112.

10. WDW to C. A. Joy, 27 May 1854; WDW to JDW, 28 February 1861, WP.

11. Quotation about Whitney from Timothy Dwight, *Memories of Yale Life and Men* (New York: Mead and Co., 1903), 48; see also Thomas R. Lounsbury, Obituary of William Dwight Whitney, *Proceedings of the American Academy of Arts and Sciences* (1895): 579–89, on p. 588.

12. WDW to Dwight Whitney Marsh, 28 November 1842, quoted in Frederick Rudolph, *Mark Hopkins and the Log: Williams College, 1836–1872* (New Haven, Conn.: Yale University Press, 1956), 221; WDW, "Ornithological Journal" (9 April 1843), WP.

13. Rudolph, *Mark Hopkins*, 142–48; *Williams College Announcements* (Williamstown, Mass., 1845), 16–17.

14. *Williams College Announcements* (1845), 16–17.

15. Washington Gladden, *Recollections* (Boston: Houghton Mifflin, 1909), 72. WDW to Dwight Whitney Marsh, 28 October 1844, quoted in Rudolph, *Mark Hopkins*, 49; WDW to JDW, Sr., 6 October 1844; WDW to Dwight Whitney Marsh, 9 February 1845, WP. Less flattering assessments of Mark Hopkins appear in G. Stanley Hall, *Life and Confessions of a Psychologist* (New York: D. Appleton and Co., 1924), 168–69, and John Bascom, *Things Learned by Living* (New York: G. P. Putnam's Sons, 1913), 58.

16. Rudolph, *Mark Hopkins*, 28; Mark Hopkins, *An Outline Study of Man* (New York: Scribners, 1878), 71. (Hopkin's lectures scarcely changed over the years.)

17. WDW to JDW, 7 January 1872, WP.

18. Rudolph, *Mark Hopkins*, 118.

19. *Williams College Announcements* (1845), 16–17; Charles Darwin, *Autobiography*, ed. Nora Barlow (1864; New York: W. W. Norton, 1969), 59.

20. Receipt from Hopkins, Bridgeman and Co., Booksellers, 30 January 1856; Elizabeth Whitney Putnam to JDW, 4 August 1845, WP.

21. JDW to WDW, 31 January 1843; WDW to JDW, 29 August 1844, 20 March 1845; WDW to Dwight Whitney Marsh, 28 October 1844, WP.

22. William Jones, *The Works of Sir William Jones*, ed. Anna Maria Jones, 13 vols. (London: John Stockdale, John Walker, 1807): 3:34–35.

23. JDW to WDW, 11 November 1850, in Edwin T. Brewster, *Life and Letters of Josiah Dwight Whitney* (Boston: Houghton Mifflin Co., 1909), 114. Elizabeth Whitney Putnam to JDW, 4 August 1845, WP.

24. WDW, "Autobiography"; WDW to JDW, 29 January 1846, WP.

25. Stanley M. Guralnick, "The American Scientist in Higher Education, 1820–1910," in *The Sciences in the American Context: New Perspectives,* ed. Nathan Reingold (Washington, D.C.: Smithsonian Institution Press, 1979), 99–141, on p. 117.

26. WDW, "Autobiography"; JDW to WDW, 25 April 1846, quoted in Diehl, *Americans and German Scholarship,* 121.

27. WDW, "Autobiography"; WDW to JDW, 30 October 1846, 29 January 1847, 31 January 1848, 20 February 1848, 31 July 1848, WP.

28. Diehl, *Americans and German Scholarship,* 120.

29. Whitney's official biographies suggest that Josiah's bringing home Bopp's Sanskrit grammar was a mere happenstance and that Whitney's deciding to learn that language was a resulting whim. Charles R. Lanman, "Memorial Address," in *The Whitney Memorial Meeting,* ed. Charles R. Lanman (Boston: Ginn and Co., 1897), 10–11; Thomas Day Seymour, "W. D. Whitney," in *Portraits of Linguists,* ed. Thomas A. Sebeok (Bloomington: Indiana University Press, 1966), 399–426, on p. 402. Yet the grammar did not arrive until late in 1847, well after Whitney had made his decision to become a philologist.

30. WDW to Freeman Bumstead, 12 May 1848, WP.

31. George E. Day to E. E. Salisbury, 10 May 1849, SP. Day's influence on Whitney's interest in Sanskrit has been overestimated: Seymour, "W. D. Whitney," 401, 411, 421.

32. JDW to WDW, 7 March 1849, in Brewster, *Life and Letters of Josiah Dwight Whitney,* 105. WDW, "Autobiography," WP.

33. WDW, Translation and abridgment of von Bohlen, "On the grammatical structure of the Sanskrit," *Bibliotheca Sacra* 6 (1849): 471–86; Frank Luther Mott, *A History of American Magazines,* 3 vols. (1937, Cambridge, Mass: Belknap Press, 1957), 1:740.

34. WDW to Elizabeth Whitney Putnam, 29 December 1849; WDW to JDW, Sr., 7 January 1850, WP; *Diary of James Hadley,* 32, 35, 58.

35. WDW to Elizabeth Whitney Putnam, 29 December 1849, emphasis in the original; WDW to Freeman Bumstead, 25 November 1849, WP, quoted in Diehl, *Americans and German Scholarship,* 122.

36. WDW to Freeman Bumstead, 6 January 1850, WP, quoted in Diehl, *Americans and German Scholarship,* 122–23.

37. Rudolph Garrigue to WDW, 6 December 1849, WP. WDW, Review of *Studies in English* by M. Schele de Vere, in *NAR* 104 (1867): 631–35, on p. 631.

38. WDW to Elizabeth Whitney Putnam, 29 December 1849, WP; WDW to JDW, Sr., 11 January 1850, quoted in Diehl, *Americans and German Scholarship,* 124.

39. WDW to Elizabeth Whitney Putnam, 31 January 1850, WP.

40. George E. Day to WDW, 13 January 1850, emphasis in the original; Stephen C. Strong to WDW, 4 March, 20 April 1847; Dwight Whitney Marsh to WDW, 7 November 1849; Clarissa Whitney to WDW, 19 February 1850; JDW, Sr., to WDW, 18 October 1850, WP.

41. JDW, Sr., to WDW, n.d. April 1858, WP, emphasis in the original.

42. WDW to Freeman Bumstead, 9 December 1849, WP.

43. WDW to Freeman Bumstead, 23 December 1849, WP.

44. WDW, "Autobiography"; WDW to Freeman Bumstead, 10 December 1850, WP. Whitney Journal, 7 January 1851, quoted in Diehl, *Americans and German Scholarship,* 127.

45. WDW to E. E. Salisbury, 15 February 1851, SP.

46. "Archaeology," in WDW, ed., *The Century Dictionary,* 6 vols. (New York: The Century Co., 1906), 1:293.

47. WDW to E. E. Salisbury, 15 February 1851, WP.

48. Whitney Journal, 7 January 1852, 15 January 1852, WP. The Whitney Family Papers (box 50, folder 36) contain notes Whitney took on lectures at Berlin and Tübingen by Albrecht Weber, Karl R. Lepsius, and Rudolph von Roth.

49. Lanman, "Memorial Address," 23–24.

50. Bruce Sinclair, "Americans Abroad: Science and Cultural Nationalism in the Early Nineteenth Century," in Reingold, *Sciences in the American Context,* 46; F. J. Child to WDW, 25 April 1851; WDW to JDW, Sr., 25 November 1850, WP; Whitney Journal, 25 October 1851, quoted in Diehl, *Americans and German Scholarship,* 181, n. 22.

51. WDW to E. E. Salisbury, 3 January 1853, SP.

52. James Hadley to WDW, 22 November 1850, WP. John Pickering, "Founding Address," *JAOS* 1 (1843): 1–60, on pp. 5–6.

53. WDW to JDW, 20 October 1861, 29 March 1863; WDW to James Whitney, 20 October 1867, WP.

54. Albrecht Weber to the Corresponding Secretary of the American Oriental Society, 28 December 1852, in *PAOS* (1853): 6.

55. E. E. Salisbury to WDW, 19 February 1853 (copy), SP.

56. WDW to E. E. Salisbury, 4 April, 7 May 1853; E. E. Salisbury to WDW, 16 June 1853 (copy), SP.

57. WDW to E. E. Salisbury, 15 August 1853, SP; James Hadley to WDW, 25 June 1853, WP. JDW to WDW, 22 May 1853, quoted in Brewster, *Life and Letters of Josiah Dwight Whitney.*

58. WDW to Elizabeth Whitney Putnam, 15 January, 16 March 1854; WDW to JDW, Sr., 18 January 1854, WP; WDW to E. E. Salisbury, 18 December 1853, 4 February 1854, SP. Josiah Whitney's book was *Metallic Wealth of the United States* (Boston: Grambo, 1854). W. D. Whitney's first book reviews appeared in *JAOS* 4 (1854): 245–61.

59. E. E. Salisbury to WDW, 3 January, 29 March, 11 May 1854; T. D. Woolsey to WDW, 11 May 1854; WDW to JDW, Sr., 15 May, 4 June 1854, WP.

60. Louise Stevenson, *Scholarly Means to Evangelical Ends: The New Haven Scholars and the Transformation of Higher Learning in America, 1830–1890* (Baltimore: Johns Hopkins University Press, 1986), esp. chs. 2, 3, and 5.

61. WDW to JDW, 11 September 1854, 27 December 1854, 28 January 1855, 7 March 1855, 1 April 1855; WDW to Elizabeth Putnam Whitney, 3 November 1854; WDW to JDW, 15 November 1863, WP.

62. WDW to JDW, 11 September 1854, 24 October 1854, 30 September 1855, 16 October 1857, WP; WDW to E. E. Salisbury, 5 June 1854, SP; WDW to Elizabeth Whitney Putnam, 18 August, 3 November 1854; WDW to JDW Sr., 19 October 1854, WP.

63. WDW to JDW, 1 April 1855, WP.

64. JDW, Sr., to WDW, 30 May 1854; WDW to JDW Sr., 4 June 1854; WDW to JDW, 24 October 1854, 9 December 1857; WDW to Charles Arad Joy, 30 December 1854, 1 May 1856 (this last letter announces Whitney's engagement); WDW, "Autobiography," WP. *DAB,* s.v., "Whitney, William Dwight"; "Baldwin, Roger Sherman." Baldwin is perhaps best remembered for his early work as a lawyer: he assisted John Quincy Adams

in successfully defending African slave ship mutineers before the U.S. Supreme Court, in the *Amistad* case of 1841.

65. WDW to Elizabeth Whitney Putnam, 2 December 1854, WP.

66. WDW to Elizabeth Wooster Baldwin, 8 April 1856; WDW to Elizabeth Whitney Putnam, 18 April 1856, WP.

67. WDW to JDW, 23 October, 4 November 1855, WP.

68. JDW, Sr., to WDW, n.d. July 1855, 4 April 1856, WP.

69. WDW to Elizabeth Wooster Baldwin, 8 April 1856, WP.

70. Ibid.

71. WDW to Elizabeth Wooster Baldwin, 9, 10 and 8 April 1856, WP.

72. WDW to Elizabeth Whitney Putnam, 18 April 1856, WP.

73. Ibid.

74. JDW, Sr., to WDW, 25 and 30 September, 7 October 1856; WDW to JDW, 12 October 1856, WP; WDW to E. E. Salisbury, 31 July 1856, SP.

75. WDW to JDW, 12 October 1856, 8 January, 13 September 1857, 27 June 1858; WDW to JDW, Sr., 15 January 1857, WP; WDW to C. E. Norton, 22 December 1857, Norton Papers. James Turner, *The Liberal Education of Charles Eliot Norton* (Baltimore: Johns Hopkins University Press, 1999), 139–41. The Whitneys' European visit lasted from November 1856 until June 1857.

76. WDW to JDW, 13 September 1857, 25 September 1859, WP. Whitney's children were: Edward Baldwin Whitney (1857–1911, Assistant U.S. Attorney General); Williston Clapp Whitney (1859–61, died in infancy); Marian Parker Whitney (1861–1946, Professor of Modern Languages at Vassar College); Roger Sherman Baldwin Whitney (1863–74, drowned while skating on Mill River, New Haven); Emily Henrietta Whitney (1864–?); Margaret Dwight Whitney (1866–?). B. W. Dwight, *History of the Descendants of John Dwight,* 2:836–37.

77. E. E. Salisbury to T. D. Woolsey, 29 March 1859; E. E. Salisbury to WDW, 4 July 1859, WP; WDW to E. E. Salisbury, 11 July 1859, SP.

78. George Ripley to WDW, 4 September 1860; WDW to Elizabeth Whitney Putnam, 27 January 1861; WDW to JDW, 19 January 1861, 16 January 1862, 24 August 1863, 6 January 1864, 17 September 1865, WP.

79. James Hadley to WDW, 7 April 1851, WP.

80. WDW to JDW, 15 November 1863, WP.

81. WDW to JDW, 12 October 1856, 21 July 1857, WP.

82. WDW to Ezra Abbot, 21 October 1856, 14 October 1857, Ezra Abbot Papers. Report of Committee on Efficiency: *JAOS* 6 (1857): 579.

83. The AOS reform campaign is described in WDW to JDW, 16 October, 9 December 1857, 4 May 1858; WDW to Elizabeth Baldwin Whitney, 30 April 1858; WDW to JDW, Sr., 2 May 1858; Charles Short to WDW, 29 October, 13 November 1858, WP. Further details appear in Whitney's letters to AOS Recording Secretary Ezra Abbot during 1857 and 1858: Ezra Abbot Papers.

84. WDW to JDW, 12 October 1856, WP. The alleged donor was G. W. Wales' brother Harry Wales, of Cambridge, Massachusetts.

85. *DAB,* s.v. "Hall, Fitzedward." WDW to JDW, 16 October, 13 November 1859, 11 March 1860, WP.

86. WDW to G. W. Wales, 4 June 1862, WP (copy).

87. G. W. Wales to WDW, 10 June 1862; WDW to E. R. Hoar, 28 June 1862, WP (copy).

88. WDW to C. E. Norton, 5 May 1864, Norton Papers.

89. WDW to JDW, 11 August 1866, WP.

T W O: Indological Foreshadowings

1. E. E. Salisbury, "Text of the Atharva-Veda," *JAOS* 3 (1853): 501; Notice of "Roth and Whitney's Edition of the Atharva-Veda," *JAOS* 3 (1856): 226; WDW, "Index to Atharva-Veda Sanhita," *Indische Studien* 4 (1857): 9–64; WDW, "Index Verborum," *JAOS* 12 (1881): 1–383.

2. WDW, "The St. Petersburg Lexicon," *JAOS* 4 (1854): 465–66. Thomas R. Lounsbury, Obituary of W. D. Whitney, *Proceedings of the American Academy of Arts and Sciences* (1895): 579–89, on p. 582.

3. An initial translation of the *Suryasiddhanta* had been made by Ebenezer Burgess, a retired missionary to India and a member of the AOS. Yet Whitney, ostensibly serving as Burgess's assistant, was obliged to revise the whole of Burgess's work, which he described as "worthless." WDW to JDW, 27 March 1858, 16 October 1859, WP. Ebenezer Burgess, "Translation of the Sūrya-Siddhānta, a Text-Book of Hindu Astronomy, with Notes and an Appendix," *JAOS* 6 (1860): 141–98. S. H. Sen, "Survey of Studies in European Languages," in *History of Astronomy in India,* ed. S. H. Sen and K. S. Shukla (New Delhi: Indian National Science Academy, 1985), 65, says that the explanatory notes by Whitney appended to the text are of "inestimable value."

4. C. H. J. Warner quoted in Arthur Versluis, *American Transcendentalism and Asian Religions* (New York: Oxford University Press, 1993), 144.

5. WDW, "Present State of the Question as to the Origin of Language," *OLS,* 1:279–91, on pp. 280–81.

6. WDW, "Pauthier: Antiquité de l'Histoire, etc., Chinoises," *NAR* 108 (January 1869): 291–96, on p. 295. The quoted phrases are from 1 Thessalonians 5:19.

7. WDW to JDW, 16 October 1859, WP.

8. WDW, "History of the Vedic Texts," *JAOS* 4 (1854): 245–61; WDW, Review of *Handbuch der Sanskritsprache* (1853) by Theodor Benfey, in *JAOS* 4 (1854): 468–70; WDW, "The Vedas," *OLS,* 1:1–45.

9. J. F. Staal, *A Reader in the Sanskrit Grammarians* (Cambridge, Mass.: MIT Press, 1972), 138–41.

10. George H. Daniels, *American Science in the Age of Jackson* (New York: Columbia University Press, 1968), 102, 113–15.

11. WDW, "The Teachings of the Vedic Pratisakhyas with respect to the Theory of Accent," *JAOS* 7 (1862): lvii; WDW, "Contributions from the Atharva-Veda to the Theory of Sanskrit Verbal Accent," *PAOS* 5 (1856): 387–88.

12. WDW, "Contributions from the Atharva-Veda," 387–88.

13. WDW, "Sanscrit," 338. Rosane Rocher, "The Past up to the Introduction of Neogrammarian Thought: Whitney and Europe," in *The European Background of American Linguistics,* ed. Henry M. Hoenigswald (Dordrecht-Holland: Furis, 1979), 5–22, on p. 6.

14. WDW, "Sanscrit," 334–35, 338.

15. WDW, "The Avesta," *OLS,* 1:149–97, on pp. 184–85.

16. WDW, "Veda," in *New American Cyclopedia,* vol. 16, 38–40; WDW, "The Vedas," *OLS,* 1:6; WDW, "Sanscrit," 337; WDW, "Müller's History of Vedic Literature," *OLS,* 1:64–99, on p. 68.

17. WDW, "The Cosmogonic Hymn, Rg-Veda X. 129," *JAOS* 11 (1882): cxi.

18. Ibid.

19. WDW, "The Vedas," *OLS,* 1:23–31. Further remarks disparaging "the Hindoo mind" appear in WDW, "Sanscrit," in *New American Cyclopedia* (New York: Appleton, 1859), 14:334–39, especially on pp. 337–38.

20. *DNB,* s.v. "Max Müller, Friedrich."

21. Ibid.

22. WDW to E. E. Salisbury, 28 December 1853, 5 July 1854, SP; F. Max Müller to WDW, 20 June 1860, WP; WDW to E. E. Salisbury, 25 June, 10 July 1860, SP. Whitney also endorsed Müller for the Boden chair before the members of the AOS: WDW, "Müller's History of Vedic Literature," *JAOS* 7 (1860): viii.

23. Fitzedward Hall to WDW, 4 July, 30 August 1860; D. C. Scudder to WDW, 17 January 1861, WP.

24. WDW to JDW, 19 and 31 January 1861, WP.

25. Biot's works on this subject were his *Études sur l'astronomie indienne* (1859) and *Études sur l'astronomie chinoise* (1862).

26. Sen, "Survey of Studies," 65–69.

27. WDW, "Hindu Astronomy," *Proceedings of the American Association for the Advancement of Science* 13 (1859): 354 (title only); WDW, "Reply to the Strictures of Professor Weber upon an Essay respecting the Asterismal System of the Hindus, Arabs, and Chinese," *JAOS* 8 (1866): 382–98, on p. 385. Whitney also tested the Indian science using a modern almanac's projection: WDW, "Comparison of the Elements of the Lunar Eclipse of Feb. 6th, 1860, as calculated according to the data and methods of the Sūrya-Siddhānta, and as determined by modern science," *PAOS* (1859): 4–5.

28. WDW, "On the Lunar Zodiac of India, Arabia, and China," *OLS,* 2:341–421, on pp. 363–64, 369–70, 376, 407.

29. WDW, "On the Views of Biot and Weber respecting the Relations of the Hindu and Chinese Systems of Asterisms; with an Addition on Müller's Views respecting the Same Subject," *JAOS* 8 (1863): 1–94. (Whitney's "Lunar Zodiac" article, published in *OLS,* vol. 2, was a revised version of this 1863 essay.)

30. WDW, "On the Origin of the Hindu Science of Astronomy," *PAOS* (1859): 8; Unsigned, "American Scientific Association," *New York Times* (10 August 1859), in Newsclippings File, WP.

31. WDW, "Lunar Zodiac," 418–19.

32. Ibid., 370.

33. A. Weber to WDW, 27 June 1867; WDW to Maria Whitney, 30 October 1870, WP.

34. WDW to JDW, 26 August 1860, WP. WDW, "Müller's History of Vedic Literature," *OLS,* 1:74.

35. WDW, "On the Views of Biot and Weber," 73–83. (See note 29 above; the entire section dealing with Müller's theory is on pp. 72–94.)

36. WDW to JDW, 7 October 1863, WP.

37. Max Müller to WDW, 18 February 1863, WP.

38. WDW to JDW, 7 October 1863, WP.

39. Max Müller to WDW, 22 November 1863, WP.

40. Max Müller to WDW, 13 January, 29 March 1864, 20 December 1867, 13 February 1871, WP.

THREE: Victorian Language Debates

1. My interpretation of Locke comes from Roy Harris and Talbot J. Taylor, *Landmarks in Linguistic Thought,* 2nd ed. (1989; New York: Routledge, 1997), 1:129–32; and Talbot J. Taylor, "Liberalism in Lockean Linguistics," *Historiographia Linguistica* 17 (1990): 99–109.

2. John Locke, *Essay Concerning Human Understanding* (1690), Book III, ch. 2, sections 1–2, quoted in Harris and Taylor, *Landmarks,* 1:126.

3. Locke, *Essay,* Book III, ch. 1, sec. 5, quoted in Harris and Taylor, *Landmarks,* 1:136.

4. Horne Tooke quoted in Harris and Taylor, *Landmarks,* 1:156–57, 161.

5. William Hazlitt quoted in Hans Aarsleff, *The Study of Language in England, 1780–1860* (Princeton, N.J.: Princeton University Press, 1967), 71. The Anglican churchman and philologist R. C. Trench noted the intellectual stimulation the *Diversions* often supplied: Richard Chenevix Trench, *On the Study of Words,* 2nd London edition, 1852), 5.

6. John William Donaldson, *The New Cratylus, or Contributions Towards a More Accurate Knowledge of the Greek Language,* 3rd ed. (London: John W. Parker and Son, 1859), 110.

7. Ralph Waldo Emerson, *Selected Writings of Ralph Waldo Emerson* (New York: New American Library, 1946), 200–201 (in ch. 4, "Language"); Henry David Thoreau, *Walden and Civil Disobedience* (1854, New York: Viking, 1983), 354–57 (in the chapter entitled "Spring").

8. Harris and Taylor, *Landmarks,* 1:153–58; James H. Stam, *Inquiries into the Origin of Language: The Fate of a Question* (New York: Harper & Row, 1978), 209–13, 224–25;

9. Herbert Hovenkamp, *Science and Religion in America, 1800–1860* (Philadelphia: University of Pennsylvania Press, 1978), 97–117.

10. Josiah W. Gibbs, *Philological Studies* (New Haven, Conn.: Durrie and Peck, 1857), 15. Overlooking their Lockean origin, Gibbs attributed his basic principles to "distinguished German philologians," particularly Karl Ferdinand Becker (see Preface).

11. Gibbs, *Philological Studies,* 16–18.

12. Ibid., 190–91.

13. Josiah W. Gibbs, "On the Natural Significancy of Articulate Sounds," *Biblical Repository,* 2nd ser. 2 (July 1839): 166–73, on pp. 166–67; Unsigned, Review of *Philological Studies* by J. W. Gibbs, in *Bibliotheca Sacra* 15 (1858): 237.

14. H. Bushnell, *God in Christ* (Hartford, Conn.: Brown and Parsons, 1849), 8, 20, 29.

15. Ibid., 37–38.

16. Ibid., 30.

17. [Robert Chambers], *Vestiges of the Natural History of Creation* (1844; New York: Humanities Press, 1969), 297–98, 305–6, 311–15. Rousseau's view appeared in two different works: his 1749 *Essay on the Origin of Language,* chs. 2 and 4, and his 1755 *Discourse on the Origin of Inequality,* Part I.

18. W. G. T. Shedd, "The Relation of Language to Thought," *Bibliotheca Sacra* 5

(1848): 650–63; Henry M. Goodwin, "Thoughts, Words, and Things," *Bibliotheca Sacra* 6 (1849): 271–300, on p. 271; Daniel R. Goodwin, "The Unity of Language and Mankind," *NAR* 73 (1851): 164–84, on pp. 165–67, 174, 178, 184; Isidor Loewenthal, "The Origin of Language," *Princeton Review* 24 (July 1852): 405–42, on pp. 414, 421.

19. Bushnell, *God in Christ*, 13–14; Francis Lieber, *The Origin and Development of the First Constituents of Civilization* (Columbia, S.C.: I. C. Morgan, 1845), 15–17; Francis Andrew March, "The Origin of Language," *PAPA* 2 (1871): 18.

20. B. W. Dwight, *Modern Philology* (New York: A. S. Barnes & Burr, 1859), 280–81, 263; James Hadley, Review of *Modern Philology* by Benjamin W. Dwight, in *New Englander* 17 (1859): 1087–89.

21. T. S. Lothrop, "The Development of Language," *Universalist Quarterly* 17 (1860): 255–58; J. S. Lee, "The Philosophy of Language," *Universalist Quarterly* 23 (1866): 457–75.

22. F. Max Müller, *The life and letters of the Right Honourable Friedrich Max Müller; edited by his wife*, 2 vols. (London, New York: Longmans, Green, 1902), 1:246–48.

23. F. Max Müller, *Lectures on the Science of Language*, First Series, 2nd London edition, revised (New York: Charles Scribner, 1862), 1:22–23, 354. Max Müller can be seen as the philological counterpart of the Swiss zoologist Louis Agassiz, the idealist and anti-Darwinian who enjoyed a celebrated career in America.

24. F. Max Müller, *Lectures on the Science of Language*, Second Series (1864; New York: Charles Scribner, 1871), 2:79, emphasis in the original.

25. Müller, *Science of Language*, 1:228. For context, see M. H. Abrams, *Natural Supernaturalism: Tradition and Revolution in Romantic Literature* (New York: Norton, 1971), 65–70, 217–25, 255.

26. Here I draw from the discussion of Max Müller in Maurice Olender, *The Languages of Paradise: Race, Religion, and Philology in the Nineteenth Century*, trans. Arthur Goldhammer (Cambridge, Mass.: Harvard University Press, 1992).

FOUR: Building a System of General Linguistics

1. WDW to Freeman Bumstead, 6 January 1850, WP.

2. WDW to JDW, 1 April 1855; WDW to Elizabeth Whitney Putnam, 18 November 1855, WP.

3. WDW, "On the Origin of Language," *PAOS* (November 1858): 8–9; WDW, "Strictures upon the Views of M. Ernst Renan respecting the Origin and Early History of Languages," *PAOS* (October 1859): 9–10. These two pieces were published only as abstracts. Renan's views had appeared in his *Origin of Language* (1848). WDW to JDW, 5 June, 13 November 1859, WP.

4. WDW, "The Scope and Method of Linguistic Science," *Proceedings of the American Association for the Advancement of Science* 13 (1859): 355 (title only). Unsigned, "The True Method in Philology," *The (Springfield) Republican* (6 August 1859), in WP.

5. WDW to JDW, 3 November 1861, WP.

6. WDW, *Max Müller and the Science of Language: A Criticism* (New York: D. Appleton and Co., 1892), 77–78.

7. [C. C. Smith], "Müller's Lectures on the Science of Language," *NAR* 95 (July 1862): 265–67. American praise for Müller's lectures also appeared in Unsigned, "The

Science of Language," *Boston Review* 2 (September 1862): 539–48; [W. F. Allen], "Science of Language," *Christian Examiner* 73 (July 1862): 140–44.

8. Joseph Henry to WDW, 16 December 1862; WDW to JDW, 3 November 1861, WP. A prospectus advertising Whitney's series appeared in the Smithsonian Institution, *Annual Report* (1863): 41–42.

9. WDW to JDW, 7 February, 20 March, 21 August, 10 October 1864; Joseph Henry to WDW, 13 November 1863; B. E. Cotting to WDW, 17 November 1864, WP; Boston *Evening Transcript* (14 January 1865), in WP.

10. WDW to C. E. Norton, 1 November, 10 December 1863, 5 November 1864, Norton Papers; C. E. Norton to WDW, 27 November 1863, WP.

11. WDW, "On Müller's Second Series of Lectures on the Science of Language," *NAR* 100 (1865): 565–81. WDW to JDW, 26 February 1865, WP.

12. WDW to JDW, 7 October 1863, WP.

13. WDW to JDW, 7 March 1865, WP; WDW to C. E. Norton, 4 March 1865, 14 October, 1866, 11 May 1867, Norton Papers.

14. WDW to Albrecht Weber, 16 June 1864, Weber Papers; WDW to JDW, 7 November 1865, WP. WDW, "Brief Abstract of a Series of Six Lectures on the Principles of Linguistic Science," Smithsonian Institution, *Annual Report* (1864): 95–116.

15. WDW to JDW, 29 November 1865, 8 March 1866; Charles Scribner to WDW, 13 March 1867; WDW to JDW, 3 and 19 March 1866; Charles Short to WDW, 24 January 1866, WP.

16. J. S. Lee, "The Philosophy of Language," *Universalist Quarterly* 33 (1866): 457–75, on p. 457. WDW to Albrecht Weber, 12 April 1864, Weber Papers.

17. WDW to JDW, 19 October 1866; Charles Scribner to WDW, 13 March 1867; N. Trübner to WDW, 20 and 29 July, 26 August 1867, WP; WDW to A. Weber, 22 September 1867, Weber Papers.

18. Whitney account books, box 53, folder 54, WP.

19. Benvenuto Terracini long ago noted the affinity between Whitney's thought and British empiricism, especially as expressed by Adam Smith and John Stuart Mill (see "Le origini della linguistica generale: Whitney," in *Guida allo studio della linguistica storica* [Rome: Dell'Ateneo, 1949], 73–110, especially pp. 91–93). I have found no evidence that Whitney read or took a special interest in Mill.

20. WDW, *LSL*, 32; WDW, *LGL*, 19.

21. Ferdinand de Saussure, *Course in General Linguistics,* trans. and annotated by Roy Harris (1916; La Salle, Ill.: Open Court, 1983), 26, 100, 110 (page numbers from the original edition).

22. *Williams College Announcements* (1845), 16–17; Hugh Blair, *Lectures on Rhetoric and Belles Lettres,* ed. Harold F. Harding (1783; Carbondale: Southern Illinois University Press, 1965), 98, also pp. 97–116, 137–42; George Campbell, *Philosophy of Rhetoric* (1776; London: Tegg and Son, 1838), 141; Levi Hedge, *Elements of Logick,* 3rd. ed. (Boston: Hilliard, Gray, and Co., 1832), 30; Richard Whately, *Elements of Logic,* rev. ed. (Boston and Cambridge: James Munroe, 1851), 19.

23. WDW, *LSL*, 14; also: WDW, *LGL*, 18, 19.

24. Saussure later showed general agreement with the eighteenth-century Scots on these issues; see *Course in General Linguistics,* 107–9.

25. Noah Webster, *The American Dictionary of the English Language,* revised by

Chauncey A. Goodrich (Springfield, Mass.: George and Charles Merriam, 1853, 1861), s.v. "language."

26. WDW to C. E. Norton, 24 August 1865, Norton Papers; emphasis in the original. The article in question was "Is the Study of Language a Physical Science?" *NAR* 101 (1865): 434–74.

27. WDW to JDW, 9 June 1872, WP.

28. A. H. Sayce, Review of *The Life and Growth of Language* by WDW, in *The (London) Academy* 8 (18 September 1875): 311–12, on p. 311.

29. WDW, "Present State of the Question as to the Origin of Language," *OLS*, 1:279–91, on pp. 288–89; also WDW, *LSL*, 435. WDW to George Curtius, 30 May 1873, Curtius Papers.

30. A private controversy arose over the similarity between Whitney's views on these subjects and those of the Dane Johan Nicolai Madvig (1804–86). Madvig's friends accused Whitney of borrowing without acknowledgment from an essay Madvig wrote in 1842. Brigitte Hauger, "Odd Man Out: The Language Theory of Johan Nicolai Madvig (1804–1886)," in *History of Linguistics, 1993*, ed. Kurt R. Jankowsky (Philadelphia: John Benjamins, 1995), 209–19. Whitney denied the charge, noting that he had not been aware of Madvig's writings until they appeared in German translation in 1875. WDW to A. H. Edgren, 12 September 1881 (copy); WDW to the editor of *Norsk Tijdshift*, 20 December 1881 (copy), WP. This confirms Hans Aarsleff's judgment in *From Locke to Saussure: Essays on the Study of Language and Intellectual History* (Minneapolis: University of Minnesota Press, 1982), 299–302.

31. WDW, *LSL*, 55, 128; also: WDW, *LGL*, 140–43.

32. Richard Chenevix Trench, *On the Study of Words* (London, 1852); Unsigned, "The Revised Webster," *Biblical Repository and Princeton Review* 37 (July 1865): 374–78, on p. 378.

33. WDW, *LSL*, 128.

34. Saussure, *Course in General Linguistics,* Part I, ch. 3: "Static Linguistics and Evolutionary Linguistics" (114–40).

35. WDW, *LGL*, 155–156; WDW, *LSL*, 151.

36. Some writers accuse Whitney of heavy-handed prescriptivism: Julie Tetel Andresen, *Linguistics in America, 1769–1924: A Critical History* (New York: Routledge, 1990), 141, 145, 149–50, 155; and William Labov, *Principles of Linguistic Change*, 2 vols. (Cambridge, Mass.: Blackwell, 1994), 1:22, 2:17, 30–31 (with qualification: 2:30n). Gavin Jones, *Strange Talk: The Politics of Dialect Literature in Gilded Age America* (Berkeley: University of California Press, 1999), ch. 1, charges Whitney with an intolerance of linguistic diversity yet rightly notes that his stance was at once prescriptivist and descriptivist.

37. WDW, Review of *Bad English* by George Washington Moon, *Nation* 7 (10 December 1868): 482–83, on p. 483. See also: WDW, Review of *Strictures on Dean Alford's Queen's English* by G. W. Moon, *New Englander* 26 (January 1867): 173–76.

38. Whitney's view of popular speech is described in Kenneth Cmiel's *Democratic Eloquence: The Fight Over Popular Speech in Nineteenth-Century America* (New York: William Morrow, 1990), 157–62. Jones, *Strange Talk*, ch. 1, finds considerable agreement between philologists such as Whitney and the genteel critics, yet he arrives at this view, in part, by attributing to Whitney a "largely favorable review" of R. G. White's *Words and Their Uses (Strange Talk,* 28, 280). The author of that article was actually Charles

Astor Bristed (1820–74). Similarly, the 1863 *NAR* article "The Evolution of Language," which Jones attributes to Whitney, was actually by John Fiske (*Strange Talk*, 279). *Index to North American Review,* Vols. 1–125, 1815–77, by William Cushing.

39. WDW, *LSL,* 171.

40. WDW, *LSL,* 149, 150, 171–72, 159; WDW, *LGL,* 158.

41. An opposing thesis, suggesting that Whitney worried about the expansion and political viability of American English, appears in Jones, *Strange Talk,* and especially Andresen, *Linguistics in America.*

42. Campbell, *Philosophy of Rhetoric,* 141–52, especially p. 143; WDW, *Essentials of English Grammar. For the Use of Schools* (Boston: Ginn and Co., 1877), 3.

43. WDW, Review of *Exemplifications of False Philology* by Fitzedward Hall, *Nation* 16:411 (15 May 1873): 334–35, on p. 335. This review of Hall's book contains a scathing critique of R. G. White's work. By contrast, Whitney had earlier described White as the best of the genteel critics: WDW, Review of *Words and Their Uses* by Richard Grant White, *New Englander* 30 (April 1871): 305–11, on p. 307.

44. WDW, "Brief Abstract," 97–98; WDW, *LSL,* 174, 182–84; WDW, *LGL,* 154–55.

45. WDW, *LSL,* 148–51, 171–74, quotation from p. 150. See also WDW, *LGL,* 156–59. Gavin Jones (*Strange Talk,* 26–27) suggests that Whitney placed less emphasis in *LGL* than in his earlier book on the ability of American English to assimilate dialects. Yet Whitney's essential stance did not change. He still argued in *LGL* that the general conformity to elite usage would *in fact* bring about a desirable unity, at least in "modern enlightened communities" (*LGL,* 158). In both books, moreover, Whitney said that an equilibrium between dialectal unity and diversity actually exists in most languages: *LSL,* 161–62, 168; *LGL,* 154–58.

46. WDW, "The Study of English Grammar," Part 1, *New England Journal of Education* 3:12 (18 March 1876): 1; WDW, *Essentials of English Grammar,* iii, v, 3–4.

47. WDW, "On Lepsius's Standard Alphabet," *PAOS* (October 1861): xlix; WDW, Review of *Sounds and Their Relations* by A. M. Bell, *The Critic* 3:25 (17 December 1881): 349; and WDW, Review of *First Lessons in Reading* by Soule and Wheeler, *NAR* 104 (1867): 655–58.

48. WDW, "The Sovereign Reason for Spelling Reform," *New York Evening Post* (19 May 1883); "Report of the Committee on Spelling Reform," *PAPA* (1876): 36; and "Simplified Spelling: A Symposium," *American Anthropologist* 6 (1893): 190–93. This last piece was the single instance I have found in which Whitney himself used simplified spelling in a publication.

49. WDW to George Curtius, 15 February 1873, Curtius Papers.

50. WDW, *LSL,* vi–vii.

51. WDW, *LGL,* 315, 318.

52. Unsigned, "The Philosophical Study of Language," *Methodist Quarterly Review* 31 (April, July, October 1849): 250–68, 471–84, 620–33, on pp. 251, 268. See also: Unsigned, "English Philology," *New Englander* 2 (1844): 350–59, on p. 351; [Mary Lowell Putnam], "The Significance of the Alphabet," *NAR* 68 (January 1849): 160–82, on pp. 160–61, 165; John Fiske, "The Evolution of Language," *NAR* 97 (1863): 411–50, on p. 413; Unsigned, "The Natural Revolutions of Language," *Methodist Quarterly Review* 39 (1857): 576–94, on p. 593.

53. WDW, "Franz Bopp" (obituary), *Proceedings of the American Academy of Arts and Sciences* 8 (June 1868): 47–49; WDW, *LSL,* 236.

54. WDW, *LGL,* 50–53, 45–47.

55. Ibid. 55–61.

56. Ibid., 83.

57. Ibid., 85.

58. Ibid., 85, 28, 82.

59. WDW, *LSL,* 28, 82; also: 55–61, 69; WDW, *LGL,* 75.

60. WDW, *LGL,* 79. Brigitte Nerlich, *Change in Language: Whitney, Bréal, and Wegener* (New York: Routledge, 1990), 64, suggests that Whitney borrowed his notion of semantic flexibility from Charles Lyell's *Geological Evidences of the Antiquity of Man* (1863). Yet Whitney held his main ideas on the subject by the time of his 1864 Smithsonian lectures; see WDW, "Brief Abstract," 101. Also, Whitney's own copy of Lyell's *Antiquity,* held in the AOS Library, is dated in Whitney's hand with the year 1864 (not 1863), suggesting that Whitney would not have had time to read that work prior to composing the lectures he gave in March of that year.

61. WDW, *LGL,* 79–82, 47, 48; also: WDW, *LSL,* 101–4.

62. WDW, *LSL,* 132; also: WDW, *LGL,* 87–88.

63. WDW, *LSL,* 128.

64. Josiah W. Gibbs, *Philological Studies* (New Haven, Conn.: Durrie and Peck, 1857): 15, 18; WDW, *LGL,* 87, emphasis added.

65. WDW, *LSL,* 73.

66. WDW, "Memoirs of the Linguistic Society of Paris," *Nation* 6 (23 April 1868): 331.

67. F. W. Farrar, *Origin of Language* (1860), and *Chapters on Language* (1865); Edward B. Tylor, "On the Origin of Language," *Fortnightly Review* 4 (1866): 544–59.

68. Although Whitney appreciated Wedgwood's origins theory, he strongly criticized his etymologies; see WDW, Review of *A Dictionary of English Etymology* by Hensleigh Wedgwood, in *NAR* 115 (1872): 425–26. Wedgwood protested (H. Wedgwood to WDW, 4 December 1872, WP), yet he joined Whitney as an ally in the subsequent fight against Max Müller.

69. WDW, "Brief Abstract," 115–16; WDW, "Origin of Language," *OLS,* 1:279–80, 283, emphasis in the original.

70. WDW, *LSL,* 255–256; F. Max Müller, *Lectures on the Science of Language,* from the 2nd London edition, revised, First Series (New York: Charles Scribner, 1862), 1:252, 286.

71. WDW, Obituary for August Schleicher, *Nation* 9 (January 28, 1869): 70; WDW, *LGL,* 199, 200; WDW, "Present State of the Question," 283; WDW, *LSL,* 264; Müller, *Science of Language,* 1:356–58.

72. WDW, *LSL,* 424–25; Müller, *Science of Language,* 1:374.

73. Adam Smith, "Considerations Concerning the First Formation of Languages," in Adam Smith, *The Theory of the Moral Sentiments,* ed. Dugald Stewart (1759; London: G. Bell and Sons, 1911), 507–9.

74. Müller, *Science of Language,* 1:374.

75. Ibid., 1:376.

76. Ibid., 1:375, 377, emphasis added.

77. Ibid., 1:358.

78. Ibid., 1:361, 365–67.

79. J. G. Herder quoted in James H. Stam, *Inquiries into the Origin of Language: The Fate of a Question* (New York: Harper and Row, 1978), 117; see also, 121–27.

80. Max Müller, *Science of Language,* 1:384–85.

81. WDW to JDW, 20 March 1845, WP.

82. Dugald Stewart, *Elements of the Philosophy of the Human Mind* (1792; Albany: E. and E. Hosford, 1822), 79–84; Blair, *Lectures on Rhetoric and Belles Lettres,* 141–42; Campbell, *Philosophy of Rhetoric,* 252–57. This moderate Common-Sense nominalism (or "conceptualism") is clearly outlined in James Browne, "Origin and Affinities of Languages," *Edinburgh Review* 51 (July 1830): 529–64.

83. WDW, *LSL,* 423, 424.

84. WDW, *LSL,* v–vi.

85. Hensleigh Wedgwood, *Dictionary of English Etymology* (London: N. Trübner, 1859), 1:ii; and *On the Origin of Language* (London: N. Trübner, 1866), 1–7, 128–31. Wedgwood faulted Müller specifically for not adhering to the uniformitarian principle: *Origin of Language,* 6–7.

86. This popular definition of "uniformitarianism" goes more precisely under the name *actualism.* For the classic discussion of these concepts, see Martin J. S. Rudwick "Uniformity and Progression: Reflections on the Structure of Geological Theory in the Age of Lyell," in *Perspectives in the History of Science and Technology,* ed. Duane H. D. Roller (Norman: University of Oklahoma Press, 1971), 209–27.

87. WDW, *LSL,* 287.

88. WDW, *LSL,* 38; WDW, *LGL,* 299.

89. WDW, *LSL,* 433–34.

90. WDW, *LSL,* 430; WDW, *LGL,* 294, emphasis added.

91. WDW, *LSL,* 297, 427, 428. Seconding Whitney's critique was the American scientific writer John Fiske: "The Genesis of Language," *NAR* 109 (October 1869): 305–67.

92. Müller, *Science of Language,* 1:viii, 428–29; WDW, "On Müller's Lectures on the Science of Language, sixth edition," *NAR* 113 (1871): 430–41, reprinted in *OLS,* 1:262–78.

93. [Noah Porter], "The New Infidelity," *New Englander* 11 (1853): 277–95; Horace Bushnell, *Nature and the Supernatural* (New York: Scribner's, 1858): 16–18.

94. J. S. Mill's book was entitled *The Positive Philosophy of Auguste Comte* (1866); Chauncey Wright, "Mill on Comte," *Nation* 2 (4 January 1866): 20–21; and "Peabody's Positive Philosophy," *NAR* 106 (1868): 285–94; John Fiske, "Mill's Positive Philosophy of Auguste Comte," *NAR* 102 (1866): 275–80, on p. 278.

95. E. L. Youmans, ed., *The Culture Demanded by Modern Life* (New York: D. Appleton, 1867), 377.

96. Unsigned, "Herbert Spencer's Philosophy; Atheism, etc.," *Biblical Repository and Princeton Review* 37 (April 1865): 243 70; G. P. Fisher, "Porter's Human Intellect," *NAR* 108 (January 1869): 280–86; Samson Talbot, "Development and Human Descent," *Baptist Quarterly* 6 (1872): 129–46, esp. pp. 144–45.

97. WDW, "Languages and Dialects," *NAR* 104 (1867): 30–64, on pp. 31, 32; WDW, "Schleicher and the Physical Theory of Language," *OLS,* 1:298–331, on p. 314. Whitney made the same point in private: WDW to C. E. Norton, 4 March, 10 October 1865, Norton Papers.

98. WDW to JDW, 30 October 1864, WP; [W. H. Green], "Modern Philology," *Princeton Review* 36 (October 1864): 629–52, on pp. 633, 634, 637, 641.

99. Unsigned, Review of *Language and the Study of Language* by W. D. Whitney, *Congregationalist Review* 8 (March 1868): 187; William A. Stevens, "Growth and History of Language," *Baptist Quarterly* 3 (1869): 419–35, on pp. 431–32. Horace Bushnell charitably treated Whitney's book as if it potentially buttressed his own view of language—if only Whitney had dwelt more on the moral and religious implications of faded metaphor—see "Our Gospel a Gift to the Imagination," in H. Bushnell, *Building Eras in Religion* (New York: Charles Scribner's Sons, 1881), 249–85, on pp. 268–69. This essay (first published in 1869) was a reworking of the "Preliminary Dissertation on Language" in Bushnell's *God in Christ* (1849). Another favorable review was: John Fiske, Review of *Language and the Study of Language* by W. D. Whitney, in *Nation* 5 (7 November 1867): 369–70.

100. [C. A. Aiken], "Whitney on Language," *Princeton Review* 40 (April 1868): 263–92, on pp. 270, 269 n; Unsigned, Review of *Language and the Study of Language* by W. D. Whitney, in *Catholic World* 6 (1867): 423–25, on p. 423.

101. WDW to JDW, 8 December 1867, WP; WDW to C. E. Norton, 22 February 1867, Norton Papers.

102. Unsigned, Review of *Language and the Study of Language* by W. D. Whitney, in *Westminster Review* 89 (January 1868): 138–39.

F I V E: Organizing a New Science

1. See, for example: William H. Sewell, *Work and Revolution in France: The Language of Labor from the Old Regime to 1848* (Cambridge, UK: Cambridge University Press, 1980); and Daniel T. Rodgers, *Contested Truths: Keywords in American Politics Since Independence* (New York: Basic Books, 1987). On the discursive formation of knowledge disciplines, see Michel Foucault, *The Order of Things: An Archaeology of the Human Sciences* (New York: Pantheon, 1970), xiv. The other classic source is Raymond Williams, *Keywords: A Vocabulary of Culture and Society,* rev. ed. (New York: Oxford University Press, 1983).

2. Noah Webster and Chauncey Goodrich, *An American Dictionary of the English Language* (Springfield, Ill.: G. and C. Merriam, 1869), s.v. "science." A canvass of the editions of Webster's Dictionary from 1847, 1853, 1857, 1861, 1865, 1873, and 1883 reveals surprisingly little change in their definitions of "science." Although the list of qualifiers, such as "*pure* science," grew as time went on, the basic definition was invariably broad: "knowledge, especially knowledge systematically arranged"; and "learning having a certain completeness; philosophical knowledge." Noah Webster, *An American Dictionary of the English Language,* revised by Chauncey A. Goodrich (Springfield, Ill.: G. and C. Merriam, 1865), emphasis in the original.

3. Simon Newcomb quoted in I. Bernard Cohen, *Science and American Society in the First Century of the Republic* (Columbus: Ohio State University Press, 1981), 23–24. Also see Noah Porter's definition of science in *The Human Intellect* (New York: Charles Scribner, 1868), 437.

4. C. Darwin to E. Haeckel, 20 December 1868, Haeckel Haus Archives, Jena; and *The Descent of Man and Selection in Relation to Sex* (1871; Princeton, N.J.: Princeton University Press, 1981), 55, where Darwin referred to "the noble science of philology."

5. R. Williams, *Keywords,* 276–80. Charles Hodge, *What is Darwinism?* (New York: Scribner and Armstrong, 1874), 128. An earlier instance of this complaint appeared in

James Warley Miles, *The Student of Philology* (Charlestown, S.C.: John Russell, 1853), 5–6.

6. WDW to JDW, 20 April 1858, WP.

7. WDW to JDW, 20 April, 4 May 1858; WDW to JDW, Sr., 2 May 1858, WP. *Proceedings of the American Association for the Advancement of Science* 12 (1858): 286–87. Whitney's paper was entitled "Analysis, Classification and Representation of the Sounds of the English Spoken Alphabet." (The ASSA *Proceedings* gives the titles but no abstracts of these papers.) J. P. Leslie's paper was "On the Insensible Gradation of Words in Comparative Philology, illustrated by Five Charts."

8. WDW to JDW, 5 June 1859, WP. WDW, "Scope and Method of Linguistic Science," *Proceedings of AAAS* (1859): 355 (title only).

9. "The True Method in Philology," *The (Springfield) Republican,* n.d., in Newsclippings File, WP.

10. "American Scientific Association," *New York Times* (10 August 1859), in Newsclippings File, WP.

11. WDW to JDW, 4 May 1858; WDW to Elizabeth Baldwin Whitney, 30 April 1858, WP.

12. WDW to JDW, 14 November 1860, WP.

13. WDW to JDW, 24 May 1863, WP, emphasis in the original. *Memoirs of the American Academy of Arts and Sciences* 8 (1863): ix–xiv.

14. WDW to C. E. Norton, 24 August 1865, Norton Papers, emphasis in the original. WDW, "Is the Study of Language a Physical Science?" *NAR* 101 (October 1865): 434–74, on p. 437.

15. WDW to C. E. Norton, 3 September 1866, Norton Papers; WDW to D. C. Gilman, 26 August 1866, Gilman Papers; WDW to JDW, 4 April 1869, WP.

16. WDW to Oliver Wolcott Gibbs, 4 August 1866 (draft copy); WDW to JDW, 31 January, 10 August 1866, 19 August 1867, 19 January 1868; WDW to Elizabeth Baldwin Whitney, 1 September 1869; Petition to the U.S. Congress from the NAS, 22 January 1868, WP. The story of the NAS reorganization, including Whitney's proposal, appears in Sally Gregory Kohlstedt, *The Formation of the American Scientific Community: The American Association for the Advancement of Science, 1848–1860* (Urbana: University of Illinois Press, 1976), 228–32.

17. *DAB,* s.v., "Silliman, Benjamin, Jr."

18. "The Yale Report of 1828," excerpted in *American Higher Education: A Documentary History,* 2 vols., ed. Richard Hofstadter and Wilson Smith (Chicago: University of Chicago Press, 1961), 1:275–91.

19. WDW to JDW, 13 March 1871, WP. C. W. Eliot, "The New Education, Part I," *Atlantic Monthly* 23 (February 1869): 203–20, on pp. 208–9.

20. WDW to JDW, 1 April 1855, 7 February 1864, WP.

21. WDW to JDW, 15 and 19 January 1861, WP. *DAB,* s.v., "Gilman, Daniel Coit."

22. Faculty Minutes of the Sheffield Scientific School, 30 September, 20 October 1868, Sterling Library, Yale University; WDW to JDW, 20 March 1868, WP.

23. WDW, "Annual Statement for 1867–68," *Third Annual Report of the Sheffield Scientific School* (New Haven, 1867–68): 10–18, on p. 13. (Whitney's Sheffield statement is excerpted, without attribution of authorship, in Hofstadter and Smith, *American Higher Education,* 2:583–86.) Whitney repeated these themes in WDW, "Language and Education," *NAR* 112 (1871): 343–74.

24. WDW, "Annual Statement," 11, 19, emphasis added.

25. Anna Manning Comfort, "Memorial Biographical Sketch: George Fisk Comfort," Archives of American Art, G. F. Comfort Collection, Smithsonian Institution, Washington, D.C. G. F. Comfort to WDW, 24 April 1868, WP; G. F. Comfort to Isaac Ferris, 1 June 1868, New York University Library.

26. G. F. Comfort to WDW, 5, 12 and 19 May, 8 June, 13 October 1868; W. H. Green to WDW, 21 October 1868; J. H. Trumbull to WDW, 2 November 1868, WDW to JDW, 22 October 1868, WP. "J. H. Trumbull" (obituary), *National Academy of Sciences Biographical Memoirs* (1913): 145–69.

27. Minutes of 1868 Preliminary Meeting, *PAPA* 1 (1869): 5–6. WDW to JDW, 15 November 1868, WP.

28. G. F. Comfort to WDW, 14 and 23 December 1868, WP. Minutes of 1868 Preliminary Meeting, 7.

29. Franklin Carter to WDW, 17 December 1868; J. H. Trumbull to WDW, 22 March 1869; WDW to JDW, 6 April 1869, WP. In addition to the nascent APA, Whitney referred here to the American Union Academy of Literature, Science, and Art, also founded in 1869: WDW to JDW, 8 January 1869, WP. On this organization, see Donald Fleming, *John William Draper and the Religion of Science* (Philadelphia: University of Pennsylvania Press, 1950), 111.

30. J. H. Trumbull to WDW, 14 June 1869; G. F. Comfort to WDW, 28 August 1869, WP.

31. Invitation to a Convention of American Philologists at Poughkeepsie, N.Y., commencing July 27, 1869, WP. *PAPA* 1 (1869): 8, 17–18. Trumbull's paper was "On the Best Method of Studying the North American Languages," *TAPA* 1 (1869–70): 55–79.

32. [WDW], "The Philological Convention," *Nation* 9 (5 August 1869): 110.

33. WDW to JDW, 1 August 1869, WP.

34. [WDW], "Philological Convention," emphasis in the original. Whitney's authorship of this and a second *Nation* piece is attested in Charles R. Lanman, "Chronological Bibliography of the Writings of William Dwight Whitney," in *The Whitney Memorial Meeting*, ed. C. R. Lanman (Boston: Ginn and Co., 1897), 124–49, on pp. 132, 133.

35. [WDW], "Philological Convention," 110.

36. T. P., "The Philological Convention," *Nation* 9 (August 12, 1869): 129. "T. P." likely stood for "the president," that is, Whitney himself.

37. G. F. Comfort to WDW, 16 and 28 August 1869, WP.

38. WDW, Presidential Address (abstract), *PAPA* 1 (1870): 5.

39. Ibid., 5, 6.

40. [WDW,] "Report on the Rochester Meeting of the American Philological Association," *Nation* 10 (11 August 1870): 92.

41. Unsigned, "The Philological Convention," *Nation* 13 (3 August 1871): 72. WDW to JDW, 13 April, 19 May, 30 June, 28 July 1872, WP.

42. "Harvard Commencement," *Boston Advertiser* (23 June 1876), in Newsclippings File, Harvard University Archives, Pusey Library. Among Whitney's main honorary degrees were: PhD, Breslau, 1861; LLD, Harvard, 1876; LLD, Edinburgh, 1889.

43. Charles Gillispie, ed., *Dictionary of Scientific Biography*, s.v. "Marsh, Othniel C."; Franklin Parker, *George Peabody: A Biography* (1956; Nashville, Tenn.: Vanderbilt Uni-

versity Press, 1971), 139–42. O. C. Marsh to WDW, 25 September 1866; WDW to JDW, 7 October 1866, WP.

44. Asa Gray to O. C. Marsh, 14 July 1866, O. C. Marsh Papers; Charles Schuchert and Clara Mae LeVene, *O. C. Marsh: Pioneer in Paleontology* (New Haven, Conn.: Yale University Press, 1940), 229–230.

45. WDW to JDW, 30 May, 20 June 1866, WP. Like Whitney, O. C. Marsh believed that Harvard's Americanist ethnology ought to have a linguistic focus: O. C. Marsh to Asa Gray, 19 September, 2 October, 1874, Asa Gray Papers, Gray Herbarium Library, Harvard University.

46. O. C. Marsh to WDW, 25 September 1866; WDW to JDW, 7 October 1866, WP. (This letter to Josiah contains Whitney's summary of his appeal to Asa Gray. No original of Whitney's letter to Gray survives in the Asa Gray Papers.) Asa Gray to WDW, 19 October 1866, WP.

47. Draft statement on the history of the Peabody Museum, Jeffries Wyman Papers, Francis A. Countway Library of Medicine, Boston. The original plan, as O. C. Marsh had understood it, was that the professorship would be established immediately from the $45,000 set aside for that purpose. O. C. Marsh to WDW, 25 September 1866, WP.

48. F. W. Putnam, "The Peabody Museum of American Archaeology and Ethnology in Cambridge," *Proceedings of the American Antiquarian Society 6* (April 1889): 180–84. *DAB*, s.v. "Wyman, Jeffries." WDW to JDW, 7 October 1866, WP.

49. WDW to JDW, 21 March 1869, 4 April 1869, 15 October 1869, WP, emphasis in the original.

50. Hugh Hawkins, *Between Harvard and America: The Educational Leadership of Charles W. Eliot* (New York: Oxford University Press, 1972), 54–55. C. W. Eliot to WDW, 9 and 14 June 1869, WP.

51. WDW to C. W. Eliot, 14 June 1869, Eliot Papers, emphasis in the original.

52. WDW to C. W. Eliot, 19 and 26 June 1869, 10 July 1869, Eliot Papers; C. W. Eliot to WDW, 24 and 30 June 1869, 4 July 1869; WDW to JDW, 4 July 1869, WP. Whitney did present visiting lectures at Harvard in 1870, but he declined to continue after this.

53. WDW to JDW, 31 October 1866, WP; WDW to E. E. Salisbury, 21 September 1869, SP. The books Whitney prepared were *A Compendious German Grammar* (New York: Henry Holt, 1869), and *A German Reader* (New York: Henry Holt, 1870). Later Whitney prepared a *Compendious German-English Dictionary,* with the assistance of August H. Edgren (New York: Henry Holt, 1877).

54. JDW to WDW, 24 September 1869, WP.

55. E. E. Salisbury to WDW, 26 September 1869, WP; WDW to E. E. Salisbury, 29 September 1869, SP.

56. WDW to E. E. Salisbury, 29 September 1869, SP; WDW to JDW, 26 September 1869, WP.

57. WDW to JDW, 30 September 1869, WP.

58. WDW to C. W. Eliot, 6 October 1869, Eliot Papers; C. W. Eliot to WDW, 7 October 1869, WP.

59. Noah Porter, "The American Colleges and the American Public, Part IV," *New Englander* 28 (October 1869): 748–82, on p. 763. The impression of Noah Porter's personality comes from Donald C. Bellomy, "The Molding of an Iconoclast: William Graham Sumner, 1840–1885," (PhD dissertation: Harvard University, 1980), 38–39.

60. A useful overview of Yale's noncollegiate departments at this time appears in [Lyman Hotchkiss Bagg], *Four Years at Yale, By a Graduate of '69* (New Haven, Conn.: Charles C. Chatfield, 1871), 32–34, 38–39.

61. D. C. Gilman to E. E. Salisbury, 30 September (emphasis in the original), 6 October 1869, SP; E. E. Salisbury to D. C. Gilman, 2 October 1869, Gilman Papers. Chittenden, *Sheffield Scientific School,* 2:486; Hawkins, *Between Harvard and America,* 62.

62. WDW to JDW, 5 May 1872, William H. Pettee Collection, Box 3 (40), Huntington Library, San Marino, Calif.

63. E. E. Salisbury to WDW, 6 October 1869; WDW to Elizabeth Baldwin Whitney, 8 October 1869, WP. The original job offer from Yale's President Woolsey gave Whitney's title as "Professor of the Sanskrit Language and its Applications to Other Languages, and of Sanskrit Literature." T. D. Woolsey to WDW, 11 May 1854, WP.

64. JDW to WDW, 7 October 1869, WP.

65. WDW to E. E. Salisbury, 10 October 1869, SP; E. E. Salisbury to WDW, 11 October 1869, WP.

66. WDW to JDW, 15 October, 1869, WP. Similar themes appear in WDW to Elizabeth Baldwin Whitney, 19 October 1869; and WDW to JDW, 28 November 1869, WP.

67. WDW to D. C. Gilman, 14 October 1869, Gilman Papers.

68. C. W. Eliot to WDW, 20 October, 8 November 1869; F. J. Child to WDW, 23 October 1869; J. R. Lowell to WDW, 27 October 1869; E. Abbot to WDW, 27 October 1869, WP, emphasis in the original. Other Harvard faculty also appealed to Whitney: E. W. Gurney to WDW, 27 October 1869; W. W. Goodwin to WDW, 26 October, 10 Nov. 1869, WP. Whitney's final answer to the Harvard offer appeared in the following letters: WDW to C. W. Eliot, 25 October, 10 November 1869, Eliot Papers.

69. WDW to E. E. Salisbury, 29 October 1869, SP; E. E. Salisbury to WDW, 2 November 1869, WP.

70. WDW to JDW, 28 November 1869, WP.

71. WDW to JDW, 5 February, 13 and 16 March, 13 August 1871, WP.

72. WDW to JDW, 15 October 1871, WP.

73. D. C. Gilman to E. E. Salisbury, 30 September, 10 November 1869, SP; Eliot, "The New Education, Part I," 207–8.

74. M. A., "Yale College and its Government," *Nation* 10 (4 August 1870): 71.

75. "Announcement of a course of instruction in philology," *Nation* 12 (27 April 1871): 290. The graduate philology faculty would include Hadley in Greek, Thomas A. Thacher in Latin, George E. Day in Semitics, Thomas R. Lounsbury in Anglo-Saxon, Edward B. Coe in the modern Romance languages, Addison Van Name in Chinese and Japanese, and J. H. Trumbull in American Indian languages. *Yale Bulletin* (1871–72), 62; ibid. (1880–81), 48–50. The name "School of Philology" used in the *Nation* announcement does not appear in the *Yale Bulletin* in this period; rather, the 1870s through the 90s saw an expanding list of course offerings in the Department of Philosophy and the Arts, under the heading "Philological Science" or "Philology; Literature."

76. WDW to JDW, 24 September 1871.

77. WDW to JDW, 24 September 1871; G. F. Comfort to WDW, 29 May 1871, WP; WDW to E. E. Salisbury, 4 October 1871, SP.

78. Louise Stevenson, *Scholarly Means to Evangelical Ends: The New Haven Scholars and the Transformation of Higher Learning in America, 1830–1890* (Baltimore: Johns Hopkins University Press, 1986), 66.

79. For a list of philology professors who had studied under Whitney in the early 1870s, see Thomas Day Seymour, "William Dwight Whitney," in *Portraits of Linguists,* ed. Thomas A. Sebeok (Bloomington: Indiana University Press, 1966), 399–426, on p. 411.

si x: Creating a Science of Language

1. James H. Stam, *Inquiries into the Origin of Language: The Fate of a Question* (New York: Harper and Row, 1978), 224–28.
2. F. Schlegel quoted in *A Reader in Nineteenth-Century Historical Indo-European Linguistics,* ed. and trans. Winfred P. Lehmann (Bloomington: Indiana University Press, 1967), 23.
3. F. Schlegel quoted in ibid., 25.
4. Franz Bopp, quoted in Stam, *Origin of Language,* 224.
5. [Frances Julia Wedgwood], "The Origin of Language: The Imitative Theory and Mr. Max Müller's Theory of Phonetic Types," *Macmillan's Magazine* 7 (November 1862): 54, emphasis in the original.
6. F. Max Müller, *Lectures on the Science of Language,* First Series, 2nd London edition, revised (New York: Charles Scribner, 1862), 2:9.
7. Ibid., 1:31–33.
8. John E. Joseph, *From Whitney to Chomsky* (Philadelphia: John Benjamins, 2003), 21.
9. Müller, *Science of Language,* 1:39, 49, 47.
10. Theodore M. Porter, *The Rise of Statistical Thinking: 1820–1900* (Princeton, N.J.: Princeton University Press, 1986), 50–51.
11. Müller, *Science of Language,* 1:49–50.
12. Ibid., 1:50.
13. F. Max Müller, *Lectures on the Science of Language,* Second Series (1863; New York: Charles Scribner, 1871), 2:15, emphasis in the original.
14. Ibid., 2:325–27, emphasis in the original.
15. A. Schleicher quoted in Abel Hovelacque, *The Science of Language: Linguistics, Philology, Etymology,* trans. A. H. Keane (1876, London: Chapman and Hall, 1877), 6, 7.
16. August Schleicher, *Die Darwinische Theorie und die Sprachwissenschaft* (1863), translated as "Darwinism Tested by the Science of Language," by Alex V. W. Bikkers (London: John Camden Hotten, 1869), 20.
17. Müller, *Science of Language,* 2:50–51; Schleicher, *Darwinische Theorie,* 20–21, emphasis added.
18. WDW, *LSL,* 22, 154, 177.
19. Ibid., 155; also: ibid., 28, 31, 104.
20. Ibid., 37, 38.
21. Ibid., 44.
22. Ibid., 45.
23. Ibid., 45, 51.
24. Dugald Stewart, *Elements of the Philosophy of the Human Mind* (1792; Albany: E. and E. Hosford, 1822), 60; Mark Hopkins, *The Law of Love and Love as a Law, or Christian Ethics,* rev. ed. (1828; New York: Charles Scribner's Sons, 1881), 150, 151.
25. WDW, *LSL,* 44, 43.

26. WDW, *LGL,* 150.

27. Adam Smith, *An Inquiry into the Nature and Causes of the Wealth of Nations* (1776), Book IV, Part 2, emphasis added.

28. WDW, *LSL,* 45.

29. *Williams College Announcements* (1845), 16–17; William Paley, *Principles of Moral and Political Philosophy,* 11th American ed. (1785; Boston: Richardson and Lord, 1825), 321.

30. Charles Darwin, *Origin of Species* (1859; facsimile edition: Cambridge, Mass.: Harvard University Press, 1963), 45; Ernst Mayr, Introduction to Darwin, *Origin of Species,* xix–xx; WDW, *LSL,* 16–22.

31. WDW to Josiah Dwight Whitney, Sr., 19 June 1855, WP.

32. WDW to Elizabeth Whitney Putnam, 1 July 1855, WP, emphasis added.

33. Noah Webster and Chauncey Goodrich, eds., *An American Dictionary of the English Language* (Springfield, Mass.: G. and C. Merriam, 1869), s.v., "moral."

34. *Williams College Announcements* (1845), 16–17; Francis Wayland, *Elements of Moral Science* (Boston: Gould, Kendall, and Lincoln, 1842), 26; George Campbell, *Philosophy of Rhetoric* (1776; London: Tegg and Son, 1838), 48–49; Mark Hopkins, *An Outline Study of Man* (New York: Scribners, 1878), 54.

35. WDW to JDW, 7 February 1864, WP, emphasis added.

36. WDW, "Brief Abstract of a Series of Six Lectures on the Principles of Linguistic Science," Smithsonian Institution, *Annual Report* (1864): 95–116, on p. 101.

37. WDW, *LSL,* 48, 49.

38. *American Dictionary of the English Language* (1869), s.v., "moral," emphasis in the original.

39. WDW, "Is the Study of Language a Physical Science?" *NAR* 101 (1865): 434–74. WDW to JDW, 16 October 1864, WP; WDW to C. E. Norton, 24 July, 17 and 24 August 1865, Norton Papers.

40. Donald C. Bellomy, " 'Social Darwinism' Revisited," *Perspectives in American History* n.s. 1 (1984): 1–129, on 69–70.

41. WDW, Obituary of August Schleicher, *Nation* 9 (28 January 1869): 70. WDW to JDW, 4 and 11 June, 20 July 1871, WP.

42. WDW, "Schleicher and the Physical Theory of Language," *OLS,* 1:298–331, on pp. 312–13.

43. G. F. Comfort to WDW, 28 August 1869; WDW to JDW, 24 May 1863, WP. WDW, *LSL,* 52–53; an almost identical passage appeared in WDW, "Is the Study of Language a Physical Science?" 473.

44. WDW, *LSL,* 49.

45. WDW, *LSL,* 52–53; D. H. Wheeler, "Growth in Language," *Methodist Quarterly Review* 51 (April 1869): 228–42, on pp. 241–42.

46. WDW, *LSL,* 49.

47. WDW, *LSL,* 47; WDW, *LGL,* 195.

48. WDW, *LSL,* 46–47. Whitney referred here to ch. 23 of Lyell's *Antiquity of Man.* He expressed his favorable judgment of this chapter also in "Is the Study of Language a Physical Science?" 470.

49. WDW, *LSL,* 49.

50. *Williams College Announcements* (1845), 16–17; Henry Home (Lord Kames), *Ele-*

*ments of Criticism* (1761; New York: A. S. Barnes and Burr, 1863), 269–74. The classic statement appears in the opening pages of Thomas Reid, *Essays on the Intellectual Powers of Man* (1785).

51. WDW, *LSL*, 10, 49; also 145–46.

52. WDW, *LSL*, 47, 48.

53. WDW, *LSL*, 49, emphasis added.

54. In WDW, "Schleicher and the Physical Theory," 319–20, Whitney rejected Schleicher's argument that language-use had originated purely as a result of the physiological development of the human speech organs. See August Schleicher, *Über die Bedeutung der Sprach für die Naturgeschichte des Menchen* (Weimar, 1865).

55. WDW, *LSL*, 49; WDW, "De Vere's Studies in English," *NAR* 104 (April 1867): 631–35, on p. 634.

56. WDW, "Schleicher and the Physical Theory," 316.

57. [Noah Porter], "Recent Works on Psychology," *New Englander* 13 (February 1855): 129–44, on p. 132; Noah Porter, *The Human Intellect* (New York: Charles Scribner, 1868), 28–29.

58. WDW, *LSL*, 112; also: WDW, "Schleicher and the Physical Theory," 318; WDW, "General Considerations on the Indo-European Case-System," *TAPA* (1882): 88–100, on p. 91.

59. WDW, *LSL*, 49, 52.

60. Otto Jespersen, *Language: Its Nature, Development and Origin* (London: G. Allen and Unwin, 1922), 86–87.

61. Hugo Schuchardt, "On Sound Law: Against the Neogrammarians" (1885), in *The Lautgesetz-Controversy: A Documentation,* ed. Terence H. Wilbur (Amsterdam: John Benjamins, 1977), 41–71, on p. 64.

62. Charles R. Lanman, ed. *The Whitney Memorial Meeting* (Boston: Ginn and Co., 1897), 78, 94, author's translation.

63. Jespersen, *Language,* 86–87, emphasis added.

SEVEN: Forging an Alliance with Anthropology

1. The biblical affirmations of monogenesis appear in Genesis 10 and Acts 17:26.

2. Max Müller, "Ethnology v. Phonology," in C. C. J. Bunsen, *Outlines of the Philosophy of Universal History* (London: Longman, Brown, Green, and Longman, 1854), 349, 352–53; T. H. Huxley, "On the Methods and Results of Ethnology," *Fortnightly Review* 1 (1865): 257–77.

3. WDW, "The Avesta," *OLS,* 1:149–97, on pp. 184–85; WDW, "Brief Abstract of a Series of Six Lectures on the Principles of Linguistic Science," Smithsonian Institution, *Annual Report* (1864): 95–116, on p. 104; see also: WDW, *LSL,* 205, 382–83. Thomas R. Trautmann gives a detailed analysis of the time revolution's impact on Whitney's thinking in *Louis Henry Morgan and the Invention of Kinship* (Berkeley: University of California Press, 1987), 226–29.

4. L. Agassiz, "The Diversity of the Origins of the Human Races," *Christian Examiner* 160 (July 1850): 139–40; idem, "Prefatory Remarks," in J. C. Nott and George R. Gliddon, *Indigenous Races of the Earth* (Philadelphia: J. B. Lippincott and Co., 1857), xiii–vx.

5. Whitney showed a similar contempt for the physicalist and polygenist Anthropological Society of London: WDW, Review of *Chapters on Man* by C. Staniland Wake, in *NAR* 108 (January 1869): 290–91.

6. WDW, *LSL*, 371–73, quotation from p. 372, emphasis added.

7. WDW, *LSL*, 380–81, 442; WDW, "Logical Consistency in Views of Language," *AJP* 1 (1880): 327–43, on pp. 330–31; WDW, "Darwinism and Language," *NAR* 119 (July 1874): 61–88, on p. 84.

8. WDW, *LGL*, 224–25; WDW, "Philology, Pt. I: Science of Language in General," *Encyclopedia Britannica*, 9th ed., 1885, reprinted in American Reprint Edition (Philadelphia: J. M. Stoddart, 1875–90), vol. 18 (1885), 778–94, on p. 788.

9. WDW, Review of *Indo-European Origins, or the Primitive Aryans* by Adolphe Pictet, *PAOS* 8 (October 1865): lxxxv–vi.

10. WDW, *LSL*, 371–74. E. B. Tylor later made this same essential argument in *Primitive Culture*, 2 vols. (1871; New York: Gordon Press, 1974), 1:43–44.

11. WDW, *LSL*, 371; George W. Stocking, Jr., *Victorian Anthropology* (New York: Free Press, 1987), 250.

12. WDW, *LSL*, 384–385. Here Whitney likely adapted an argument from Charles Lyell's *Antiquity of Man* (1863): see Stocking, *Victorian Anthropology*, 75–76.

13. Thomas R. Trautmann, *Aryans and British India* (Berkeley: University of California Press, 1997), 52–56, 133–34.

14. WDW, "On Johannes Schmidt's New Theory of the Relationship of Indo-European Languages," *JAOS* 10 (1873): lxxvii–viii; WDW, *LSL*, 378, 379; also: WDW, *LGL*, 175–76.

15. WDW, *LSL*, 359–60.

16. WDW, *LSL*, 204–8.

17. WDW, *LSL*, 205; also: WDW, "On the Testimony of Language respecting the Unity of the Human Race," *NAR* 105 (1867): 214–41, on p. 230.

18. Thomas Jefferson, *Notes on the State of Virginia*, in *Thomas Jefferson: Writings* (1787; New York: Viking Press, 1984), 227 (ch. 11, on "Aborigines").

19. A. C. Kendrick to WDW, 4 January 1859, WP.

20. Oliver Wolcott Gibbs to WDW, 7 November 1860; Joseph Henry to WDW, 1 August 1861; WDW to JDW, 8 December 1861, WP. The instrument for gathering Indian word lists appeared in George Gibbs, *Instructions for Research relative to the Ethnology and Philology of America* (Smithsonian Institution, 1863). Here Whitney elaborated an earlier critique: WDW, "On Lepsius' Standard Alphabet," *JAOS* 7 (1861): 299–332. WDW to JDW, 4 May 1858, WP.

21. J. H. Trumbull to WDW, 23 September 1867, 31 January 1870, 26 June 1871; John Wesley Powell to WDW, 17 and 31 July 1877; Alexander Bell to WDW, 30 August 1877; WDW to JDW, 1 October 1876, WP. WDW to John Wesley Powell, 25 July 1877, quoted in Curtis M. Hinsley, Jr., *Savages and Scientists: The Smithsonian Institution and the Development of American Anthropology, 1846–1910* (Washington, D.C.: Smithsonian Institution Press, 1981), 160. Powell publicly thanked Whitney for his aid in preparing the alphabet for the first edition of his book, although his amanuensis misidentified him as J. D. Whitney: J. W. Powell, *Introduction to the Study of Indian Languages*, 2nd ed. (Washington, D.C.: Government Printing Office, 1880), vi.

22. J. H. Trumbull to WDW, 31 January 1870, WP. WDW, *LSL*, 351–52.

23. F. Max Müller, *Lectures on the Science of Language*, from the 2nd London edi-

tion, revised, First Series (New York: Charles Scribner, 1862), 1:58; WDW, "Unity of the Human Race," 222–23.

24. WDW, Review of *Outlines of Indian Philology* by John Beame, in *Nation* 7 (24 December 1868): 535; WDW, Presidential Address, *PAPA* 1 (1870): 5; also, WDW, *LSL*, 352. Daniel Crane Brinton later acknowledged Whitney's encouragement of the study of American Indian languages: *Essays of an Americanist* (Philadelphia: Porter and Coates, 1890), 327.

25. Jefferson had made a remark strikingly similar to Whitney's: "It is to be lamented then, very much lamented, that we have suffered so many of the Indian tribes already to extinguish, without our having previously collected and deposited in the records of literature, the general rudiments at least of the languages they spoke" (*Notes on the State of Virginia*, ch. 11, on "Aborigines," p. 227).

26. WDW, *LSL*, 352n.

27. Stephen Jay Gould, *Dinosaur in a Haystack: Reflections on Natural History* (New York: Harmony Books, 1995), 350; also H. W. Conn, *Evolution of Today* (New York: G. P. Putnam's Sons, 1886), 307.

28. WDW, Review of *The Alphabet: An Account of the Origin and Development of Letters*, by Isaac Taylor, in *Science* 2 (September 28, 1883): 438–39, on p. 439.

29. WDW, "Bleek and the Simious Theory of Language," *OLS*, 1:292–97, on p. 297.

30. Donald Bellomy, "William Graham Sumner: The Making of an Iconoclast" (PhD dissertation, Harvard University, 1980), 236–37; WDW to JDW, 11 January 1874, WP.

31. WDW, "Bleek and the Simious Theory," 293.

32. John O. Means, "Recent Theories on the Origin of Language," *Bibliotheca Sacra* 27 (January 1870): 162–79, on p. 163.

33. WDW, "Bleek and the Simious Theory," 296.

34. H. Wedgwood, *On the Origin of Language* (London: N. Trübner and Co., 1866), 3–4; see also 137–38.

35. C. Darwin, *The Descent of Man and Selection in Relation to Sex* (1871; Princeton, N.J.: Princeton University Press, 1981), 56.

36. Ibid., 57.

37. WDW, "Schleicher and the Physical Theory of Language," *OLS*, 1:298–331, on p. 324; WDW, "Darwinism and Language," *NAR* 119 (July 1874): 61–88, on p. 87.

38. WDW, *LGL*, 306; WDW, "Philology: The Science of Language in General," 783. In one sense, Whitney did accept Darwin's perspective. In *Descent*, 57, Darwin said that a fair amount of mental development must have taken place prior to the origin of speech. Whitney presumably was responding to this point when he said: "If there once existed creatures above the apes and below man . . . there is no difficulty in supposing them to have possessed forms of speech, [albeit] more rudimentary and imperfect than ours." WDW, "Philology, Part I: Science of Language in General," 783.

39. WDW to JDW, 17 March 1872, WP.

40. An article by E. B. Tylor on the origin of language mainly repeated the general outlook of Hensleigh Wedgwood: "The Science of Language," *Quarterly Review* 119 (April 1866): 208–30.

41. On the link between political economy and evolutionary anthropology, see J. W. Burrow, *Evolution and Society* (Cambridge, UK: Cambridge University Press, 1966), 21–22, 218–20, 251, 263–64.

42. Hugh Blair, *Lectures on Rhetoric and Belles Lettres,* ed. Harold F. Harding (1783; Carbondale: Southern Illinois University Press, 1965), 100, 101.

43. W. B. Winning, *A Manual of Comparative Philology* (London: J. G. and F. Rivington, 1838), 288–90; Richard Chenevix Trench, *On the Study of Words* (London, 1852), 17. Tylor lamented the continued strength of the declension thesis in *Primitive Culture,* 1:32.

44. Thomas R. Trautmann, "The Revolution in Ethnological Time," *Man* 27:2 (June 1992): 379–97, on pp. 386–89.

45. WDW, "On Müller's Chips from a German Workshop," *OLS,* 2:126–48, on p. 130; WDW, *LSL,* 398, 434; WDW, "Steinthal and the Psychological Theory of Language," *OLS,* 1:332–75, on p. 341; WDW, *LGL,* 144–45, 226: "law of simplicity."

46. Whitney's "cultural" view of language was first remarked on in print in *Whitney on Language,* ed. Michael Silverstein (Cambridge: MIT Press, 1971), viii. Since they omit works written before 1900 (prior to the Boasian era), Alfred L. Kroeber and Clyde Kluckhohn do not include Whitney from their discussion of linguists in *Culture: A Critical Review of Concepts and Definitions* (New York: Knopf, 1952), 242.

47. Tylor, *Primitive Culture,* 1:1, emphasis added; WDW, *LSL,* 17, 441, emphasis added; WDW, Review of J. F. Clark's *Ten Great Religions,* in *Nation* 13 (17 August 1871): 109–10.

48. Burrow, *Evolution and Society,* 218–20, 227; Peter Mandler, "'Race' and 'Nation' in Mid-Victorian Thought," in Stefan Collini et al., *History, Religion, and Culture: British Intellectual History: 1750–1950* (New York: Cambridge University Press, 2000), 224–44.

49. WDW, *LSL,* 359–60. For Max Müller's version of the three morphological stages, see Müller, *Science of Language,* 1:286–93. Standard criticism of the three-stage theory appears in Otto Jespersen, *Language: Its Nature, Development and Origin* (London: G. Allen and Unwin, 1922), 367–68.

50. WDW, *LGL,* 277. Whitney was likewise skeptical of Herbert Spencer's and L. H. Morgan's theory of sharp breaks between the stages of savagery, barbarism, and civilization: "Tylor's Anthropology," *Nation* 33 (1 September 1881): 181; Tylor, *Primitive Culture,* 1:14, 19, 28, 29, 34.

51. WDW, *LGL,* 191; *LSL,* 202; also: *LSL,* 237, 289–90.

52. Roger Smith, "The Language of Human Nature," in *Inventing Human Science: Eighteenth-Century Domains,* ed. Christopher Fox et al. (Berkeley: University of California Press, 1995), 92, 97–98, 103–5; Dugald Stewart, *Elements of the Philosophy of the Human Mind* (1792; Albany, N.Y.: E. and A. Hosford, 1822), 60, 63.

53. WDW, *LGL,* 146; WDW, "Present State of the Question as to the Origin of Language," *OLS,* 1:279–91, on p. 281, emphasis added.

54. WDW, "Steinthal and the Psychological Theory," 354–55; Francis Wayland, *Elements of Political Economy,* 4th ed. (Boston: Gould, Kendall, and Lincoln, 1841), 15, 27, 58, 76, 29; *Williams College Announcements* (1845), 16–17.

55. WDW, *LGL,* 50; also WDW, *LSL,* 69–70.

56. WDW, *LSL,* 47, emphasis added.

57. Philip Baldi, *An Introduction to the Indo-European Languages* (Carbondale: Southern Illinois University Press, 1983), 3–13.

58. WDW, "Grimm's Law," *Nation* 26 (2 August 1877): 75–76; WDW, "Cockneyisms," *TAPA* (1877): 26–28, on p. 28; WDW, *LSL,* 152.

59. WDW, *LGL,* 57–59, 73. Twentieth-century linguists have suggested a plausible social-psychological explanation for this phenomenon in terms of "chains" of sound displacement; see Jean Aitchison, *Language Change: Progress or Decay?* (New York: Universe Books, 1981), 160–61.

60. WDW, *LSL,* 229, 233; WDW, *LGL,* 19–20, 224.

61. WDW, "On Combination and Adaptation, as Illustrated by the Exchanges of Primary and Secondary Suffixes," *TAPA* (1885): 111–23, on p. 111; WDW, "On E. Kuhn's Origin and Languages of the Transgangetic Peoples," *AJP* 5 (1884): 89–92, on p. 92.

62. WDW, *LGL,* 319; also: WDW, "Logical Consistency," 338.

63. WDW, "Philology, Part I: Science of Language in General," 786.

64. Ian Hacking, *The Taming of Chance* (Cambridge, UK: Cambridge University Press), 161–62; E. B. Tylor, *Researches,* 3.

65. Trautmann, *Lewis Henry Morgan,* 72–73, 216; Jon Roberts and James Turner, *The Sacred and the Secular University* (Princeton, N.J.: Princeton University Press, 2000), 96–97. The political-economy/philology dichotomy and the physical/moral sciences dichotomy were distinct. The former was based on the kind of output produced, the one generating laws and the other generating meanings; the latter was based on what kind of causation was involved, the one material, the other human.

66. Stefan Collini, Donald Winch, and John Burrow, *That Noble Science of Politics: A Study in Nineteenth-century Intellectual History* (New York: Cambridge University Press, 1983), 213, 215.

67. James Turner, *The Liberal Education of Charles Eliot Norton* (Baltimore: Johns Hopkins University Press, 1999), 258, 283; Clifford Geertz, "Thick Description: Toward an Interpretive Theory of Culture," in *The Interpretation of Cultures* (New York: Basic Books, 1973), 3–30, especially pp. 5, 9–10.

68. WDW, "On Pictet's Work: Indo-European Origins, or the Primitive Aryans," *PAOS* 8 (October 1865): lxxxv–vi; WDW, "On the So-Called Science of Religion," *Princeton Review* (May 1881): 429–52, on p. 429.

69. Müller presented his system in outline in his 1856 Oxford lecture on "Comparative Mythology," then gave it extensive treatment in the last four chapters of his *Science of Language,* vol. 2.

70. WDW to C. E. Norton, 21 December 1867, Norton papers. Whitney reiterated a month later: "It gave me the sincerest pleasure to be able to speak with decided commendation, in the 'Nation,' of Muller's 'Chips': the Lord knows that I have been longing enough watching and waiting for something of his which I could commend without reserve, or nearly so." WDW to C. E. Norton, 19 January 1868, Norton Papers. According to Charles R. Lanman's bibliography (item no. 90), Whitney did this initial review of *Chips* vols. 1 and 2 for the *Nation* sometime in 1868. Charles R. Lanman, "Chronological Bibliography of the Writings of William Dwight Whitney," *Whitney Memorial Meeting* (Boston: Ginn and Co., 1897), 131. I have not been able to locate this review.

71. [F. Max Müller], Review of *The Aitareya Brāhmanam of the Rigveda,* edited and translated by Martin Haug, in *Saturday Review* 17 (19 March 1864): 360–62, on p. 361.

72. WDW, "Müller's *Chips from a German Workshop,*" *OLS,* 2:126–48, on p. 132; also "Müller on the Science of Religion," *Nation* 11 (13 October 1870): 242–44; and "Max Müller and the Philosophy of Mythology," *The (New York) Independent* 24 (25 January 1872): 6.

73. WDW, "Müller's *Chips from a German Workshop*," *OLS*, 2:131.

74. Heymann Steinthal, Review of *Language and the Study of Language* by W. D. Whitney, in *Zeitschrift für Völkerpsychologie und Sprachwissenschaft* 5 (1868): 364–66, on p. 265; author's translation. Whitney had sent a copy of the newly published *LSL* to Steinthal. Account books showing distribution of Whitney's writings: Box 53, file 54, WP.

75. H. Steinthal quoted in James H. Stam, *Inquiries into the Origin of Language: The Fate of a Question* (New York: Harper and Row, 1978), 230. WDW to JDW, 7 January 1872, WP. An in-depth analysis of this topic appears in Patricia Casey Sutcliffe, "Humboldt's *Ergon* and *Energeia* in Friedrich Max Müller's and William Dwight Whitney's Theories of Language," *Logos and Language* 2:2 (2001): 21–35.

76. WDW to JDW, 28 January, 9 June 1872, WP.

77. WDW to JDW, 28 January, 25 February 1872, WP.

78. WDW to JDW, 7 January 1872, WP, emphasis added. Also: WDW, *LGL*, v.

79. WDW, "Steinthal and the Psychological Theory," 365, 364.

80. H. Steinthal quoted in Stam, *Origin of Language*, 230.

81. WDW, "Steinthal and the Psychological Theory," 355.

82. Ibid., 353–54.

83. The product-oriented perspective appeared in its purest form in the anthropologist Alfred L. Kroeber's "The Superorganic," in *The Nature of Culture* (Chicago: University of Chicago Press, 1952), 40; and "Eighteen Professions," *American Anthropologist* 17 (1915): 283.

84. WDW to JDW, 17 November 1872, WP; WDW to Albrecht Weber, 9 December 1872, 2 February 1874, Weber Papers. Salisbury's daughter died in April of 1875.

85. WDW to Albrecht Weber, 12 February 1877, Weber Papers.

EIGHT: The Battle with Max Müller

1. WDW to JDW, 29 March 1867, WP. The work the Royal Asiatic Society honored was "On the Jyotisha Observation of the Place of the Colures, and the Date Derivable from It," *Journal of the Royal Asiatic Society of Great Britain and Ireland* n.s. 1 (1865): 316–31.

2. "Literary Notes," *Nation* 10 (9 June 1870): 369. WDW to E. E. Salisbury, 13 February 1871, SP. WDW, "Tāittirīya-Prātiśākhya with commentary: text, translation, and notes," *JAOS* 9 (1871): 1–469.

3. E. B. Cowell, ed., *Miscellaneous Essays by Henry Thomas Colebrooke* (London: Trübner and Co., 1873), vi–vii; WDW, "Colebrooke's Essays," *The (New York) Independent* 26 (16 April 1874): 9.

4. WDW, "Translation of the Veda," *OLS*, 1:121–32, on p. 113; WDW, "Müller's Rig-Veda Translation," *OLS*, 1:133–48, on p. 139; WDW, "Roth's *Rig-Veda* Specimen," *Nation* 12 (23 March 1871): 199. These reviews dealt mainly with Müller's Sanskrit edition of the *Ṛg Veda*, to which Müller added sections of his English translation of the text, first published in 1869. *DNB*, s.v. "Max Müller, Friedrich."

5. WDW, *LSL*, vi–vii, 35, 427. WDW to A. Weber, 22 September 1867, Weber Papers.

6. Henry Adams to WDW, 2 March, 6 June 1871; WDW to JDW, 4 and 11 June 1871, WP. WDW, "Müller's Lectures on Language," *OLS*, 1:239–78, on p. 272.

7. WDW to C. E. Norton, 20 February 1868, Norton Papers; Reinhold Rost to WDW, 11 June 1868; John Muir to WDW, 29 March 1872, WP.

8. WDW to JDW, 20 December 1867; N. Trübner to WDW (n.d.) September 1869, WP. A list of Whitney's European correspondents who were to receive copies of his Orientalist works appears in N. Trübner to WDW, 24 June 1868, WP.

9. Wilhelm Clemm, Review of *LSL*, by W. D. Whitney, in *Zeitschrift für vergleichende Sprachforschung* 18 (1869): 119–25, on p. 125, author's translation.

10. Unsigned, Review of *LSL*, by W. D. Whitney, in *Westminster Review* 89 (January 1868): 138–39; Unsigned, Review of *LSL*, by W. D. Whitney, in *The Atheneum* 2093 (12 December 1867): 758–59. At first, *The Atheneum* had been unfavorable toward Müller: see Unsigned, Review of *Lectures on the Science of Language* by F. Max Müller, in *The Atheneum* 1919 (6 August 1864): 172–73. The review in the *Scotsman* is mentioned in J. Muir to WDW, 28 April 1868, WP.

11. [F. Max Müller], "The Science of Language," *Saturday Review* 24 (30 November 1867): 699–700. WDW to JDW, 29 December 1867; Fitzedward Hall to WDW, 24 August 1867, 24 October 1868, WP.

12. WDW to A. Weber, 3 January 1872, Weber Papers; Fitzedward Hall to WDW, 9 January 1872, WP.

13. F. J. Furnivall to WDW, 16 November, 27 December 1872, WP. A second *OLS* volume, published in 1874, contained little on general linguistics.

14. Philological Society notices, *Academy* n.s. 132 (14 November 1874): 154; ibid. (28 November 1874): 591; Thomas Hewitt Key, *Language: Its Origin and Development* (London: George Bell and Sons, 1874), 5–6.

15. M. B. [Michel Bréal], "Whitney: Oriental and Linguistic Studies," *Revue Critique d'Histoire et de Littérature* 8 (22 February 1873): 8.

16. Bertholdt Delbrück, Review of *OLS*, vol. 1, by W. D. Whitney, in *Academy* 6:78 (14 August 1873): 314. Two favorable reviews of *OLS*, vol. 1, appeared in Germany: F. Spiegel, *Heidelberger Jahrbücher der Literatur* 58 (1872): 918–22; and Julius Jolly, *Göttingische gelehrte Anzeigen* 7 (18 February 1874): 193–218.

17. Account books showing distribution of gift copies of Whitney's writings: Box 53, folder 54, WP. WDW, "Steinthal and the Psychological Theory of Language," *OLS*, 1:332–75, on p. 373.

18. WDW to JDW, 19 May 1872, 9 June 1872, WP; WDW to A. Weber, 24 June 1872, Weber Papers.

19. Heymann Steinthal, *Antikritik. Wie Einer den Nagel auf en Kopf trifft. Ein Freundschaflichen Dialog* (Berlin, 1874). Henry Adams to WDW, 15 October 1874, WP.

20. Unsigned, Review of Steinthal pamphlet, *The Atheneum* 2443 (22 August 1874): 245; Unsigned, Review of "Anticriticism, or How Someone Hit the Nail on the Head" by H. Steinthal, in *Academy* 121, n.s. (29 August 1874): 234.

21. Unsigned, Review of "Anticriticism," 234.

22. Unsigned, Review of *OLS*, vol. 1, by W. D. Whitney, in *NAR* 116 (1873): 177.

23. WDW to A. Weber, 3 November 1873, Weber Papers, emphasis in the original. *DAB* s.v. "Hayden, Ferdinand Vandiveer."

24. A copy of Josiah's 17-page indictment to be submitted to the NAS, written in W. D. Whitney's hand and dated 18 October 1873, is held in the WP; also WDW to the Council of the NAS (cover letter, copy), 18 October 1873, WP.

25. WDW to JDW, 11 January 1874, WP.

26. WDW to JDW, 11 January, 23 April 1874, WP.

27. F. Max Müller, "The Science of Language," *Nature* 1 (6 January 1870): 256–58, on p. 256.

28. F. Max Müller, *Lectures on the Science of Language,* from the 2nd London edition, revised, First Series (New York: Charles Scribner, 1862), 1:354; Max Müller, "Lectures on Mr. Darwin's Philosophy of Language," *Frazer's Magazine* (June 1873): 666–67; ibid., n.s. 8 (July 1873): 1–24, on p. 12, emphasis in the original.

29. Unsigned, "Max Müller on Darwin's Philosophy of Language," *Nature* 7 (26 December 1872): 145. This review was of an earlier performance of Müller's new lectures, delivered to the Liverpool Literary and Philosophical Society.

30. WDW to JDW, 23 February 1873, WP.

31. WDW, "Darwinism and Language," *NAR* 119 (July 1874): 61–88, on p. 74.

32. Ibid., 83–84, 88.

33. Ibid., 88, emphasis added.

34. Ibid.

35. WDW to A. Weber, 2 February 1874, Weber Papers.

36. Whitney sent copies of *OLS,* vol. 1, as well as his "Darwinism and Language" to both Darwin and Hensleigh Wedgwood. Later he sent them each a copy of *LGL.* Account books showing distribution of gift copies of Whitney's writings: box 53, folder 54, WP.

37. C. Darwin, *The Descent of Man,* rev. ed. (London: John Murray, 1874), 104, n. 63. The Whitney quotation is from WDW, "Bleek and the Simious Theory of Language," *OLS,* 1:297.

38. Surprisingly, in the first of the two new footnotes using Whitney's essays, Darwin drew upon Whitney to bolster his thesis that language is not an intentionally made "art" but rather grows unconsciously. Darwin was already aware that Whitney typically stressed human agency with a vengeance: C. Darwin to Chauncey Wright, 3 June 1872, in *The Life and Letters of Charles Darwin,* ed. Francis Darwin, 3 vols. (London: John Murray, 1888), 2:343. Still, in *Descent,* Darwin quoted, from Whitney's anti-Steinthal article, the unusually pointed acknowledgment that language change "works both consciously and unconsciously; consciously as regards the immediate end to be attained; unconsciously as regards the further consequences of the act" ("Steinthal and the Psychological Theory," 355): Darwin, *Descent of Man,* rev. ed., 102, n. 53. Max Müller, of course, had said similar things many times, yet Darwin took what he needed from Whitney, the philologist who had not come out against his transmutation theory. The passages Darwin scored in his copy of *OLS* indicates his particular interest in two topics: the language-thought identity (*OLS,* 1:285, 287, 297), and the "unconscious" nature of language change (ibid., 353–55). See Mario A. Di Gregorio and Nicholas Gill, eds., *Charles Darwin's Marginalia,* 2 vols. (New York: Garland, 1990), 1:871.

39. F. J. Furnivall to WDW, 6 August, 30 September, 7 November 1874; Richard Morris to F. J. Furnivall, 1 October 1874 (forwarded to WDW), WP.

40. C. Darwin to J. Knowles, 31 July 1874, Wellcome Library, London.

41. J. Knowles to C. Darwin, 4 August 1874, Darwin Collection, Cambridge University Library; C. Darwin to J. Knowles, 5 August 1874, Wellcome Library, London.

42. C. Darwin to WDW, 5 August 1874, WP.

43. [St. George Mivart], "Tylor and Lubbock on Primitive Man," *London Quarterly Review* 137 (July 1874): 22–42, on p. 41.

44. G. H. Darwin, "Professor Whitney on the Origin of Language," *Contemporary Review* 24 (November 1874): 894–904, on p. 900. George Darwin probably used (and marked) his father's copy of Whitney's *OLS*, vol. 1, in preparing his article. According to Di Gregorio and Gill, *Darwin's Marginalia*, 871, Darwin's copy of Whitney's volume contains "many markings presumed not to be by CD."

45. G. H. Darwin, "Professor Whitney on the Origin of Language," 902; C. Darwin to G. H. Darwin, 5 November 1874, in *A Calendar of the Correspondence of Charles Darwin, 1821–1882*, ed. Frederick Burkhardt and Sydney Smith (New York: Garland, 1985).

46. George Darwin thanked Whitney for his approval of his *Contemporary Review* article: G. H. Darwin to WDW, 8 February 1875, WP.

47. F. Max Müller, "My Reply to Mr. Darwin," *Contemporary Review* 25 (January 1875): 305–26, on p. 305.

48. WDW to JDW, 10 June 1876, WP.

49. Müller, "My Reply to Mr. Darwin," 307.

50. Ibid., 308.

51. Ibid., 313, 324.

52. Ibid., 311, 312; quotations from WDW, *LSL*, 49.

53. Müller, "My Reply to Mr. Darwin," 308; quotation from Müller, *Science of Language*, 2:43.

54. Müller, "My Reply to Mr. Darwin," 311, emphasis added; Müller, "Science of Language" (1870), 258, emphasis added.

55. Ibid., 310, emphasis in the original; embedded quotations are from WDW, *LSL*, 45, 52.

56. George Darwin forwarded Whitney's letter to Knowles: G. H. Darwin to J. Knowles, 8 February 1875, Darwin Collection, Cambridge University Library. *The Calendar of the Correspondence of Charles Darwin* lists an additional letter on this subject from Charles Darwin to Knowles, also on 8 February 1875.

57. J. Knowles to C. Darwin, 9 February 1875, WP. (The remainder of Knowles' postscript is illegible.)

58. G. H. Darwin to WDW, 10 March 1875; J. H. Trumbull to WDW, 5 March 1875, WP.

59. WDW, "Are Languages Institutions?" *Contemporary Review* 25 (April 1875): 713–32, on p. 727.

60. Ibid., 715.

61. N. Trübner to WDW, 18 March 1875, WP. Morris received credit as the ostensible editor of the abridgment: Richard Morris, ed., *Language and its Study, with special reference to the Indo-European family of languages: Seven lectures by William Dwight Whitney* (London: Trübner and Co., 1876). WDW to JDW, 31 March 1872, WP.

62. R. Rost to WDW, 31 December 1875; C. Darwin to WDW, 8 May 1875; Emma Darwin to WDW, 9 May 1875, WP.

63. Whitney Journal, 11 May 1875, WP.

64. WDW to Elizabeth Baldwin Whitney, 13 June 1875, WP.

65. G. Curtius to WDW, 7 June 1875, WP; WDW to G. Curtius, 6 June 1875, Curtius Papers; WDW to C. R. Lanman, 19 December 1875, LP. Whitney had sent Leskien a

copy of the newly published *LGL* in May of 1875: Account books showing distribution of gift copies of Whitney's writings: Box 53, folder 54, WP. Leskien's work appeared as *Leben und Wachsthum der Sprache* (Leipzig: F. A. Brockhaus, 1876). Other translations of *LGL* followed: German, French and Italian in 1876, Dutch in 1879, Swedish in 1880, and Japanese in 1899.

66. Whitney praised the efforts of *LSL*'s German translator, Julius Jolly: WDW to A. Weber, 3 November 1873, 2 February 1874, Weber Papers. Jolly's work appeared as *Die Sprachwissenschaft: W. D. Whitney's Vorlesungen über die Principien der vergleichenden Sprachforschung* (München: T. Ackermann, 1874). Dutch was the only language besides German into which *LSL* eventually was translated (in two volumes, 1877–81).

67. WDW, *A Sanskrit Grammar* (Boston: Ginn, Heath and Co., 1879), v. Whitney Journal, 26 May 1875, WP; WDW to E. E. Salisbury, 25 June 1875, SP; WDW to Elizabeth Baldwin Whitney, 18 June 1875, WP.

68. F. Max Müller, "The Life of Language," *Nature* 12 (22 July 1875): 226.

69. WDW to E. E. Salisbury, 29 July 1875, SP.

70. Unsigned, "Streitfragen der heutigen Sprachwissenschaft," *Deutsche Rundschau* 4 (August 1875): 259–79. Julius Redenberg to WDW, 6 July 1875, WP.

71. WDW to Elizabeth Baldwin Whitney, 31 August 1875, WP. Unsigned, Review of *LGL* by W. D. Whitney, in *Academy* 174 n.s. (4 September 1875): 248. This review was followed two weeks later by A. H. Sayce, Review of *LGL* by W. D. Whitney, *Academy* 176 n.s. (18 September 1875): 311–12.

72. WDW, "Professor Whitney on Language," *Academy* 175 n.s. (11 September 1875): 282. F. J. Furnivall to WDW, 7 September 1875; R. Rost to WDW, 12 September 1875, WP.

73. F. Max Müller, "In Self-defence," *Chips from a German Workshop,* 4 vols. (New York: Scribner, Armstrong and Co., 1876), 4:456–531, on p. 527. Müller's most convincing charge related to Whitney's "epitheta ornantia" against Heymann Steinthal: ibid., 505–7. Whitney gave Steinthal's first name as "Hajjim" in his anti-Steinthal article, presumably as an anti-Semitic jibe (WDW, "Steinthal and the Psychological Theory," 1:332). Even Whitney's AOS colleague Ezra Abbot felt obliged to question him about this: Ezra Abbot to WDW, 14 and 22 October 1877, WP.

74. Müller, "In Self-defence," 517, 465.

75. Ibid., 528, 529, 530.

76. Ibid., 526–27.

77. Unsigned, Announcement of *Chips from a German Workshop,* vol. 4, by Max Müller, in *Academy* 179 n. s. (October 9, 1875): 379. A. H. Sayce, Review of *Chips* vol. 4, by Max Müller, in *Academy* 184 n.s. (13 November 1875): 507; Charles Kegan Paul to WDW, 18 May 1876, WP; WDW to A. Weber, 17 December 1875, 5 June 1876, Weber Papers. Sayce wrote to Whitney to defend his remarks: A. H. Sayce to WDW, 18 December 1875, 15 April, 13 July 1876; WDW to A. H. Sayce, 5 June 1876, WP (copy).

78. Whitney Journal, 29 November, 8 and 11 December, 1875, 15 February 1876; WDW to JDW, 19 December 1875, WP. Whitney noted the identities of various friends who wrote in his defense: WDW to E. L. Godkin, 8 January 1877, E. L. Godkin Papers, Houghton Library, Harvard University. George Ripley (editor of *The American Cyclopedia*) to WDW, 7 April 1876; Wendell Philips Garrison (*Nation*) to WDW, 27 March 1876; Henry Adams to WDW, 1 May 1876, WP. The language critic Richard Grant White wrote a pro-Müller piece: [R. G. White], *New York Times* (18 April 1876), in Newsclippings File, WP.

79. A. Weber to WDW, 25 December 1875; John Muir to WDW, 29 March 1876; William Newton to WDW, 13 March 1876; Fitzedward Hall to WDW, 28 January, 21 March 1876; E. B. Cowell to WDW, 20 June 1876, WP.

80. R. Rost to WDW, 7 November, 31 December 1875, WP.

81. G. H. Darwin to WDW, 21 December 1875, WP.

82. C. E. Norton to WDW, 28 December 1875, WP.

83. WDW, "A Rejoinder," *Academy* 191 n.s. (1 January 1876): 12. C. Appleton to WDW, 31 December 1875, WP. Letters confirming Whitney's account include: Max Müller to WDW, 20 June 1860 (the Boden request), 22 November 1863, 13 January 1864, 29 March 1864, 39 December 1867, WP.

84. WDW, "A Rejoinder": the emphasis appears in Whitney's quotation of the passage from Max Müller, although not in Müller's original. The original passage appeared in Müller, *Science of Language,* 1:50 (quoted in ch. 6 above). Whitney quoted the revised passage from Max Müller, "In Self-defence," 476. Seconding Whitney's account were [A. W. Wheeler], "Müller versus Whitney," *New England Journal of Education* 3:9 (26 February 1876): 98; Unsigned, "Müller's Chips from a German Workshop," *Nation* 22 (23 March 1876): 195–97; and [T. R. Lounsbury], "Review of Müller's *Chips from a German Workshop,* vol. iv," *NAR* 123 (July 1876): 193–210, on p. 202.

85. WDW, "A Rejoinder."

86. Max Müller, "Light, Delight, Alight," *Academy* 192 n.s. (8 January 1876), in WP. Charles Appleton, Editorial, *Academy* 200 n.s. (4 March 1876): 215, in WP. [WDW], "Mr. Max Müller and Professor Whitney," *The Examiner* (4 March 1876): 264. The publisher Charles Kegan Paul acted as Whitney's agent in securing space in the *Examiner.* C. K. Paul to WDW, 29 February 1876; Watson R. Sperry to WDW, 22 March 1876, WP.

87. Angelo de Gubernatis, "Una Questione in Famiglia," *Rivista Europa* 7 (1876): 311–19. WDW to A. de Gubernatis, 17 February 1876, Weber Papers. (The quotation appears in a copy of the letter to Gubernatis that Whitney sent to Albrecht Weber.)

88. WDW to A. Weber, 6 April 1876, Weber Papers; T. Aufrecht to WDW, 30 May 1876; K. R. Lepsius to WDW, 29 May 1876, WP. De Gubernatis later apologized for printing the letter: A. de Gubernatis to WDW, 27 August 1878, WP.

89. Whitney Journal, 20 January 1876, WP.

90. Max Müller to M. Conway, 10 and 11 May 1876, Conway Papers.

91. Max Müller to M. Conway, 11 and 13 May 1876, Conway Papers, emphasis in the original.

92. Max Müller to M. Conway, 14 May 1876, Conway Papers, emphasis in the original.

93. WDW to A. Weber, 9 December 1872, Weber Papers. WDW, "On the Main Results of the Later Vedic Researches in Germany," *JAOS* 3 (1853): 289–328, on p. 293. Whitney had similarly snubbed Müller by omitting his work from the bibliography to his article "Veda," in the *New American Cyclopedia* (New York: Appleton, 1861), vol. 16, 38–40, on p. 40. Finally, when Whitney reprinted the 1853 piece as "The Vedas" (*OLS,* 1:1–45), he added a footnote (ibid., 3) indicating that Max Müller was indeed the editor of the Ṛg-Veda.

94. Max Müller to M. Conway, 15 May 1876, Conway Papers.

95. WDW to M. Conway (copy) 31 May 1876, WP.

96. Moncure Conway, "The Whitney-Müller Controversy," *The Palladium* (7 June 1876), in Newsclippings File, WP.

97. [Lounsbury], "Müller's Chips volume iv." Another careful summation of the controversy, sympathetic to Whitney, was E. A. [Ezra Abbot], "American Oriental Society," *Bibliotheca Sacra* 34 (July 1877): 557–62. Henry Adams to T. R. Lounsbury, 21 May 1876, in *The Letters of Henry Adams,* eds. J. C. Levenson et al., 6 vols. (Cambridge, Mass.: Belknap Press, 1982–88), 2:268.

98. H. Adams to WDW, 15 October 1875; 1 May, 8 and 9 September, 1876, WP; WDW to C. E. Norton, 22 December 1875, 14 and 28 September 1876, Norton Papers; C. E. Norton to WDW, 28 December 1875, 19 September 1876, WP.

99. WDW, "Müller's Rig-Veda and Commentary," *New Englander* 35 (October 1876): 772–91.

100. Henry Sweet to WDW, 14 February 1882, WP. Unsigned, Review of *The Life and Letters of the Right Honourable Friedrich Max Müller,* edited by his wife, in *The (New York) Methodist Review* 85 (July 1903): 676–78. This review, perhaps the best-informed assessment of Max Müller's career by a contemporary, likely was written by A. H. Sayce.

101. Müller, *Science of Language,* 2:43.

102. C. A. Aiken, "Whitney on Language," *Princeton Review* (April 1868): 263–92, on p. 277; [George Frederick Wright], "Whitney-Müller Controversy," *Bibliotheca Sacra* (1877): 185.

103. [G. F. Wright], "Whitney-Müller Controversy," 185; Unsigned, Review of *LGL* by WDW, in *Saturday Review* (13 May 1876): 625.

104. On the concept in general, see Edna Ullmann-Margalit, "Invisible-Hand Explanations," *Synthese* 39 (1978): 263–91. On the concept applied to language, see Helmut Lüdtke, "Invisible-hand Processes and the Universal Laws of Language Change," in *Language Change,* ed. Leiv Breivik and Ernst Håkon Jahr (New York: de Gruyter, 1989), 131–36; Brigitte Nerlich, *Change in Language: Whitney, Bréal, and Wegener* (New York: Routledge, 1990), 144; and Rudi Keller, *On Language Change: The Invisible Hand in Language,* trans. Brigitte Nerlich (New York: Routledge, 1994), ch. 4, especially pp. 68–69.

105. For perspectives different from my own about the relative contributions of Whitney and Müller, see Keller, *On Language Change,* 53, 78–79, 155; and Nerlich, *Change in Language,* 94, 105.

106. Keller, *On Language Change,* 68–69; WDW, *LGL,* 146.

107. D. H. Wheeler, "Growth in Language," *Methodist Quarterly Review* 51 (April 1869): 228–42, on pp. 238, 241–42. For the kind of careful definitions of "intention" and "conscious/unconscious" that often were lacking in Whitney's time, see Keller, *On Language Change,* 9–13.

108. F. A. March, Review of *OLS,* vol. 1, by W. D. Whitney, in *Nation* 16 (6 February 1873): 96–97. In the wake of the controversy with Müller, the British historian Edward A. Freeman (1823–92) implicitly defended Whitney by taking a generous view of what counted as "willed" behavior: E. A. Freeman, "Race and Language," *Contemporary Review* 29 (May 1877): 711–24, on p. 720.

109. Chauncey Wright, "The Evolution of Self-Consciousness," *NAR* 116 (April 1873): 245–310, on p. 304.

110. WDW, "Steinthal and the Psychological Theory," 151–52.

111. WDW, *LGL,* 147, emphasis added.

112. Ibid., 146, 286. Whitney probably was responding as well to a critique of his voluntarism by J. S. Blackie, Review of *OLS,* vol. 1, by W. D. Whitney, in *The Scotsman* 9216 (7 February 1873): 2.

113. WDW, "Logical Consistency in Views of Language," *AJP* 1 (1880): 327–43, on p. 335.

114. Keller, *On Language Change,* 155.

NINE: The Elder Statesman and the *Junggrammatiker*

1. WDW to E. B. Cowell, 22 May 1876, E. B. Cowell Papers, Cambridge University Library.

2. Kurt R. Jankowsky, *The Neogrammarians: A Re-evaluation of their Place in the Development of Linguistic Science* (The Hague: Mouton, 1972), 169, 207; Randy Allen Harris, *The Linguistic Wars* (New York: Oxford University Press, 1993), 19.

3. D. C. Gilman to G. J. Brush, 30 January 1875, quoted in Fabian Franklin, *The Life of Daniel Coit Gilman* (New York: Dodd, Mead and Co., 1910), 191–92. D. C. Gilman to WDW, 30 January 1875, WP. Gilman's letter to Whitney (marked "private and unofficial") set forth some of his earliest plans for the new university.

4. WDW to D. C. Gilman, 14 March 1875, Gilman Papers, emphasis in the original.

5. The list Whitney recommended to Gilman was extensive for its day: the only language families omitted, yet included among those described in *LGL,* ch. 12, were Malayan-Polynesian, Papuan, Australian, Dravidian, Bantu, Middle African, and Basque.

6. D. C. Gilman to WDW, 21 and 30 November 1875, 30 March 1876, WP; WDW to D. C. Gilman, 7 November, 12 December, 1875, Gilman Papers. *DAB,* s.v. "Lanman, Charles Rockwell."

7. WDW to C. R. Lanman, 19 December 1875, 29 May 1876, LP.

8. WDW to D. C. Gilman, 14 March 1875, 1 April 1876, 28 April 1877, 9 May 1877, Gilman Papers; D. C. Gilman to WDW, 25 January, 4 April 1876, WP. Announcement of Visiting Lectures at The Johns Hopkins University, 1876–77, WP.

9. WDW to C. R. Lanman, 11 April 1880, LP; WDW to JDW, 9 January 1881, WP.

10. *DAB* s.v. "Hopkins, Edward Washburn." E. W. Hopkins to WDW, 9 July 1881, WP; WDW to D. C. Gilman, 3 June, 31 July 1880, Gilman Papers; D. C. Gilman to B. L. Gildersleeve, 31 July 1880, Gildersleeve Papers.

11. *DAB* s.v. "Bloomfield, Maurice." C. R. Lanman to WDW, 17 August 1880, emphasis in original, WP; C. R. Lanman to D. C. Gilman, 30 November 1880, Gilman Papers; WDW to D. C. Gilman, 17 December 1880, Gilman Papers.

12. D. C. Gilman to WDW, 4 December 1880, WP.

13. WDW to D. C. Gilman, 27 October 1881, Gilman Papers, emphasis in the original; C. R. Lanman to H. Collitz, 13 April 1905, Herman Collitz Papers, Milton S. Eisenhower Library, Johns Hopkins University.

14. W. R. Harper to WDW, 26 May 1880, WP; WDW to D. C. Gilman, 3 June, 31 July 1880, Gilman Papers.

15. WDW to D. C. Gilman, 1880, Gilman Papers.

16. C. R. Lanman to WDW, 11 June 1885; F. A. P. Barnard to WDW, 18 October 1880; James McCosh to WDW, 29 May 1877, WP.

17. WDW to C. R. Lanman, 17 June 1881, LP.

18. Whitney gave this advice in his 1870 APA presidential address: *PAPA* 1 (1870): 4–7.

19. C. R. Lanman to WDW, 7 October 1881, WP; WDW to C. R. Lanman, 21 October 1881, LP; Albert Harkness to WDW, 21 March 1876; WDW to JDW 20 July 1881, WP. Charles A. Bristed, "Literary Note," *Nation* 15 (29 August 1872): 135.

20. B. L. Gildersleeve, "The Special Province of the American Philologian," *PAPA* 10 (1878): 22–23. Gildersleeve's address reappeared as "University Work in America and Classical Philology," *Princeton Review* 55 (May 1879): 511–26, reprinted in B. L. Gildersleeve, *Essays and Studies* (Baltimore, Md.: N. Murray, 1890), 87–123, relevant section on pp. 96–97. B. L. Gildersleeve to WDW, 17 March, 23 May 1879, WP. B. L. Gildersleeve to James Morgan Hart, 6 June 1879, in *The Letters of Basil Lanneau Gildersleeve*, ed. Ward W. Briggs, Jr. (Baltimore: Johns Hopkins University Press, 1987), 84.

21. Gildersleeve, "University Work in America," 97. B. L. Gildersleeve to D. C. Gilman, 16 July 1881, in *Letters of B. L. Gildersleeve*, 145.

22. WDW to E. E. Salisbury, 26 June 1875, SP.

23. U.S. Passport for WDW, issued 11 July 1878, WP.

24. Bertoldt Delbrück to WDW, 22 July, 24 August 1878; WDW to JDW, 27 October 1878, 20 September 1879, WP; WDW to C. R. Lanman (postcard), 1 October 1878, LP. John E. Joseph, *From Whitney to Chomsky* (Philadelphia: John Benjamins, 2003), 34–35.

25. Joseph, *Whitney to Chomsky*, 36–37.

26. WDW to JDW, 10 July, 2 and 20 August 1878, WP.

27. WDW to C. R. Lanman, 2 February 1882, LP. *DNB*, s.v. "Wilde, Oscar O'Flahertie."

28. Ferdinand de Saussure, *Course in General Linguistics*, trans. and annotated by Roy Harris (1916; La Salle, Ill.: Open Court, 1983), 17.

29. Ibid., 18, 19.

30. F. de Saussure, *Deuxieme cours de linguistique générale (1908–1909)*, ed., Eisuke Komatsu, Eng. trans. by George Wolf (New York: Pergamon, 1997), 92a; also 160a.

31. Curtius quoted in Paul Kiparsky, "From Paleogrammarians to Neogrammarians," *Studies in the History of Linguistics*, ed. Dell Hymes (Bloomington: Indiana University Press, 1974), 331–45, on pp. 337–38.

32. Franz Bopp quoted in James H. Stam, *Inquiries into the Origin of Language: The Fate of a Question* (New York: Harper & Row, 1978), 224.

33. August Schliecher, *Die Deutsche Sprache*, 4th ed. (1859; Stuttgart: J. G Gotta'schen, 1879), 35; Winfred P. Lehmann, ed. and trans., *A Reader in Nineteenth-Century Historical Indo-European Linguistics* (Bloomington: Indiana University Press), 91–92.

34. Franz Bopp, *A Comparative Grammar of Sanskrit, Zend, Greek, Latin, Lithuanian, Gothic, German, and Sclavonic Languages*, 3 vols., translated by Edward B. Eastwick, third edition (Edinburgh: Williams and Norgate, 1862), 2:471.

35. William M. Norman, "The Neogrammarians and Comparative Linguistics" (PhD diss., Princeton University, 1972), 31–33.

36. WDW, "Schleicher and the Physical Theory of Language," *OLS*, 1:298–331, on p. 328.

37. WDW to Georg Curtius, 30 May 1873, Curtius Papers. Whitney had first dealt with this issue in one of his earliest forays into general linguistics, a paper about

Ernest Renan's theory of language's early efflorescence: "Strictures upon the Views of M. Ernest Renan respecting the Origin and Early History of Languages," *PAOS* 7 (October 1859): 9–10. This paper appeared only in abstract.

38. WDW, "Müller's Chips from a German Workshop," *OLS*, 2:131.

39. WDW, *LSL*, 184, 286; also *LGL*, 196.

40. Craig Christy, *Uniformitarianism in Linguistics* (Philadelphia: John Benjamins, 1983), 35.

41. Leskien's work was his *Die Declination im Slavisch-Litauischen und im Germanishen* (1876).

42. WDW, *LGL*, 74.

43. Karl Brugmann, Preface to *Morphologische Untersuchungen auf dem Gebiete der indogermanischen Sprachen*, quoted in *Reader in Nineteenth-Century Historical Indo-European Linguistics*, 203–4; Norman, "The Neogrammarians," 55–62; Christy, *Uniformitarianism in Linguistics*, 73–75.

44. See ch. 7 above.

45. WDW, "On Peile's Greek and Latin Etymology," *Transactions of the Philological Society of London* (1873–74), part iii, 312.

46. WDW, *LSL*, 28, 82, 85; WDW, *LGL*, 75, 148. Craig Christy notes that Whitney's jaundiced view of analogy likely prejudiced the Neogrammarians' reception of his views to some degree (*Uniformitarianism in Linguistics*, 82, 86).

47. WDW, *LGL*, 74, 75.

48. Ibid., 74.

49. Pedersen, *Discovery of Language*, 291; Brugmann, Preface to *Morphologische Untersuchungen*, 198, 203.

50. E. Sievers, "Philology, Part II: Comparative Philology of the Aryan Languages," in *Encyclopedia Britannica*, 9th ed. (1875–90) vol. 18 (1885), 794–803, on p. 797. Whitney was the author of Part I of this article: "The Science of Language in General."

51. Christy, *Uniformitarianism in Linguistics*, 78–80; W. Scherer quoted in ibid., 80, author's translation.

52. Brugmann, Preface to *Morphologische Untersuchungen*, 204.

53. Ibid., 205.

54. Brugmann in Charles R. Lanman, ed. *The Whitney Memorial Meeting* (Boston: Ginn and Co., 1897), 78, 76–77, author's translation.

55. Brugmann quoted in Christy, *Uniformitarianism in Linguistics*, 82.

56. The exceptions are Christy, *Uniformitarianism in Linguistics*, 58, which shows that the rise of uniformitarian theory necessarily entailed a "chronological revolution"; and Thomas Trautmann, *Louis Henry Morgan and the Invention of Kinship* (Berkeley: University of California Press, 1987), 229, which describes the multiple links between the Neogrammarian program and the *human* time revolution specifically.

57. The connections Saussure drew between Whitney's critique of early comparative philology, the role of analogy, and the Neogrammarians can be seen clearly in the student notes. Material on these topics is widely separated in the published *Course in General Linguistics*, where the discussion of analogy on p. 223 completes the thought begun on pp. 17–19 about the Neogrammarians. This same material is presented in connected sequence in Saussure, *Deuxieme cours de linguistique générale*, 86–87, 91–92.

58. Kiparsky, "Paleogrammarians to Neogrammarians," 340.

59. WDW, "The Principle of Economy as a Phonetic Force," *PAPA* (1877): 14 (ab-

stract). Account books showing distribution of gift copies of Whitney's writings: Box 53, folder 54, WP.

60. WDW, *LSL,* 152, 95; also: WDW, "The Principle of Economy as a Phonetic Force," *TAPA* (1878): 123–34.

61. Brugmann, Preface to *Morphologische Untersuchungen,* 205, 207.

62. Ibid., 203–4.

63. WDW to Georg Curtius, 18 May 1879, Curtius Papers.

64. Bertoldt Delbrück, *Introduction to the Study of Language,* trans. E. Channing (1882; Amsterdam: John Benjamins, 1974), 58, 60.

65. Hermann Paul, *Principles of the History of Language,* trans. Herbert A. Strong (London: Swan Sonnenchein, Lowrey, and Co., 1888), 3–8, 26, 50–53, 59–64.

66. Brugmann, Preface to *Morphologische Untersuchungen,* 201.

67. Delbrück, *Introduction,* 123, 129, emphasis added.

68. E. W. Hopkins, Review of B. Delbrück, *Introduction to the Study of Language,* trans. E. Channing, in *AJP* 3 (1882): 235–36. The translator, Eva Channing, was a New England native who had studied at Leipzig. An acquaintance of Whitney's, she was elected the first female member of both the American Oriental Society and the American Philological Association. Eva Channing to WDW, 16 October 1878, 23 December 1881, WP.

69. WDW to Georg Curtius, 30 October 1881, Curtius Papers.

70. WDW, "Further Words as to Surds and Sonants, and the Law of Economy as a Phonetic Force," *PAPA* 13 (1882): xiii–xiv; also "On the Relation of Surd and Sonant," *TAPA* (1878): 41–57. Earlier, Whitney had argued that it was a Germanic bias to consider sonancy as weaknesses: WDW, "On Lepsius's Standard Alphabet," *JAOS* 7 (1861): 299–332.

71. Maria Whitney to WDW, 14 November 1880, 29 December 1881, WP. Maria Whitney had taught modern languages at Smith College during the two years prior to her stay in Germany, yet she did not return to her teaching post there afterwards (*Bulletin of Smith College Alumni and Officers, 1875–1925*). Gabriel Engelsman to WDW, 4 February 1882, WP.

72. Maurice Bloomfield, "On the Probability of the Existence of Phonetic Laws," *AJP* 5:18 (1884): 178–85, on p. 178; F. A. March, "Response," *PAPA* 17 (1886): xxxvi. (See note 75 for the context of the March article.)

73. Morton W. Easton, "Analogy and Uniformity," *AJP* 5:18 (1884): 164–77, on pp. 171, 176. The dialectologist Hugo Schuchardt briefly praised Whitney's outlook in his polemic "On Sound Law: Against the Neogrammarians" (1885), in *The Lautgesetz-Controversy: A Documentation,* ed. Terence H. Wilbur (Amsterdam: John Benjamins, 1977), 41–71, on p. 51.

74. *DAB,* s.v. "Tarbell, Frank B."

75. WDW, "The Method of Phonetic Change in Language," *PAPA* 17 (1886): xxxiii–v, on p. xxxv; WDW, "Response to F. A. March," *PAPA* 16 (1885): xix–xx, on p. xx. (Whitney's "Method" paper was published only in the form of a detailed abstract, probably due to Whitney's illness at this time.)

76. WDW, "Method of Phonetic Change," xxxv.

77. Ibid.

78. Frank B. Tarbell, "Phonetic Law," *TAPA* 17 (1886): 5–16, on pp. 13–14.

79. Ibid., 13.

80. Ibid., 14.

81. Pliny Earle Chase to WDW, 5 November 1867, WP.

82. William Paley, *Natural Theology*, 12th ed. (1803; London: J. Faulder, 1809), 415–16, 446; William Whewell, *Astronomy and General Physics Considered with Reference to Natural Theology* (London: W. Pickering, 1833), 301, 361, 374. Useful background on this subject appears in Ronald L. Numbers, *Creation by Natural Law: Laplace's Nebular Hypothesis in American Thought* (Seattle: University of Washington Press, 1977), 78–83.

83. Karl Pearson, *The Grammar of Science*, 2nd ed. (London: Adam and Charles Black, 1900), 79, 86–89, 99; Dorothy Ross, *The Origins of American Social Science* (New York: Cambridge University Press, 1991), 16–17, 227–28.

84. Ross, *Origins of American Social Science*, 59–60.

85. In the *Grammar*'s Preface, Whitney said that he put his data into statistical form "whenever possible": *A Sanskrit Grammar* (Boston: Ginn, Heath and Co., 1879), vi. At times he shows actual tabulations or percentages, for instance, pp. 26, 47. But more often (e. g., pp. 210–11), he states his results based on data he has gathered without including numerical evidence.

86. Here I use the title of the abstract version: "The Proportional Elements of English Utterance," *PAPA* (1874): 14–17. The fuller presentation appeared as "The Elements of English Pronunciation," *OLS*, 2:202–76.

87. Ian Hacking, *The Taming of Chance* (Cambridge, UK: Cambridge University Press, 1990), 181.

TEN: Enduring Legacies

1. WDW to E. F. Salisbury, 21 September 1869, SP; WDW to C. R. Lanman, 2 May 1886, LP.

2. WDW to E. B. Cowell, 22 May 1876, E. B. Cowell Papers, Cambridge University Library; WDW to Albrecht Weber, 19 November 1876, Weber Papers. Whitney's *Essentials of English Grammar* would go through eighteen printings by 1903.

3. Roswell Smith to WDW, 1 April 1890; WDW to JDW, October 1884, 21 January 1885, 26 June 1889, WP. WDW, "Preface," *Century Dictionary*, vi. Richard W. Bailey, "The *Century Dictionary*," in *The Oxford Companion to the English Language*, ed., Tom McArthur (Oxford: Oxford University Press, 1992), 206. Thomas R. Lounsbury, Obituary of William Dwight Whitney, *Proceedings of the American Academy of Arts and Sciences* (1894): 579–89, on p. 587.

4. Simon Newcomb, letters to *Nation* 48 (13 June 1889): 488; and (27 June 1889): 524. WDW to B. E. Smith, 15 June 1889, Benjamin Eli Smith Papers, Amherst College Archives.

5. JDW to WDW, 1 July, 5 September 1889; WDW to JDW, 10 September 1889, WP; C. S. Peirce, letter to *Nation* 48: 1251 (20 June 1889): 504; WDW to Benjamin Eli Smith, 20 October 1891, Benjamin Eli Smith Papers, Amherst College Archives.

6. WDW, "Philology, Pt. I: Science of Language in General." The invitation to Whitney to do this article came in 1881: Thomas S. Baynes to WDW, 16 December 1881, WP. "Professor Whitney on Philology," *Atheneum*, reprinted in *(New York) Critic* 3:74 (30 March 1885): 262. The 1929 edition of *Encyclopedia Britannica* replaced Whitney's article with a new article on "Philology" by the Danish linguist Otto Jespersen.

7. G. J. Romanes, *Mental Evolution in Man* (London: Kegan Paul, Trench & Co., 1888), 83, 290, 369.

8. Praise for Whitney's origins theory appeared in André Lefevre, *Race and Language* (London: Kegan Paul, 1894), 37–38, while Leonard Bloomfield rejected the imitation and interjection theories in his *Introduction to the Study of Language* (New York: Henry Holt and Co., 1914), 13–14.

9. WDW, *Max Müller and the Science of Language: A Criticism* (New York: D. Appleton and Co., 1892). Account books showing distribution of gift copies of Whitney's writings: Box 53, folder 54; WDW to JDW, 2 March 1892; F. A. March to WDW, 2 April 1892, WP.

10. Some later works in this vein include: "The Cosmogonic Hymn, Rig-Veda X. 129," *JAOS* 11 (1882): cxi; "On the Latest Translation of the Upanishads," *PAOS* 13 (1885): lxvii–viii; and "The Native Commentary of the Atharva-Veda," *Festgruss an Roth* (Stuttgart: Kohlhammer, 1893), 95–96.

11. Maurice Bloomfield to WDW, 23 May 1891, WP. B. I. Wheeler, "The Progress of the History of Language during the Last Century," in *International Congress of Arts and Sciences,* ed. Howard J. Rogers, 8 vols. (New York: Houghton-Mifflin, 1906), 3:17–28.

12. A. Burnell to WDW, 19 August 1878; WDW to E. B. Cowell, 7 July 1879, E. B. Cowell Papers, Cambridge University Library; WDW to JDW, 26 December 1880; Henry Sweet to WDW, 14 February 1882, WP. Sweet's praise for Whitney's grammar appeared also in "Report on General Philology," in *The Collected Papers of Henry Sweet,* ed. H. C. Wyld (Oxford: Clarendon Press, 1913), 157.

13. WDW to A. Weber, 24 June 1872, Weber Papers; Karl R. Lepsius to WDW, 29 May 1876, WP. W. D. Whitney, *Sanskrit Grammar* (1882; Cambridge, Mass.: Harvard University Press, 1975).

14. WDW, "Report of Progress of the edition of the Atharva-Veda," *PAOS* 10 (1875): cxviii–ix. WDW to JDW, 29 December 1879, WP.

15. WDW to C. R. Lanman, 17 June 1881, LP; WDW to George Curtius, 30 October 1881, Curtius Papers; WDW to Rudolph von Roth, 5 February 1882 (copy); WDW to JDW, 22 February 1882, WP.

16. E. E. Salisbury to WDW, 27 May 1884, WP.

17. WDW to C. R. Lanman, n.d. October 1884, 27 October 1886, 1 May 1887, 23 October 1889, LP; WDW to JDW, 11 January 1885; WDW to James Lyman Whitney, 19 May 1889, WP. Lounsbury, "Obituary of William Dwight Whitney," 585–87.

18. WDW to C. R. Lanman, 1 February 1886, 12 January 1888, emphasis in the original, LP.

19. WDW to C. R. Lanman, 19 April 1885, 8 June 1886, 13 January 1890, 12 July 1891, LP; WDW to W. R. Harper, 22 November 1890, 1 January 1891, W. R. Harper Papers.

20. WDW to C. R. Lanman, 19 November 1888, 11 August 1889, 21 November 1890, LP; WDW to W. R. Harper, 8 December 1888, W. R. Harper Papers.

21. Cyrus Adler to WDW, 20 January 1886, WP.

22. WDW to C. R. Lanman, 13 March 1890, LP; C. R. Lanman to WDW, 8 and 15 May 1890, WP.

23. Minutes of Annual Meeting, *PAOS* 15 (May 1890): i–iv.

24. C. R. Lanman to WDW, 2 May 1890, WP; WDW to C. R. Lanman, 4 May, LP; C. R. Lanman to D. C. Gilman, 17 October 1890, Gilman Papers; D. C. Gilman to C. R.

Lanman, 21 October 1890, American Oriental Society Correspondence File, Sterling Library, Yale University; WDW to C. R. Lanman, 21 October 1890, LP.

25. Minutes of Semi-Annual Meeting, *PAOS* 15 (October 1890): xxxviii. C. R. Lanman to WDW, 17 January, 15 March 1890; R. Gottheil to WDW, 13 and 17 March 1890, WP.

26. WDW to C. R. Lanman, 7 December 1890, LP; C. R. Lanman to WDW, 10 December 1890, WP; WDW to D. C. Gilman, 10 March 1891, Gilman Papers; D. C. Gilman to WDW, 13 March 1891, WP.

27. Minutes of Semi-Annual Meeting, *PAOS* 15 (October 1890): xxxviii. WDW to C. R. Lanman, 29 June 1890, LP; C. R. Lanman to WDW, 29 October, 23 November 1890, WP. Under the amended charter, the AOS could hold its meetings in any state or territory of the United States, provided that it met within the Commonwealth of Massachusetts at least once every three years. Minutes of Annual Meeting, *PAOS* 15 (May 1891): lxxx.

28. WDW to C. R. Lanman, 1 November 1891, 12 January 1892, LP. Minutes of Annual Meeting, *PAOS* 15 (April 1892): cxliii.

29. C. R. Lanman to D. C. Gilman, 20 February, 29 March 1893; D. C. Gilman to W. H. Ward, 30 March 1893; W. H. Ward to D. C. Gilman, 1 April 1893, Gilman Papers; W. H. Ward to WDW, 1 April 1893, WP; WDW to C. R. Lanman, 5 April 1893, LP. Minutes of Annual Meeting, *PAOS* 16 (April 1893): v–vi.

30. C. R. Lanman to WDW, 8 April 1893, WP.

31. WDW, "Announcement as to a Second Volume of the Roth-Whitney edition of the Atharva-Veda," *PAOS* 15 (1892): clxxi–xxiii. WDW to Rudolph von Roth, 16 June 1893, 19 April 1894, LP.

32. A. V. Williams Jackson, "William Dwight Whitney and his Influence upon American Philological Scholarship," *Anzeiger für Indogermanishe Sprach und Altertumskunde* 5 (1895): 275–77, on p. 277.

33. Charles R. Lanman, ed. *The Whitney Memorial Meeting* (Boston: Ginn and Co., 1897), 150. The completed second volume of the *Atharva* came out in 1897, and in 1905 it was included in the Harvard Oriental Series, which Lanman edited.

34. WDW to C. R. Lanman, 11 May 1894, LP.

35. WDW, "Examples of Sporadic and Partial Phonetic Change in English," *Indogermanische Forschungen* 4 (1894): 32–36; Frank B. Tarbell, "Phonetic Law," *TAPA* 17 (1886): 5–16, on pp. 13–14.

36. WDW, "Sporadic and Partial Phonetic Change," 36.

37. In addition to the APA, the 1894 American Congress of Philologists included the AOS, the Spelling Reform Association (est. 1876), the Archaeological Institute of America (est. 1879), the Society of Biblical Literature and Exegesis (est. 1880), the Modern Language Association of America (est. 1883), and the American Dialect Society (est. 1889).

38. C. R. Lanman, ed., *Whitney Memorial Meeting* (Boston: Ginn and Co., 1897), 75, 84–85, author's translation.

39. John E. Joseph, *From Whitney to Chomsky* (Philadelphia: John Benjamins, 2003), 42–43. In an Appendix to this volume, Joseph reproduces a letter from Saussure to Whitney, dated 7 April 1879, thanking Whitney for his offer to send Saussure copies of some of his writings plus some notes he had made on Saussure's dissertation.

This letter also attests to the fact of the meeting between the two men. Whitney later obtained the published version of Saussure's 1879 treatise: WDW to C. R. Lanman, 15 August 1882, LP.

40. Ferdinand de Saussure, *Écrits de linguistique générale,* ed. Simon Bouquet and Rudolf Engler, with the collaboration of D'Antoinette Weil (Paris: Gallimard, 2002), 213.

41. The complete text of Saussure's 1894 "Notes pour un article sur Whitney" appears in Saussure, *Écrits de linguistique générale* (ed. Bouquet and Engler), 203–22. The most important passages have been translated alongside the French originals in a useful essay: Roman Jakobson, "The World Response to Whitney's Principles of Linguistic Science," in *Whitney on Language,* ed. Michael Silverstein (Cambridge: MIT Press, 1971), xxv–xlv. In the notes that follow, for material from Saussure's "Notes sur Whitney," I first give a reference to the Jakobson essay, then a reference to the full version in the Bouquet and Engler edition. I add, when relevant, one of the other two works showing the sources of Saussure's *Cours.* The latter are: Robert Godel, *Les sources manuscrites du Cours de linguistique générale de F. de Saussur* (Genève: Droz, 1957), 43–46, 51; and Ferdinand de Saussure, *Cours de linguistique générale, édition critique par Rudolph Engler,* 2 vols. (Wiesbaden: Harrassowitz, 1967–74). (The latter is cited hereafter as *Cours, Engler edition.*)

42. Those passages from Saussure's "Notes sur Whitney" adapted for use in the published *Cours* are arrayed throughout volume 1 of *Cours, Engler edition* under the heading of source N-10. The most important theoretical contributions to the final published version appear on pp. 106, 110, 126–27, and 163.

43. Jakobson, "World Response," xxix, xxxi, xxxii; Saussure, "Notes sur Whitney," 204, 213, 222.

44. Jakobson, "World Response," xxxi; Saussure, "Notes sur Whitney," 213.

45. Ferdinand de Saussure, *Course in General Linguistics,* trans. and annotated by Roy Harris (1916; La Salle, Ill.: Open Court, 1983), 5, 76; additional praise of Whitney appears ibid., 10; Jakobson, "World Response," xxxii.

46. WDW, *LGL,* 137. Roy Harris and Talbot J. Taylor, *Landmarks in Linguistic Thought* (New York: Routledge, 1989), 188, labels this traditional view of the sign "surrogationism." Roy Harris, *Reading Saussure* (London: Duckworth, 1987), 67, says that Whitney's view of arbitrariness "still suggests that what is 'arbitrary' stands simply opposed to what is naturally determined."

47. Saussure, "Notes sur Whitney," 210; Godel, *Le sources manuscrites,* 43–46; Saussure, *Course in General Linguistics,* 98–101, 158, 160.

48. Jakobson, "World Response," xli, xlii, emphasis in the original; Saussure, "Notes sur Whitney," 218–19; *Cours, Engler edition,* 197–98.

49. The full version of Saussure's discussion of the chess game can be found in the "Notes sur Whitney," 207–8, 216–17. For a comparison with what appeared in the published *Cours,* see *Cours, Engler edition,* 126–27.

50. WDW, *LSL,* 54, 74; also 32, 128. On the basis of these passages from Whitney's first book, a convincing case has been made against any deep continuity between Whitney's outlook and Saussurean structuralism: Bridgitte Nerlich, *Change in Language: Whitney, Bréal, and Wegener* (New York: Routledge, 1990), 74–76, 79–81; Roy Harris, *Reading Saussure,* 66–69; and Julie Tetel Andresen, *Linguistics in America, 1769–1924: A Critical History* (New York: Routledge, 1990), 157–61.

51. WDW, *LSL*, 251–55.

52. WDW, *LGL*, 214 (Whitney treated this entire subject in *LGL*, ch. 11: "Linguistic Structure: Material and Form in Language"); WDW, "On Material and Form in Language," *TAPA* 3 (1872): 77–96.

53. Here I follow the essential point made in E. F. K. Koerner, *Ferdinand de Saussure* (Braunschweig: Vieweg, 1973), 90–91; Richard W. Bailey, "William Dwight Whitney and the Origins of Semiotics," in *The Sign: Semiotics Around the World*, ed. R. W. Bailey, L. Matejka, and P. Steiner (Ann Arbor: Michigan Slavic Publications, 1978), 74; and E. F. Konrad Koerner, "L'Importance de William Dwight Whitney pour les jeunes linguistes de Leipzig," *Etudes saussuriennes* (Geneva: Editions Slatkine, 1988), 1–16, on pp. 10–11. In this last piece, Koerner suggests that the 1876 French translation of Whitney's *LGL*, with its added wording on "oppositions" between paired terms, likely influenced Saussure. (Whitney himself, as it happened, intensely disliked the translation: "As for that French version, hardly anything is too bad to say of it: I didn't at all realize its enormity." WDW to C. R. Lanman, 19 December 1875, LP. On this subject, see Joseph, *Whitney to Chomsky*, 41–42.)

54. Saussure, "Notes sur Whitney," 207; Godel, *Le sources manuscrites*, 44.

55. WDW, "Are Languages Institutions?" *Contemporary Review* 25 (April 1875): 713–32, on p. 717.

56. Problematically, Saussure suggested the same point: *Course in General Linguistics*, 157.

57. George Campbell, *Philosophy of Rhetoric* (1776; London: Tegg and Son, 1838), 250–52.

58. Jakobson, "World Response," xxxvii; Godel, *Le sources manuscrites*, 51. John Joseph details further aspects of Saussure's dissent from Whitney's language theory in *Whitney to Chomsky*, 37–43.

59. Saussure's consideration of the Neogrammarians, beginning in *Course in General Linguistics*, 17–19, is continued in the discussion of analogy on pp. 223–25. The same material appears in the student notes: Saussure, *Deuxieme cours de linguistique générale*, 86–87, 91–92.

60. Saussure, *Course in General Linguistics*, 223, emphasis added.

61. Several writers have traced this connection from Paul (or the Neogrammarians as a whole) to Saussure: Konrad Koerner, "Hermann Paul and Synchronic Linguistics," *Lingua* 29 (1972): 274–307, on pp. 288–89; Kurt R. Jankowsky, *The Neogrammarians: A Re-evaluation of their Place in the Development of Linguistic Science* (The Hague: Mouton, 1972), 193; Craig Christy, *Uniformitarianism in Linguistics* (Philadelphia: John Benjamins, 1983), 256–57; and A. M. Davies, *History of Linguistics*, Vol. 4: *Nineteenth-Century Linguistics*, 256–57. John Joseph provides a thoughtful note of skepticism: Review of *Saussurean Studies* by Konrad Koerner, in *Language* 65:3 (1989): 595–602, on p. 599.

62. Jankowsky, *The Neogrammarians*, 137, 148–50, 193.

63. Paul Kiparsky, "From Paleogrammarians to Neogrammarians," *Studies in the History of Linguistics*, ed. Dell Hymes (Bloomington: Indiana University Press, 1974), 331–45, on pp. 340–41.

64. Ibid., 78, author's translation.

65. Lanman, *Whitney Memorial Meeting*, 94, author's translation.

66. Edgar H. Sturtevant, *Linguistic Change* (1917; Chicago: University of Chicago,

1962), xiii; Konrad Koerner, ed., *First Person Singular II: Autobiographies by North American Scholars in the Language Sciences* (Philadelphia: John Benjamins, 1991), 275.

67. Leonard Bloomfield, "On Recent Work in General Linguistics," *Modern Philology* 25 (1927): 211–12 n. A sixth English edition of Whitney's *Language and the Study of Language* came out in 1901.

68. Oertel, *Lectures on the Study of Language*, 82, 144–45, 271–72; Sturtevant, *Linguistic Change*, 25–29, 61–65; Leonard Bloomfield, *Introduction to the Study of Language* (1914; Philadelphia: John Benjamins, 1983), 77–82, 236.

69. Boyd H. Davis and Raymond K. O'Cain, eds., *First Person Singular* (Amsterdam: John Benjamins, 1980), 106; Bloomfield, *Introduction*, vi, 312, 308 n., 315.

70. Bloomfield, *Introduction*, 315, 312. Bloomfield's praise of Whitney's theoretical views in his book *Language* (New York: Henry Holt, 1933), 16, likewise need to be placed into larger context.

71. Bloomfield, *Introduction*, 197, 219, 221, 259, 312.

72. Oertel, *Study of Language*, 150–88. Tarde's book was *Les lois de l'imitation* (1890).

73. Oertel, *Study of Language*, 80, 136–38, 268–71; Sturtevant, *Linguistic Change*, 29–30, 75–77. Hermann Paul, *Principles of the History of Language*, trans. Herbert A. Strong (London: Swan Sonnenchein, Lowrey, and Co., 1888), ch. 2.

74. Sturtevant, *Linguistic Change*, 74, 84; Holgar Pedersen, *The Discovery of Language: Linguistic Science in the Nineteenth Century* [1924], trans. John W. Spargo (Bloomington: Indiana University Press, 1931), 297, 301–2.

75. Dell Hymes and John Fought, *American Structuralism* (New York: Mouton, 1975), 50–56.

76. Bloomfield, *Language*, 78–85, 129–38; Edward Sapir, "Language," *Encyclopedia of the Social Sciences*, ed. E. R. A. Seligman (New York: Macmillan, 1933), 9:155–69, on pp. 155–56.

77. WDW, "On the Comparative Frequency of Occurrence of the Alphabetic Element in Sanskrit," *PAOS* (1877): xx–xxii.

78. WDW, "The Proportional Elements of English Utterance" *PAPA* (1874): 14–17, on p. 14; Bloomfield, *Language*, 136–37.

79. John G. Fought, "American Structuralism," in *A Concise History of the Language Sciences*, ed. E. F. K. Koerner and R. E. Asher (New York: Pergamon, 1995), 295–306, on p. 303.

80. WDW, *A Sanskrit Grammar* (Boston: Ginn, Heath and Co., 1879), vi.

81. Bloomfield, *Language*, 33, 145; Leonard Bloomfield, "Language or Ideas?" *Language* 2 (1936): 89–95.

82. John E. Joseph, "Bloomfield's Saussurianism," *Cahiers Ferdinand de Saussure* 43 (1989): 43–53; Rudolf P. Botha, *Twentieth-century Conceptions of Language* (Cambridge, Mass.: Blackwell, 1992), 40.

83. WDW, *LSL*, 175, 241, 369.

84. WDW to Albrecht Weber, 3 November 1873, Weber Papers; WDW to C. R. Lanman, 13 October 1877, LP. WDW, "On Johannes Schmidt's New Theory of the Relationship of Indo-European Languages," *JAOS* 10 (1873): lxxvii–viii.

85. WDW, "The Method of Phonetic Change in Language," *PAPA* 17 (1886): xxxiii–v, on p. xxxv.

86. Whitney did reject Max Müller's and Ernest Renan's extreme theory of an original diversity of dialects prior to the emergence of unified languages. This view, he said,

did not go back far enough to find the relative unity that must have preceded dialectal variety. WDW, "Languages and Dialects," *NAR* 104 (1867): 30–64.

87. Gauchat's work is described in William Labov, *Principles of Linguistic Change*, 2 vols. (Cambridge, Mass.: Blackwell, 1994, 2001), 1:18–19.

88. Bloomfield, *Introduction*, 216–18.

89. Sturtevant, *Linguistic Change*, 78–79, 82; idem, *An Introduction to Linguistic Science* (New Haven, Conn.: Yale University Press, 1947), 77, 83.

90. William S. -Y. Wang, "Competing Changes as a Cause of Residue," *Language* 45:1 (1969): 9–25, on p. 10.

91. Wang, "Competing Changes," nn. 11, 14. I have found only one source that cites Whitney's 1894 article as an anticipation of the lexical diffusion idea: N. E. Collinge, "Historical Linguistics: History," *Encyclopedia of Languages and Linguistics*, 3:1564. The pioneering work of Sturtevant and Hugo Schuchardt receives credit in C. Lien, "Lexical Diffusion," in ibid., 3:2142.

92. C. Lien, "Lexical Diffusion"; for example, William S. -Y. Wang and C. F. Lien, "Bidirectional Diffusion in Sound Change," in *Historical Linguistics: Problems and Perspectives*, ed. C. Jones (London: Longman, 1993).

93. William Labov, *Sociolinguistic Patterns* (Philadelphia: University of Pennsylvania Press, 1972), 264; James Milroy, *Linguistic Variation and Change* (Oxford: Blackwell, 1991), 4.

94. Konrad Koerner offers a more extensive genealogy of sociolinguistic theory and practice in *Toward a History of American Linguistics* (New York: Routledge, 2002), 263–68.

95. Labov, *Sociolinguistic Patterns*, 266; Milroy, *Linguistic Variation and Change*, 23.

96. Saussure, *Course in General Linguistics*, 30; John E. Joseph, *Limiting the Arbitrary* (Philadelphia: John Benjamins, 2000), 127; Labov, *Sociolinguistic Patterns*, 164.

97. Labov, *Sociolinguistic Patterns*, 160–64, 185–87, 260–70. Chomsky quoted in ibid., 267.

98. Labov, *Principles of Linguistic Change*, 1:21–23; Labov, *Sociolinguistic Patterns*, 261.

99. William S. -Y. Wang, *Explorations in Language* (San Francisco: Pyramid Press, 1991), 20–25; Milroy, *Linguistic Variation and Change*, 26–27.

100. Dorothy Ross, *The Origins of American Social Science* (New York: Cambridge University Press, 1991), 219–22, 236–39; Jaap van Ginnekin, *Crowds, Psychology, and Politics, 1871–1899* (New York: Cambridge University Press, 1992), 196–97, 222–28.

101. *DAB*, s.v., "Sumner, William Graham." W. G. Sumner to WDW, 8 December 1881, WP; "Funeral of Prof. Whitney," *Boston Herald* (10 June 1894), in "Whitney, William Dwight": Newsclippings File, Harvard University Archives, Pusey Library.

102. William Graham Sumner, *Folkways* (1906; Boston: Ginn and Co., 1940), 35.

103. Sumner, *Folkways*, 135, 136.

104. WDW, *LGL*, 21–22; see also 82, 110.

105. H. Stuart Hughes, *Consciousness and Society: The Reorientation of European Social Thought, 1890–1930* (New York: Random House, 1958).

106. James Turner, *The Liberal Education of Charles Eliot Norton* (Baltimore: Johns Hopkins University Press, 1999), 340–41; see Part II of Jon H. Roberts and James Turner, *The Sacred and the Secular University* (Princeton: Princeton University Press, 2000); Rosane Rocher, "The Past up to the Introduction of Neogrammarian Thought:

Whitney and Europe," *The European Background of American Linguistics,* ed. Henry M. Hoenigswald (Dordrecht, Holland: Furis Publishers, 1979), 5–22, on p. 8.

107. C. R. Lanman, Preface to WDW, *Atharva-Veda Sanhita* (Cambridge, Mass.: Harvard University Press, 1905). Here was a close parallel to the fact-gathering ethos touted by the organizers of the American historical profession in the 1880s: Peter Novick, *That Noble Dream: The "Objectivity Question" and the American Historical Profession* (New York: Cambridge University Press, 1988), 51–52.

108. Statistics on Yale's Department of Philosophy and the Arts and other parts of the university appear in Edward E. Atwater, ed., *History of the City of New Haven* (New York: W. W. Munsell, 1887), 181. On the wider impact of the DPA, see Nathan Reingold, "Graduate School and the Doctoral Degree: European Models and American Realities," in *Science, American Style* (New Brunswick, N.J.: Rutgers University Press, 1991), 171–89, on pp. 177–81.

109. George Marsden, *The Soul of the American University* (New York: Oxford University Press, 1994), 154–55.

110. On the importance of the AOS to Gilman, see Thomas L. Haskell, *The Emergence of Professional Social Science: The American Social Science Association and the Nineteenth-Century Crisis of Authority* (Urbana: University of Illinois Press, 1977), 152, 170, 171 n.

# W. D. Whitney's Main Works in General Linguistics

"On the Origin of Language." *PAOS* 6 (1858): 8–9.

"On the Scope and Method of Linguistic Science." *Proceedings of the American Association for the Advancement of Science* 13 (1859): 335.

"Strictures upon the views of M. Ernest Renan respecting the Origin and Early History of Languages." *PAOS* 6 (1859): 9–10.

"On the Relation of Language to the Problem of Human Unity." *PAOS* 8 (1863): xxii–iii.

"Brief Abstract of a Series of Six Lectures on the Principles of Linguistic Science." Smithsonian Institution. *Annual Report* (1863): 95–116.

"On the Origin of Language." *PAOS* 8 (1864): lv.

"On Müller's second series of lectures on the Science of Language." *NAR* 100 (1865): 565–81. Reprinted in *OLS*, vol. 1.

"Is the Study of Language a Physical Science?" *NAR* 101 (1865): 434–74.

"On the Classification of Languages." *PAOS* 9 (1866): xi.

*Language and the Study of Language: Twelve Lectures on the Principles of Linguistic Science* 6th ed. (New York: Scribner and Co., [1867] 1901.

"The Value of Linguistic Science to Ethnology." *New Englander* 26 (1867): 30–52.

"Languages and Dialects." *NAR* 104 (1867): 30–64.

"On the Testimony of Language respecting the Unity of the Human Race." *NAR* 105 (1867): 214–41.

"Key and Oppert on Indo-European philology." *NAR* 105 (1867): 521–54.

Review of *Studies in English* by M. Schele de Vere. In *NAR* 104 (1867): 631–35.

Review of *Man's Origin and Destiny* by J. P. Lesley. In *NAR* 107 (1868): 358–70.

"On the Present State of the Question as to the Origin of Language." *TAPA* (1869–70): 20–45.

Review of *Chips from a German Workshop*, vols. 1 and 2, by F. Max Müller. In *NAR* 109 (1869): 544–56. Reprinted in *OLS*, vol. 2.

"Obituary of August Schleicher." *Nation* (28 January 1869): 70.

"The Present State of the Discussion of the Origin of Language." *PAPA* (1871): 84–94.

"On Müller's Lectures on the Science of Language, 6th ed." *NAR* 113 (1871): 430–41. Reprinted in *OLS*, vol. 1.

"Strictures on the Views of August Schleicher respecting the Nature of Language and Kindred Subjects." *TAPA* (1872): 35–64. Reprinted in *OLS*, vol. 1.

"Steinthal on the Origin of Language." *NAR* 114 (1872): 272–308. Reprinted in *OLS*, vol. 1.

"On the so-called Vowel-increment, with Special Reference to the Views of Mr. J. Peile."
   *PAOS* 10 (1873): lxvii–viii.
"On Johannes Schmidt's New Theory of the Relationship of Indo-European Lan-
   guages." *PAOS* 10 (1873): lxxvii–viii.
Review of *A Dictionary of English Etymology* by H. Wedgewood. In *NAR* 115 (1872):
   423–28.
*Oriental and Linguistic Studies,* Vol. 1. New York: Charles Scribner, 1873.
"On Material and Form in Language." *TAPA,* (1873), 77–96.
"On Darwinism and Language." *NAR* 119 (1874): 61–88.
*Oriental and Linguistic Studies,* Vol. 2. New York: Charles Scribner, 1874.
*The Life and Growth of Language.* London: Henry S. King and Co., 1875.
"Are Languages Institutions?" *Contemporary Review* 25 (1875): 713–32.
"Steitfragen der heutigen Sprachphilosophie." *Deutsche Rundschau* 4 (August 1875):
   259–79.
"Language." *New Universal Cyclopedia,* Vol. 2. New York: A. J. Johnson and Son, 1876–
   78.
"On the Relation of Surd and Sonant." *TAPA* (1878): 41–57.
"The Principle of Economy as a Phonetic Force." *TAPA* (1878) 41–57.
"Logical Consistency in Views of Language." *AJP* 1 (1880): 327–343.
"On Mixture in Language." *TAPA* (1881): 5–26.
Review of *Anthropology* by E. B. Tylor. In *Nation* 33: 844 (1 September 1881): 181.
"Further Words as to Surds and Sonants, and the Law of Economy as a Phonetic Force."
   *PAPA* 13 (1882): xiii–xiv.
"Philology." *Encyclopedia Britannica,* 9th ed., vol. 18 (1885). American reprint: Phila-
   delphia: J. M. Stoddart, 1875–1890.
"On Combination and Adaptation as Illustrated by the Exchanges of Primary and Sec-
   ondary Suffixes." *TAPA* (1885): 111.
"Remarks [on F. A. March's Paper on the Neo-grammarians]." *PAPA* 16 (1885): xxi.
"The Method of Phonetic Change in Language." *PAPA* 17 (1886): xxxiii–v.
*Max Müller and the Science of Language: a Criticism.* New York: D. Appleton and
   Co., 1892.
"Examples of Sporadic and Partial Phonetic Change in English." *Indogermanische For-
   schungen* 4 (1894): 32–36.

ORIGINAL CITATIONS FOR ESSAYS IN
ORIENTAL AND LINGUISTIC STUDIES

"The Vedas," *OLS,* 1:1–45; originally "On the Main Results of the Later Vedic Researches
   in Germany," *JAOS* 3 (1953): 289–328.
WDW, "Müller's History of Vedic Literature," *OLS,* 1:64–99; originally published
   under the same title in *Christian Examiner* 70 (1861): 251–81.
"The Translation of the Veda," *OLS,* 1:100–132; originally published under the same
   title in *NAR* 106 (1868): 515–42.

"Müller's Rig-Veda Translation," *OLS*, 1:133–48; originally "Müller's Translation of the Rig-Veda," *NAR* 113 (1871): 174–87.

"The Avesta," *OLS*, 1:149–97; originally "On the Avesta or the Sacred Scriptures of the Zoroastian Religion," *JAOS* 5 (1856): 337–83.

"Müller's Lectures on Language," *OLS*, 1:239–78; originally "On Müller's Lectures on the Science of Language, 6th ed.," *NAR* 113 (1871): 430–41.

"Bleek and the Simious Theory of Language," *OLS*, 1:292–97; originally "A Bad Book in Linguistics," *Nation* 9 (11 November 1869): 414–15.

"Schleicher and the Physical Theory of Language," *OLS*, 1:298–331; originally "Strictures on the views of August Schleicher respecting the nature of language and kindred subjects," *TAPA* (1872): 35–64.

"Steinthal and the Psychological Theory of Language," *OLS*, 1:332–75; originally "Steinthal on the Origin of Language," *NAR* 114 (1872): 272–308.

"Müller's Chips from a German Workshop," *OLS*, 2:126–48; originally "On Müller's Chips from a German Workshop, I, II," *NAR* 109 (1869): 544–56.

# Essay on Sources

The notes to this book refer to the primary sources as well as to secondary works dealing with isolated points of information. This essay surveys the remaining secondary works of most importance, starting with those relevant to the entire book and proceeding to specific topics. The latter are arranged roughly in the order of the chapters.

The best works dealing with William Dwight Whitney's linguistic thought have been brief in scope: these include Michael Silverstein, "Preface" to *Whitney on Language*, ed. Michael Silverstein (Cambridge: MIT Press, 1971); Charles F. Hockett, "Introduction to the Dover Edition" of W. D. Whitney, *The Life and Growth of Language* (1875; New York: Dover Publications, 1979), iv–xx; Rosane Rocher, "The Past up to the Introduction of Neogrammarian Thought: Whitney and Europe," *The European Background of American Linguistics*, ed. Henry M. Hoenigswald (Dordrecht, Holland: Furis Publishers, 1979), 5–22; and John E. Joseph, "'The American Whitney' and his European Heritages and Legacies," in *From Whitney to Chomsky* (Philadelphia: John Benjamins, 2003), 19–43. A longer work giving an overview of Whitney's ideas is Joel Herbert Siegel, "W. D. Whitney's Views on the Nature of Language and Language Study," (PhD diss., University of Indiana, 1980).

Works on particular aspects of Whitney's life and thought include Richard W. Bailey, "William Dwight Whitney and the Origins of Semiotics," in R. W. Bailey et al., *The Sign: Semiotics Around the World* (Ann Arbor: Michigan Slavic Publications, 1978), 68–80; John E. Joseph, "Saussure's Meeting with Whitney, Berlin, 1879," *Cahiers de Ferdinand Saussure* 42 (1988): 205–14; E. F. Konrad Koerner, "L'Importance de William Dwight Whitney pour les jeunes linguistes de Leipzig," *Etudes saussuriennes* (Geneva: Editions Slatkine, 1988), 1–16; Koerner, "William Dwight Whitney and the Influence of Geology on Linguistic Theory in the Nineteenth Century," in *Language and Earth: Studies in the History of the Language Sciences* 66, ed. Bernd Naumann, Frans Plank, and Gottfried Hofbauer (Philadelphia: John Benjamins, 1992), 271–87; and Patricia Casey Sutcliffe, "Humboldt's *Ergon* and *Energeia* in Friedrich Max Müller's and William Dwight Whitney's Theories of Language," *Logos and Language* 2:2 (2001): 21–35.

A number of writings on broader subjects also give attention to W. D. Whitney. The most important of these are T. Craig Christy, *Uniformitarianism in Linguistics* (Philadelphia: John Benjamins, 1983); and Bridgitte Nerlich, *Change in Language: Whitney, Bréal, and Wegener* (London: Routledge, 1990). Additional material on Whitney can be found in Brigitte Nerlich, *Semantic Theories in Europe, 1830–1930: From Etymology to Contextuality* (Philadelphia: John Benjamins, 1992); and Anna Morpurgo Davies, *History of Linguistics*, Vol. 4: *Nineteenth-Century Linguistics*, ed. Giulio Lepschy (London: Longman, 1994). Julie Tetel Andresen's informative *Linguistics in America, 1769–1924: A Critical History* (London: Routledge, 1990), includes an extensive discussion of Whitney's ideas, although its interpretive framework requires that it be used with caution.

Among the best works on nineteenth-century linguistics are Otto Jespersen, *Language: Its Nature, Development and Origin* (London: G. Allen and Unwin, 1922); Holgar Pedersen, *The Discovery of Language: Linguistic Science in the Nineteenth Century* [1924], trans. John W. Spargo (Bloomington: Indiana University Press, 1931); Paul Kiparsky, "From Paleogrammarians to Neogrammarians," *Studies in the History of Linguistics*, ed. Dell Hymes (Bloomington: Indiana University Press, 1974), 331–45; James H. Stam, *Inquiries into the Origin of Language: the Fate of a Question* (New York: Harper & Row, 1978); Hans Aarsleff, *From Locke to Saussure: Essays on the Study of Language and Intellectual History* (Minneapolis: University of Minnesota Press, 1982); Roy Harris and Talbot J. Taylor, *Landmarks in Linguistic Thought, I: The Western Tradition from Socrates to Saussure*, 2nd ed. (1989; London: Routledge, 1997); Maurice Olender, *The Languages of Paradise: Race, Religion, and Philology in the Nineteenth Century*, trans. Arthur Goldhammer (Cambridge: Harvard University Press, 1992); and Tullio de Mauro and Lia Formigari, eds., *Leibniz, Humboldt, and the Origins of Comparativism* (Philadelphia: John Benjamins, 1990).

To the above should be added the writings of E. F. K. Koerner, which have been a major force in the historiography of modern linguistics. A sample of his best work, much of it relevant to Whitney and especially to the Neogrammarians, appears in Koerner, *Practicing Linguistic Historiography: Selected Essays* (Philadelphia: John Benjamins, 1989). For appreciative yet critical overviews of Koerner's contributions, see the following works by John E. Joseph: Review of *Saussurean Studies* by Konrad Koerner, in *Language* 65:3 (1989): 595–602; and "Introduction," to *The Emergence of the Modern Language Sciences*, ed. Sheila Embleton, John E. Joseph, and Hans-Jesef Niederehe, 2 vols. (Philadelphia: John Benjamins, 1999). The latter includes a full bibliography.

Works on early-twentieth-century American linguistics include Erwin A. Esper, *Mentalism and Objectivism in Linguistics: The Sources of Leonard Bloomfield's Psychology of Language* (New York: American Elsevier, 1968); Giulio C. Lepschy, *A Survey of Structuralist Linguistics* (London: Faber and Faber, 1970); Dell Hymes and John Fought, *American Structuralism* (New York: Mouton Publishers, 1981); and E. F. K. Koerner, *Toward a History of American Linguistics* (London: Routledge, 2002).

Background on all of the above topics can be found in articles from recent encyclopedias and surveys, including William Bright, ed., *International Encyclopedia of Linguistics*, 4 vols. (Oxford: Oxford University Press, 1992); R. E. Asher, ed., *The Encyclopedia of Language and Linguistics*, 10 vols. (Oxford: Pergamon Press, 1994); and E. F. K. Koerner and R. E. Asher, eds., *A Concise History of the Language Sciences*, (Oxford: Pergamon, 1995).

For nineteenth-century American language study in its wider sense, see especially Donald A. Crosby, *Horace Bushnell's Theory of Language* (The Hague: Mouton, 1975); Philip Gura, *The Wisdom of Words* (Middleton, Conn.: Wesleyan University Press, 1981); Kenneth Cmiel, *Democratic Eloquence: The Fight Over Popular Speech in Nineteenth-Century America* (New York: William Morrow, 1990); and Caroline Winterer, *The Culture of Classicism* (Princeton, N.J.: Princeton University Press, 2000). For the British context, see J. W. Burrow, "The Uses of Philology in Victorian England," in *Ideas and Institutions of Victorian Britain,* ed. Robert Robson (London: G. Bell and Sons, 1962), 180–204; Hans Aarsleff, *The Study of Language in England, 1780–1860* (Princeton, N.J.: Princeton University Press, 1967); and, for the seventeenth and eighteenth century, Stephen K. Land, *The Philosophy of Language in Britain: Major Theories from Hobbes to Thomas Reid* (New York: AMS Press, 1986).

Works dealing with W. D. Whitney's broader intellectual environment include Frederick Rudolph, *Mark Hopkins and the Log: Williams College, 1836–1872* (New Haven, Conn.: Yale University Press, 1956); Edward Lurie, *Louis Agassiz: A Life in Science* (Chicago: University of Chicago Press, 1960); Carl Diehl, *Americans and German Scholarship: 1770–1870* (New Haven, Conn.: Yale University Press, 1978); Louise Stevenson, *Scholarly Means to Evangelical Ends: The New Haven Scholars and the Transformation of Higher Learning in America, 1830–1890* (Baltimore: Johns Hopkins University Press, 1986); Charles D. Cashdollar, *The Transformation of Theology, 1830–1890: Positivism and Protestant Thought in Britain and America* (Princeton, N.J.: Princeton University Press, 1989); and James Turner, *The Liberal Education of Charles Eliot Norton* (Baltimore: Johns Hopkins University Press, 1999). On Boston's Lowell Institute lectures in the nineteenth century, see Harriett Knight Smith, *The History of the Lowell Institute* (Boston: Lamson, Wolffe, 1898).

The most stimulating introductions to the social sciences in this period are Thomas L. Haskell, *The Emergence of Professional Social Science: The American Social Science Association and the Nineteenth-Century Crisis of Authority* (1977; Baltimore: Johns Hopkins University Press, 2001), and Dorothy Ross, *The Origins of American Social Science* (Cambridge, UK: Cambridge University Press, 1991).

General histories of Yale include George Wilson Pierson, *Yale College: An Educational History, 1871–1921* (New Haven, Conn.: Yale University Press, 1952), and Brooks Mather Kelley, *Yale: A History* (New Haven, Conn.: Yale University Press, 1974). (These, however, say little about the philology curriculum.) On the Sheffield School in particular, see Russell H. Chittenden, *History of the Sheffield Scientific School of Yale University, 1846–1922* (New Haven, Conn.: Yale University Press, 1928), and Charles Schuchert and Clara Mae LeVene, *O. C. Marsh: Pioneer in Paleontology* (New Haven, Conn.: Yale University Press, 1940).

The beginnings of the American Oriental Society are recounted in Nathaniel Schmidt, "Early Oriental Studies in Europe and the Work of the American Oriental Society, 1842–1922," *Journal of the American Oriental Society* 43 (1923): 1–14. Basic histories of the American Philological Association appear in Frank Gardner Moore, "A History of the American Philological Association," *Transactions of the American Philo-*

*logical Association* 50 (1919): 5–32; and Lucius Rogers Shaw, "The American Philological Association, an Historical Sketch," *The Fourth International Congress of Classical Studies* (Philadelphia, 1964): 1–11.

The literature on nineteenth-century American science is extensive. Emphasizing the collegiate context and other special topics are Stanley M. Guralnik, *Science and the Ante-Bellum American College* (Philadelphia: American Philosophical Society, 1975); and Nathan Reingold, ed., *The Sciences in the American Context: New Perspectives* (Washington, D.C.: Smithsonian Institution Press, 1979). For a more general treatment, see Robert V. Bruce, *The Launching of Modern American Science, 1846–1876* (New York: Alfred A. Knopf, 1987). An incisive guide to the science-oriented natural theology of this period appears in James Turner, *Without God, Without Creed: The Origins of Unbelief in America* (Baltimore: Johns Hopkins University Press, 1985). The Baconian orientation toward science is described in George H. Daniels, *American Science in the Age of Jackson* (New York: Columbia University Press, 1968); and Theodore Dwight Bozeman, *Protestants in an Age of Science* (Chapel Hill: University of North Carolina Press, 1977).

Standard works on the scientific associations in this era include Ralph S. Bates, *Scientific Societies in the United States,* 2nd ed. (New York: Columbia University Press, 1958); Sally Gregory Kohlstedt, *The Formation of the American Scientific Community: The American Association for the Advancement of Science, 1848–1860* (Urbana: University of Illinois Press, 1976); Rexmond C. Cochrane, *The National Academy of Sciences: The First Hundred Years, 1863–1963* (Washington, D.C.: The National Academy of Sciences, 1978); and A. Hunter Dupree, "The National Academy of Sciences and the American Definition of Science," in *The Organization of Knowledge in Modern America,* ed. Alexandra Oleson and John Voss (Baltimore: Johns Hopkins University Press: 1979), 342–63.

A number of works detail the Silliman oil controversy. For the basic story, see Gerald D. Nash, "The Conflict Between Pure and Applied Science in Nineteenth-Century Public Policy: The California State Geological Survey, 1860–1874," in *Science in America since 1820,* ed. Nathan Reingold (New York: Science History Publications, 1976), 174–85; and Paul Lucier, "Commercial Interests and Scientific Disinterestedness: Consulting Geologists in Antebellum America," *Isis* 86 (1995): 245–67.

Thoughtful works exploring the development of the research university include Lawrence Veysey, *The Emergence of the American University* (Chicago: University of Chicago Press, 1967); Julie Reuben, *The Making of the Modern University* (Chicago: The University of Chicago Press, 1996); and Jon H. Roberts and James Turner, *The Sacred and the Secular University* (Princeton, N.J.: Princeton University Press, 2000). Books by Hugh Hawkins examine particular institutions: *Pioneer: The Early Years of the Johns Hopkins University, 1874–1889* (Ithaca, N.Y.: Cornell University Press, 1960); and *Between Harvard and America: The Educational Leadership of Charles W. Eliot* (Oxford: Oxford University Press, 1972). A useful collection of primary materials appears in Richard Hofstadter and Wilson Smith, eds., *American Higher Education: A Documentary History,* 2 vols. (Chicago: University of Chicago Press, 1961).

The classic guide to nineteenth-century Europe's fascination with Middle Eastern and Asian cultures is Raymond Schwab's *The Oriental Renaissance: Europe's Rediscovery of the India and the East, 1680–1880,* trans. Gene Patterson-Black and Victor Reinking (New York: Columbia University Press, 1984). Thomas R. Trautmann's *Aryans and British India* (Berkeley: University of California Press, 1997) is an erudite revisionist treatment. The American versions of the renaissance, including the second-generation Transcendentalists, are described in Carl T. Jackson, *The Oriental Religions and American Thought: Nineteenth Century Explorations* (Westport, Conn.: Greenwood Press, 1981); and Arthur Versluis, *American Transcendentalism and Asian Religions* (Oxford: Oxford University Press, 1993).

Background on the mid-nineteenth-century Indian astronomy debate appears in Edwin Burrows Smith, "Jean-Sylvain Bailly: Astronomer, Mystic, Revolutionary, 1736–1793," *Transactions of the American Philosophical Society* n.s. 44 (1954), part 4: 429–538; and S. H. Sen and K. S. Shukla, eds., *History of Astronomy in India* (New Delhi: Indian National Science Academy, 1985).

The best brief description of F. Max Müller's career appears in George W. Stocking, Jr., *Victorian Anthropology* (New York: Free Press, 1987). Also useful are Elizabeth Knoll, "The Science of Language and the Evolutionary Mind: Max Müller's Quarrel with Darwinism," *Journal of the History of the Behavioral Sciences* 22 (January 1986): 3–22; Gregory Schrempp, "The Re-Education of Friedrich Max Müller: Intellectual Appropriation and Epistemological Antinomy in Mid-Victorian Evolutionary Thought," *Man* 18 n.s. (1983): 90–110; and Linda Dowling, *Language and Decadence in the Victorian Fin-de-Siècle* (Princeton, N.J.: Princeton University Press, 1986).

Olender's *Languages of Paradise* (cited above) provides insight into Müller's ideological project. The only full-length treatment of Max Müller's life is Nirad C. Chaudhuri's highly laudatory *Scholar Extraordinary: The Life of Professor the Rt. Hon. Friedrich Max Müller* (Oxford: Oxford University Press, 1974). A perspective different from my own on the Whitney-Müller controversy appears in David A. Valone, "Language, Race, and History: The Origin of the Whitney-Müller Debate and the Transformation of the Human Sciences," *Journal of the History of the Behavioral Sciences* 32 (April 1996): 119–34.

The links between language study and Darwinism are explored in Robert J. Richards, *Darwin and the Emergence of Evolutionary Theories of Mind and Behavior* (Chicago: University of Chicago Press, 1987); and Stephen G. Alter, *Darwinism and the Linguistic Image: Language, Race and Natural Theology in the Nineteenth Century* (Baltimore: Johns Hopkins University Press, 1999).

On the International Scientific Series as a phenomenon in Victorian scientific publishing, see William E. Leverette, Jr., "E. L. Youmans' Crusade for Scientific Autonomy and Respectability," *American Quarterly* 17 (1965): 12–32; and Roy M. MacLeod, "Evolutionism, Internationalism and Commercial Enterprise in Science: The International Scientific Series, 1871–1910," in *The Development of Scientific Publishing in Europe,* ed. A. J. Meadows (Amsterdam: Elsevier Scientific Publishers, 1980), 63–91.

Much has been written on the development of anthropological study in this period.

Thomas R. Trautmann's *Louis Henry Morgan and the Invention of Kinship* (Berkeley: University of California Press, 1987) provides an invaluable guide to the theoretical landscape, particularly the links between philology and ethnology. On the revised human chronology, see Stocking, *Victorian Anthropology* (cited above), and especially Thomas R. Trautmann, "The Revolution in Ethnological Time," *Man* 27:2 (June 1992): 379–97. Although superceded by Stocking's book, J. W. Burrow's *Evolution and Society* (Cambridge: Cambridge University Press, 1966) contains valuable insights on nineteenth-century British anthropology. On the racialist "American school" of ethnology, see William Stanton, *The Leopard's Spots: Scientific Attitudes Toward Race in America, 1815–1859* (Chicago: University of Chicago Press, 1960). For the standard introduction to the Boasian revolution in anthropology, see the essays in George W. Stocking, Jr., *Race, Culture, and Evolution* (1968; Chicago: University of Chicago Press, 1982).

A number of works have dealt with the study of Native American languages and ethnology in the nineteenth century. The early period is covered in John C. Greene, *American Science in the Age of Jefferson* (Ames: Iowa State University Press, 1984); and Anthony F. C. Wallace, *Jefferson and the Indians* (Cambridge, Mass.: Belknap Press, 1999). For the middle part of the century, see Curtis M. Hinsley, Jr., *Savages and Scientists: The Smithsonian Institution and the Development of American Anthropology, 1846–1910* (Washington, D.C.: Smithsonian Institution Press, 1981); and Donald Worster, *A River Running West: The Life of John Wesley Powell* (Oxford: Oxford University Press, 2001). The story of Harvard's Peabody Museum of American Archeology and Ethnology is told in Floyd G. Lounsbury, "One Hundred Years of Anthropological Linguistics," in *One Hundred Years of American Anthropology*, ed., John Otis Brew (Cambridge, Mass.: Harvard University Press, 1968), 153–226.

My reading of W. D. Whitney's influence on the Neogrammarian movement draws upon three works especially, all of them cited above. Foremost is Craig Christy's outstanding *Uniformitarianism in Linguistics*, complemented by Paul Kiparsky's "From Paleogrammarians to Neogrammarians." Unique among the works on this subject, Thomas Trautmann's *Lewis Henry Morgan* shows how the *ethnological* time revolution prepared the way for the Neogrammarian methodology.

The most reliable general overview of the Neogrammarians and their theoretical work appears in the Introduction to Terence H. Wilbur, *The Lautgesetz-Controversy: A Documentation* (Amsterdam: John Benjamins, 1977). Also useful are Kurt R. Jankowsky, *The Neogrammarians: A Re-evaluation of their Place in the Development of Linguistic Science* (The Hague: Mouton, 1972); William M. Norman, "The Neogrammarians and Comparative Linguistics," (PhD diss., Princeton University, 1972); and Terence H. Wilbur, "Hugo Schuchardt and the Neogrammarians," in *Schuchart, the Neogrammarians, and the Transformational Theory of Phonological Change*, ed. Theo Vennemann and Terence H. Wilbur (Frankfurt am Main: Athenäum, 1972), 75–113.

Of the many works on Saussurean linguistics, those I have found most helpful include E. F. K. Koerner, *Ferdinand de Saussure: The Origin and Development of his Lin-*

*guistic Thought in Western Studies of Language* (Braunschweig: Vieweg, 1973); David Holdcroft, *Saussure: Signs, System and Arbitrariness* (Cambridge: Cambridge University Press, 1991); and various writings by John E. Joseph, including the relevant material in Koerner and Asher, *Concise History of the Language Sciences* (cited above).

# Index